Advanced SharePoint Services Solutions

SCOT P. HILLIER

Apress®

Advanced SharePoint Services Solutions

Copyright © 2005 by Scot P. Hillier

ISBN (pbk): 1-59059-456-8

Printed and bound in the United States of America 9 8 7 6 5 4 3 2 1

Trademarked names may appear in this book. Rather than use a trademark symbol with every occurrence of a trademarked name, we use the names only in an editorial fashion and to the benefit of the trademark owner, with no intention of infringement of the trademark.

Lead Editor: Jim Sumser

Technical Reviewer: Seth Bates

Editorial Board: Steve Anglin, Dan Appleman, Ewan Buckingham, Gary Cornell, Tony Davis, Jason Gilmore, Chris Mills, Dominic Shakeshaft, Jim Sumser

Project Manager: Beth Christmas

Copy Edit Manager: Nicole LeClerc

Copy Editor: Liz Welch

Production Manager: Kari Brooks-Copony

Production Editor: Mary Keith Trawick

Compositor: Linda Weidemann, Wolf Creek Press

Proofreader: April Eddy

Indexer: Michael Brinkman

Artist: Kinetic Publishing Services, LLC

Cover Designer: Kurt Krames

Manufacturing Manager: Tom Debolski

Distributed to the book trade in the United States by Springer-Verlag New York, Inc., 233 Spring Street, 6th Floor, New York, NY 10013, and outside the United States by Springer-Verlag GmbH & Co. KG, Tiergartenstr. 17, 69112 Heidelberg, Germany.

In the United States: phone 1-800-SPRINGER, fax 201-348-4505, e-mail orders@springer-ny.com, or visit http://www.springer-ny.com. Outside the United States: fax +49 6221 345229, e-mail orders@springer.de, or visit http://www.springer.de.

For information on translations, please contact Apress directly at 2560 Ninth Street, Suite 219, Berkeley, CA 94710. Phone 510-549-5930, fax 510-549-5939, e-mail info@apress.com, or visit http://www.apress.com.

The information in this book is distributed on an "as is" basis, without warranty. Although every precaution has been taken in the preparation of this work, neither the author(s) nor Apress shall have any liability to any person or entity with respect to any loss or damage caused or alleged to be caused directly or indirectly by the information contained in this work.

The source code for this book is available to readers at http://www.apress.com in the Downloads section.

For Nan, who makes everything wonderful

Contents at a Glance

Contents

■CHAPTER 4   Advanced SharePoint Portal Server Solutions 145

■CHAPTER 5   The Information Bridge Framework 195

About the Author

SCOT HILLIER is the vice president of DataLan Corporation, a Microsoft Gold–Certified partner located in White Plains, New York. DataLan Corporation provides end-to-end solutions for information workers using the complete range of Microsoft products and was recently named the *2004 New York/New Jersey Platform Partner of the Year*. Scot is the author of eight books on Microsoft technologies written over the last ten years. When not working, Scot can be found at home with his family playing games and taking walks. Scot can be reached at shillier@datalan.com, and support for this book may be found at www.sharepointstuff.com.

About the Technical Reviewer

SETH BATES is a software architect and practice manager for DataLan Corporation, the 2004 NY/NJ Microsoft Platform Partner of the Year located in White Plains, NY. He has over six years of experience engineering business solutions primarily using Microsoft technologies. With experience in all phases of the software engineering life cycle, Seth brings a broad mix of analysis, design, and implementation expertise to his work. Seth would like to thank his wife and son for their love and support.

Acknowledgments

My experience as an author with Apress just keeps getting better. Across the spectrum the people at Apress are outstanding, and I'd like to thank several of them by name. First, I'd like to thank Gary Cornell and Dan Appleman for founding Apress. They have done a great job bringing the "author's press" to life; I've always felt that our relationship was a partnership. I'd also like to thank Jim Sumser for managing that relationship and dealing with my regular inquiries. Beth Christmas was the project manager for this book and made sure all the different tasks were well coordinated even as the schedule was changing. Thanks as well to Liz Welch for copyediting and Mary Keith Trawick for managing the production.

Along with the folks at Apress, I also had significant help from my colleagues at DataLan Corporation. First and foremost, I'd like to thank Seth Bates, who was the technical editor for the book. Once again, he had to work through every example and exercise. The book is more accurate and valuable thanks to his efforts. I'd also like to thank everyone else at DataLan who participated in our efforts to take this technology to market with our customers. That real-world experience ultimately gave the book focus and helped me decide what areas were most important.

Each time I return to the keyboard, I am reminded that no one can be successful without a supportive family. Nan, after knowing you for 24 years and being married for 18, it just keeps getting better. Ashley, you are a blessing; who says teenagers are difficult to raise? We are so proud of your many accomplishments, personal character, and peer leadership. Matt, you're a great son. We all marvel at how you can be so proficient at so many different endeavors. Thank you, guys. Now it's time for all of us to have some fun again, because I'm finished with this book!

Introduction

No sooner had I finished my first book on SharePoint technologies titled *Microsoft Share-Point: Building Office 2003 Solutions* than Gary Cornell sent me an e-mail asking for a sequel. I thought about the concept for a while and began to realize that there was a definite need in the SharePoint community for a book that went beyond the basics of team sites and web part construction. Based on feedback from customers, postings on the Web, e-mail inquiries, and blogs, I realized that people were struggling to create real solutions with SharePoint technologies. Everyone understands the basics, but many are having difficulty overcoming certain limitations, customizing sites, and integrating with other Microsoft technologies.

As SharePoint gains hold, I am increasingly seeing development teams stretching the product to behave in new ways. Much of this effort involves changing the underlying XML structure of SharePoint or manipulating the content database directly. This is an area where some guidance is required because you can easily destroy a SharePoint installation by manipulating either of these subsystems.

Many teams are also drastically changing the navigation system that SharePoint uses. Popular alternatives involve the use of tabs or treeview controls to present views of sites and information. Additionally, developers often want to significantly customize search capabilities and present the results in unique ways. These modifications can dramatically impact performance if not done correctly.

Finally, developers are beginning to realize that SharePoint is more than just an intranet. In fact, Microsoft is integrating many significant products with SharePoint technologies. For many teams, it is difficult to find good documentation on these integration points with systems like BizTalk Server and Content Management Server. These are all areas where I hope to shed enough light to move the community forward.

Who This Book Is For

Because this book is a sequel, I must assume that you have complete knowledge of all the material covered in my first book. This means that I will assume you already know how to set up Windows SharePoint Services (WSS) and SharePoint Portal Server (SPS). I will also assume that you can write and deploy web parts without assistance, set up team sites, and manage security. If you are weak in any of these areas, you should revisit the appropriate chapters in the first book.

Beyond having strong knowledge of SharePoint itself, this book also assumes that you are an intermediate to advanced developer with strong skills in all key development technologies. You should have strong .NET development skills including XML, web services, scripting, code access security, ASP.NET, and SQL. Throughout the book, I present code samples and techniques that assume a high level of proficiency in these topics.

Ultimately, this book is for intermediate to advanced developers who want to radically change SharePoint or integrate it with other key Microsoft technologies.

How This Book Is Organized

As I noted in my first book, my writing style is strongly influenced by my early experience as a technical trainer. In this environment, I found that people learned best when presented with a lecture, followed by a demonstration, and then a hands-on exercise. Each chapter in this book takes that approach. You will find that each chapter presents key concepts in the beginning with examples followed by a complete exercise at the end.

Generally speaking, I assume that you have read each chapter in the book in order. This allows me to build the concepts without repeating information, which makes the learning experience more efficient. In my first book, this concept was critical. In this book, it is less important because several of the topics stand alone. Nonetheless, I strongly recommend that you read the book cover to cover to get the most value. A brief description of each chapter follows.

Chapter 1: Collaborative Application Markup Language

This chapter provides complete coverage of Collaborative Application Markup Language (CAML). CAML is the language that defines all of the sites and lists within SharePoint. Manipulating the underlying CAML structure allows you to create radically new functionality for SharePoint.

Chapter 2: Databases, Web Services, and Protocols

This chapter is an examination of the key database tables, web services, and communication protocols that SharePoint supports. The chapter focuses on practical uses of these interfaces for manipulating documents and information. You'll learn how to retrieve information directly from the SharePoint database and create utilities to help with system integration.

Chapter 3: Advanced Web Part Techniques

This chapter is dedicated to web part construction. In particular, I will develop a graphical technique for creating web part user interfaces that speeds development. At the end of the chapter, you will create a new project type specifically for building graphical web parts.

Chapter 4: Advanced SharePoint Portal Server Solutions

This chapter focuses specifically on SPS. You'll learn to create custom search applications, improve SPS navigation, and manipulate audiences. The chapter is designed to overcome the common limitations of SPS that most developers encounter.

Chapter 5: The Information Bridge Framework

This chapter presents the Information Bridge Framework (IBF). IBF is a new paradigm for creating Microsoft Office solutions that can integrate with SharePoint. In the chapter, you'll learn to create projects that can interact with systems directly from Word, Excel, or Outlook. These projects can then be integrated with SharePoint to provide a complete solution for information workers.

Chapter 6: The Business Scorecards Accelerator

Integrating business intelligence systems with SharePoint is critical for creating complete solutions. In this chapter, I'll examine the Business Scorecards Accelerator and show how you can create management dashboards in SharePoint. These dashboards are strong solutions for managers who want to view and analyze key organization metrics.

Chapter 7: SharePoint and BizTalk Server 2004

This chapter provides fundamental coverage of BizTalk Server 2004 integration with SharePoint technologies. The chapter assumes no prior knowledge of BizTalk Server. The examples and exercises focus on using InfoPath forms, BizTalk Server, and SharePoint libraries to create workflow solutions.

Chapter 8: SharePoint and Microsoft Content Management Server

This chapter provides fundamental coverage of Microsoft Content Management Server 2002 and how it integrates with SharePoint. The chapter assumes no prior knowledge of Content Management Server. You'll learn to create and manage content using InfoPath forms and Visual Studio .NET.

CHAPTER 1

Collaborative Application Markup Language

Although Windows SharePoint Services (WSS) sites have a professional look and feel right out of the box, inevitably you will want to customize the site structures to fit particular business needs. Significant customization of WSS sites is possible because a language known as the Collaborative Application Markup Language (CAML) defines all of the sites. CAML is a language based on XML elements that define all aspects of a WSS site from link structure to available web parts. Each time you create a new WSS site, a CAML template is used to generate the pages associated with the site. By modifying these CAML structures, you can make small changes to a site layout or even create radically new site structures.

■**Caution** Making incorrect changes to CAML structures can destroy a WSS installation. Additionally, modifications to these files may be overwritten by future service packs. I strongly recommend that you experiment on a test platform extensively before putting any CAML changes into production.

Understanding Key WSS Files

If you want to create your own site definition using CAML, you first have to understand the collection of files utilized by WSS to create and manage sites. The site definition files include not only CAML files but also other files that are utilized by WSS to create entries in the database. All of these files are located in the directory `\Program Files\Common Files\ Microsoft Shared\web server extensions\60\TEMPLATE`. Inside the `\TEMPLATE` directory you will find several folders that contain most of the key elements of a WSS installation. Table 1-1 lists these directories and their content.

■**Caution** Be extremely careful when examining the files located in these directories. Improperly editing these files can result in destroying your WSS installation.

Table 1-1. *Key WSS Directories*

Directory	Description
culture	Contains the definitions for every type of site that can be created. Each subdirectory defines a site template.
ADMIN	Contains the pages for administration of WSS sites and the Microsoft Single Sign-On (SSO) service (if installed).
IMAGES	Contains images used in WSS sites.
LAYOUTS	Contains style sheets and page headers that may be used with site definitions along with Site Settings administration pages.
SQL	Contains SQL scripts used to create WSS databases.
THEMES	Contains the various themes that may be administratively applied to a site.
XML	Contains the file DOCICON.XML for associating document types with icons and htmltransinfo.xml for supporting users who do not have Office 2003 installed.

Although there are several WSS directories, we are most concerned with the site definitions contained in the \culture directory. The \culture directory is named by the decimal representation of the local culture. On U.S. English machines, for example, this is 1033. When you look into the \culture directory, you will see several additional folders. Most of these folders contain complete site definitions with the exception of the \XML folder. This folder contains items that are utilized by all site definitions and for other WSS functionality. Table 1-2 lists these files and their purpose.

Table 1-2. *Key Schema Files in the* \culture*XML Directory*

File	Description
BASE.XML	Contains the schema definitions for the Lists, Documents, and UserInfo tables that are created in the content database when a top-level site is created. This file should never be edited.
DEADWEB.XML	Defines the message that is sent to the site owner asking for site usage confirmation. This message is only used if you have enabled site confirmation and deletion from the Central Administration pages.
FLDTYPES.XML	Used during site and list creation to determine how lists will appear in different views.
NotifItem.xml, NotifListHdr.xml, NotifSiteFtr.xml, NotifSiteHdr.xml	These files define the structure of the alert e-mail message that is sent to a subscriber.
RGNLSTNG.XML	Holds the definitions for regional settings used in sites such as time zone, language, and currency formats.
WEBTEMP.XML	Contains the list of site definition templates that are presented to a user when a new site is created.
WEBTEMPSPS.XML	Contains additional site definitions that apply to SharePoint Portal Server (SPS). This file will only be present when SPS is installed.

Along with the files located in the \XML directory, you will see various site definitions contained in folders. The number of site definitions will differ depending on whether or not you have SPS installed along with WSS. Table 1-3 lists these directories and which sites they define.

Table 1-3. *Site Definition Folders*

Folder	Description	Platform
MPS	Defines the template for a Meeting Workplace	WSS/SPS
SPS	Defines the template for the portal home page	SPS
SPSBWEB	Defines the template for a Bucket Web, which is a site used internally by SPS	SPS
SPSCOMMU	Defines the template for a Community Area	SPS
SPSMSITE	Defines the template for My Site	SPS
SPSNEWS	Defines the template for a News Area	SPS
SPSNHOME	Defines the template for the News Home page	SPS
SPSPERS	Defines the template for a Personal Workspace	SPS
SPSSITES	Defines the template for the Sites Directory	SPS
SPSTOC	Defines the template for a Content Area	SPS
SPSTOPIC	Defines the template for a Topic Area	SPS
STS	Defines the template for a Team site	WSS/SPS

Inside each site definition folder, you will find subfolders that define the elements the site will contain. These elements include definitions for all of the Document Libraries and Lists, which are found in the \DOCTEMP and \LISTS folders, respectively. In this same location, you will also find the \XML folder that contains three files. Table 1-4 lists these files and their purpose.

Table 1-4. *Key Files in the* \culture\site definition*XML Directory*

File	Description
ONET.XML	This file contains site configuration data and ties together most of the other files in the site definition. This file is essentially the master file for the site definition. This file should never be edited for any site definition installed by WSS or SPS.
STDVIEW.XML	Defines the view of the site. This file should never be edited for any site definition installed by WSS or SPS.
VWSTYLES.XML	Defines the styles that are used for viewing list data. This file should never be edited for any site definition installed by WSS or SPS.

Creating a New Site Definition

While it is theoretically possible to create your own site definition from scratch, there really is no reason to attempt it. Once you have identified the site definition folders, you can simply use any of them as a template for your own site definition. All you have to do is copy one of the directories and give it a new name. When you create your new folder, make sure that it is located in the \Program Files\Common Files\Microsoft Shared\web server extensions\60\ TEMPLATE*culture* directory and be sure to use all capital letters in the name. Figure 1-1 shows a new site definition folder named DATALAN.

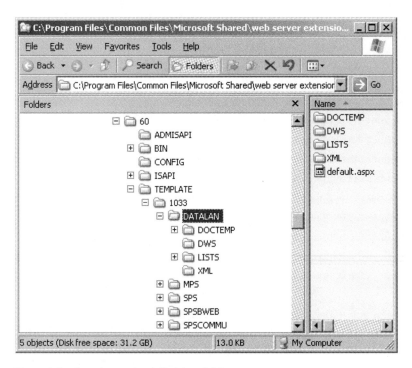

Figure 1-1. *Creating a site definition folder*

Copying an existing site definition folder will give you all of the elements necessary to render a new site template in WSS; however, simply copying the folder does not make the new site template available for use. In order to make the template available, you must create a new web template file.

The base web template file for WSS is WEBTEMP.XML in the *culture*\XML directory. This file contains the information about the two basic site templates that are part of any WSS installation. These site templates are STS and MPS templates described in Table 1-3. If you also have SPS installed alongside WSS, then you will have a second file named WEBTEMPSPS.XML that contains all the templates that are specific to an SPS installation. You can also add information about your own templates by simply copying WEBTEMP.XML and appending a unique string at the end. This is because WSS combines all the template files that begin with WEBTEMP to create the complete set of templates. As an example, I simply copied WEBTEMP.XML and renamed it WEBTEMPDL.XML. You can make as many template files as you want using this technique.

Once you have created your own XML template file, you can simply open it in Visual Studio .NET for editing. When you open the new template file, you'll see that it is made up of Template and Configuration elements. Each site template may consist of multiple configurations. These configurations determine, for example, what web parts are displayed on the page by default. The STS template has, for example, three different configurations: Team Site, Blank Site, and Document Workspace.

The Template element has a Name attribute that must be the exact name of the site definition folder you created earlier and it must also be in all capital letters. The ID attribute must contain a unique number that is greater than 10,000 because WSS reserves all smaller numbers for itself. In order to ensure that your templates and configurations are consistent, use the Template element that was originally associated with the site definition you copied. If you copied the STS definition, for example, then work with the STS Template element in the XML file. Listing 1-1 shows the WEBTEMPDL.XML file from my example.

Listing 1-1. *WEBTEMPDL.XML*

```
<?xml version="1.0" encoding="utf-8" ?>
<!-- _lcid="1033" _version="11.0.5510" _dal="1" -->
<!-- _LocalBinding -->
<Templates xmlns:ows="Microsoft SharePoint">
   <Template Name="DATALAN" ID="10001">
      <Configuration ID="0" Title="DataLan Team Site"
      Hidden="FALSE" ImageUrl="/_layouts/images/stsprev.png"
      Description="This template creates a site for teams."></Configuration>
      <Configuration ID="1" Title="DataLan Blank Site"
      Hidden="FALSE" ImageUrl="/_layouts/images/stsprev.png"
      Description="This template creates a blank home page."></Configuration>
      <Configuration ID="2" Title="DataLan Document Workspace"
      Hidden="FALSE" ImageUrl="/_layouts/images/dwsprev.png"
      Description="This template creates a site."></Configuration>
   </Template>
</Templates>
```

The Configuration element does not have to be changed in order to create your own site definition, but you may want to customize some of the text to make clear how your templates differ from the originals. You can give your templates titles and descriptions, and associate an image with them. Table 1-5 explains each attribute of the Configuration element.

Table 1-5. *The Configuration Element*

Attribute	Type	Description
ID	Integer	This is the only required attribute. It must be a unique number.
Title	Text	A title for the configuration.
Description	Text	A description for the configuration.
Hidden	Boolean	True hides the configuration and it is not available for use in WSS. False makes the configuration available.
ImageURL	Text	The URL of the preview image used in the template page. These are typically located in the directory \Program Files\Common Files\ Microsoft Shared\web server extensions\60\TEMPLATE\IMAGES.
Type	Text	Associates a configuration with a specific site definition.

Customizing the Site Definition

Once the new site definition is completed, you should restart Internet Information Server (IIS) to make the new templates available. In fact, you should get in the habit of restarting IIS after any changes to a site definition. Once IIS is restarted, your templates will show up in WSS when you create a new site. The problem is that you really haven't done anything except rename the same site templates you had before.

In order to customize the configurations, we will have to make changes to ONET.XML. ONET.XML is the backbone of the site definition in WSS. Each site definition folder contains its own ONET.XML file that describes all of the key aspects of the site. You can locate the ONET.XML file under your site definition folder in the \XML directory.

The top-level element in ONET.XML is the Project element. Most of the time, you will only see the Title and ListDir attributes specified, but there are several other attributes that will be valuable later in our discussion. Table 1-6 lists all of the Project attributes and their purpose.

Table 1-6. *The Project Element*

Attribute	Type	Description
AlternateCSS	Text	Allows you to specify a different Cascading Style Sheet (CSS) to use with your site definition. These style sheets are all located in the directory directory \Program Files\ Common Files\Microsoft Shared\web server extensions\ 60\TEMPLATE\LAYOUTS*culture*\STYLES.
AlternateHeader	Text	Allows you to specify an alternate header to use with your site definition. The header should be an ASPX file located in \Program Files\Common Files\Microsoft Shared\ web server extensions\60\TEMPLATE\LAYOUTS*culture*.
CustomJSUrl	Text	Allows you to specify a custom JavaScript file that can be executed within your sites definition. These files should be located in \Program Files\Common Files\Microsoft Shared\web server extensions\60\TEMPLATE\LAYOUTS\ *culture*.
DisableWebDesignFeatures	Text	Allows you to specify that certain features in Microsoft FrontPage cannot be used to edit your sites. This attribute is a semicolon-delimited list with any of the following values: wdfbackup; wdfrestore; wdfpackageimport; wdfpackageexport; wdfthemeweb; wdfthemepage; wdfnavigationbars; wdfnavigationview; wdfpublishview; wdfpublishselectedfile; wdfopensite; and wdfnewsubsite.
ListDir	Text	The subdirectory in your site definition folder where the list definitions are located. This is usually "Lists".
Title	Text	The default title for sites built from the template.

Using an Alternate Style Sheet

The AlternateCSS attribute of the Project element allows you to specify a style sheet that should be applied to site pages that is different than the one associated with the current site theme. This alternate style sheet is applied to all of the administration pages associated with the site including the list management pages, the Create page, and the Site Settings page.

To use an alternate style sheet, follow these steps:

1. Open the Windows File Explorer and navigate to `\Program Files\Common Files\` `Microsoft Shared\web server extensions\60\TEMPLATE\`*culture*.

2. In the `\`*culture* directory, make a copy of the `STS` folder and name it **CSS**.

3. From the `\CSS\XML` directory, open the `ONET.XML` file in Visual Studio .NET.

4. In the `ONET.XML` file, locate the `Project` element and add the `AlternateCSS` attribute to reference an existing style sheet as shown in the following code:

   ```
   <Project Title"Team Web Site" ListDir="Lists" AlternateCSS="OWS.CSS"
   xmlns:ows="Microsoft SharePoint">
   ```

5. Save and close `ONET.XML`.

6. In the `\`*culture*`\XML` directory, make a copy of the `WEBTEMP.XML` file and name it **WEBTEMPCSS.XML**.

7. Open `WEBTEMPCSS.XML` in Visual Studio .NET.

8. In `WEBTEMPCSS.XML`, delete the `Template` element that defines the MPS site.

9. Rename the `Template` element that defines the STS site to **CSS** and change the `ID` attribute to **20001**.

10. Change the `Title` attributes for each configuration in the file so that you can identify them when you are creating a new site. Listing 1-2 shows the complete `WEBTEMPCSS.XML` file.

11. Save `WEBTEMPCSS.XML`.

12. Restart IIS.

13. Create a new site based on the new templates you designed. When you navigate to any of the administration pages, you should see the effect of the new style sheet. Figure 1-2 shows the results.

Listing 1-2. *WEBTEMPCSS.XML*

```
<?xml version="1.0" encoding="utf-8" ?>
<!-- _lcid="1033" _version="11.0.5510" _dal="1" -->
<!-- _LocalBinding -->
<Templates xmlns:ows="Microsoft SharePoint">
    <Template Name="CSS"    ID="20001">
       <Configuration ID="0" Title="CSS Team Site" Hidden="FALSE"
ImageUrl="/_layouts/images/stsprev.png"
Description="Alternate Style Sheet example.">   </Configuration>
       <Configuration ID="1" Title="CSS Blank Site" Hidden="FALSE"
ImageUrl="/_layouts/images/stsprev.png"
Description="Alternate Style Sheet example">   </Configuration>
```

```
        <Configuration ID="2" Title="CSS Document Workspace" Hidden="FALSE"
    ImageUrl="/_layouts/images/dwsprev.png"
    Description="Alternate Style Sheet example">   </Configuration>
        </Template>
    </Templates>
```

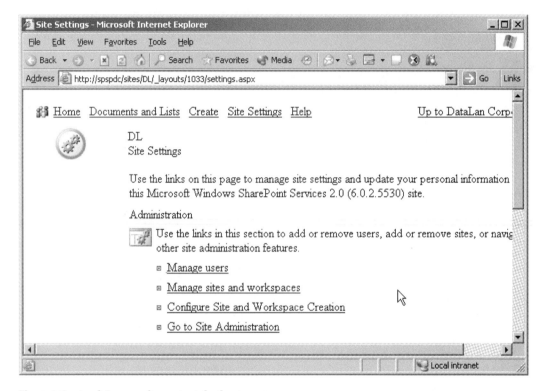

Figure 1-2. *Applying an alternate style sheet*

Using an Alternate Header

The AlternateHeader attribute of the Project element allows you to specify a header section that should appear with site pages. Just like the style sheet, this alternate header appears with all of the administration pages associated with the site.

To use an alternate header, follow these steps:

1. From the directory *culture*\CSS\XML, open the ONET.XML file in Visual Studio .NET.

2. Remove the AlternateCSS attribute that you defined previously and insert an AlternateHeader attribute so that the Project element appears as follows:

   ```
   <Project Title"Team Web Site" ListDir="Lists" AlternateHeader="MyHeader.aspx"
   xmlns:ows="Microsoft SharePoint">
   ```

3. Using Visual Studio .NET, create a new file named MyHeader.aspx. Place the code from Listing 1-3 into this file.

4. Save the file into \Program Files\Common Files\Microsoft Shared\web server extensions\ 60\TEMPLATE\LAYOUTS*culture*.

5. Restart IIS.

6. Create a new site based on this new template. When you navigate to any of the administration pages, you should see the effect of the new header. Figure 1-3 shows the results.

Listing 1-3. *MyHeader.aspx*

```
<HTML>
<HEAD>
<Title>Alternate Header</Title>
</HEAD>
<BODY>
<form runat="server" name="frmAlternate" ID="frmAlternate">
<p>This is my alternate header!</p>
</form>
</BODY>
</HTML>
```

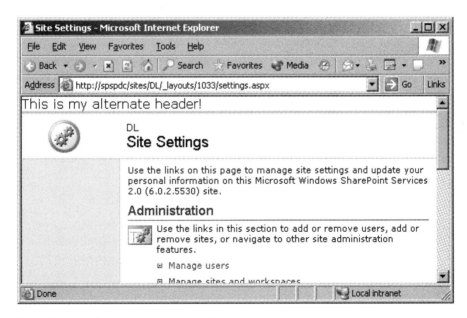

Figure 1-3. *Applying an alternate header*

Customizing the Site Navigation

Once you have a working site definition, you'll want to make several changes to the final site structure. One of the most common changes you'll make is to the site navigation. By making changes to the NavBars element section in ONET.XML, you can alter both the top navigation elements and the side navigation elements in a WSS site. The NavBars element has no attributes, but contains one or more NavBar elements that define the navigation elements in the site. A NavBar element in turn contains one or more NavBarLink elements that define a particular navigation link. Table 1-7 lists the attributes of the NavBar and NavBarLink elements.

Table 1-7. *The NavBar and NavBarLink Elements*

Element	Attribute	Type	Description
NavBar	Body	Text	The HTML that makes up the main part of the navigation bar
NavBar	ID	Integer	A numeric identifier for the navigation bar
NavBar	Name	Text	The name of the navigation bar
NavBar	Prefix	Text	The opening HTML TABLE elements that are rendered before the navigation bar is rendered
NavBar	Separator	Text	The HTML to be used between items in the navigation bar
NavBar	Suffix	Text	The closing HTML TABLE elements that are rendered after the navigation bar is rendered
NavBarLink	Name	Text	The name of the link
NavBarLink	Url	Text	The address of the link

Opening ONET.XML in Visual Studio .NET immediately exposes the NavBars element because it is near the top of the file. Within the NavBars element you'll see a NavBar element for the top navigation area and a separate NavBar element for each of the five quick launch areas defined for the basic WSS site. You'll also notice that only the first NavBars element contains NavBarLink elements. This is because only the top navigation section has links defined. The quick launch areas do not have links until an associated web part is added to the site.

Adding a new link to any NavBar is a simple matter of inserting a new NavBarLink element. You can insert the new link in either the top navigation area or in any of the quick launch areas. As an example, I added a link to the Apress web site to the top navigation bar in my site definition using the following code:

```
<NavBarLink Name="Apress" Url="http://www.apress.com"></NavBarLink>
```

While adding and removing specific links is straightforward, working with the quick launch areas can be a bit more challenging. As an example of customizing the quick launch areas, let's remove the Pictures, Discussions, and Surveys quick launch areas from our site definition. I have always found these particular elements to be of limited use in most business sites, so it makes good sense to remove them. This way, our sites will be created with only the Documents and Lists quick links.

Instead of modifying ONET.XML, hiding the quick launch areas requires modifications to the home page for the site. The definition for the site home page can be found in the default.aspx file located in the site definition folder. If you open this file in Visual Studio .NET, you can locate the quick launch HTML code in a section marked by the comment <!-- Navigation -->. Listing 1-4 shows the HTML that generates the quick launch area for Picture Libraries.

Listing 1-4. *The Navigation Section*

```
    <TR>
<TD class="ms-navheader"><A
HREF="_layouts/<%=System.Threading.Thread.CurrentThread.CurrentUICulture.LCID%>
/viewlsts.aspx?BaseType=1&ListTemplate=109">Pictures</A></TD></TR>
    <TR>
<TD style="height: 6px"><!--webbot bot="Navigation" S-Btn-Nobr="FALSE"
S-Type="sequence" S-Rendering="html" S-Orientation="Vertical"
B-Include-Home="FALSE" B-Include-Up="FALSE" U-Page="sid:1005" S-Bar-Pfx=
"<table border=0 cellpadding=4 cellspacing=0>" S-Bar-Sfx="</table>"
S-Btn-Nml="<tr><td><table border=0 cellpadding=0 cellspacing=0><tr><td>
<img src='_layouts/images/blank.gif' ID='100' alt='Icon'
border=0> </td><td valign=top><a ID=onetleftnavbar#LABEL_ID#
href='#URL#'>#LABEL#</a></tr></table></td></tr>" S-Target TAG="BODY"
startspan --><SharePoint:Navigation LinkBarId="1005" runat="server"/>
<!--webbot bot="Navigation" endspan --></TD></TR>
```

Each quick launch area defined in the home page is represented by two rows in the HTML table. The first row defines the quick launch area and its associated link. The second row inserts the navigation bar onto the page. In order to completely remove the unwanted quick launch areas, these rows must be hidden. Listing 1-5 shows the final HTML for the Picture Library area with Style attributes added to the TR elements to hide the links.

▪**Caution** Don't try to delete any of the quick launch areas from ONET.XML or default.aspx. If you do, the site will not render.

Listing 1-5. *The Modified Navigation Section*

```
    <TR style="visibility:hidden">
<TD class="ms-navheader"><A
HREF="_layouts/<%=System.Threading.Thread.CurrentThread.CurrentUICulture.LCID%>
/viewlsts.aspx?BaseType=1&ListTemplate=109">Pictures</A></TD></TR>
    <TR style="visibility:hidden">
<TD style="height: 6px"><!--webbot bot="Navigation" S-Btn-Nobr="FALSE"
S-Type="sequence" S-Rendering="html" S-Orientation="Vertical"
B-Include-Home="FALSE" B-Include-Up="FALSE" U-Page="sid:1005" S-Bar-Pfx=
"<table border=0 cellpadding=4 cellspacing=0>" S-Bar-Sfx="</table>"
S-Btn-Nml="<tr><td><table border=0 cellpadding=0 cellspacing=0><tr><td>
<img src='_layouts/images/blank.gif' ID='100' alt='Icon'
border=0> </td><td valign=top><a ID=onetleftnavbar#LABEL_ID#
href='#URL#'>#LABEL#</a></tr></table></td></tr>" S-Target TAG="BODY"
startspan --><SharePoint:Navigation LinkBarId="1005" runat="server"/>
<!--webbot bot="Navigation" endspan --></TD></TR>
```

When the new site is created based on the modified template, the Pictures, Discussions, and Surveys quick launch areas are no longer visible. Interestingly, you can still select to add new picture libraries, discussions, or surveys to the quick launch area when you create them, but the links will never appear. I'll correct this problem later when we modify the list templates. Figure 1-4 shows the final site with the modifications.

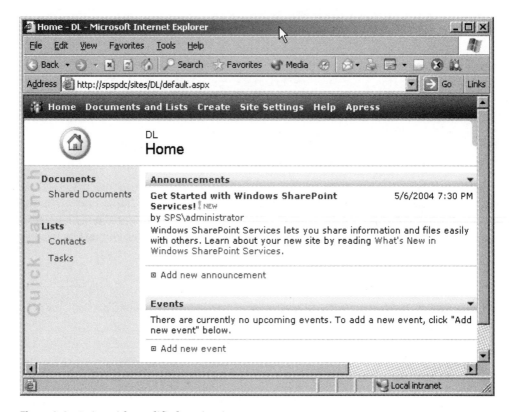

Figure 1-4. *A site with modified navigation areas*

Working with List and Document Templates

The ListTemplates element in ONET.XML contains the definitions for all of the lists that are part of the site definition. The ListTemplates element has no attributes but contains a set of ListTemplate elements. Each ListTemplate element references a list definition that is contained within the \Lists directory of the site definition. Table 1-8 lists all of the attributes of the ListTemplate element.

Table 1-8. *The ListTemplate Element*

Attribute	Type	Description
BaseType	Integer	Specifies the base list type that defines the schema for the list. The base list types are defined in the BaseTypes section of ONET.XML and are: 0-Custom List, 1-Document Library, 2-Not Used, 3-Discussion Form, 4-Survey, and 5-Issues List.
Catalog	Boolean	True if this list can be part of a gallery.
Default	Boolean	True if this list will be created automatically with new sites.
Description	Text	A description of the list.
DisplayName	Text	The display name of the list.
DocumentTemplate	Integer	This attribute is not used and should be left blank.
DontSaveInTemplate	Boolean	True prevents the contents of the list from being saved in a template.
Hidden	Boolean	True if the list will not appear on the Create page.
HiddenList	Boolean	True if list instances created from the definition are to be hidden.
Image	Text	A URL to an image to be used as an icon for the list.
MultipleMtgDataList	Boolean	True if the list contains data to be used across multiple meeting sites.
MustSaveRootFiles	Boolean	For internal use only.
Name	Text	The name of the list.
OnQuickLaunch	Boolean	True if lists created from this definition will appear in the quick launch area by default.
Path	Text	The name of the site definition folder that contains the list (e.g., MPS or STS).
RootWebOnly	Boolean	True if this list can only exist in a top-level site.
SecurityBits	Text	Not used.
Type	Integer	A unique identifier for the list definition.
Unique	Boolean	True if the list can only be used during the site-creation process.

Earlier I had created an example that hid the Pictures, Discussions, and Surveys quick launch areas. However, I noted that when new lists were created we were still presented with the option to show them in the associated quick launch area. Using the ListTemplate element, we can correct this behavior by setting the Hidden attribute to True for the associated lists so that they do not appear on the Create page. This effectively removes the Pictures, Discussions, and Surveys capability from the site altogether.

The DocumentTemplates element in ONET.XML contains the definition for all of the Document Libraries that are part of the site definition. Just like the ListTemplates element, the DocumentTemplates element does not have any attributes. Instead it contains a set of DocumentTemplate elements. Each DocumentTemplate element defines a Document Library. Table 1-9 defines each attribute of the DocumentTemplate element.

Table 1-9. *The DocumentTemplate Element*

Attribute	Type	Description
Default	Boolean	True if this is the library type that is selected by default when creating a new Document Library
Description	Text	A description of the library
DisplayName	Text	The display name of the library
Name	Text	The name of the library
Path	Text	The name of the site definition folder that contains the library (e.g., MPS or STS)
Type	Integer	A unique identifier for the library definition
XMLForm	Boolean	True if the library contains InfoPath forms

Working with Configurations and Modules

Previously, I showed that the web template file contained a set of possible configurations for each site template. For example, we discovered that the STS template, which defines the standard team site template in WSS, has three possible configurations. These are the Team Site, Blank Site, and Document Workspace configurations. Each of these configurations was also assigned a unique identifier. This unique identifier is the connection between the WEBTEMP.XML file and the ONET.XML file. Each configuration identifier contained in WEBTEMP.XML is referenced in the Configurations element of the ONET.XML file. Figure 1-5 shows a graphical representation of this relationship.

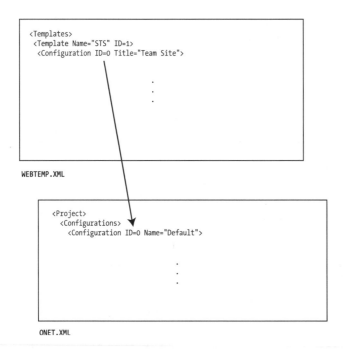

Figure 1-5. *WEBTEMP.XML and ONET.XML are related by the Configuration element.*

The Configurations element is used as a child of the Project element and contains the set of Configuration elements that are related to the configurations specified in the web template file. Each Configuration element in turn contains Lists and Modules elements that define the components that make up the site.

The Lists element has no attributes, but contains a set of List elements that define the lists that will be initially created with the site. In the default configuration for a standard WSS site, a discussion forum is created automatically. Table 1-10 displays the attributes of the List element. In keeping with my desire to eliminate the discussion forum from my customized site template, I can simply delete this List element from the configuration.

Table 1-10. *The List Element*

Attribute	Type	Description
BaseType	Text	Set to Integer to store integer values for the list, or Text to store text values.
Default	Boolean	True specifies that the list is created when a new site is created.
Description	Text	A description of the list.
Direction	Text	Sets the reading order of the list. Can be set to none, RTL (right-to-left), or LTR (left-to-right).
DisableAttachments	Boolean	True prevents the use of attachments with the list.
EventSinkAssembly	Text	Specifies the strong name of an assembly that receives events from this list. This only applies to Document Libraries.
EventSinkClass	Text	Specifies the fully qualified, case-sensitive name of a class that implements the IListEventSink interface to receive list events. This only applies to Document Libraries.
EventSinkData	Text	Sets a text value that is passed to the assembly referenced in the EventSinkAssembly attribute when a list event occurs. This only applies to Document Libraries.
Name	Text	The name of the list.
OrderedList	Boolean	True allows users to reorder the list.
PrivateList	Boolean	True specifies that the list is private to the site.
QuickLaunchUrl	Text	Sets the name of the page to open when the list is accessed from a quick launch area.
RootWebOnly	Boolean	True specifies that the list only belongs to the top-level site in the collection.
ThumbnailSize	Integer	Sets the size of the thumbnail images for a picture library.
Title	Text	The title of the list.

(Continues)

Table 1-10. *The List Element (Continued)*

Attribute	Type	Description
Type	Integer	Specifies the type of list. Possible values are: 100 Generic list, 101 Document library, 102 Survey, 103 Links, 104 Announcements, 105 Contacts, 106 Events, 107 Tasks, 108 Discussion, 109 Picture library, 110 Data sources, 111 Site template gallery, 113 Web Part gallery, 114 List template gallery, 115 InfoPath Form library, 120 Custom grid, 200 Meeting Series, 201 Meeting Agenda, 202 Meeting Attendees, 204 Meeting Decisions, 207 Meeting Objectives, 210 Meeting text box, 211 Meeting Things To Bring, 212 Meeting Workspace Pages, 300 Portal Sites list, 1100 Issue tracking, 2002 Personal document library, and 2003 Private document library.
Url	Text	Specifies the folder where the list definition can be found within the site defection folder.
UrlEncode	Boolean	True to encode the URL.
VersioningEnabled	Boolean	True specifies that versioning on the library is enabled by default.
WebImageHeight	Integer	Sets the height of an image in a Picture Library.
WebImageWidth	Integer	Sets the width of an image in a Picture Library.

The `Modules` element is used in two different places inside of the `ONET.XML` file. It can be a child element of either the `Project` element or the `Configuration` element. When used as a child of the `Project` element, the `Modules` element specifies components, such as web parts, to include in the site definition. When used as a child of the `Configuration` element, the `Modules` element ties a specific module to a site configuration.

The `Modules` element has no attributes but contains a set of `Module` elements. When used as a child of the `Project` element, the `Module` element contains a set of `File` elements that define external files that are part of the site definition. These external files can be either ASP.NET files or web part description files. Listing 1-6 shows two module definitions. One creates a home page for the site and the other adds several web part description files to the site.

Listing 1-6. *Module Definitions*

```
<Modules>
    <Module Name="Default" Url="" Path="">
        <File Url="default.aspx" NavBarHome="True">
            <View List="104" BaseViewID="0" WebPartZoneID="Left"/>
            <View List="106" BaseViewID="0" WebPartZoneID="Left"
WebPartOrder="2"/>
            <AllUsersWebPart WebPartZoneID="Right" WebPartOrder="1">
              <![CDATA[
                <WebPart xmlns=http://schemas.microsoft.com/WebPart/v2
xmlns:iwp="http://schemas.microsoft.com/WebPart/v2/Image">
```

```
              <Assembly>Microsoft.SharePoint, Version=11.0.0.0,
Culture=neutral, PublicKeyToken=71e9bce111e9429c</Assembly>
           <TypeName>Microsoft.SharePoint.WebPartPages.ImageWebPart</TypeName>
           <FrameType>None</FrameType>
           <Title>Site Image</Title>
           <iwp:ImageLink>/_layouts/images/homepage.gif</iwp:ImageLink>
          </WebPart>
              ]]>
           </AllUsersWebPart>
           <View List="103" BaseViewID="0" WebPartZoneID="Right"
WebPartOrder="2"/>
           <NavBarPage Name="Home" ID="1002" Position="Start">
</NavBarPage>
           <NavBarPage Name="Home" ID="0" Position="Start">
</NavBarPage>
        </File>
    </Module>
    <Module Name="WebPartPopulation" List="113" Url="_catalogs/wp"
Path="lists\wplib\dwp" RootWebOnly="TRUE">
        <File Url="MSContentEditor.dwp" Type="GhostableInLibrary"/>
        <File Url="MSPageViewer.dwp" Type="GhostableInLibrary"/>
        <File Url="MSImage.dwp" Type="GhostableInLibrary"/>
        <File Url="MSMembers.dwp" Type="GhostableInLibrary"/>
        <File Url="MSSimpleForm.dwp" Type="GhostableInLibrary"/>
        <File Url="MSXml.dwp" Type="GhostableInLibrary"/>
    </Module>
</Modules>
```

The File element is reasonably straightforward, requiring only that you specify the name of the file to add. Within the File element, however, you may include several child elements such as View, AllUsersWebPart, and NavBarPage. The View element allows you to add a list to the page. The AllUsersWebPart element lets you add a web part to the page, and the NavBarPage element is included if the file is the site home page.

Examining Listing 1-6, you'll notice that the home page for the site defines two lists that are made visible on the home page using the View element. These lists are identified as lists "104" and "106". The list identifiers are defined in the Lists element in the Configuration section. Examining the Configuration section reveals that list "104" is an announcements list and list "106" is an events list. These two lists always appear on the home page of a WSS team site. I'm sure you've seen them many times. The attributes of the View element are shown in Table 1-11.

Table 1-11. *The View Element*

Attribute	Type	Description
AggregateView	Boolean	True if this is a "Merge View" for a library containing InfoPath forms.
BaseViewID	Integer	The identifier of the base list view.
DefaultView	Boolean	True if this view is the default list view.
DisplayName	Text	The display name of the list.
FailIfEmpty	Boolean	True to return a blank page and an error when no items are in the view.
FileDialog	Boolean	True if the view is used within the file dialog box in applications, like Word 2003, that can interact with WSS sites.
FPModified	Boolean	True if the list was modified in FrontPage 2003 and can no longer be modified directly in WSS.
FreeForm	Boolean	True if alternate formatting is used for the list.
Hidden	Boolean	True if the view is hidden.
List	Integer	The identifier of the list type associated with this view.
Name	Text	The name of the view.
OrderedView	Boolean	True if the view is ordered.
Path	Text	Specifies the name of the file for the view.
ReadOnly	Boolean	True if the view is read only.
RecurrenceRowset	Boolean	True if the list will display all recurring entries (e.g., recurring meetings).
RowLimit	Integer	Specifies the maximum number of rows to return. If set to none, then all rows are returned.
Scope	Text	Determines the files and folders displayed in a Document library view. Possible values are: FilesOnly – to show only files in a specific folder, Recursive – to show all files of all folders, and RecursiveAll – to show all files and all subfolders of all folders.
ShowHeaderUI	Boolean	True if the column headers in the view are enabled as sorting hyperlinks.
Threaded	Boolean	True to indicate that the view is threaded as in a discussion forum.
Type	Text	Specifies how the view should be rendered. Possible values are HTML, Chart, and Pivot.
Url	Text	The URL of the view.
WebPartOrder	Integer	Specifies the vertical ordering of the web part within a web part zone.
WebPartZoneID	Text	Specifies the web part zone where the view is rendered.

Whenever I create a team site using the standard Team Site template, I always remove these announcements and events lists. Then I substitute the Document Library and tasks list. I can make this change part of my site definition by simply changing the values in the View elements to "101" and "107", which correspond to the library and task lists. Listing 1-7 shows the changes.

Listing 1-7. *Changing the Visible Lists*

```
<Module Name="Default" Url="" Path="">
    <File Url="default.aspx" NavBarHome="True">
        <View List="101" BaseViewID="0" WebPartZoneID="Left"/>
        <View List="107" BaseViewID="0" WebPartZoneID="Left" WebPartOrder="2"/>
        <AllUsersWebPart WebPartZoneID="Right" WebPartOrder="1">
            <![CDATA[
            <WebPart xmlns=http://schemas.microsoft.com/WebPart/v2
            xmlns:iwp="http://schemas.microsoft.com/WebPart/v2/Image">
                <Assembly>Microsoft.SharePoint, Version=11.0.0.0,
                Culture=neutral, PublicKeyToken=71e9bce111e9429c</Assembly>
        <TypeName>Microsoft.SharePoint.WebPartPages.ImageWebPart</TypeName>
                <FrameType>None</FrameType>
                <Title>Site Image</Title>
                <iwp:ImageLink>/_layouts/images/homepage.gif</iwp:ImageLink>
            </WebPart>
            ]]>
        </AllUsersWebPart>
        <View List="103" BaseViewID="0" WebPartZoneID="Right" WebPartOrder="2"/>
        <NavBarPage Name="Home" ID="1002" Position="Start">  </NavBarPage>
        <NavBarPage Name="Home" ID="0" Position="Start">  </NavBarPage>
    </File>
</Module>
```

Along with changing the lists that are displayed, I also typically add a couple of web parts to each new site that I create. In particular, I add a web part that lists all of the subsites beneath the current site as well as a web part that allows a user to see their personal information and edit it. I can add both of these web parts to my site definition by including the appropriate web part description file in the module. Because I copied the STS site definition, I already have a module defined specifically for web parts. The STS site definition calls this module WebPartPopulation. Listing 1-8 shows the module definition.

Listing 1-8. *The WebPartPopulation Module*

```
<Module Name="WebPartPopulation" List="113" Url="_catalogs/wp"
Path="lists\wplib\dwp" RootWebOnly="TRUE">
    <File Url="MSContentEditor.dwp" Type="GhostableInLibrary"/>
    <File Url="MSPageViewer.dwp" Type="GhostableInLibrary"/>
    <File Url="MSImage.dwp" Type="GhostableInLibrary"/>
    <File Url="MSMembers.dwp" Type="GhostableInLibrary"/>
    <File Url="MSSimpleForm.dwp" Type="GhostableInLibrary"/>
    <File Url="MSXml.dwp" Type="GhostableInLibrary"/>
</Module>
```

In order to include my own web part description files, I must first copy them into the \LISTS\WPLIB\DWP directory underneath my site definition folder. Then I can modify the module definition to include my files. Of course, the actual web part assembly must first be correctly installed and marked as safe in the web.config file before they can be added to the site, but I'm assuming that you know how to do that already. Listing 1-9 shows the modified module.

Listing 1-9. *The Modified WebPartPopulation Module*

```
<Module Name="WebPartPopulation" List="113" Url="_catalogs/wp"
Path="lists\wplib\dwp" RootWebOnly="TRUE">
    <File Url="MSContentEditor.dwp" Type="GhostableInLibrary"/>
    <File Url="MSPageViewer.dwp" Type="GhostableInLibrary"/>
    <File Url="MSImage.dwp" Type="GhostableInLibrary"/>
    <File Url="MSMembers.dwp" Type="GhostableInLibrary"/>
    <File Url="MSSimpleForm.dwp" Type="GhostableInLibrary"/>
    <File Url="MSXml.dwp" Type="GhostableInLibrary"/>
    <File Url="SPSIdentity.dwp" Type="GhostableInLibrary"/>
    <File Url="SPSSubSites.dwp" Type="GhostableInLibrary"/>
</Module>
```

The changes made to the WebPartPopulation module will make my custom web parts available to the site administrator, but if I want them added to the home page by default, then I need to use the AllUsersWebPart element. This element allows you to add non-list web parts to the page. Within this element, you must specify the web part assembly information that will be used by the file when it loads. For this reason, the information is contained within a CDATA block. Listing 1-10 shows a block that adds the image web part to the site home page.

Listing 1-10. *Adding a Non-List Web Part to a Page*

```
<AllUsersWebPart WebPartZoneID="Right" WebPartOrder="1">
    <![CDATA[
    <WebPart xmlns=http://schemas.microsoft.com/WebPart/v2
xmlns:iwp="http://schemas.microsoft.com/WebPart/v2/Image">
        <Assembly>Microsoft.SharePoint, Version=11.0.0.0, Culture=neutral,
PublicKeyToken=71e9bce111e9429c</Assembly>
        <TypeName>Microsoft.SharePoint.WebPartPages.ImageWebPart</TypeName>
        <FrameType>None</FrameType>
        <Title>Site Image</Title>
        <iwp:ImageLink>/_layouts/images/homepage.gif</iwp:ImageLink>
    </WebPart>
    ]]>
</AllUsersWebPart>
```

Modifying the CDATA block is reasonably straightforward. Simply substitute the information for your web part in place of the existing entries. When modifying the code from Listing 1-10, you can remove the reference to the iwp namespace as well as the ImageLink element. These are both specific to the image web part. You can also eliminate the FrameType element to make your web part appear in a frame by default. Listing 1-11 shows an example that inserts a custom web part into the home page.

Listing 1-11. *Customizing the AllUsersWebPart Element*

```
<AllUsersWebPart WebPartZoneID="Left" WebPartOrder="3">
    <![CDATA[
    <WebPart xmlns="http://schemas.microsoft.com/WebPart/v2">
        <Assembly>SPSSubSites, Version 1.0.0.0, Culture=neutral,
PublicKeyToken=315a4c3e9164ed11</Assembly>
        <TypeName>SPSSubSites.Lister</TypeName>
        <Title>Sites Under this Site</Title>
    </WebPart>
    ]]>
</AllUsersWebPart>
```

As a result of creating my own site template, I have made many changes to the basic team site. I removed the Pictures, Surveys, and Discussions quick launch areas. I made it so none of these lists could be added after the initial site is created. I changed the home page to show documents and tasks instead of announcements and events. I also added two of my favorite web parts to the site definition. With all of that accomplished, I now have a team site that suits my tastes. Figure 1-6 shows the final results.

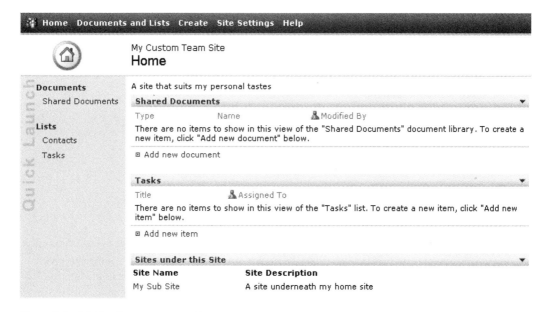

Figure 1-6. *My final custom team site*

Creating a New List Definition

Just as you can create new site definitions from existing ones, you can also create new list definitions in much the same way. All of the list definitions for a site are contained in folders under the \Lists directory for the site definition. You can simply pick the list that most closely resembles the functionality that you are trying to create, copy the entire folder, and give it a new name using all capital letters.

For this discussion, I created a list with links to published reports found in a SQL Reporting Services installation. SQL Reporting Services is an enterprise reporting system that has a web-based repository. Therefore, I was able to modify the links list under the folder named FAVORITE to provide references to these reports. Figure 1-7 shows my new list definition folder named SQLREPORTS.

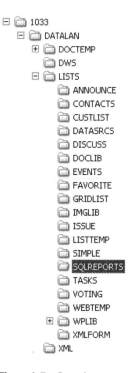

Figure 1-7. *Creating a new list definition*

Within the list definition folder, you will find several files that represent the functionality necessary to view and edit the list. All of these files are ASP.NET files. In this same directory, you will also find a single XML file named SCHEMA.XML. This file contains the definition for the list. Most of the modifications you perform will be in this file.

The top-level element in the SCHEMA.XML file is the List element. This element is the same element described in Table 1-10, but in this usage it defines the schema and views of the new list. The following code shows my modified List element for the SQL Reports list:

```
<List xmlns:ows="Microsoft SharePoint" Name="SQLReports"
Title="SQL Reporting Services reports" Direction="0" OrderedList="TRUE"
Url="Lists/SQLREPORTS" BaseType="0" DisableAttachments="TRUE" >
```

The List element contains two child elements. The MetaData element defines the schema for the fields in the list, and the Data element defines specific rows that are present in the list when it is first created. The MetaData element is required for the list definition, but you only need to include the Data element if you want data to appear in the list by default.

The MetaData element contains the child elements DefaultDescription, Fields, Views, Toolbar, and Forms. The DefaultDescription element defines a description that is used on the site. The following code shows the default description for the SQL Reports list:

```
<DefaultDescription>
    Use the SQL Reports list for links to enterprise reports.
</DefaultDescription>
```

Understanding the Field Element

The Fields element contains a set of Field elements that define the schema for the list columns. Field elements have a significant number of attributes associated with them, which allows you to define a wide variety of field types for your lists. Table 1-12 lists the attributes of the Field element along with a summary description.

Table 1-12. *The Field Element*

Attribute	Type	Description
Aggregation	Text	Used with InfoPath forms to provide aggregate functions associated with fields on the form. Possible values include: sum, count, average, min, max, merge, text, first, and last.
AllowHyperlink	Boolean	True if hyperlinks can exist in the field.
AllowMultiVote	Boolean	True if multiple responses are allowed to this field when it is associated with a survey.
AuthoringInfo	Text	Sets a description of the field that is shown when the value is being edited.
BaseType	Text	Specifies the data type of the field. Possible values are: Integer or Text.
CanToggleHidden	Boolean	True if the field can be hidden through the list administration pages.
ClassInfo	Text	Specifies a style sheet to be used for the field.
ColName	Text	Maps the field to a specific database field.
Commas	Boolean	True if commas are used to separate thousands n numeric values.
Decimals	Integer	The number of decimal places to display for numeric values in the list.
Description	Text	Sets the description for the field in the list.
Dir	Text	Specifies the reading direction for the field. Possible values are RTL (right-to-left), LTR (left-to-right), and none.
DisplayImage	Text	Sets the name of the icon used to represent the field.
DisplayName	Text	The display name of the field.
DisplayNameSrcField	Text	Sets the name of a field that is used as the basis for a calculated field.

(Continues)

Table 1-12. *The Field Element (Continued)*

Attribute	Type	Description
Div	Number	Sets a division scaling factor applied to the field value before it is displayed. Ultimately, the displayed value is multiplied by the value set in the Mult attribute and then divided by the value set in the Div attribute.
FieldRef	Text	Sets the name of a field to which this field refers such as when the field value comes from a lookup on another list.
FillInChoice	Boolean	True if users can add their own values to the field.
Filterable	Boolean	True if the field can be filtered.
ForcedDisplay	Text	Sets the text to display in place of the actual field value. This attribute is used to hide the respondent's name in a survey.
Format	Text	Sets the format for a field. Possible values are: DateOnly, DateTime, ISO8601, ISO8601Basic, DropDown, RadioButtons, Hyperlink, and Image.
FromBaseType	Boolean	Deprecated.
HeaderImage	Text	Sets the name of the image for the column.
Hidden	Boolean	True to hide the field.
HTMLEncode	Boolean	True to HTML encode the field.
JoinColName	Text	Sets the name of a field to be used in a join associated with a lookup list.
JoinType	Text	Sets the type of join between lists. Possible values are: Inner, LeftOuter, and RightOuter.
LCID	Integer	The number of the culture to use when formatting currency values.
List	Text	The internal name of the parent list.
Max	Number	Sets the maximum value for the field.
MaxLength	Integer	Sets the maximum character length for the field.
Min	Number	Sets the minimum value for the field.
Mult	Number	Sets a multiplier scaling factor applied to the field value before it is displayed. Ultimately, the displayed value is multiplied by the value set in the Mult attribute and then divided by the value set in the Div attribute.
Name	Text	Sets the name of the field.
NegativeFormat	Text	Sets the format for displaying negative values. Possible values are: MinusSign and Parens.
Node	Text	Specifies the XPath expression for a promoted node in an InfoPath form.
NoEditFormBreak	Boolean	True to prevent line breaks from being entered in the field.
NumLines	Integer	The number of lines to show in a TEXTAREA element during field editing.
Percentage	Boolean	True to show the field as a percentage.
PIAttribute	Text	Processing instructions for locating the Document Library link in an InfoPath form.

Table 1-12. *The Field Element*

Attribute	Type	Description
PITarget	Text	Processing instructions for locating the template form for an InfoPath form.
Presence	Boolean	True if presence information is in the field.
PrimaryKey	Boolean	True if this field is the primary key relating two lists.
ReadOnly	Boolean	True if the field is read only.
RenderXMLUsingPattern	Boolean	Sets the display format of computed fields.
Required	Boolean	True if a field value is required.
RichText	Boolean	True if the field contains rich text.
Sealed	Boolean	True if the field cannot be deleted from the list schema.
SeparateLine	Boolean	Internal use only.
ShowAddressBookButton	Boolean	Internal use only.
ShowField	Text	Sets the name of the field to be shown as a hyperlink or used in a lookup list.
ShowInEditForm	Boolean	True if the field is shown in edit mode.
ShowInFileDlg	Boolean	True if the field shows in the property dialog when an associated document is saved from an Office 2003 product.
ShowInNewForm	Boolean	True if the field shows in the New Item page.
Sortable	Boolean	True if the field can be sorted.
StorageTZ		When present, this attribute ensures that date/time values are stored in Coordinated Universal Time format.
StripWS	Boolean	True to trim white space from the field.
SuppressNameDisplay	Boolean	True to prevent the user name from being displayed in a User field.
TextOnly	Boolean	True if the field can only accept text values.
Type	Text	The field data type. Possible values are: Attachments, Boolean, Choice, Computed, Counter, CrossProjectLink, Currency, DateTime, File, Guid, Integer, Lookup, ModStat, Note, Number, Recurrence, Text, Threading, URL, and User.
URLEncode	Boolean	True if the field is URL encoded.
URLEncodeAsURL	Boolean	True if the URL encoding is being applied to a path.
Viewable	Boolean	True if the field is part of the default view.
xName	Text	Internal use only.

For my example, I wanted to add an additional field to the list to display a contact person for each report. You can add additional columns to the list by inserting a new Field element as a child of the Fields element. The following code shows the new field definition I added:

```
<Field Type="User" List="UserInfo" Name="ReportOwner"
DisplayName="Report Owner"></Field>
```

Understanding Basic Field Data Types

CAML recognizes all of the fundamental data types that developers have always used. These data types include Boolean, Currency, DateTime, Integer, Number, and Text. For the most part, these data types work exactly as you would expect. The only issue that will concern you is formatting.

In general, field values are formatted in accordance with the rules that apply to the particular locale. However, you can control some aspects of the formatting by using additional attributes of the Field element.

With Currency types, you can specify the Decimals, Min, and Max attributes. This allows you to specify the number of decimal places to show, the minimum value of the field, and the maximum value of the field, respectively.

DateTime types use the Format attribute to change the display format of the field. Using this attribute, you can select to display just the date or a complete date/time stamp.

The Integer type supports positive and negative integer values. You can modify the display format of this type by using the NegativeFormat or Commas attribute. The NegativeFormat attribute allows you to specify whether the integer is shown with a negative sign or inside parentheses when its value is less than zero. The Commas attribute allows you to specify that commas should be used to separate thousands when the value is displayed.

The Number type is a floating value that supports decimals. The value of this field may be formatted using the Decimals, Min, Max, Percentage, Div, and Mult attributes. The Percentage attribute formats the number as a percentage. The Div and Mult attributes specify a scaling factor that is applied to the field value before it is displayed.

The Text type holds standard string values. You can use the MaxLength attribute to specify the maximum number of characters in the field.

Using Lists Items in Fields

CAML supports several types of fields whose value may be set from group of items. The simplest form of this field is the Choice type. Choice types provide a set of predefined items in a list from which the user may select the value of the field. The items are defined directly using the CHOICES element. The following code shows an example taken from the standard issues list definition:

```
<Field Type="Choice" Name="Priority" DisplayName="Priority" >
    <CHOICES>
        <CHOICE>(1) High</CHOICE>
        <CHOICE>(2) Normal</CHOICE>
        <CHOICE>(3) Low</CHOICE>
    </CHOICES>
    <Default>(2) Normal</Default>
</Field>
```

The Lookup field type allows you to use another list defined in the site as a set of items from which to choose the value of the field. The List attribute specifies the name of the list that provides the choices for the field. The ShowField attribute specifies the field from the connected list that should be used to generate the possible field values.

The ModStat field type is a specialized field used to track item approval. This type of field supports the values Approved, Rejected, and Pending. Internally, these values are stored in the database as 0, 1, and 2, respectively. You can find ModStat fields associated with many of the base list types in WSS. The following code shows how the field is defined in the basic Document Library:

```
<Field ColName="tp_ModerationStatus" ReadOnly="TRUE" Type="ModStat"
Name="_ModerationStatus" DisplayName="Approval Status" Hidden="TRUE"
CanToggleHidden="TRUE" Required="FALSE">
    <CHOICES>
        <CHOICE>0;#Approved</CHOICE>
        <CHOICE>1;#Rejected</CHOICE>
        <CHOICE>2;#Pending</CHOICE>
    </CHOICES>
    <Default>0</Default>
</Field>
```

Understanding Computed Fields

A Computed type is a field that derives its value from one or more fields in the same list. A common use of computed fields is to create hyperlinks in the display of a list. One field in the list might hold the address for the link while another field contains the title of the link. A computed field would combine these two fields to create the hyperlink.

In order to use the address and title fields, the computed field must reference these fields. The reference is made using a FieldRef element in the definition of the field. The following code shows how this might look in our example:

```
<Field Name="LinkField" Type="Computed">
    <FieldRefs>
        <FieldRef Name="Address"/>
        <FieldRef Name="Title"/>
    </FieldRefs>
        .
        .
        .
</Field>
```

After the references are established to the address and title fields, we must specify how these fields are combined. This is done inside a DisplayPattern element. This element is a child of the Field element and appears immediately after the field references.

When defining the display pattern for a field, you are actually specifying the HTML that should be generated for the field. This is done by enclosing HTML tags within the HTML CAML element. The HTML element tells the CAML parsing engine to skip over the display tags. Furthermore, the actual HTML is enclosed inside a CDATA block. The following line of code shows a simple example of defining HTML within CAML:

```
<HTML><![CDATA[<p>This is HTML, not CAML</p>]]></HTML>
```

Along with the raw HTML, you will also need to generate the values of the referenced fields in order to create a hyperlink field. CAML allows you to access the raw values of fields in a list as well as their column names and much more. The following code uses the Column element to insert the raw data from the address and title fields, thus creating a complete definition for our computed field:

```
<Field Name="LinkField" Type="Computed">
   <FieldRefs>
      <FieldRef Name="Address"/>
      <FieldRef Name="Title"/>
   </FieldRefs>
   <DisplayPattern>
   <HTML><![CDATA[<a href="]]></HTML>
   <Column Name="Address"/>
   <HTML><![CDATA[ ">]]></HTML>
   <Column Name="Title"/>
   <HTML><![CDATA[ </a>]]></HTML>
   </DisplayPattern>
</Field>
```

In most computed fields, the display pattern is conditional upon other elements. For example, we may want to show the address and title separately during editing so the user can change either field. Applying conditional processing is done with CAML fields that form logical constructs. In many ways, these fields form a programming language that can be used with CAML. Listing 1-12 shows an actual computed field definition for a URL from the favorites link list.

Listing 1-12. *A Computed Field with Conditional Display*

```
<Field ReadOnly="TRUE" Filterable="FALSE" Type="Computed" Name="URLwMenu"
DisplayName="URL" DisplayNameSrcField="URL"
AuthoringInfo="(URL with edit menu)">
   <FieldRefs>
      <FieldRef Name="URL"/>
   </FieldRefs>
   <DisplayPattern>
      <FieldSwitch>
         <Expr><GetVar Name="FreeForm"/></Expr>
         <Case Value="TRUE"><Field Name="URL"/></Case>
         <Default>
            <HTML><![CDATA[<table height="100%" cellspacing=0
            class="ms-unselectedtitle" onmouseover="OnItem(this)"
            CTXName="ctx]]></HTML>
            <Counter Type="View"/><HTML>" ItemId="</HTML>
            <Column Name="ID" HTMLEncode="TRUE"/>
            <HTML><![CDATA["><tr><td width="100%" Class="ms-vb">]]></HTML>
            <Switch>
               <Expr><Column Name="URL"/></Expr>
               <Case Value="">
                  <Column2 Name="URL" HTMLEncode="TRUE"/>
               </Case>
```

```
        <Default>
            <FieldSwitch>
            <Expr><FieldProperty Name="URL" Select="Format"/></Expr>
            <Case Value="Image">
                <HTML><![CDATA[<IMG onfocus="OnLink(this)"
                SRC="]]></HTML>
                <Column Name="URL" HTMLEncode="TRUE"/>
                <HTML>" ALT="</HTML>
                <Column2 Name="URL" HTMLEncode="TRUE"/>
                <HTML><![CDATA[">]]></HTML>
            </Case>
            <Default>
                <HTML><![CDATA[<A onfocus="OnLink(this)"
                HREF="]]></HTML>
                <Column Name="URL" HTMLEncode="TRUE"/>
                <HTML><![CDATA[">]]></HTML>
                <Switch>
                <Expr><Column2 Name="URL"/></Expr>
                <Case Value=""><Column Name="URL"
                HTMLEncode="TRUE"/></Case>
                <Default>
                    <Column2 Name="URL" HTMLEncode="TRUE"/>
                </Default>
                </Switch>
                <HTML><![CDATA[</A>]]></HTML>
            </Default>
            </FieldSwitch>
        </Default>
        </Switch>
        <HTML><![CDATA[</td><td><IMG SRC="/_layouts/images/blank.gif"
        width=13 height=13 alt=""></td></tr></table>]]></HTML>
        </Default>
    </FieldSwitch>
    </DisplayPattern>
</Field>
```

Examining Listing 1-12 shows us that there are several new CAML tags inside the DisplayPattern element. The first new element is the FieldSwitch element. The FieldSwitch element and its cousin the Switch element are both switch-case constructs familiar to any C# programmer. If you are a VB.NET programmer, these constructs are the same as a Select-Case construct in Visual Basic. The difference between the FieldSwitch element and the Switch element is that the Switch element is intended to be evaluated once whereas the FieldSwitch element is evaluated for every field in the DisplayPattern element. Therefore, you will often find FieldSwitch constructs in DisplayPattern elements.

Both the FieldSwitch and the Switch elements contain a single Expr element that specifies the expression to be evaluated. They also contain any number of Case elements whose value is compared to the Expr element. If the values match, then the CAML inside the Case element is executed. If none of the Case element values match the Expr value, then the CAML inside the Default element is processed.

Looking more closely at Listing 1-12, we can see that a FieldSwitch element is evaluating an expression for the variable FreeForm. The FreeForm variable is True if the display is not rendering the field inside a table. In this case FreeForm will only be False when the URL field is being edited. If the FreeForm variable is True, then the URL is displayed in its entirety using the following code:

```
<Case Value="TRUE"><Field Name="URL"/></Case>
```

If the value of the FreeForm variable is False, then the Default case will be processed because no other cases are defined. This case will render the URL in an appropriate format depending on whether the URL is currently defined and what data is in the field. In Listing 1-13, I have removed most of the details of the Default case and substituted comments so that you can analyze the code.

Listing 1-13. *Understanding the* Default *Case*

```
<Default>
    <HTML>GENERATE AN HTML TABLE OPEN</HTML>
    <HTML>GENERATE A TABLE ROW OPEN</HTML>
    <Switch>
        <Expr>GET THE VALUE OF THE URL FIELD</Expr>
        <Case IF THE FIELD IS EMPTY>
            RENDER THE FIELD WITH NO SPECIAL PROCESSING
        </Case>
        <Default>
            <FieldSwitch>
            <Expr GET THE FORMAT OF THE URL FIELD></Expr>
            <Case IF IT'S AN IMAGE VALUE>
                <HTML>GENERATE AN IMAGE HYPERLINK</HTML>
            </Case>
            <Default IF IT'S NOT AN IMAGE>
                <HTML>GENERATE A NORMAL HYPERLINK</HTML>
            </Default>
            </FieldSwitch>
        </Default>
    </Switch>
    <HTML>GENERATE AN HTML TABLE ROW CLOSE</HTML>
    <HTML>GENERATE AN HTML TABLE CLOSE</HTML>
</Default>
```

Understanding Miscellaneous Field Types

Along with the broad categories of field types I discussed earlier, CAML supports a number of other field types. Some of these field types are specific to a kind of list and mostly used internally. Others can be used to customize existing lists.

Attachments

The Attachments field type specifies whether there are any attachments associated with the list item. This field type is found in the definition for the base WSS lists that accept attachments.

The field itself is closely tied to the tp_HasAttachment field of the UserData table in the WSS content database. The following code shows an example of a field definition based on this type:

```
<Field ColName="tp_HasAttachment" Type="Attachments" Name="Attachments"
DisplayName="Attachments"></Field>
```

Counter

The Counter field type is used as an internal identifier only. It is used to guarantee a unique identifier for each item in a list. The following code shows an example of a field definition used for this purpose:

```
<Field ColName="tp_ID" ReadOnly="TRUE" Type="Counter" Name="ID"
DisplayName="ID"></Field>
```

CrossProjectLink

The CrossProjectLink field type is used to connect a list with a meeting workspace site. This connection allows a meeting workspace site to be created for selected items in a list.

File

The File field type is used to contain a file. This field type is found in the definition of Document Libraries. The following code shows an example of this field definition taken from the standard Document Library:

```
<Field ShowInFileDlg="FALSE" Type="File" Name="FileLeafRef" DisplayName="Name"
AuthoringInfo="(for use in forms)" List="Docs" FieldRef="ID"
ShowField="LeafName" JoinColName="DoclibRowId" JoinType="INNER"
Required="TRUE"></Field>
```

Guid

The Guid field type accepts a Globally Unique Identifier (GUID). This field type is used to give a unique number to items in a list. You can find an example of this field in the definition of the discussion list. The identifier is used to track the discussion items and associated threads. The following code shows how this field is defined in the discussion list:

```
<Field ColName="tp_GUID" ReadOnly="TRUE" Hidden="TRUE" Type="Guid"
Name="GUID" DisplayName="GUID"></Field>
```

Note

The Note field type accepts multiple lines of text. The text in a Note field is essentially handled the same way as a TextArea element in HTML.

Recurrence

The Recurrence field type is specifically used to define the recurrence patterns of events. This highly specialized field is used internally when a new event is added to a calendar.

Threading

The Threading field type is used specifically to provide a threaded view of items, as in a discussion list. Threading fields are not directly editable. Instead, they cause a special threaded list view to be generated. Threading fields are closely associated with the tp_Ordering field of the UserData table in the content database. The following code shows a definition of this field type in a discussion list:

```
<Field ColName="tp_Ordering" Hidden="TRUE" Name="Ordering"
Type="Threading" DisplayName="Ordering"></Field>
```

URL

The URL field type is used to contain a hyperlink. URL field types store their hyperlink information in the content database. The following code shows an example from a favorites link list:

```
<Field Name="URL" Type="URL" DisplayName="URL"></Field>
```

User

The User field type is used to provide a list of site users. The User field type is bound to the UserInfo database table to provide the list. In Document Libraries, the resulting value can be stored in the Lists table. The following code shows an example of a User field type that allows someone to select a user whose name is saved in the tp_Author field of the Lists table in the content database. This is used in Document Libraries to specify the author of a document.

```
<Field ColName="tp_Author" ReadOnly="TRUE" Type="User"
List="UserInfo" Name="Author" DisplayName="Created By" ></Field>
```

Understanding the View Element

The Views element contains a set of View elements that define the available data views for a list. Each list may have a number of different data views, but they almost always have views for presenting a summary, adding new items, and editing items. The View element used in SCHEMA.XML is the same element described in Table 1-11.

Each definition of a view consists of a header, body, and footer section. These sections are defined by the ViewHeader, ViewBody, and ViewFooter, respectively. The ViewHeader and ViewFooter sections are rendered a single time in each view while the ViewBody section is rendered once for each row contained in the view. The fields contained in the view are specified by the ViewFields element. Listing 1-14 shows a simple tabular view where column headings are rendered using the Fields element within the ViewHeader element.

Listing 1-14. *A Simple View Definition*

```
<View Name="Summary" DisplayName="Summary View" Type="HTML">

    <ViewHeader>
      <HTML><![CDATA[<TABLE><TR>]]></HTML>
      <Fields>
        <HTML><![CDATA[<TH>]]></HTML>
        <Field/>
        <HTML><![CDATA[</TH>]]></HTML>
      </Fields>
      <HTML><![CDATA[</TR>]]></HTML>
    </ViewHeader>

    <ViewBody>
      <HTML><![CDATA[<TR>]]></HTML>
        <Fields>
          <HTML><![CDATA[<TD>]]></HTML>
          <Field/>
          <HTML><![CDATA[</TD>]]></HTML>
        </Fields>
      <HTML><![CDATA[</TR>]]></HTML>
    </ViewBody>

    <ViewFooter>
      <HTML><![CDATA[</TABLE>]]></HTML>
    </ViewFooter>

    <ViewFields>
      <FieldRef Name="Title"/>
      <FieldRef Name="Size"/>
    </ViewFields>

</View>
```

When a data view is created, a dataset is generated from the underlying list. This dataset is generated as the result of a query defined in a Query element. The Query element is a child of the View element and uses CAML tags to define a SQL SELECT statement to run against the underlying list data. The SELECT statement is often as simple as specifying the field order for the view, as shown in the following code:

```
<Query>
    <OrderBy>
        <FieldRef Name="title" Ascending="TRUE"></FieldRef>
    </OrderBy>
</Query>
```

CAML queries can return a subset of list data by using a WHERE element to specify a conditional clause. The WHERE element supports the operations AND, =, >=, >, <=, <, <>, and OR through the child elements And, Eq, Geq, Gt, Leq, Lt, Neq, and Or, respectively. If the results of the query do not return any results, then the list may display alternate text using the ViewEmpty element. The following code shows the message displayed from my custom SQL Reports list when it is empty:

```
<ViewEmpty>
    <HTML><![CDATA[
    <TABLE class="ms-summarycustombody" cellpadding=0 cellspacing=0 border=0>
    <TR><TD class="ms-vb">]]></HTML>
    <HTML>There are currently no report links to display. To add a new report,
    click "Add new report link" below.</HTML>
    <HTML><![CDATA[
    </TD></TR><tr><td height="5"><img src="/_layouts/images/blank.gif" width="1"
    height="5" alt=""></td></tr></TABLE>]]></HTML>
</ViewEmpty>
```

Understanding the Toolbar Element

The Toolbar element defines additional content that is rendered outside the view definition. The rendered content may appear before or after the ViewBody element is rendered. Typically, standard toolbars are rendered before the ViewBody element and appear as an HTML representation of a standard Windows toolbar. Figure 1-8 shows a typical standard toolbar.

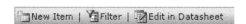

Figure 1-8. *A standard toolbar*

Freeform toolbars usually appear after the ViewBody element and consist of simple hyperlinks. These types of toolbars often appear in the summary view of a list. The toolbars often contain a link to add a new item to the list. Listing 1-15 shows the definition for a freeform toolbar that appears on the summary view of the link list.

Listing 1-15. *A Freeform Toolbar Definition*

```
<Toolbar Position="After" Type="Freeform">
  <HTML><![CDATA[
    <table width=100% cellpadding=0 cellspacing=0 border=0 >
      <tr>
        <td colspan="2" class="ms-partline">
        <IMG SRC="/_layouts/images/blank.gif" width=1 height=1 alt="">
        </td>
      </tr>
```

```
        <tr>
          <td class="ms-addnew" style="padding-bottom: 3px">
            <img src="/_layouts/images/rect.gif" alt=""> 
            <a class="ms-addnew" ID="idHomePageNewLink" href="]]>
  </HTML>
            <URL Cmd="New"/>
  <HTML><![CDATA[
          "ONCLICK="javascript:NewItem(']]>
  </HTML>
            <URL Cmd="New"/>
  <HTML><![CDATA[
          ', true);javascript:return false;" target="_self">]]>
  </HTML>
  <HTML>
          Add new link
  </HTML>
  <HTML><![CDATA[
            </a>
          </td>
        </tr>
        <tr>
          <td>
            <IMG SRC="/_layouts/images/blank.gif" width=1 height=5
            alt=""></td></tr> </table>
    ]]></HTML>
  </Toolbar>
```

A list definition will generally contain several toolbar definitions. Standard toolbars will be defined for displaying item views, editing, and adding new items. At least one freeform toolbar will be defined for the summary view. You can easily add your own items to an existing toolbar in the SCHEMA.XML list definition. The trick is to identify the correct toolbar definition for the view where you want the new item to appear. For my SQL Reports list, I wanted to add a toolbar link to the SQL Reporting Services home page so that users could perform additional operations outside SharePoint.

If you examine the Toolbar element in Listing 1-15, you'll notice that the Position attribute specifies that the toolbar should appear after the ViewBody element. The subsequent HTML code defines a table containing a link for adding a new item to the list. I can make a simple change to the toolbar by editing the hyperlink text. In my case, I simply changed the text "Add new link" to "Add new report link". These are often the kinds of simple changes you will make to customize toolbars.

If you would like, however, you can add new links to the toolbar definition. This is a matter of copying the existing link and modifying it. Although this is simple in concept, it is often difficult to identify exactly what elements you should copy in order to maintain the toolbar structure. Essentially, you have to carefully identify row boundaries within the table and copy the entire row definition. This may require you to add some additional HTML or CDATA elements to the code in order to get the break points you want and keep the XML well formed. Listing 1-16 shows the final CAML code with the modifications. Examine the code carefully and note where I have added additional HTML and CDATA elements along with the link definitions.

Listing 1-16. *Adding a Custom Toolbar Button*

```
<Toolbar Position="After" Type="Freeform">
  <HTML><![CDATA[
    <table width=100% cellpadding=0 cellspacing=0 border=0 >
      <tr>
        <td colspan="2" class="ms-partline">
        <IMG SRC="/_layouts/images/blank.gif" width=1 height=1 alt="">
        </td>
      </tr>
      <tr>
        <td class="ms-addnew" style="padding-bottom: 3px">
        <img src="/_layouts/images/rect.gif" alt=""> 
        <a class="ms-addnew" ID="idHomePageNewLink" href="]]>
  </HTML>
        <URL Cmd="New"/>
  <HTML><![CDATA[
        " ONCLICK="javascript:NewItem(']]>
  </HTML>
        <URL Cmd="New"/>
  <HTML><![CDATA[
        ', true);javascript:return false;" target="_self">]]>
  </HTML>
  <HTML>
        Add new report link
  </HTML>
  <HTML><![CDATA[
        </a>
        </td>
      </tr>
      <tr>
        <td>
        <IMG SRC="/_layouts/images/blank.gif" width=1 height=5
        alt=""></td></tr>]]>
  </HTML>
  <HTML><![CDATA[
      <tr>
        <td class="ms-addnew" style="padding-bottom: 3px">
        <img src="/_layouts/images/rect.gif" alt=""> 
        <a class="ms-addnew" ID="idReportsHome"
        href="http://spspdc/Reports">SQL Reports Home</a>
        </td>
      </tr>
  ]]></HTML>
  <HTML><![CDATA[
    </table>]]>
  </HTML>
</Toolbar>
```

Adding items to the standard toolbars found on list views and edit pages follows the same process as I outlined above. The only real difference is that you will need to add an image file to the directory `\Program Files\Common Files\Microsoft Shared\web server extensions\60\TEMPLATE\IMAGES` for the new toolbar button. Figure 1-9 shows a new button on a standard toolbar that also accesses the SQL Reporting Services home page.

Figure 1-9. *A custom toolbar*

Understanding the Form Element

The `Forms` element contains a set of `Form` elements that define the forms used to display, edit, and add items on lists. Forms are always associated with an ASP.NET file that acts as a container for the form in a WSS site. Views are merged into the forms to create the list rendering that appears in the browser.

The `Form` element supports the child elements `ListFormOpening`, `ListFormBody`, and `ListFormClosing`, which define sections of the web page. The form structure is similar to the view structure; it even has a toolbar, which is defined by the `ListFormButtons` element. The difference between the view and the form is that the view is used to show all items whereas the form is most often used to edit a single item at a time. You can use the same techniques described earlier, however, to modify the form presentation or add items to the toolbars.

Adding Lists to Site Definitions

Once the new list is defined, it must be referenced in the `ListTemplates` element of `ONET.XML` before it can be used with the site template. Once again, the simplest way to create this code is to copy an existing entry. To create an entry for my own custom list, I just copied the entry for the links list.

Once I copied the entry, I made changes to the `Name`, `DisplayName`, `Type`, and `Description` attributes. The `Name`, `DisplayName`, and `Description` are simple enough to understand, but the `Type` attribute requires some special attention. This attribute is the unique identifier for the list template and should be set to a value greater than 1000. The following code shows my entry for the SQL reports list:

```
<ListTemplate Name="SQLREPORTS" DisplayName="SQL Reporting Services" Type="1001"
BaseType="0" OnQuickLaunch="TRUE" SecurityBits="11"
Description="Create a report for sharing SQL Reports."
Image="/_layouts/images/itlink.gif"></ListTemplate>
```

Working with Shortcut Menus

Using CAML, we have made changes to the structure and presentation of a list and its data. These structural changes affect the way that WSS sites are constructed on the server before being presented to an end user. When users subsequently add or edit items in the list, they utilize server-side processing in the form of ASP.NET pages. However, not all list functionality is implemented in ASP.NET. In particular, the shortcut menu that drops down from a list item is implemented using client-side JavaScript. This JavaScript is contained in a file named OWS.JS located in the directory \Program Files\Common Files\Microsoft Shared\web server extensions\ 60\TEMPLATE\LAYOUTS*culture*. Using the code from this file, we can modify the behavior of existing menu items or create new items.

The JavaScript code contained in OWS.JS is extensive and affects every site in the installation; therefore, the file should never be edited directly. Instead, we will override functionality located in this file by creating our own JavaScript file that is a copy of the code we want to modify. This modified code will then be used only by particular site definitions that we designate. The function CreateMenu is the root of the menu building process and is shown in Listing 1-17.

Listing 1-17. *The CreateMenu Function*

```
function CreateMenu()
{
    if (! IsContextSet())
        return;
    var ctx = currentCtx;
    if (itemTable == null || imageCell == null ||
        (onKeyPress == false &&
         (event.srcElement.tagName=="A" ||
          event.srcElement.parentNode.tagName == "A")))
        return;
    IsMenuShown = true;
    window.document.body.onclick="";
    m = CMenu(currentItemID + "_menu");
    currenMenu = m;
        if (ctx.isVersions)
            AddVersionMenuItems(m, ctx);
    else if (ctx.listBaseType == BASETYPE_DOCUMENT_LIBRARY)
        AddDocLibMenuItems(m, ctx);
    else if (ctx.listTemplate == LISTTEMPLATE_MEETINGS)
        AddMeetingMenuItems(m, ctx);
    else
        AddListMenuItems(m, ctx);
    OMenu(m, itemTable, null, null, -1);
    document.body.onclick=HideSelectedRow;
    return false;
}
```

Examining the code in Listing 1-17, you'll notice that the CreateMenu function calls one of four other functions to build the shortcut menu. These functions—AddVersionMenuItems, AddDocLibMenuItems, AddMeetingMenuItems, and AddListMenuItems—contain the code that creates the individual items for each shortcut menu. Generally, you will override one of these functions to create a custom menu item.

Individual menu items are created by making a call to the CAMOpt function. This function takes as arguments the menu where the item will be created, the text for the menu item, the JavaScript function to be executed when the item is selected, and a path to an image to be

used on the menu item. The following code from the function `AddDocLibMenuItems` defines
a new menu item for editing the properties of a document:

```
strDisplayText = L_EditProperties_Text;
strAction = "STSNavigate('" + ctx.editFormUrl+"?ID="+ currentItemID +
            "&Source=" + GetSource() + RootFolder + "')";
strImagePath = ctx.imagesPath + "edititem.gif";
CAMOpt(m, strDisplayText, strAction, strImagePath);
```

The JavaScript file uses a constant to define the text for the menu item, which it stores in
the variable `strDisplayText`. When the menu item is selected by a user, the JavaScript function
`STSNavigate` will be called, which will open the form used to edit the document properties. The
image for the item is stored in the directory `\Program Files\Common Files\Microsoft Shared\`
`web server extensions\60\TEMPLATE\IMAGES`, which is retrieved from the `imagesPath` property
of the context object. These values are all passed to the function `CAMOpt` along with the menu
object, designated by the variable `m`.

As an example of how to add a new item to the shortcut menu, I created a new menu item
for Document Libraries called "Mail Document". Selecting this item from the shortcut menu
associated with a document will create a new message in Microsoft Outlook 2003 and attach
the document. End users can then enter an e-mail address to send the document to someone.
I intended this functionality to be similar to the Send To ➤ Mail Recipient functionality already
found in Microsoft Word. Figure 1-10 shows my final menu with the new item selected.

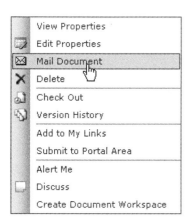

Figure 1-10. *A custom menu item*

As I said earlier, in order to add a new item to a shortcut menu you must override the
existing JavaScript code in `OWS.JS`. This is accomplished by creating your own JavaScript file
with a new definition for the function you wish to override. In my example, I need to override
the function `AddDocLibMenuItems`; this function defines the items in the shortcut menu for a
standard Document Library. To begin the process, I simply copied the code for the entire file
and saved it in a separate file named `MailDocument.js` and saved this file into the directory
`\Program Files\Common Files\Microsoft Shared\web server extensions\60\TEMPLATE\`
`LAYOUTS\`*culture*.

Once the entire function is copied, we are free to make any changes we want without worrying about impacting other sites. Using the format from an existing menu item, I inserted code to add a new item. The following code shows the definition for my new item:

```
//My new code
strDisplayText = "Mail Document";
strAction = "mailDocument('" + currentItemFileUrl + "')";
strImagePath = ctx.imagesPath + "mapi16.gif";
CAMOpt(m, strDisplayText, strAction, strImagePath);
```

The menu item I created has an action set to call a JavaScript function named mailDocument. This function does not exist; I had to create it. Fortunately, I can easily create the required function directly in the MailDocument.js file. Listing 1-18 shows the code for the mailDocument function called by the new menu item.

Listing 1-18. *The mailDocument Function*

```
function mailDocument(documentUrl)
{
    try{
        var protocolParts = location.href.split("//");
        var urlParts = protocolParts[1].split("/");
        var fileUrl = "http://" + urlParts[0] + documentUrl;

        var outlook = new ActiveXObject("Outlook.Application.11");
        var outlookMessage = outlook.CreateItem(0);
        var outlookAttachment = outlookMessage.Attachments.Add(fileUrl);
        outlookMessage.Display();

        outlookAttachment = null;
        outlookMessage = null;
        outlook = null;

        CollectGarbage();
    }
    catch(e){
        alert("This functionality requires Microsoft Outlook to be installed➥
and the associated Windows SharePoint Services site to be trusted.");
    }
}
```

Once you have modified the copied code and added any new functions to your custom JavaScript file, you must add the functionality to your site definition. Adding the new JavaScript file to the site definition is accomplished using the CustomJSUrl attribute of the Project element found in the ONET.XML file for the site definition. Once the custom JavaScript file is specified in the attribute, any functions defined in the file will override functions with the same name in OWS.JS. The following code shows the Project element for my example:

```
<Project Title="Team Web Site" ListDir="Lists" xmlns:ows="Microsoft SharePoint"
CustomJSUrl="/_layouts/
[%=System.Threading.Thread.CurrentThread.CurrentUICulture.LCID%]
/MailDocument.js">
```

■**Caution** The above code should all appear on a single line.

Working with the Content Editor Web Part

Once you understand the general structure of a WSS site and how the JavaScript functions
are used to provide client-side functionality, you can make changes to a site using the Content Editor web part. The Content Editor web part allows you to add HTML or JavaScript
directly to a page. Once you understand how shortcut menus are created, you can use this
web part to add new items to any menu.

The key to making this technique work lies in some special functionality provided by
OWS.JS. The functions AddDocLibMenuItems and AddListMenuItems both support a hook for
adding new items to the shortcut menu. These hooks look for the presence of custom functions named Custom_AddDocLibMenuItems and Custom_AddListMenuItems. If either of these
functions are present, then the code within them is processed as part of the menu construction routine. The following code shows the hook for Document Library menus:

```
function AddDocLibMenuItems(m, ctx)
{
   if (typeof(Custom_AddDocLibMenuItems) != "undefined")
   {
      if (Custom_AddDocLibMenuItems(m, ctx))
         return;
   }
}
```

Using the Content Editor web part, you can create a JavaScript function for either of the
hooks and add your own menu item. You can then code a custom function to handle the item
when it is selected. The code for the Content Editor will be exactly the same as the code we
used previously for the custom JavaScript file.

Use the following steps to create a new menu item:

1. Create a new WSS Team Site that contains a Document Library.

2. On the home page of the site, select Modify Shared Web Page ➤ Add Web Parts ➤
   Browse.

3. Drag the Document Library and the Content Editor web parts into the same zone on
   the page. Figure 1-11 shows the web parts.

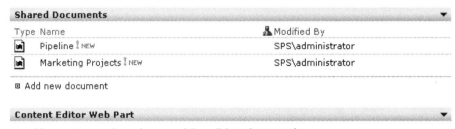

Figure 1-11. *Adding the web parts*

4. In the Content Editor web part, click the link titled Open the Tool Pane.

5. In the web part pane, click the Source Editor button.

6. Add the following code to the Text Entry box to create a new item for mailing documents:

```
<SCRIPT LANGUAGE="JavaScript">
function Custom_AddDocLibMenuItems(m,ctx)
{
    //Menu item
    strDisplayText = "Mail Document";
    strAction = "mailDocument(currentItemFileUrl)";
    strImagePath = ctx.imagesPath + "mapi16.gif";
    CAMOpt(m, strDisplayText, strAction, strImagePath);

    //Separator bar
    CAMSep(m);
    return false;
}
```

7. Add the code from Listing 1-18 to the Text Entry box to handle mailing the document.

8. At the end of the code, close the script section by adding the following code:

```
</SCRIPT>
```

9. Click the Save button.

10. In the Content Editor property pane, expand the Layout section.

11. In the Layout section, uncheck the Visible on Page box.

12. Click the OK button.

13. Select Modify Shared Web Part from the Document Library menu.

14. In the Document Library property pane, select **All Documents** from the Selected View list.

15. Click the OK button.

When you have finished, the Content Editor web part will be hidden and the new menu item will appear on the Document Library. This technique is a simple way to add items to a shortcut menu, but it has a few drawbacks. First, this technique cannot be used to make global changes; it must be applied to every site where you want it. Second, the technique only works on pages where you can add the Content Editor web part. In order to achieve more global and consistent changes to list functionality, you will ultimately have to modify the site CAML.

Exercise 1-1. Creating a Custom Site Definition

Creating a custom site definition is an excellent way to make global modifications to navigation links and list elements. In this exercise, you will create your own site definition with a modified task list to support Outlook integration. Using the new list, you will be able to export an item from a WSS task list to your Outlook 2003 task list.

Creating the Base Site Template

The first step in creating a new site definition is to copy an existing template. Because the CAML language is complex and difficult to work with, copying an existing site definition is the best way to start a new template. In this section, you will make a new template from the basic WSS site template.

To create the base site template, follow these steps:

1. Open the Windows File Explorer and navigate to \Program Files\Common Files\Microsoft Shared\web server extensions\60\TEMPLATE*culture*.

2. In the *culture* directory, make a copy of the STS folder and name it **MYTEMPLATE**.

3. From the \MYTEMPLATE\XML directory, open the ONET.XML file in Visual Studio. NET.

4. In the ONET.XML file, locate the Project element and change the Title attribute to the value **My New Template** and add a reference to the custom JavaScript file you will create later. The following code shows how the Project element should appear:

```
<Project Title"My New template" ListDir="Lists"
xmlns:ows="Microsoft SharePoint" CustomJSUrl="/_layouts/
[%=System.Threading.Thread.CurrentThread.CurrentUICulture.LCID%]
/CustomTaskList.js">
```

■**Caution** The above code should all appear on a single line.

---

5. Save and close ONET.XML.

6. In the *culture*\XML directory, make a copy of the WEBTEMP.XML file and name it **WEBTEMPNEW.XML**.

7. Open WEBTEMPNEW.XML in Visual Studio .NET.

8. In WEBTEMPNEW.XML, delete the Template element that defines the MPS site.

9. Rename the Template element that defines the STS site to **MYTEMPLATE** and change the ID attribute to **30001**.

10. Change the `Title` attributes for each template by adding the words **My New** before each of them. Listing 1-19 shows the complete `WEBTEMPNEW.XML` file.

11. Save `WEBTEMPNEW.XML`.

Listing 1-19. *The Final Version of WEBTEMPNEW.XML*

```xml
<?xml version="1.0" encoding="utf-8" ?>
<!-- _lcid="1033" _version="11.0.5510" _dal="1" -->
<!-- _LocalBinding -->
<Templates xmlns:ows="Microsoft SharePoint">
    <Template Name="MYTEMPLATE"      ID="30001">
        <Configuration ID="0" Title="My New Team Site" Hidden="FALSE"
        ImageUrl="/_layouts/images/stsprev.png"
        Description="This template creates a site for teams to create, organize,
        and share information quickly and easily. It includes a Document Library,
        and basic lists such as Announcements, Events, Contacts, and Quick
        Links.">
        </Configuration>
        <Configuration ID="1" Title="My New Blank Site" Hidden="FALSE"
        ImageUrl="/_layouts/images/stsprev.png"
        Description="This template creates a Windows SharePoint Services-enabled
        Web site with a blank home page. You can use a Windows SharePoint
        Services-compatible Web page editor to add interactive lists or any other
        Windows SharePoint Services features.">
        </Configuration>
        <Configuration ID="2" Title="My New Document Workspace" Hidden="FALSE"
        ImageUrl="/_layouts/images/dwsprev.png" Description="This template creates
        a site for colleagues to work together on documents. It provides a
        document library for storing the primary document and supporting files, a
        Task list for assigning to-do items, and a Links list for resources
        related to the document.">
        </Configuration>
    </Template>
</Templates>
```

Creating the New Menu Item

Once the base site template has been created, you can use the associated list definitions to create custom lists. In this section, you are going to modify the shortcut menu on the standard task list. You will copy an existing menu item from the standard contacts list and use it as the basis for a new menu item.

Use the following steps to create the new menu item:

1. Open the Windows File Explorer and navigate to the directory `\Program Files\ Common Files\Microsoft Shared\web server extensions\60\TEMPLATE\LAYOUTS\ culture`.

2. Open the file `OWS.JS` in Visual Studio .NET.

3. In Visual Studio .NET, select Edit ➤ Find and Replace ➤ Find to open the Find dialog.

4. In the Find dialog, type **AddListMenuItems** and click the Find Next button until you locate the function definition for AddListMenuItems.

5. Close the Find dialog.

6. In Visual Studio .NET, select File ➤ New ➤ File from the menu.

7. In the New File dialog, select to create a new Text File and click the Open button.

8. Copy the entire function definition for AddListMenuItems from OWS.JS and paste it into the new file you just opened.

9. Save the new file as CustomTaskList.js into the directory \Program Files\Common Files\Microsoft Shared\web server extensions\60\TEMPLATE\LAYOUTS*culture*.

10. Close OWS.JS, but keep CustomTaskList.js open in Visual Studio .NET.

11. Locate the following code in CustomTaskList.js, which defines a new menu item for a contact list:

```
if (ctx.listTemplate == LISTTEMPLATE_CONTACTS)
{
    strDisplayText = L_ExportContact_Text;
    strAction = "STSNavigate('" + ctx.HttpPath +
    "&Cmd=Display&CacheControl=1&List=" + ctx.listName +
    "&ID=" + currentItemID + "&Using=" +
    escapeProperly(ctx.listUrlDir) + "/vcard.vcf" + "')";
    strImagePath = ctx.imagesPath + "exptitem.gif";
    CAMOpt(m, strDisplayText, strAction, strImagePath);
}
```

12. Copy the code and paste it directly beneath the original code.

13. Modify the copied code to add a new menu item for task lists that calls a JavaScript function named exportTask. Your modified code should look like the following code:

```
if (ctx.listTemplate == LISTTEMPLATE_TASKS)
{
    strDisplayText = "Export Task";
    strAction = "exportTask('" + ctx.HttpRoot + "','" + ctx.listName + "','" +
                        currentItemID + "')";
    strImagePath = ctx.imagesPath + "exptitem.gif";
    CAMOpt(m, strDisplayText, strAction, strImagePath);
}
```

Accessing the Task Information

When you created the new menu item, you defined JavaScript code to call when the item is selected from the shortcut menu. In this section, you will create a function named exportTask, which takes as arguments the URL of the site, the GUID identifying the list, and the identifier of the selected list item. These arguments are then used to access information about the selected task through web services.

To create the new function, follow these steps:

1. Open the file `CustomTaskList.js` in Visual Studio .NET if it is not already open.

2. Scroll to the bottom of the file and add the following variable definition, which will support making a `POST` to the SharePoint Lists web service:

```
var objHttp;
```

3. Directly beneath the variable definition, add the signature for the new function using the following code:

```
function exportTask(SitePath,listName,currentItemID)
{
}
```

4. Add the code from Listing 1-20 to the body of the `exportTask` function to retrieve the task information for the selected task.

Listing 1-20. *The exportTask Function*

```
try
 {

    //Use MSXML to make web service call
    objHttp = new ActiveXObject("MSXML2.XMLHTTP");

    //Create the SOAP envelope
    strEnvelope =
    "<soap:Envelope xmlns:xsi=\"http://www.w3.org/2001/XMLSchema-instance\"" +
    " xmlns:xsd=\"http://www.w3.org/2001/XMLSchema\"" +
    " xmlns:soap=\"http://schemas.xmlsoap.org/soap/envelope/\">" +
    "  <soap:Body>" +
    "     <GetListItems
xmlns=\"http://schemas.microsoft.com/sharepoint/soap/\">" +
    "        <listName>" + listName + "</listName>" +
    "        <query>" +
    "           <Query><Where>" +
    "             <Eq><FieldRef Name=\"ID\" />" +
    "             <Value Type=\"Counter\">" + currentItemID + "</Value></Eq>" +
    "           </Where></Query>" +
    "        </query>" +
```

```
    "       <viewFields><ViewFields>" +
    "           <FieldRef Name=\"ID\"/><FieldRef Name=\"Title\"/>" +
    "           <FieldRef Name=\"Status\"/><FieldRef Name=\"Priority\"/>" +
    "           <FieldRef Name=\"StartDate\"/><FieldRef Name=\"DueDate\"/>" +
    "           <FieldRef Name=\"Body\"/><FieldRef Name=\"PercentComplete\"/>" +
    "       </ViewFields></viewFields>" +
    "     </GetListItems>" +
    "   </soap:Body>" +
    "</soap:Envelope>";

    //Make the call
    objHttp.open("post", SitePath + "/_vti_bin/Lists.asmx");
    objHttp.setRequestHeader("Content-Type", "text/xml; charset=utf-8");
    objHttp.setRequestHeader("SOAPAction",
 "http://schemas.microsoft.com/sharepoint/soap/GetListItems");
    objHttp.send(strEnvelope);

    //Wait for return XML
    window.setTimeout(showResults, 1);

}

catch(e)
{
   alert(e.message);
}
```

Examining the code from Listing 1-20, you'll see that it constructs a Simple Object Access Protocol (SOAP) call to the SharePoint Lists web service. The Lists web service returns information about items in a list. The code makes use of the GetListItems method to return information about the selected task item. I cover SharePoint web services in detail later in the book.

Exporting the Task to Microsoft Outlook

After the web service call is made, our code has to wait for the response that contains the data. Therefore, the last part of Listing 1-20 sets a timeout to call a function showResults, which will process the return data. In this section, you will create the showResults function.

Use the following steps to build the function:

1. Open the file CustomTaskList.js in Visual Studio .NET if it is not already open.

2. Scroll to the bottom of the file and add the following code signature for the showResults function:

```
function showResults(){
}
```

3. Within the body of the showResults function, add the code from Listing 1-21 to parse the returned XML and export the task to Microsoft Outlook.

Listing 1-21. *The showResults Function*

```
try
{

  if(objHttp.readyState==4)
  {

    //Parse XML
    var responseXML = objHttp.responseText;
    objHttp = null;

    var title = nodeValue("Title",responseXML);
    var status = nodeValue("Status",responseXML);
    var priority = nodeValue("Priority",responseXML);
    var startdate = nodeValue("StartDate",responseXML);
    var duedate = nodeValue("DueDate",responseXML);
    var body = nodeValue("Body",responseXML);
    var percent = nodeValue("PercentComplete",responseXML);

    //Create a new task in Outlook 2003
    var ol = new ActiveXObject("Outlook.Application.11");
    var olTask = ol.CreateItem(3);

    //Subject
    try{olTask.Subject = title; }catch(e){}

    //Start Date
    try{olTask.StartDate = startdate;}catch(e){}

    //Due Date
    try{olTask.DueDate = duedate;}catch(e){}

    //Body
    try{olTask.Body = body; }catch(e){}

    //Status
    switch(status)
    {
      case 'Not Started':
        try{olTask.Status = 0; }catch(e){}
        break;
      case 'In Progress':
        try{olTask.Status = 1; }catch(e){}
        break;
      case 'Completed':
        try{olTask.Status = 2; }catch(e){}
        break;
      case 'Deferred':
        try{olTask.Status = 4; }catch(e){}
```

```
        break;
      case 'Waiting on some else':
        try{olTask.Status = 3; }catch(e){}
        break;
    }

    //Priority
    switch(priority)
    {
      case '(1) High':
        try{olTask.Importance = 2; }catch(e){}
        break;
      case '(2) Normal':
        try{olTask.Importance = 1; }catch(e){}
        break;
      case '(3) Low':
        try{olTask.Importance = 0; }catch(e){}
        break;
    }

    //Percent Complete
    try{olTask.PercentComplete = percent * 100; }catch(e){}

    //Show the new task
    olTask.Display();
    olTask = null;
    ol = null;

  }

  else
    window.setTimeout(showResults, 1);

}

catch(e){
  alert(e.message);
}

finally
{
  CollectGarbage();
}
```

Adding the Helper Function

The showResults function calls a helper function named nodeValue to parse the returned XML. This function returns the value of the various task attributes so they can be used in automating Microsoft Outlook. Add the code from Listing 1-22 to the bottom of the CustomTaskList.js file to complete the task processing.

Listing 1-22. *The nodeValue Function*

```
function nodeValue(nodeName,xmlString){

  try
  {
    //Parses return XML
    var singleQuote="'";
    var searchString = "ows_" + nodeName + "=" + singleQuote;
    if (xmlString.indexOf(searchString,0) == -1)
    {
      return '';
    }
    else
    {
      var searchBegin = xmlString.indexOf(searchString,0) +
      searchString.length;
      var searchEnd = xmlString.indexOf(singleQuote,searchBegin);
      return xmlString.substring(searchBegin,searchEnd);
    }
  }

  catch(e)
  {
    alert(e);
  }

}
```

Using the New Site Definition

Once the site definition and custom JavaScript files are completed, you are ready to use them to create a SharePoint site. Before you can use them, however, you must save the files and restart IIS. Once this is done, you should be able to create a new site with the templates. Standard task lists made from the template will now contain a new menu item to export tasks. Figure 1-12 shows the shortcut menu with the new item selected.

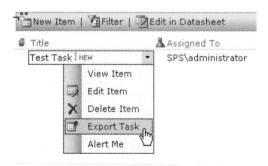

Figure 1-12. *The new menu item*

CHAPTER 2

■■■

Databases, Web Services, and Protocols

Anyone who has installed Windows SharePoint Services (WSS) knows that it requires Microsoft SQL Server to operate. This is because nearly all of the content displayed and managed by WSS is stored in SQL Server databases. All of the web pages, documents, and lists are stored in database tables and then produced dynamically when requested through a site. With the small exception of some configuration files and web part description files, everything else is stored in these databases.

WSS manages two basic database types known as the *configuration* and *content* databases. A single configuration database is created for a WSS installation while a separate content database is created for each virtual server in a WSS installation. If you also have SharePoint Portal Server (SPS) installed, your installation will have additional databases for things like the Microsoft Single Sign-On (SSO) service and user profiles.

Although the Software Development Kit (SDK) documents every table and field for the configuration and content databases, manipulating the information in these databases still remains a mystery to most developers. This is because Microsoft does not support direct manipulation of the databases. In fact, improperly changing theses databases can destroy a WSS installation and should never be done lightly. While the recommended approach for manipulating WSS databases is to utilize the object model or the web services provided by Microsoft as part of the SDK, there are times when I have had to directly access one of the databases to accomplish a task.

In this chapter, I'll take a look at some advanced techniques to manipulate WSS content. I'll access the databases directly, utilize web services, and investigate some HTTP techniques. While all the possible avenues of study could easily comprise a separate book, I'll focus on accomplishing useful tasks that help you manage and maintain WSS installations.

Working with Documents

Document management is one of the pillars of the Microsoft Office System and is a part of nearly every solution design involving WSS. Although the Document Libraries offered by WSS provide the fundamental features (check-in, checkout, version control, and approval) expected in a document management system, the WSS architecture often frustrates developers trying to access and manage the document storage system. This is because sites are logically related but physically separated. For example, documents located in one site cannot be easily moved to another site because sites represent security boundaries. Additionally, you can't see all of the documents in a WSS installation through a single hierarchical tree that represents the data store as a whole. Because documents represent such a significant part of a WSS installation, we often need advanced techniques to access and manipulate them.

The Docs Table

All of the documents maintained in a WSS installation are located in the Docs table of the content database. This table contains not only the documents stored in libraries but also the web pages that make up the WSS sites. Table 2-1 lists the columns found in the Docs table and their associated descriptions.

Table 2-1. *The Docs Table*

Column	Data Type	Description
Id	uniqueidentifier	The Globally Unique Identifier (GUID) used to identify the document in the database.
SiteId	uniqueidentifier	The GUID of the top-level site under which the document is logically located.
DirName	nvarchar	The directory relative to the server in which the file is logically located.
LeafName	nvarchar	The name of the document or folder under the directory name.
WebId	uniqueidentifier	The GUID of the web under the top-level site to which the document belongs. This field maps to the Id field of the Webs table in the content database.
ListId	uniqueidentifier	The GUID of the list or library with which the document is associated.
DoclibRowId	int	The row number of the document in the library. Row numbers are assigned in the order in which documents are added.
Type	tinyint	The type of leaf. Possible values are 1 for a folder or 0 for a file.
Size	int	The size of the document.
MetaInfoSize	int	The size of the metadata information associated with the document.
Version	int	The most recent version number of the document.
UIVersion	int	The document version number that is displayed.
Dirty	bit	The value that indicates if a content page needs to be reparsed. Possible values are True and False. When set to True, links inside the document are processed.

Table 2-1. *The Docs Table*

Column	Data Type	Description
CacheParseId	uniqueidentifier	The GUID value used for optimistic concurrency checking during conflict resolution.
DocFlags	tinyint	Bit field used internally.
ThicketFlag	bit	The value indicating whether the document has additional supporting files.
CharSet	int	Microsoft Windows character set of the document.
TimeCreated	datetime	Nonlocalized date and time the file was created.
TimeLastModified	datetime	Nonlocalized date and time the file was modified.
NextToLastTimeModified	datetime	Nonlocalized date and time the file was modified prior to TimeLastModified.
MetaInfoTimeLastModified	datetime	Nonlocalized date and time the metadata was updated.
TimeLastWritten	datetime	Nonlocalized date and time the document was written.
SetupPath	nvarchar	The path from which the file was originally installed.
CheckoutUserId	int	Id of the user in the UserInfo table who has the file checked out.
CheckoutDate	datetime	Nonlocalized date and time that the file was checked out.
CheckoutExpires	datetime	Nonlocalized date and time that the checkout expires.
CheckoutSize	int	The size of the file when it was checked out.
VersionCreatedSinceSTCheckout	bit	A flag that prevents multiple document versions from being created on a single short-term checkout.
LTCheckoutUserId	int	The Id of the user in the UserInfo table who has the file checked out.
VirusVendorID	int	The Id of the antivirus vendor in use.
VirusStatus	int	The status of the virus scan on the document.
VirusInfo	nvarchar	The details regarding a detected virus.
MetaInfo	image	The document metadata stored in binary format.
Content	image	The document content in binary format.
CheckoutContent	image	The content of the document when it is checked out. This content overwrites the existing content when the document is checked in.

As new sites are created and documents are loaded, the Docs table is populated. WSS then uses these entries to present content to end users when it is requested through the site. If you examine the contents of this table through a typical site creation process, you can see how WSS populates the table.

Follow these steps to see how WSS uses the Docs table:

1. Select Start ➤ All Programs ➤ Administrative Tools ➤ SharePoint Central Administration. (This step assumes that SharePoint Portal Server is not installed along with WSS.)

2. From the Windows SharePoint Services Central Administration page, select Virtual Server Configuration ➤ Create a Top-Level Web Site.

3. On the Virtual Server List page, select the virtual server where you will create a new site.

4. On the Create Top-Level Web Site page, fill in values to create a new top-level site named **Docs**.

5. Click the OK button, and stop on the Top-Level Site Successfully Created page.

6. Start the SQL Query Analyzer and connect to the content database that contains the Docs table.

7. In the SQL Query Analyzer, execute the following statement against the content database:

```
SELECT DirName, LeafName, TimeCreated FROM Docs
ORDER BY TimeCreated DESC, DirName, LeafName
```

8. Examine the results of the query and note that WSS has created the structure of the site but that no content is present yet.

9. Return to the Top-Level Site Successfully Created page and click the link for the new site.

10. On the template Selection page, choose to use the Team Site template and click the OK button.

11. Once the site is created, return to the SQL Query Analyzer and rerun the query.

12. Examine the query results and you will see that the table now contains the site content. You should be able to locate entries for the same ASPX pages that I presented in Chapter 1.

13. Return to the new site you created and upload a document into the Shared Documents library.

14. Return to the SQL Query Analyzer and rerun the query. You should now see the uploaded document in the Docs table, proving that the site content and the managed documents are all stored together.

Once you understand the basics of the Docs table, it is simple to return a list of documents contained in WSS. Listing 2-1 shows how to return the set of all Microsoft Word documents contained in a WSS installation and display them in a list box using Visual Basic .NET. This same code stores the Id field for each document as the ValueMember of the list. This way you can select a document and use its unique identifier to access the individual document in the Docs table.

Listing 2-1. *Returning Microsoft Word Documents*

```
Private Const SHAREPOINT_ROOT As String = "http://myserver/"

Private Sub FillList()

    'List all of the word documents in SharePoint
    Dim strConnection As String = "Integrated Security=SSPI;" & _
    "Initial Catalog=MyContentDatabase;Data Source=MySQLServer;"

    Dim strSQL As String = "SELECT CONVERT(nvarchar(36), Id) AS ID," & _
    " '" & SHAREPOINT_ROOT & "' + DirName + '/' + LeafName AS Name " & _
    "FROM dbo.Docs " & _
    "WHERE (LeafName NOT LIKE 'template%') AND " & _
    "LeafName LIKE '%.doc' " & _
    "ORDER BY DirName, LeafName"

    Try

        Dim objDataset As New DataSet("root")

        'Run Query
        With New SqlDataAdapter
            .SelectCommand = New SqlCommand(strSQL, _
            New SqlConnection(strConnection))
            .Fill(objDataset, "Docs")
        End With

        'Fill List
        lstDocs.DataSource = objDataset.Tables("Docs")
        lstDocs.DisplayMember = "Name"
        lstDocs.ValueMember = "ID"

    Catch x As Exception
        MsgBox(x.Message, MsgBoxStyle.Exclamation)
    End Try

End Sub
```

The Docs table is designed with three primary key fields: SiteId, DirName, and LeafName. Using these three fields, you can join other tables to the query to enhance the information you can access. The following query returns all of the ASPX files contained in a WSS installation. Additionally, the Docs table is joined to the Sites table to return a complete URL to the web site:

```
SELECT dbo.Docs.Id, dbo.Sites.FullUrl, dbo.Docs.LeafName
FROM dbo.Sites INNER JOIN
    dbo.Docs ON dbo.Sites.Id = dbo.Docs.SiteId
WHERE (dbo.Docs.Type = 0)
        AND (dbo.Docs.LeafName LIKE '%.aspx')
        AND (dbo.Docs.LeafName NOT LIKE 'template%')
```

Accessing Binary Information

Once you have returned the Id field of a document, you can use it to access both the document content and the metadata. WSS stores content and metadata information as binary large objects (BLOB) using image fields in the Docs table. Accessing these BLOBs in SQL Server can prove very handy when you're creating utilities that help manage WSS installations.

Accessing binary data from a WSS installation is done using the SqlDataReader object. The SqlDataReader object is part of ADO.NET and functions to return a stream of data from a database. This stands in contrast to the DataSet object, which returns a set of data from the database. The beauty of the SqlDataReader object is that it can act as a lightweight, forward-only, read-only stream that rapidly and efficiently accesses BLOB data. This configuration is often called a "firehose cursor" because the data streams rapidly out of the database.

Accessing the content for an individual document begins by returning the Content field using the Id of the document. This is a simple query to write, but you must take care to provide the Id field in the correct format because it is a GUID. To create the correct query, simply enclose the GUID in single quotes, including the curly braces, as shown in the following code:

```
SELECT Content From Docs Where Id='{046921FB-448F-47DA-87DF-1BCC8B85DEAA}'
```

If you have used the SqlDataReader before to return numeric and text data, you'll find that returning BLOB data from WSS is somewhat different. After the connection to the database is opened, you use the ExecuteReader method to execute the query and build the SqlDataReader. When accessing BLOB data, however, you must utilize the CommandBehavior argument of the ExecuteReader method to specify SequentialAccess.

Specifying CommandBehavior.SequentialAccess allows the data reader to load the large binary fields as a stream. You can then set up a buffer to fill with the streaming bytes until you have retrieved the entire document. When you specify SequentialAccess, you must read from the column data in the order that the columns are returned. However, you are not required to read each column. You can skip any column you wish, but you cannot return to a column once you have skipped it.

When filling the buffer with the bytes representing the document content, you will typically use a Stream object to put the content in a useful format like a file. This requires setting up FileStream and BinaryWriter objects to move the content from the buffer into the file system. Listing 2-2 shows a complete example of reading a Word document from the Docs table and creating a file on your desktop.

Listing 2-2. *Reading a Document*

```
'Set up the database connection
Dim strConnection As String = "Integrated Security=SSPI;" & _
                        "Initial Catalog=MyContentDatabase;" & _
                        "Data Source=MySQLServer;"
Dim strSQL As String = "SELECT Content FROM dbo.Docs " & _
                        "WHERE Id = '{046921FB-448F-47DA-87DF-1BCC8B85DEAA}'"
Dim objConnection As New SqlConnection(strConnection)
Dim objCommand As New SqlCommand(strSQL, objConnection)
Dim objReader As SqlDataReader

'Create a file name
Dim strDesktop As String = _
System.Environment.GetFolderPath(Environment.SpecialFolder.Desktop)
Dim strFile As String = strDesktop & "\FileName.doc"

'Create a filesteam
Dim objStream As New FileStream(strFile, FileMode.OpenOrCreate, _
                            FileAccess.Write)
Dim objWriter As New BinaryWriter(objStream)

'Set up the buffer to receive the byte data
Dim intSize As Integer = 8192
Dim bytBuffer(intSize - 1) As Byte
Dim lngIndex As Long
Dim lngReturn As Long

Try

    'Open the connection
    objConnection.Open()
    objReader = objCommand.ExecuteReader(CommandBehavior.SequentialAccess)

    Do While objReader.Read

        lngIndex = 0

        'Read first chunk into the buffer
        lngReturn = objReader.GetBytes(0, lngIndex, bytBuffer, 0, intSize)

        Do While lngReturn = intSize

            'Write out the chunk
            objWriter.Write(bytBuffer)
            objWriter.Flush()
```

```
                    'Get next chunk
                    lngIndex += intSize
                    lngReturn = objReader.GetBytes(0, lngIndex, bytBuffer, 0, intSize)

            Loop

                    'Write the last chunk to the file
                    objWriter.Write(bytBuffer)
                    objWriter.Flush()

                    'Close the stream
                    objWriter.Close()
                    objStream.Close()

            Loop

            MsgBox("Content placed on your desktop.", MsgBoxStyle.Information)

    Catch x As Exception
            MsgBox(x.Message, MsgBoxStyle.Exclamation)

    Finally
            objReader.Close()
            objStream = Nothing
            objConnection.Close()

    End Try
```

Document content data is not the only information that WSS stores in binary fields. Along with content, WSS also stores metadata information in BLOB format. Using the same technique as outlined in Listing 2-2, you can also access the MetaInfo field to retrieve associated information. When you access this field, you will find that it contains both standard document metadata as well as the particular field values that were defined for the Document Library where the document is stored. Listing 2-3 shows a typical metadata text file retrieved directly from the database. Note that the values designated with SW are the custom fields associated with the Document Library.

Listing 2-3. *Typical Document Metadata*

```
vti_approvallevel:SR|
vti_categories:VW|
Routing Status:SW|In Progress
vti_assignedto:SR|
Document Status:SW|Under Review
K2Process:SW|
vti_cachedcustomprops:VX|vti_approvallevel vti_categories Routing\\ Status
vti_assignedto Document\\ Status K2Process vti_title Route\\ for\\ Approval
vti_modifiedby:SR|SPS\\administrator
```

```
vti_cachedtitle:SR|1Q2004 Quarterly Report
vti_title:SR|1Q2004 Quarterly Report
Route for Approval:SW|1
vti_author:SR|SPS\\administrator
```

Accessing the binary information stored in the Docs table is a good way to read documents and metadata outside of the WSS site structure, but it is dangerous to attempt to use the same techniques to write to the database. It is tempting, for example, to try to use these techniques to automatically migrate existing documents into WSS libraries from a file server. The problem is that the database dependencies between tables, fields, and data are not well documented. It is very easy to destroy a WSS installation by writing directly to the database. Fortunately, we have other techniques for manipulating documents that are both useful and safe.

Downloading and Uploading Documents

We know as users of WSS Document Libraries that every document stored in a library is accessible through a Uniform Resource Identifier (URI). We also know from examining the Docs table that we can easily retrieve the URI for any document by joining the Docs table with the Sites table. Once we have a document URI, we can access the document programmatically and download it. Similarly, if we know the URI for a Document Library, we can programmatically upload documents into the library.

Downloading and uploading documents is much safer than direct manipulation of the database because we are interacting with WSS in the expected manner. In other words, programmatically downloading and uploading simply automates the same actions we ordinarily perform manually. This approach yields a reliable mechanism for bulk loading documents into libraries.

Automating the transfer process relies on the use of the WebClient class in the .NET Framework. The WebClient class provides methods for uploading and downloading files and data streams between Internet, intranet, and file targets. Table 2-2 lists the members of the WebClient class.

Table 2-2. *The WebClient Class*

Member	Property or Method	Description
BaseAddress	Property	The base URI for requests made by a WebClient
Credentials	Property	The network credentials used for authentication
Headers	Property	The collection of header name-value pairs
QueryString	Property	The collection of query name-value pairs
ResponseHeaders	Property	The collection of header name-value pairs from a response
DownloadData	Method	Downloads data from a URI
DownloadFile	Method	Downloads data from a URI to a local file
OpenRead	Method	Opens a stream for data download
OpenWrite	Method	Opens a stream for data upload
UploadData	Method	Uploads a data buffer
UploadFile	Method	Uploads a local file to a URI
UploadValues	Method	Uploads a name-value collection to a URI

When using the methods of the WebClient class, you must provide a set of credentials that have permission to access the target Document Library. If these credentials will represent the current user, you can utilize the CredentialCache object to return the DefaultCredentials property. The DefaultCredentials property always represents the system credentials for the current security context.

Once the Credentials property of the WebClient is set, you must build the source URI and the destination filename to where the document will be downloaded. After the URI of the document is known, downloading it to the local file system is as easy as calling the DownloadFile method. Listing 2-4 shows an example function in C# that downloads from a given source to the desktop.

Listing 2-4. *Downloading Documents from a Library*

```
private void Download_Click(string strSourceFileURL)
{
    try
    {

        //Build the destination path
        string strDesktop =
        System.Environment.GetFolderPath(Environment.SpecialFolder.Desktop);
        string strDestinationFilePath = strDesktop + "\\"
        + strSourceFileURL.Substring(strSourceFileURL.LastIndexOf("/")+1);

        //Download file
        WebClient objWebClient = new WebClient();
        objWebClient.Credentials = CredentialCache.DefaultCredentials;
        objWebClient.DownloadFile(strSourceFileURL, strDestinationFilePath);

        MessageBox.Show("File downloaded to your desktop.");
    }
    catch (Exception x)
    {
        MessageBox.Show(x.Message);
    }

}
```

Uploading files to a Document Library is nearly as easy as downloading. The difference is that you must open the local file and create a byte array. Once the byte array is created, it may be uploaded using the UploadData method of the WebClient. Listing 2-5 shows an example of uploading a file selected using a common dialog to a target Document Library specified in the code.

Listing 2-5. *Uploading Documents to a Library*

```
if(diaOpen.ShowDialog() == DialogResult.OK)
{
    try
    {

        //Load File into a byte array
        FileStream objStream = new FileStream(
        diaOpen.FileName, FileMode.Open, FileAccess.Read);
        BinaryReader objReader = new BinaryReader(objStream);
        byte [] arrFileBytes = objReader.ReadBytes((int)objStream.Length);
        objReader.Close();
        objStream.Close();

        //Upload file
        string strTarget = "http://spspdc/sites/Test/Shared%20Documents/";
        string strDestination = strTarget
        + diaOpen.FileName.Substring(diaOpen.FileName.LastIndexOf("\\")+1);
        WebClient objWebClient = new WebClient();
        objWebClient.Credentials = CredentialCache.DefaultCredentials;
        objWebClient.UploadData(strDestination,"PUT",arrFileBytes);

        MessageBox.Show("Document uploaded.");
    }
    catch (Exception x)
    {
        MessageBox.Show(x.Message);
    }
}
```

Working with Document Properties

I showed earlier that it is possible to access the metadata for any document if you know the document GUID. Using the GUID, you can access the MetaInfo BLOB in the Docs table and download it. I noted, however, that modifying the MetaInfo field was not a good idea. In fact, modifying the MetaInfo field won't really accomplish anything because the actual metadata for a document is stored in the document itself. The MetaInfo field is simply a copy of the document metadata.

You can prove to yourself that the metadata is actually stored in the document by downloading a document from a library using the technique described earlier and then examining the document properties. Custom fields that you add to a Document Library are shown under the Custom tab of the Properties dialog. Figure 2-1 shows the properties for a document I downloaded from a Document Library with some custom fields defined.

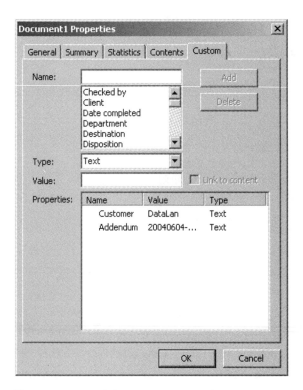

Figure 2-1. *Examining custom properties*

If you are interested in examining and modifying the properties of documents in WSS libraries, then you will need to make use of the Lists web service. The Lists web service provides methods you can use to access any list in WSS along with the items and fields it contains. Using the Lists service is not trivial, but it does offer a significant amount of control over list schema and data. In fact, we briefly used the Lists service through JavaScript in Chapter 1 to export tasks from a list to Microsoft Outlook. In this section, I'll look at the Lists service in more detail and utilize it with projects in Visual Studio .NET.

In order to get started using the Lists service in Visual Studio .NET, you must set a web reference to the Lists service in a project. Setting the web reference is done in the standard way by selecting Project ➤ Add Web Reference from Visual Studio .NET. The only difference is that a Lists web service is associated with each individual WSS site. Therefore, you must set the reference using the specific URL of the site you want to manipulate. The form of the web reference is shown in the following code:

```
http://Server_Name/Site_Path/_vti_bin/Lists.asmx?WSDL
```

When you enter the URL for the web reference, you will see the complete interface definition for the Lists web service. You can then give the web reference a name and click the Add Reference button. Table 2-3 lists all of the methods of the Lists web service.

Table 2-3. *The Lists Web Service*

Method	Description
AddAttachment	Adds an attachment to a list item in a list
AddList	Creates a new list on the site using a list template
DeleteAttachment	Deletes an attachment from a list item
DeleteList	Deletes a list
GetAttachmentCollection	Returns a set of URLs for attachments associated with a list item
GetList	Returns the schema for the fields in a list
GetListAndView	Returns the list and view schemas for a list
GetListCollection	Returns the text names and GUIDs for all the lists on the site
GetListItemChanges	Returns changes to the list since the specified date and time
GetListItems	Returns list items based on a query
UpdateList	Updates a list schema
UpdateListItems	Updates list items based on their ID

Once the web reference is set, you are ready to create an instance of the proxy object that will call the web service. When you set the web reference, you were forced to specify an exact site that you wanted to target, but the truth is that you can use the same code to access any site by first changing the URL property of the web service. For example, suppose you set a web reference and named it MyService. Using the following VB.NET code, you can create an instance of the web service and redirect it to any site you want. Then you can set the access credentials for the service to be the same as the current user.

```
Dim objService As New MyService.Lists
objService.Url = "http://Server_Name/Site_Path/_vti_bin/Lists.asmx"
objService.Credentials = System.Net.CredentialCache.DefaultCredentials
```

After you create an instance of the web service proxy, you will want to retrieve the set of all lists that are on the target site. You can then use this set to select the Document Library that you want to manipulate. The GetListCollection method is used to return a Collaborative Application Markup Language (CAML) fragment that defines all of the lists available on a site. The return value of the method is simply stored in an XmlNode object, as shown in the following Visual Basic .NET code:

```
Dim objCAML As XmlNode = objService.GetListCollection()
```

In order to show the information contained in the CAML fragment, I ran the service against a standard WSS team site. The return CAML fragment is a set of List elements. One List element is returned for each list on the target site. Listing 2-6 shows only the first List element of the return CAML fragment, but all of the subsequent List elements contain similar information.

Listing 2-6. *A Portion of the GetListCollection CAML Fragment*

```
<Lists xmlns="http://schemas.microsoft.com/sharepoint/soap/">
    <List
        DocTemplateUrl=""
        DefaultViewUrl="/sites/Test/Lists/Announcements/AllItems.aspx"
        ID="{970DF0FB-CC31-40C3-AF4C-6515C37CE582}"
        Title="Announcements"
        Description="Use the Announcements list to post messages on
        the home page of your site."
        ImageUrl="/_layouts/images/itann.gif"
        Name="{970DF0FB-CC31-40C3-AF4C-6515C37CE582}"
        BaseType="0"
        ServerTemplate="104"
        Created="20040603 16:00:26"
        Modified="20040603 16:00:26"
        LastDeleted="20040603 16:00:26"
        Version="0"
        Direction="none"
        ThumbnailSize=""
        WebImageWidth=""
        WebImageHeight=""
        Flags="4096"
        ItemCount="1"
        AnonymousPermMask=""
        RootFolder=""
        ReadSecurity="1"
        WriteSecurity="1"
        Author="1"
        EventSinkAssembly="" EventSinkClass="" EventSinkData=""
        EmailInsertsFolder=""
        AllowDeletion="True"
        AllowMultiResponses="False"
        EnableAttachments="True"
        EnableModeration="False"
        EnableVersioning="False"
        Hidden="False"
        MultipleDataList="False"
        Ordered="False"
        ShowUser="True" />
</Lists>
```

Once you have retrieved the CAML fragment containing all of the List elements, you can use the information in Listing 2-6 to help you pick out the data that you want. For example, you may want to add the titles of each list to a ListBox control so that you can select the list to manipulate. The following code shows how to do this by accessing the attributes of each List element:

```
For Each objNode As XmlNode In objCAML.ChildNodes
    Dim intIndex As Integer = _
    MyLists.Items.Add(objNode.Attributes("Title").Value)
Next
```

Once you have selected a list, you can also access the fields associated with the list. This is accomplished by calling the GetList method. The GetList method takes the title or GUID of the list as an argument and returns a CAML fragment that contains a single List element along with a collection of Field elements that provide information about each field in the list. The CAML fragment returned from the GetList method can be quite long depending on how many fields are defined in the list. Listing 2-7 only shows the first Field element of a CAML fragment associated with a standard Document Library.

Listing 2-7. *A Portion of the Returned GetList CAML Fragment*

```
<List ...>
    <Fields>
        <Field ColName="tp_ID" ReadOnly="TRUE" Type="Counter" Name="ID"
DisplayName="ID" FromBaseType="TRUE" /><Field ColName="tp_Created"
Hidden="TRUE" ReadOnly="TRUE" Type="DateTime" Name="Created
DisplayName="Created Date" StorageTZ="TRUE" FromBaseType="TRUE" />
.
.
.
    <Fields>
    <RegionalSettings>
        <Language>1033</Language>
        <Locale>1033</Locale>
        <AdvanceHijri>0</AdvanceHijri>
        <CalendarType>1</CalendarType>
        <Time24>False</Time24>
        <TimeZone>300</TimeZone>
        <SortOrder>2070</SortOrder>
        <Presence>True</Presence>
    </RegionalSettings>
</List>
```

Because the CAML fragment structure is well formed, it is easy to retrieve information about the list schema. Using the same technique as we did previously with the GetListCollection CAML fragment, we could easily show the names of the fields associated with a list. The following code fills a ListBox with the display names of the fields:

```
Dim objCAML As XmlNode = objService.GetList(MyLists.SelectedItem.ToString)

For Each objNode As XmlNode In objCAML.ChildNodes(0).ChildNodes
    MyProperties.Items.Add(objNode.Attributes("DisplayName").Value)
Next
```

Once you understand the schema that is associated with the list, you will want to return specific items from the list. In the case of Document Libraries, these items represent the documents stored in the library. Returning items from a list is accomplished using the GetListItems method of the web service.

Like all the other method calls we have examined, the return value from the GetListItems method is a CAML fragment. The set of items returned is enclosed within a data element and each item is defined using a row element. The attributes of the row element will vary based on how you construct the method call, but you should note the ID, Title, and FileRef attributes because they will be critical later when we're working with the returned items. Listing 2-8 shows a typical return CAML fragment containing the information for a single document.

Listing 2-8. *Returned GetListItems CAML Fragment*

```
<listitems xmlns:s="uuid:BDC6E3F0-6DA3-11d1-A2A3-00AA00C14882"
    xmlns:dt="uuid:C2F41010-65B3-11d1-A29F-00AA00C14882"
    xmlns:rs="urn:schemas-microsoft-com:rowset" xmlns:z="#RowsetSchema"
    xmlns="http://schemas.microsoft.com/sharepoint/soap/">

    <rs:data ItemCount="1">
        <z:row ows_FileRef="1;#sites/Test/Shared Documents/Document1.doc"
        ows_Title="New Document"
        ows_Customer="DataLan"
        ows_Last_x0020_Modified="1;#2004-06-03 17:54:01"
        ows_ID="1"
        ows_owshiddenversion="8" ows_FSObjType="1;#0"
        ows_FileLeafRef="1;#Document1.doc"
        ows_Modified="2004-06-03 17:54:01"
        ows_Editor="1;#SPS\administrator"
        ows_DocIcon="doc" />
    </rs:data>
</listitems>
```

The GetListItems method takes several arguments and requires more effort to call than methods we have already discussed. This is primarily because several of the parameters are actually CAML fragments themselves and must be constructed in code before the method call is made. The following code shows the form of the method call:

```
Dim objCAML As XmlNode = objService.GetListItems _
([listName], [viewName], [query], [viewFields], [rowLimit], [queryOptions])
```

The listName parameter is either the list name (e.g., Shared Documents) or the GUID of the target list from which items are to be returned. This is the same parameter that is used throughout the various methods of the Lists web service. This parameter is required.

The viewName parameter is the GUID of the view to be used when determining what fields to return. This parameter is optional and can be replaced with the keyword Nothing in Visual Basic .NET or null in C#. When no view is specified, the method will return the fields contained in the default list view unless you override this behavior by specifying different fields. Generally, it is easier not to supply this parameter and specify the desired fields later.

The query parameter is a properly formatted CAML Query element that specifies what items to return from the list. This parameter is optional and can be replaced with the keyword Nothing in Visual Basic .NET or null in C#. When provided, the defined query overrides the query normally associated with the default view. The Query element was discussed in Chapter 1 and is unchanged when used with the Lists web service. The only difference is that you must construct the Query element in code as opposed to writing it by hand in a CAML file. The element is generally created by first creating an XmlDocument object and then building an XmlNode object, which may be passed directly as a parameter of the GetListItems method. The following Visual Basic .NET code shows how to build a Query element that will return information for all the documents in a library in alphabetical order:

```
Dim objDocument As New XmlDocument
Dim objQuery As XmlNode
objQuery = objDocument.CreateNode(XmlNodeType.Element, "Query", "")
objQuery.InnerXml = "<OrderBy><FieldRef Name='Title'></FieldRef></OrderBy>"
```

The viewFields parameter is a properly formatted CAML ViewFields element that specifies what fields are to be returned with each item. This parameter is optional and can be replaced with the keyword Nothing in Visual Basic .NET or null in C#. When provided, the defined field set overrides the field set normally associated with the default view. The ViewFields element was also discussed in Chapter 1. It is constructed and used in a manner similar to the Query element. The following Visual Basic .NET code shows how to build a ViewFields element that will return the ID and Title fields:

```
Dim objFields As XmlNode
objFields = objDocument.CreateNode(XmlNodeType.Element, "ViewFields", "")
objFields.InnerXml += "<FieldRef Name='ID'/><FieldRef Name='Title'/>"
```

The rowLimit parameter is a string representing the number of items to return from the method call. This parameter is optional and can be replaced with the keyword Nothing in Visual Basic .NET or null in C#. When provided, rowLimit overrides the limits associated with the default view. The rowLimit parameter can also be used to set up paging when used in conjunction with the queryOptions parameter.

The queryOptions parameter is a properly formatted XML QueryOptions element. This parameter is optional and can be replaced with the keyword Nothing in Visual Basic .NET or null in C#. The QueryOptions element acts as a container for other elements that specify the options for the method call. Table 2-4 lists and describes the possible query options.

Table 2-4. *Query Options*

Element	Description
DateInUtc	Sets the date format to Coordinated Universal Time (UTC). Possible values are True and False.
Folder	Specifies a URL that represents a folder within a Document Library. When specified, only documents from the folder will be returned.
Paging	This is a bookmark used in the paging scheme.
IncludeMandatoryColumns	Specifies that required columns must always be returned regardless of the view. Possible values are True and False.
MeetingInstanceID	An integer that represents a specific meeting instance to query.

For the most part, specifying query options is just a matter of building the correct XML node. The only place where this is different concerns paging. When you implement paging by specifying a rowLimit parameter, the returned data element will contain a ListItemCollectionPositionNext attribute. The value of this attribute is the internal bookmark that must be passed back through the query options to retrieve the next page. The following code shows an example of creating a typical QueryOptions element using Visual Basic .NET:

```
Dim objOptions As XmlNode
objOptions = objDocument.CreateNode(XmlNodeType.Element, "QueryOptions", "")
objOptions.InnerXml +="<IncludeMandatoryColumns>FALSE</IncludeMandatoryColumns>"
objOptions.InnerXml += "<DateInUtc>TRUE</DateInUtc>"
objOptions.InnerXml += "<Paging ListItemCollectionPositionNext=" & _
"'Paged=TRUE&p_ID=100&View=%7bC68F4A6A%2d9AFD%2d406C%2&PageFirstRow=101' />"
```

In the same way that we parsed the returned CAML fragment from previous method calls, we can do the same to display the information returned from the GetListItems method; however, you should note that the field names returned from this method call are prefixed with ows_, which must be taken into consideration when writing the code. Listing 2-9 shows a complete example that returns all the documents from a library and displays their titles in a list.

Listing 2-9. *Returning Documents from a Library*

```
Dim objService As New MyService.Lists
objService.Url = "http://Server_Name/Site_Path/_vti_bin/Lists.asmx"
objService.Credentials = System.Net.CredentialCache.DefaultCredentials

Dim objDocument As New XmlDocument

Dim objQuery As XmlNode
objQuery = objDocument.CreateNode(XmlNodeType.Element, "Query", "")
objQuery.InnerXml = "<OrderBy><FieldRef Name='Title'></FieldRef></OrderBy>"

Dim objFields As XmlNode
objFields = objDocument.CreateNode(XmlNodeType.Element, "ViewFields", "")
objFields.InnerXml = "<FieldRef Name='Title'/>"

Dim objCAML As XmlNode
objCAML = objService.GetListItems _
(MyLists.SelectedItem.ToString, Nothing, objQuery, objFields, Nothing, Nothing)

For Each objNode As XmlNode In objCAML.ChildNodes(1).ChildNodes
    If Not (objNode.Attributes Is Nothing) AndAlso _
            Not (objNode.Attributes("ows_Title") Is Nothing) Then
        MyDocs.Items.Add(objNode.Attributes("ows_Title").Value)
    End If
Next
```

After you have identified the fields for a given document, you will want to update them and save those changes back to the Document Library. You can update any field associated with a document using the UpdateListItems method of the Lists web service. This method takes as parameters the title or GUID of the list and a CAML Batch element that defines the operations to be performed on the list items. The following Visual Basic .NET code shows the format for the call:

```
Dim objReturn As XmlNode = objService.UpdateListItems([listName],[batch])
```

The Batch element is a container for one or more Method elements that define the individual operations to be performed as a single batch. This structure allows you to perform multiple insert, update, and delete operations with a single call to the UpdateListItems method of the web service. The Method element provides an identifier attribute for the individual operation and a command attribute to specify an insert, update, or delete operation. Each Method element in turn contains a set of Field elements that provide data for the method and identify the item to receive the operation. As an example, the following code shows a Batch element that defines an update to the Title field of the document associated with ID=3:

```
<Batch>
    <Method ID='MyIdentifier' Cmd='Update'>
        <Field Name='ID'>3</Field>
        <Field Name='FileRef'>
            http://MyServer/MySite/MyDocs/Document1.doc
        </Field>
        <Field Name='Title'>My New Title</Field>
    </Method>
</Batch>
```

When you first examine the Batch element, it is easy to be confused because the elements are overloaded to perform different functions. For example, the Field elements that reference the ID field and the FileRef field are used to identify the document that will receive the update. The data in the Field element referencing the Title field is actually the new data that will be applied during the update.

As a general strategy, you should return the ID and FileRef fields using the GetListItems method and use these values later to update the document properties. The only thing you need to watch out for is that the format of the FileRef field returned from the GetListItems method is a slightly different format than what is required within the Method element. Specifically, the returned format of the FileRef field includes the ID as a prefix, but the Method element expects you to supply just a complete URL to the target document. Table 2-5 lists the attributes for both the Batch and Method elements as a reference when calling the UpdateListItems method.

Table 2-5. *The Batch and Method Elements*

Element	Attribute	Description
Batch	ListVersion	The version number of the target list. This attribute is optional.
Batch	OnError	The action to take when a method fails. Possible values are Return or Continue.
Batch	Version	The version number of Microsoft WSS. This attribute is optional.
Batch	ViewName	The GUID of the target view. This attribute is optional.
Method	Cmd	The operation to perform. Possible values are Delete, New, or Update.
Method	ID	A text string used to identify the method. Can be any text and is referenced in the return value of the UpdateListItems method to indicate the results of the operation.

Working with Lists

After documents, lists are the next most significant container for content in a WSS site. Although the document management capabilities of WSS we examined earlier use lists to show document metadata, behind the scenes Document Libraries are significantly different from other lists. The field values in a standard list, for example, are stored in a separate table from the Document Libraries. Therefore, we must examine some new approaches to access and use list data in our solutions.

The Lists and UserData Tables

All of the lists in a WSS installation are maintained using the Lists and UserData tables of the content database. The Lists table contains information about the list itself, such as the title and author. The UserData table contains the data that is entered into the fields of the list.

The Lists table is most useful because it contains the unique identifier, in the form of a GUID, for each list. This identifier may be used to join the Lists table to other tables or as an input to various web services. This allows you to present information such as a hierarchical view of lists associated with each site in a WSS installation. Table 2-6 shows the columns found in the Lists table and gives a description for each.

Table 2-6. *The Lists Table*

Column	Data Type	Description
tp_WebId	uniqueidentifier	The identifier for the parent web site.
tp_ID	uniqueidentifier	The GUID identifying the list.
tp_Title	nvarchar	The name of the list.
tp_Created	datetime	The date and time the list was created.
tp_Modified	datetime	The date and time the list was last modified.
tp_LastDeleted	datetime	The time of the last delete operation on the list.
tp_DeleteCount	int	Not used.
tp_LastSecurityChange	datetime	The date and time when any security settings on the list were last changed.
tp_Version	int	The version number of the list.

Table 2-6. *The Lists Table*

Column	Data Type	Description
tp_Author	int	The identifier of the person who created the list.
tp_BaseType	int	The type of the list. Possible values are: 0 for custom, 1 for document libraries, 3 for discussion boards, and 4 for surveys.
tp_ServerTemplate	int	The identifier of the template used to create the list from the CAML site definition.
tp_RootFolder	uniqueidentifier	The ID of the parent directory in the Docs table.
tp_Template	uniqueidentifier	The ID of the file in the Docs table associated with the New Item link.
tp_ImageUrl	nvarchar	Image associated with the list.
tp_ReadSecurity	int	A value used to restrict read access to the items the current user created.
tp_WriteSecurity	int	A value used to restrict editing to the items the current user created.
tp_AnonymousPermMask	int	A value that identifies the list access rights for anonymous users.
tp_Subscribed	bit	A value specifying whether there are any alerts for the list. Possible values are 1 or 0.
tp_Direction	int	A value indicating whether the list direction is left-to-right or right-to-left.
tp_Flags	int	A combination of list properties used internally.
tp_ThumbnailSize	int	The size of thumbnail images associated with the list.
tp_WebImageWidth	int	The image width in the browser.
tp_WebImageHeight	int	The image height in the browser.
tp_ItemCount	int	The number of items in the list.
tp_NextAvailableId	int	The next ID used when an item is added to the list.
tp_Description	ntext	The description of the list.
tp_EmailInsertsFolder	nvarchar	The name of a Public folder that is examined for e-mail inserts into this document library.
tp_EmailInserts LastSyncTime	nvarchar	The last time the list was synchronized with the associated public folder.
tp_ACL	image	The access permissions for the list.
tp_EventSinkAssembly	nvarchar	The name of the assembly to receive document library events.
tp_EventSinkClass	nvarchar	The class name of the assembly to receive document library events.
tp_EventSinkData	nvarchar	Additional data for use by the Document Library event handler.
tp_Fields	ntext	Additional fields in the list added by users after the list was created.

While the Lists table contains important information about the list itself, the UserData table contains the actual information entered into each field. What's interesting about this table is that it has multiple columns for every possible data type in a list. Specifically, the UserData table has 64 nvarchar columns, 16 int columns, 32 float columns, 16 datetime columns, 16 bit columns, 1 uniqueidentifier column, 32 ntext columns, and 8 sql_variant columns. All of these extra columns are present so that list creators can design just about any schema they want. The problem, however, is that most of these columns contain null values, so there are a lot of unused table columns for every WSS list. Table 2-7 shows the columns found in the UserData table along with a description for each.

Table 2-7. *The UserData Table*

Column	Data Type	Description
tp_ID	int	The identifier for this table row.
tp_ListId	uniqueidentifier	GUID of the parent list.
tp_SiteId	uniqueidentifier	GUID of parent site to which the data belongs.
tp_Version	int	The version of the data.
tp_Author	int	The ID of the user who entered the data.
tp_Editor	int	The ID of the user who last modified the data.
tp_Modified	datetime	The date and time the list item was last modified.
tp_Created	datetime	The date and time the list item was created.
tp_Ordering	varchar	A value identifying the order of threaded discussions.
tp_HasAttachment	bit	A value indicating if the list item has an attached document.
tp_ModerationStatus	int	A value specifying the status of the list item. Possible values are: 0 – approved; 2 – pending; and 1 – rejected.
tp_IsCurrent	bit	A value indicating whether this is the current item in the issue tracking list.
tp_ItemOrder	float	The sort value for the list.
tp_InstanceID	int	The ID for an occurrence in a Meeting Workspace site that has a recurring event or multiple single events linked to it.
tp_GUID	uniqueidentifier	A GUID value used to support full-text search.
tp_Size	int	The size of the data item.
nvarchar1 - nvarchar64	nvarchar	Data for a list item.
int1 - int16	int	Data for a list item.
float1 - float32	float	Data for a list item.
datetime1 - datetime16	datetime	Data for a list item.
bit1 - bit16	bit	Data for a list item.
uniqueidentifier1	uniqueidentifier	Data for a list item.
ntext1 - ntext32	ntext	Data for a list item.
sql_variant1 - sql_variant8	sql_variant	Data for a list item.

Once you understand the general structure of the List and UserData tables, it is fairly straightforward to write SQL queries directly against the content database that return meaningful data sets. As with all operations involving the WSS databases, it's generally better to limit your SQL queries to SELECT statements. I have to admit, though, that I have written directly to the tp_EventSinkAssembly, tp_EventSinkClass, and tp_EventSinkData fields of the Lists table to automatically connect workflow engines to Document Libraries. So, there are occasionally reasons to write to the database. I can't emphasize enough, however, that you must be careful and thoroughly test your solution before using it in production.

One of the more common operations you will perform is to retrieve the set of lists from a WSS site. In some cases, you may want to retrieve all of the lists for a site, but I find that I am usually interested in lists of a specific type. For example, I might retrieve a set of task lists associated with a web site. The following query shows how to return the tasks lists associated with a site when you know the GUID that identifies the web site of interest:

```
SELECT dbo.Lists.tp_ID As Id, dbo.Lists.tp_Title As Title,
       dbo.Webs.FullUrl As URL,dbo.Lists.tp_Description As Description
FROM dbo.Lists INNER JOIN dbo.Webs
    ON dbo.Lists.tp_WebId = dbo.Webs.Id
WHERE (dbo.Lists.tp_ServerTemplate =107)
AND (dbo.Lists.tp_WebID = '{Web GUID}')
ORDER BY dbo.Lists.tp_Title
```

The key to returning lists of a certain type is to understand the values contained in the tp_ServerTemplate field of the Lists table. This field contains the numeric identifier for the list type. These values are closely related to the identifiers that we used in the first chapter to create site definitions with CAML. Table 2-8 lists the values for the field and the associated list type.

Table 2-8. *The tp_ServerTemplate Field*

Value	List Type
104	Announcement
105	Contacts
108	Discussion Board
101	Document Library
106	Events
100	Generic List
1100	Issues List
103	Links List
109	Image Library
115	InfoPath Form Library
102	Survey
107	Task List

Returning the data contained in a list is a bit more challenging than returning the list itself. This is caused by the design of the UserData table itself. Because the UserData table has so many columns—most of which are null—it is difficult to know exactly where the data of interest is located. For instance, consider the due date for a task item. At first glance, it seems obvious that this must be maintained as a datetime stamp in the UserData table. The problem, however, is that there are 16 possible columns for datetime stamps in each row of the UserData table. Is it the first column or does that column contain the date the task was created? It's not always easy to tell, and often requires some significant investigation to get the right answer. As it turns out, the due date is stored in the column datetime2. After some additional investigation, you would finally be able to create the following query, which shows how to return all the key pieces of information associated with a task:

```
SELECT dbo.UserData.tp_Id As Id, dbo.UserData.nvarchar1 AS Title,
       dbo.UserData.datetime2 AS DueDate, dbo.UserData.nvarchar2 AS Priority,
       dbo.UserData.nvarchar3 AS Status,
       CONVERT(nvarchar(3), dbo.UserData.float1 * 100) + '%' AS PercentComplete,
       dbo.UserData.datetime1 AS CreationDate,
       dbo.UserInfo.tp_Login AS Assignment
FROM dbo.UserInfo INNER JOIN dbo.UserData
     ON dbo.UserInfo.tp_SiteID = dbo.UserData.tp_SiteId
     AND dbo.UserInfo.tp_ID = dbo.UserData.int1 INNER JOIN dbo.Lists
     ON dbo.UserData.tp_ListId = dbo.Lists.tp_ID
WHERE(dbo.Lists.tp_ServerTemplate = 107)
AND (tp_ListID='{List GUID}')
```

Working with Remote Procedure Calls

Along with the techniques we have discussed previously, you can also utilize POST and GET commands to interact with WSS lists. The formats of the POST and GET commands are defined by the WSS Remote Procedure Call (RPC) protocol. The WSS RPC protocol supports a number of different methods for retrieving and updating data. Generally speaking, methods that only return information use the GET format and methods that update data use the POST format.

Using the GET Format

Methods that utilize the GET format specify a URL followed by a set of arguments separated by ampersands. The nice thing about the GET format is that you can utilize the commands from any browser, and security checking is accomplished by challenging your normal credentials. In this section, I'll present some of the more useful GET methods and show how they can be used to help solve real WSS issues. Table 2-9 lists the methods that are available using the GET format and describes each one.

Table 2-9. *Available GET Methods*

Method	Description
Dialogview	Accesses the information contained in Document Libraries to render open and save dialogs that look like the ones available in Microsoft Office 2003. Additionally, this method can show the property sheet for any document.
Display	Used to execute a query against a list and display the results.
ExportList	Exports a list schema in CAML format.
GetProjSchema	Returns the XML schema for a web site.
GetUsageBlob	Returns usage data in binary format.
HitCounter	Causes a hit on a page.
RenderView	Returns a view of a list.

The Display Method

The Display method is used to execute a query and return the results in an XML or HTML format. This method is one of the easiest to use and returns data in a format that can be used by either web parts directly or in code through DataSets. The following example shows how simple this method can be to use.

Follow these steps to return list data:

1. Navigate to any WSS site that has a list with several items in it.

2. Open the All Items view for the target list.

3. Click the Modify Settings and Columns link in the Actions pane.

4. Look in the address bar of the browser and copy the GUID, which is the list identifier. Figure 2-2 shows an example.

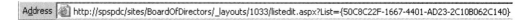

Figure 2-2. *Retrieving the list identifier*

5. Create a URL that combines the method to run, the target site, and the list GUID in the following format:

```
http://[ServerName]/[Site Path]/_vti_bin/owssvr.dll?Cmd=Display&
List={List GUID}&XMLDATA=TRUE
```

6. Enter this URL in the address bar of the browser to return the target list schema and data in XML format.

Clearly the Display method makes it very simple to return raw list data, but we certainly don't want to present XML to our users. The Display method is particularly handy, however, because it can be used in conjunction with data views in Microsoft FrontPage. Data views allow you to take the raw XML and create tabular views of lists.

Follow these steps to create a data view:

1. Start Microsoft FrontPage.

2. Select File ➤ Open Site from the menu.

3. Open a WSS site in FrontPage that you can use to test the data view capability.

4. Select Data ➤ Insert Data View to open the Data Source Catalog.

5. Click the link under Server-side Scripts titled Add to Catalog.

6. In the URL field of the Data Source Properties dialog, enter the URL that you constructed earlier to return list data in XML format. Figure 2-3 shows an example.

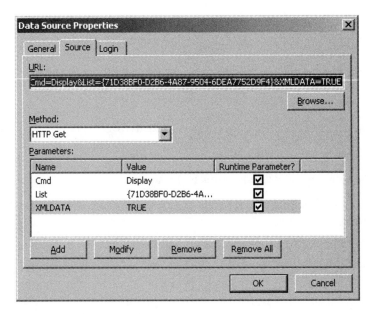

Figure 2-3. *Setting up the data source*

7. Click the OK button to add the new source to the catalog.

8. Open the default home page for your site in FrontPage.

9. Drag the new data source onto the home page, and the list information should appear in a table.

■**Note** If you receive an error when dropping the data source on the page, try providing a specific set of credentials on the Login tab of the Data Source Properties dialog.

The Display method accepts several parameters that control how the data is returned. These parameters affect what fields are returned and can even allow you to download list data to applications like Microsoft Outlook or Excel. Table 2-10 lists the method parameters and provides a description of each.

Table 2-10. *The Display Method*

Parameter	Description
ID	An identifier for a target list item when the operation does not involve the entire list.
List	The GUID identifying the target list.
XMLDATA	Set to True to return data in XML format.
View	The GUID of the view that determines the fields to return.
Query	A list of fields separated by spaces that specify what fields to return.
Using	A relative URL that specifies a file to use when exporting a list. The files are always related to exporting lists to Microsoft Outlook or Excel.
CacheControl	Prevents exported items from being cached on the client.

Along with creating tabular views of lists, the Display method can also be used to export list items to Microsoft Outlook or Excel. Exporting lists requires that you reference the correct supporting file through the Using parameter. The following code format will export any list directly into Microsoft Excel:

```
http://[ServerName]/[Site Path]/_vti_bin/owssvr.dll?Cmd=Display&
List={List GUID}&Using=_/layouts/query.iqy&CacheControl=1
```

If the list contains contacts or events, then you can also use the Display method to download a particular item into Microsoft Outlook. If the item is an event, you must reference the event.ics file; if the item is a contact, then you must reference the vcard.vcf file. Additionally, you must use the ID parameter to specify the identifier of the item to download. The following code shows the format for downloading an event from a calendar. By substituting a reference to vcard.vcf, you can use the same format to download a contact:

```
http://[ServerName]/[Site Path]/_vti_bin/owssvr.dll?Cmd=Display&ID=n&
List={List GUID}&Using=_/layouts/event.ics&CacheControl=1
```

The dialogview Method

One of the most common complaints I hear about WSS is that there is no immediate way to have a single Document Library show up on multiple web pages. It often seems as though documents are locked into the boundary defined by the hosting site, which can make it difficult to find documents. The only simple way to solve this problem seems to be to use a Web Page Viewer web part to point at the Document Library of interest. The problem with this approach, however, is that the entire page—including the navigation elements—is shown in the web part. Fortunately, a better solution exists in the form of an RPC call to the dialogview method.

The dialogview method is an RPC call that gives you direct access to the open, save, and property views used by Microsoft Office products. When you utilize this call, you'll immediately notice that the results are identical to what you see when opening or saving a document in Microsoft Office. The dialogview method takes only three parameters, which are described in Table 2-11.

Table 2-11. *The dialogview Method*

Parameter	Description
dialogview	This parameter determines whether to show the open, save, or property dialog view. Possible values are FileOpen, FileSave, or SaveForm.
location	This parameter specifies the document library or file for the operation.
FileDialogFilterValue	This parameter specifies a filter based on the file extension.

In order to create a document view from one site in another, you must utilize the Web Page Viewer web part. Instead of specifying a complete URL to the Document Library, however, we will create a valid call to the dialogview method. Simply drop the Web Page View web part onto a WSS page and set its URL using the following format:

```
http://[ServerName]/[Site Path]/_vti_bin/owssvr.dll?dialogview=FileOpen
&location=Shared%20Documents
```

The key to creating the view you want is the combination of the dialogview and location parameters. If you set dialogview to FileOpen and then specify a Document Library for the location parameter, you will create a view of the documents in that library. If you want, you can also specify a subfolder in the library and view the contents of the folder. You can also pass the location parameter with no value to show a list of all libraries on the target site. In any case, all of the hyperlinks in the target library are active so that you can easily navigate the libraries and folders. You can even open the documents from the view, and the best part is that all of the extraneous navigation elements are not rendered. Figure 2-4 shows a sample where a host site named "Multi-Practice Team" is showing documents from a target site named "Collaboration Team".

Multi-Practice Team
Home

This is a site for creating offerings that cross multiple practice areas

Collaboration Team
Shared Documents

Type	Name	Modified By	Modified	Checked Out To
	Collaboration Offerings	Scot Hillier	1/30/2004 3:22 PM	
	RMSDataSheet	Scot Hillier	5/13/2004 5:10 PM	
	Sharepoint Licensing	Scot Hillier	5/13/2004 5:09 PM	

Figure 2-4. *Hosting a Document Library*

While the `dialogview` method is a great way to show libraries from other sites, its original purpose was to support the integration of WSS libraries into document-based applications. This means you can use the method in your custom applications to provide the same look and feel that end users get when using Microsoft Office. If you want to understand this difference, simply open the Notepad application and select File ➤ Open from the menu. In the Open File dialog, enter an address for a WSS site. You will notice that the dialog presents the sites and libraries as folders in a tree, which is a decidedly different view than is provided by Office 2003 applications. Figure 2-5 shows a typical view of a WSS installation accessed from Notepad.

Figure 2-5. *Viewing WSS libraries from Notepad*

If you write custom document applications and wish to have them behave like Office 2003 applications, you must incorporate the `dialogview` method. The basic approach is to programmatically make web requests against the method and then extract the information you need from the resulting HTML. Listing 2-10 shows a simple example of this concept using an HTML Application (HTA) file. Using this code, you can select a file from a Document Library and display the address of the document.

Listing 2-10. *Creating a File Open Dialog*

```
<HTML>
<TITLE>My File Open Dialog</TITLE>
<HEAD>
<SCRIPT Language="JavaScript">
  function showPath(){
    try{
      if(window.frames("MyDialog").selectedElement.fileattribute == "file")
        alert(window.frames("MyDialog").selectedElement.id);
      else
        alert("Folder selected");
    }
    catch(x){
      alert("Nothing selected!");
    }
    } </SCRIPT>
</HEAD>
<BODY>
<IFRAME Name="MyDialog" ID="MyDialog" WIDTH="700px" HEIGHT="200px"
    SRC="http://[ServerName]/[SitePath]/_vti_bin/owssvr.dll?
dialogview=FileOpen&location=Shared%20Documents">
</IFRAME>
<FORM>
<INPUT Type="Button" Value="Show File Path" OnClick="showPath();">
</FORM>
</BODY>
</HTML>
```

Listing 2-10 uses an HTA file because I placed the `dialogview` results in an `IFrame` element and then used JavaScript to access the results. In a normal HTML page, this type of operation, known as cross-site scripting, is forbidden because it is a security risk. HTA applications, on the other hand, are always trusted. As a more complex option, you could use .NET code to initiate a request and return the HTML stream.

Regardless of how you access the information, you are interested in the `selectedElement` variable, which is defined in the return value of the `dialogview` method. First, you should examine the `fileattribute` property of the `selectedElement` variable. If this property has a value of `file`, then the user has selected a file. The `id` property will then contain the complete path to the selected file.

Using the POST Format

RPC methods that utilize the POST format are much more challenging to implement than methods that utilize the GET format. This is primarily because POST methods are intended to create, update, or delete list items, which means that they are subject to strict security requirements. The security requirements go beyond the basic username and password requirements by implementing a *form digest*.

The form digest is a security validation token generated by WSS whenever a page is created. This validation token guarantees that the page was created by WSS. When the page is submitted to WSS—as in a list item update—the form digest is checked and validated. If the token is not valid or has expired, WSS generates the timeout page shown in Figure 2-6. I'm sure you've seen this page many times when using WSS sites.

Error

The security validation for this page is invalid. Click Back in your Web browser, refresh the page, and try your operation again.

Troubleshoot issues with Windows SharePoint Services.

Figure 2-6. *Responding to an expired form digest token*

The WSS object model contains a special class that is responsible for generating the form digest. It is called, appropriately, the FormDigest class. If you select to view the source on any WSS page and search it for the term REQUESTDIGEST, you can find the token this class generates. The following code shows an example of a form digest:

```
<input type="hidden" name="__REQUESTDIGEST"
value="0x2F7DCB9B409F835723CC4DCCD2473356,10 Jun 2004 21:49:56 -0000" />
```

In order to utilize any of the POST methods, we will have to provide a valid form digest associated with the form we build to make the method call. Furthermore, the only way to get a valid form digest is for our web pages to actually be part of WSS. This means that we must build forms that make the appropriate method calls, that include a FormDigest class, and that are stored in a WSS Document Library so that a valid form digest can be generated when we access the page. Table 2-12 lists all of the methods that we can call using the POST format.

Table 2-12. *Available POST Methods*

Method	Description
Cltreq	Manages all aspects of web discussions
Delete	Deletes an item from a list
DELETEFIELD	Deletes a field from a list
DeleteList	Deletes a list
DeleteView	Deletes a list view
DisplayPost	Allows the performance of multiple methods in a single batch
ExportList	Exports a list schema
MODLISTSETTINGS	Changes list properties
MtgKeep	Clears the orphaned state of a meeting
MtgMove	Deletes an orphaned meeting occurrence
NEWFIELD	Adds a field to a list
NewList	Creates a new list

(Continues)

Table 2-12. *Available POST Methods (Continued)*

Method	Description
NewView	Creates a new view for a list
NewViewPage	Adds a view page to a site
NewWebPage	Creates a new Web Part Page
RenderView	Requests the contents of a view for a list
ReorderFields	Changes the order in which fields are displayed in the data entry form for the list
Save	Adds or modifies an item in a list
SiteProvision	Adds the default set of lists to an existing web site
UPDATEFIELD	Modifies the schema of an existing field in a list
UpdateView	Modifies a view

Regardless of which POST method you want to call, you must first start by creating the basic form for calling the method. First, the form must be contained within an ASPX page. Second, the page must contain a reference to the Microsoft.SharePoint.WebControls namespace, which contains the FormDigest control. Third, the form itself must have its Action attribute pointing to the site where the target list is located. Listing 2-11 shows the structure for the web page.

Listing 2-11. *The Basic POST Method Web Page*

```
<%@ Register TagPrefix="SharePoint" Namespace="Microsoft.SharePoint.WebControls"
Assembly="Microsoft.SharePoint, Version=11.0.0.0, Culture=neutral,
PublicKeyToken=71e9bce111e9429c" %>
<HTML>
    <HEAD>
       <title>POST Form</title>
    </HEAD>
    <body>
       <form
       method="post" action="http://[ServerName]/[SitePath]/_vti_bin/owssvr.dll">
          <SharePoint:FormDigest runat="server"></SharePoint:FormDigest>
       </form>
    </body>
</HTML>
```

Once you understand how to create the basic page, you can begin to add fields to the form that will carry the required parameters for the method call. Each method call has its own required parameters, and they are outlined completely in the SDK. In this section, I'll select a few of the methods to discuss so that you can understand the process involved in calling them.

The Save Method

The Save method makes an excellent example of how to use a POST method and will prove to be very useful in advanced WSS solutions. This method allows you to modify or create new list items. Using this method, you can create your own custom item entry page. In order to use the method, we must create a field within the basic form structure for each required parameter of the method. Table 2-13 lists the possible parameters and provides a description of each.

Table 2-13. *The Save Method*

Parameter	Description
Cmd	The name of the method. This is always Save.
Id	Set to New to add items to the list. Set to the ID of the list item to modify the item.
List	The GUID of the target list.
NextUsing	The URL where the browser will be redirected after the method call.
Field names	Any one of many possible field names depending upon the list schema.
owsfileref	The name of a file or folder whose name will be changed.
owsnewfileref	The new name of the file or folder.
fileupload0	The file to attach to the list item.

As an example of how to use the Save method, I created a simple page to add a new item to a task list. I started out by creating the basic page shown in Listing 2-11. Then I added the parameters from Table 2-13 to the page. Finally, I uploaded the page to a Document Library on the target site. Listing 2-12 shows the complete code for my solution.

Listing 2-12. *Adding a New Task Item*

```
<%@ Register TagPrefix="SharePoint" Namespace="Microsoft.SharePoint.WebControls"
Assembly="Microsoft.SharePoint, Version=11.0.0.0, Culture=neutral,
PublicKeyToken=71e9bce111e9429c" %>
<HTML>
   <HEAD>
      <title>WebForm1</title>
   </HEAD>
   <body>
      <form method="post" action="http://spspdc/sites/test/_vti_bin/owssvr.dll">
      <SharePoint:FormDigest runat="server"></SharePoint:FormDigest>
      <input type="hidden" name="Cmd" value="Save">
      <input type="hidden" name="ID" value="New">
 <input type="hidden" name="List" value="2DBAFFF2-583D-49F4-9546-C80F4B57E58B">
      <input type="text" name="urn:schemas-microsoft-com:office:office#Title">
      <input type="submit" value="Submit">
      <input type="reset" value="Reset">
      </form>
   </body>
</HTML>
```

Notice in Listing 2-12 that each required parameter is stored in a hidden field except for the title of the task. Also note the structure of the parameter name for the task title. The field names in many lists are defined in Microsoft Office schemas. There are a few dozen of these special fields, and I will not repeat all of them here. In order to get the exact name for a field, you should consult the Save method in the WSS SDK.

The DisplayPost method

The DisplayPost method is an excellent way to experiment with POST methods. That's because this method allows you to execute multiple POST methods all in a batch. Using this method, you can create a simple page that will let you test other POST methods to see their effects. That's because the DisplayPost method has a PostBody parameter, which will accept any number of methods formatted in CAML code. By creating a web page with a TextArea element, we can build a test harness for method calls.

To create the DisplayPost test page, follow these steps:

1. Open a new blank file in Visual Studio .NET.

2. Add the code from Listing 2-11. Be sure to substitute your WSS site information in the template code.

3. Modify the Form element to properly support the two method parameters Cmd and PostBody. Be sure to substitute your WSS site information in the template code:

```
<form method="post" onSubmit="addFormDigest(this);"
action="http://[ServerName]/[SitePath]/_vti_bin/owssvr.dll">
    <SharePoint:FormDigest runat="server"></SharePoint:FormDigest>
    <input type="hidden" name="Cmd" value="DisplayPost">
    <textarea rows="18" name="PostBody" cols="72"></textarea><br>
    <input type="submit" value="Submit"> <input type="reset" value="Reset">
</form>
```

4. Add the following code to the Head element of the page to ensure that each method in the batch is properly authenticated using the form digest:

```
<script type="text/javascript" language="JavaScript">

function addFormDigest(form)
{
    try {

    var digest = '<SetVar Name="__REQUESTDIGEST">' +
    form.elements["__REQUESTDIGEST"].value + "</SetVar>\n";
    var postBody = form.elements["PostBody"];
    var pattern = /<\/Method>/g;
    postBody.value = postBody.value.replace(pattern, digest + "</Method>");

    }
    catch(x) {
        alert(x.message);
    }

}

</script>
```

5. Save the file and upload it into a Document Library.

6. Open the file in the browser by clicking on it in the Document Library. It should look like the file in Figure 2-7.

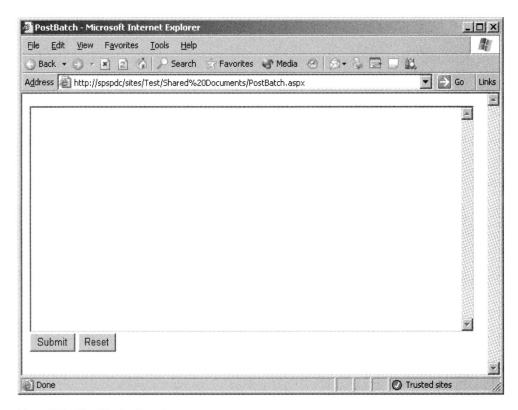

Figure 2-7. *The DisplayPost form*

Once you have the web page in place, you can test CAML constructs to call various methods. These constructs use nearly the same parameters as we used in the GET and POST forms, but they are formatted as CAML fragments. As an example, you can take the following code and execute the Save method twice in a single batch to add two tasks to a list. Just be sure to substitute the GUID of your task list for the one in the code sample:

```
<ows:Batch Version="6.0.2.5608" OnError="Return">
<Method ID="0,Save">
<SetList Scope="Request">2DBAFFF2-583D-49F4-9546-C80F4B57E58B</SetList>
  <SetVar Name="Cmd">Save</SetVar>
  <SetVar Name="ID">New</SetVar>
  <SetVar Name="urn:schemas-microsoft-com:office:office#Title">Task1</SetVar>
</Method>
<Method ID="1,Save">
<SetList Scope="Request">2DBAFFF2-583D-49F4-9546-C80F4B57E58B</SetList>
```

```
    <SetVar Name="Cmd">Save</SetVar>
    <SetVar Name="ID">New</SetVar>
    <SetVar Name="urn:schemas-microsoft-com:office:office#Title">Task2</SetVar>
</Method>
</ows:Batch>
```

While we've covered the basics of the WSS RPC protocol, there are still many different methods and parameters to investigate. This web page will help you test various methods. When you use it in combination with the information contained in the SDK, you should be able to arrive at the correct syntax for any supported operation.

Working with Areas, Sites, and Webs

Along with lists and libraries, WSS developers are interested in understanding and managing areas, sites, webs, and their relationships. This is especially true if you have installed SharePoint Portal Server (SPS) on top of WSS. Because SPS functions to aggregate sites and information into areas, developers are often interested in displaying the logical site hierarchy. Figure 2-8 shows an example of displaying the site hierarchy using a tree.

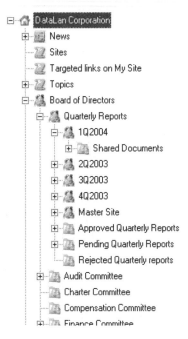

Figure 2-8. *A site hierarchy*

The Sites and Webs Tables

The information for all WSS sites is maintained in the Sites table. The term "site" in WSS always refers to a top-level web site that has a security boundary associated with it. Additionally, the portal home page associated with SPS is also a site. This means that SPS and every WSS site are actually peers whose information is all stored in the Sites table. The Sites table schema is made up of fields that contain information about the various sites, but you will use little of this information in custom applications. Instead, you will make use of the Webs table.

The information for all areas, sites, and webs is maintained in the Webs table. The term "webs" in WSS refers to any and all browser destinations. This includes top-level sites, subsites, areas, and the portal home. This is all very confusing because "sites" and "webs" are terms that people use every day in different ways. The best way to think about it is that a site is a web, but a web is not necessarily a site. All of this means that some of the information in the Sites table also appears in the Webs table.

Unlike the Sites table, however, the Webs table is intended to be accessed recursively to build a hierarchy. This is possible because the Webs table has a `ParentWebId` field that contains the identifier for the parent web. With this knowledge, you can identify the root of the site hierarchy using the following query:

```
SELECT Id, Title, FullUrl AS URL, Description
FROM dbo.Webs
WHERE (ParentWebId IS NULL) AND (FullUrl = '')
```

Because the portal home and all WSS top-level sites are peers, you will find that the `ParentWebID` field is `null` for all of these sites. However, the difference lies in the `FullUrl` field, which is an empty string for the portal home, but not for top-level sites. Using this knowledge, you can return the complete set of top-level WSS sites using the following query:

```
SELECT Id, Title, FullUrl AS URL, Description
FROM dbo.Webs
WHERE (ParentWebId IS NULL) AND (FullUrl <> '') AND (FullUrl IS NOT NULL)
ORDER BY WebTemplate,Title
```

Once you have returned the portal home and top-level sites, you can build out the web tree underneath by recursively querying the Webs table with the identifier returned from the previous query. When you return the webs, always be sure to return the `WebTemplate` field with the query. The `WebTemplate` field identifies the type of web that is returned, such as team site, meeting site, or document workspace. Table 2-14 lists the values for the `WebTemplate` field and the type of web represented.

Table 2-14. *WebTemplate Values*

Site Type	Field Value
Portal home	20
Portal area	31
Team site	1
Personal site	21
Meeting site	2
News home	33
News	32
Sites directory	34

Using the Webs Web Services

Just like the Docs and Lists tables I presented earlier, the Sites and Webs tables have associated web services provided by WSS. The primary difference between using the web services and directly accessing the database tables is that web services always assume that you are dealing with a single top-level site and its collection of subsites. This means that there is no simple way to return the collection of all top-level sites in a WSS installation. This is another example of where I have had to go directly to the database to solve an issue.

Once you know what site collection you are interested in, you can use the Webs web service to return the hierarchical information for that particular collection. Using this web service, you can return all of the sites in the collection at once, or call methods recursively to build a hierarchy. Table 2-15 lists the available methods of the Webs web service and describes each.

Table 2-15. *The Webs Web Service*

Method	Description
GetAllSubWebCollection	Returns the titles and URLs of all webs in the site collection
GetListTemplates	Returns the collection of list template definitions for the current site collection
GetWeb	Returns metadata about the current site
GetWebCollection	Returns the titles and URLs of all webs directly beneath the current site
WebUrlFromPageUrl	Returns the URL of the parent site for given web page

Like all of the web services provided by WSS, you typically set a reference to them through the particular item of interest. In this case, you will reference the web whose information you want to return. The following code shows the format for the web reference in Visual Studio .NET:

```
http://[ServerName]/[SitePath]/_vti_bin/Webs.asmx?WSDL
```

Once the web reference is made, it is a simple matter to return a collection of all webs in the referenced site collection. This can be done by calling the GetAllSubWebCollection method. Calling this method returns an XmlNode that contains the titles and addresses of every web in the current collection. This method is certainly simple to use, but it is not convenient if your goal is to build a hierarchical view of the site collection.

In order to create a tree view of a site collection, you will have to make recursive calls to the GetWebCollection method. This method simply returns all of the subwebs beneath the current web referenced by the web service. Using this technique to build a tree is reasonably simple if you assume that you know the address and name of the top-level site collection. With this knowledge, you can start building a tree by adding the top-level site collection to a TreeView control. The following code shows how to do this in Visual Basic .NET:

```
Private Const ROOT_SITE_URL As String = [SiteUrl]
Private Const ROOT_SITE_TITLE As String = [SiteTitle]

Dim objSiteNode As New TreeNode
objSiteNode.Text = ROOT_SITE_TITLE
objSiteNode.Tag = ROOT_SITE_URL
TreeView1.Nodes.Add(objSiteNode)
FillTree(objSiteNode)
```

Note that when the top-level site is added to the `TreeView` control, the `Tag` property is used to hold the site address. This value will be used to redirect the web service to each subweb as we recursively build the tree. The building is accomplished by the call to the `FillTree` routine. This routine redirects the web service and then returns the child webs. Each child web then makes a recursive call to the same routine to build the tree. Listing 2-13 shows the routine.

Listing 2-13. *The FillTree Routine*

```
Private Sub FillTree(ByVal objParentNode As TreeNode)

    'Get sub webs
    Dim objService As New MyService.Webs
    objService.Url = objParentNode.Tag.ToString & "/_vti_bin/Webs.asmx"
    objService.Credentials = CredentialCache.DefaultCredentials
    Dim objWebNodes As XmlNode = objService.GetWebCollection()

    'Add these webs to the tree and recursively call this routine
    For Each objWebNode As XmlNode In objWebNodes
        Dim objChildNode As New TreeNode
        objChildNode.Text = objWebNode.Attributes("Title").Value
        objChildNode.Tag = objWebNode.Attributes("Url").Value
        objParentNode.Nodes.Add(objChildNode)
        FillTree(objChildNode)
    Next

End Sub
```

Exercise 2-1. Building a Document Web Service

WSS comes with several companion web services, and this chapter has investigated some of the more useful functionality; however, these web services do not have all of the functionality that a developer may want. For example, WSS has no web service for loading documents into libraries. There is a web service for managing images, but not one specifically for documents. In this exercise, you will build your own document web service that will allow you to upload documents to a library and set their properties.

Creating the WSS Team Site

Before we begin creating the web service, we'll need a test WSS site for uploading documents. The site will be a simple team site with a single Document Library. After the site is created, we'll add a custom field to the Document Library whose value will be set during the upload process.

Follow these steps to create the test site:

1. Open the Windows SharePoint Services Central Administration page.

2. On the Central Administration page, select Virtual Server Configuration ➤ Create a Top-Level Web Site.

3. On the Virtual Server List page, click the virtual server where you want to create the new site.

4. On the Create Top-Level Web Site page, fill in the information necessary to create a site named **DocumentWebService** and click the OK button.

5. On the Top-Level Site Successfully Created page, click the link for the new site.

6. On the Template Selection page, select the Team Site template and click the OK button.

7. On the home page for the new team site, click the Shared Documents link in the quick launch area.

8. On the Shared Documents page, click the Modify Settings and Columns link.

9. On the Customize Shared Documents page, click the Add a New Column link.

10. On the Shared Documents: Add Column page, name the new column **Project**, and click the OK button.

11. On the Customize Shared Documents page, click the Go Back to Shared Documents link.

12. Verify the new field is visible in the default view of the Document Library.

Creating the IIS Web Site

Whenever you create your own web service, you must decide whether you will deploy the service under the same IIS web site where WSS is installed. If you choose to install the web service alongside WSS, then you will later need to add your web service to the exclusions list. Adding your web service to the exclusions list prevents WSS from intercepting calls to the service and processing them as if they were standard WSS page requests. You can exclude your web service by using the STSADM command-line tool and the following syntax:

```
STSADM.EXE -o addpath -url http://MyServer/MyPath -type exclusion
```

If you do not deploy your web service alongside WSS, then you will need to create a new IIS web site. If you create a new site, then you do not have to exclude the site from WSS management. In our exercise, we will create a separate IIS web site for the service.

Follow these steps to create a new IIS web site:

1. Select Start ➤ Administrative Tools ➤ Internet Information Services (IIS) Manager.

2. In the IIS Manager, expand the Application Pools folder.

3. Right-click the Application Pools folder and select New ➤ Application Pool from the context menu.

4. In the Add New Application Pool dialog, name the new pool **TestPool** and click the OK button.

5. In the IIS Manager, expand the Application Pools folder.

6. Right-click the TestPool node and select Properties from the context menu.

7. On the Identity tab for the pool, change the identity of the pool from the default to an account that has permission to access the target web site, and click the OK button.

8. In the IIS Manager, expand the Web Sites folder.

9. Right-click the Web Sites folder and select New ➤ Web Site from the context menu.

10. On the Welcome to the Web Site Creation Wizard screen, click the Next button.

11. On the Web Site Description screen, name the new site **ASP.NET** and click the Next button.

12. On the IP Address and Port Settings screen, set the new web site to use port 8080 and click the Next button.

13. On the Web Site Home Directory screen, be sure the Allow Anonymous Access to this Web Site box is checked.

14. Click the Browse button.

15. In the Browse for Folder dialog, select an existing folder, or create a new folder to be the root of the new web site, and then click the OK button.

16. Accept the remaining defaults settings and complete the wizard.

17. Under the Web Sites folder, locate the new site, right-click it, and select Properties from the context menu.

18. On the Home Directory tab, locate the Application Pool list and select **TestPool** as the application pool for the site.

19. Click the OK button.

20. Restart IIS to ensure your changes take effect.

Starting the Web Service Project

In this exercise, we will use Visual Studio .NET and the C# language to create a web service. We will then deploy the web service to the new IIS web site we created. Finally, we'll create a simple Windows client to upload documents from the file system to the test WSS site.

Follow these steps to start the new project:

1. Start Visual Studio .NET.

2. In Visual Studio .NET, select File ➤ New ➤ Project from the menu.

3. In the Project Types window of the New Project dialog, click on the Visual C# Projects folder.

4. In the Templates window, select ASP.NET Web Service.

5. In the Location text box, enter **http://localhost:8080/Library** and click the OK button.

6. When the new project is created, rename the file Service1.asmx to **Library.asmx**.

7. Open the file Library.asmx for editing in Visual Studio.

8. Add the following statements to the top of the file to reference namespaces you will need for the service:

```
using System.Xml;
using System.Net;
using System.Security.Principal;
```

9. When the web service project is first created, Visual Studio .NET sets up a template method. Replace the template method with the code from Listing 2-14 to define a single method for the web service. Note the name of the class and the function signature of the method.

■**Caution** For simplicity, Listing 2-14 does not show the Designer-Generated code, which must be retained for the project to compile.

Listing 2-14. *Starting Code*

```
namespace Library
{

public class DocService : System.Web.Services.WebService
{
    public DocService()
    {
        //CODEGEN: This call is required by the ASP.NET Web Services Designer
        InitializeComponent();
    }

    [WebMethod]
    public string Upload(string siteRef, string listName, string fileName,
                         byte[] fileBuffer, XmlNode fields)
    /*
     * siteRef is format "http://spspdc/sites/test"
     * listName is in format "Shared Documents"
     * fileName is format "Document1.doc"
     * fileBuffer is the document in a byte array
     * fields is in format
     <Fields><Field Name='Title'>My Document</Field>...</Fields>
                             */
    {
    }
}
}
```

Adding the Web Reference

Our web service makes use of the WSS Lists web service internally to manage library properties. Therefore, we have to set a web reference to this service. This means that our web service will in turn call a web service. This approach simplifies our development considerably.

Follow these steps to set the web reference:

1. In Visual Studio .NET, select Project ➤ Add Web Reference from the menu.

2. In the Add Web Reference dialog, type **http://[server]/[path]/DocumentWebService/ _vti_bin/Lists.asmx?WSDL** and click the Go arrow.

3. When the Lists web service is located, type **SPSService** in the Web Reference Name box and click the Add Reference button.

Coding the Web Service

Once the reference is set, you are ready to code the Upload method. Our web service is designed to accept five parameters. These parameters identify the site, library, and file to be uploaded. The method also accepts the document itself in the form of a byte array along with metadata contained in an XmlNode object.

The siteRef parameter accepts a string that contains the complete path to the upload target site. You should note that the format does not include a trailing forward slash. Including a slash will cause the Upload method to fail.

The listName parameter accepts a string that contains the name of the target Document Library. You should note that while most WSS web service will accept the list name or GUID, our service expects the name. Using the list GUID as a value for the listName parameter will cause the Upload method to fail.

The fileName parameter accepts a string that contains the name of the document to upload. The filename should be a complete name that includes the file extension.

The fileBuffer parameter accepts an array of bytes that contains the actual document to upload. Any client that uses the web service will have to convert the target document to a byte array before calling the web service. We will perform this operation when we create a Windows client for the service.

The fields parameter accepts an XmlNode object that contains the field name and values to be uploaded with the document. The format of the XmlNode object closely follows the format expected by the Lists web service. The following code shows an example of a valid fields parameter:

```
<Fields>
   <Field Name='Title'>My Document</Field>
   .
   .
   .
</Fields>
```

When the Upload method is called by a client, it will execute three distinct subprocesses to accomplish the upload. The first operation is the actual document upload. In this operation, the document is transferred into the target Document Library. After the new document is loaded, the Lists web service is called to retrieve the ID of the newly uploaded document. Finally, the ID is used to apply values to the document properties. We'll also enclose all of these operations within a single try-catch block.

Uploading the File to the Library

The first operation within the Upload method transfers the document content from the byte array to the target library. This operation relies on the uploading technique I presented earlier in the chapter. As part of this operation, I also log the identity of the operation to the Windows Event Log. This information can be useful when troubleshooting permission issues. Add the code from Listing 2-15 to the Upload method to transfer the byte array.

Listing 2-15. *Uploading the byte Array*

```
try
{

    //Log activity
    System.Diagnostics.EventLog log = new System.Diagnostics.EventLog();
    log.Source = "Library web service";
    log.WriteEntry("Service running under account "
    + WindowsIdentity.GetCurrent().Name + ".",
    System.Diagnostics.EventLogEntryType.Information);

    //Build the destination file path
    string fileRef = siteRef + "/" + listName + "/" + fileName;

    //Upload file
    WebClient webClient = new WebClient();
    webClient.Credentials = CredentialCache.DefaultCredentials;
    webClient.UploadData(fileRef,"PUT",fileBuffer);
    log.WriteEntry(fileName + " uploaded to " + listName,
    System.Diagnostics.EventLogEntryType.Information);
```

Retrieving the Document Identifier

Whenever a new document is added to a library, you will want to know the document ID so that you can interact with the properties. In order to return this information, our web service must call the Lists web service. The solution is to call the Lists web service and return the documents from the target library sorted by the date they were modified. Uploaded documents will always be the most-recently modified document in the library. Along with sorting the documents, we also instruct the Lists web service to limit the result set to a single document. This way we only get the information for the recently uploaded document. Add the code from Listing 2-16 to the end of the Upload method to retrieve the document ID.

Listing 2-16. *Retrieving the Document ID*

```
//Connect to the Lists web service for the target site
SPSService.Lists listService = new SPSService.Lists();
listService.Url = siteRef + "/_vti_bin/Lists.asmx";
listService.Credentials = System.Net.CredentialCache.DefaultCredentials;

//Create the Query for retrieving the recent document
XmlDocument xmlDoc = new XmlDocument();
XmlNode query = xmlDoc.CreateNode(XmlNodeType.Element, "Query", "");
query.InnerXml = "<OrderBy><FieldRef Name='Modified' "
                + "Ascending='FALSE'></FieldRef></OrderBy>";

//Return information for the recent document
XmlNode caml = listService.GetListItems(listName,null,query,null,"1",null);
string id = caml.ChildNodes[1].ChildNodes[1].Attributes["ows_ID"].Value;
```

Setting the Document Properties

Once the document identifier has been retrieved, we can use it to set the values of properties on the documents. This is where we will make use of the `fields` parameter. This parameter contains the names of the field and the values to set. Because this node is already properly formatted, we can use it directly in a call to the Lists web service. After this operation is complete, our web service will return the results as a string. Add the code from Listing 2-17 to complete the `Upload` method.

Listing 2-17. *Setting the Document Properties*

```
    //Create the Batch CAML element for updating
    XmlNode batch = xmlDoc.CreateNode(XmlNodeType.Element, "Batch", "");

    string temp = "<Method ID='DocService.Upload' Cmd='Update'>";
    temp += "<Field Name='FileRef'>" + fileRef + "</Field>";
    temp += "<Field Name='ID'>" + id + "</Field>";
    foreach(XmlNode field in fields.ChildNodes)
    {
        temp += field.OuterXml;
    }
    temp += "</Method>";
    batch.InnerXml =temp;

    XmlNode xmlReturn= listService.UpdateListItems(listName,batch);
    return xmlReturn.OuterXml;

}
catch (Exception x)
{
    return x.Message;
}
```

Deploying the Web Service

After you have completed coding the Upload method, you can compile the web service. After debugging, make sure to compile the web service in the Release configuration. The service should now be ready to receive client requests.

Creating the Web Service Client

Once the web service is created, you can use it from a wide variety of clients, including ASP.Net applications, web parts, and script clients. In this exercise, you will create a simple Windows client to select a file from the file system and upload it to the target library. For simplicity, we will hard-code some values, but you should be able to see clearly how to extend the concepts to other projects.

Follow these steps to create the new client project:

1. In Visual Studio .NET, select File ➤ Add Project ➤ New Project from the menu.

2. In the Project Types window of the New Project dialog, click on the Visual C# Projects folder.

3. In the Templates window, select Windows Application.

4. In the Name text box, type **LibraryClient** and click the OK button.

5. When the new project is created, select Project ➤ Add Web Reference from the menu.

6. In the Add Web Reference dialog, type **http://localhost:8080/Library/Library.asmx?WSDL** and click the Go arrow.

7. When the web service is located, type **LibraryService** in the Web Reference Name box and click the Add Reference button.

8. Once the web reference is set, open Form1 in Visual Studio .NET so you can add some controls to it.

9. Place a button named btnUpload, a TextBox named txtProperty, and an OpenDialog named openDialog on the form, as shown in Figure 2-9.

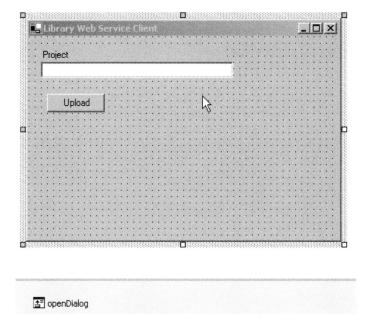

openDialog

Figure 2-9. *Creating the user interface*

10. Open the code window for Form1.cs and add the following statements:

```
using System.IO;
using System.Xml;
```

11. Add the code from Listing 2-18 to invoke the web service from the client.

Listing 2-18. *Coding the Window Client*

```
private void btnUpload_Click(object sender, System.EventArgs e)
{

    //Get Document to upload
    if(openDialog.ShowDialog() != DialogResult.OK)return;

    //Load File into a byte array
    FileStream stream = new FileStream(openDialog.FileName,
                                    FileMode.Open, FileAccess.Read);
    BinaryReader reader = new BinaryReader(stream);
    byte [] fileBuffer = reader.ReadBytes((int)stream.Length);
    reader.Close();
    stream.Close();
```

```
//Build parameters
string siteRef = "http://localhost/sites/DocumentWebService";
string listName = "Shared Documents";
string fileName = openDialog.FileName.Substring(
                            openDialog.FileName.LastIndexOf("\\")+1);
XmlDocument xmlDoc = new XmlDocument();
XmlNode fields = xmlDoc.CreateNode(XmlNodeType.Element, "Fields", "");
fields.InnerXml = "<Field Name='Project'>" + txtProperty.Text + "</Field>";

//Call web service
LibraryService.DocService service = new LibraryService.DocService();
string returnString = service.Upload(
                        siteRef,listName,fileName,fileBuffer,fields);
MessageBox.Show(returnString);

}
```

Using the Web Service

Once the client is completed, you should be able to compile the code and run the project. All you have to do is enter a name in the project field and click the Upload button. You will then be prompted to select a file for uploading. If the operation is successful, then you will see a return XML string. If the operation is unsuccessful, you will receive an error message.

Exercise 2-2. Building a Site Explorer

Although WSS provides significant capabilities within a site, there is no convenient way to view an entire WSS installation. Because of this, there is no way for administrators to understand the scope of a WSS installation. In this exercise, we will build a simple explorer that allows you to see all of the site collections and subwebs.

Starting the Project

This project will be a Windows application built using C#. We will use a combination of direct calls to the database and webs services to create a hierarchical listing of all sites and webs in a given WSS installation.

To start the project, follow these steps:

1. Start Visual Studio .NET.

2. In Visual Studio .NET, select File ➤ New ➤ Project from the menu.

3. In the Project Types window of the New Project dialog, click on the Visual C# Projects folder.

4. In the Templates window, select Windows Application.

5. Name the new project **Site Explorer** and click the OK button.

6. When the new project is opened, drop a `TreeView` control onto Form1.

7. Open the code window for Form1.cs and add the following statements:

```
using System.Data.SqlClient;
using System.Net;
using System.Xml;
```

Adding the Web Reference

This project makes use of the Webs web service to return information about sites and webs. In this section, you will set a reference to this web service. It does not matter which site you reference when setting up the service, because we will change it in code later.

Follow these steps to set the web reference:

1. In Visual Studio .NET, select Project ➤ Add Web Reference from the menu.

2. In the Add Web Reference dialog, type **http://[ServerName]/[SitePath]/_vti_bin/ Webs.asmx?WSDL** and click the Go arrow.

3. When the Webs web service is located, type **SPSService** in the Web Reference Name box and click the Add Reference button.

Returning All Sites

Before we can create the hierarchical view of the WSS installation, we must return the set of all sites that are contained in the installation. Because the available web services do not provide a mechanism for returning this information, we must go directly to the database. Add the code from Listing 2-19 to return the top-level sites and add them to the tree.

■**Note** Be sure to modify the connection string in Listing 2-19 to suit your environment.

Listing 2-19. *Returning Top-Level Sites*

```
private void Form1_Load(object sender, System.EventArgs e)
{
    string conn =
    "Integrated Security=SSPI;" +
    "Initial Catalog=[your catalog]" +
    ";Data Source=[your server]";

    string sql = "SELECT Title, FullUrl " +
    "FROM dbo.Webs " +
    "WHERE (ParentWebId IS NULL) AND (FullUrl <> '') " +
    "AND (FullUrl IS NOT NULL) " +
    "ORDER BY Title";
```

```csharp
        try
        {
            //Return the sites
            SqlDataAdapter adapter = new SqlDataAdapter();
            SqlConnection connection = new SqlConnection(conn);
            DataSet dataSet = new DataSet("root");
            adapter.SelectCommand = new SqlCommand(sql,connection);
            adapter.Fill(dataSet,"Sites");

            //Put top-level sites in tree
            DataRowCollection siteRows = dataSet.Tables["Sites"].Rows;

            foreach(DataRow siteRow in siteRows)
            {
                TreeNode treeNode = new TreeNode();
                treeNode.Text = siteRow["Title"].ToString();
                treeNode.Tag = "http://[ServerName]/" +
                siteRow["FullUrl"].ToString();
                treeView1.Nodes.Add(treeNode);
                fillTree(treeNode);
            }
        }
        catch (Exception x)
        {
            MessageBox.Show(x.Message);
        }

}
```

Adding Child Sites

Once the top-level sites are returned, we can use the Webs web service to return all of the child webs beneath each site. This is done through a recursive call to the web service. These calls are made until each branch is filled out to the leaf. Add the code from Listing 2-20 to build the tree.

Listing 2-20. *Adding Child Webs*

```csharp
private void fillTree(TreeNode parent)
{
    //Redirect web service
    SPSService.Webs service = new SPSService.Webs();
    service.Url = parent.Tag.ToString() + "/_vti_bin/Webs.asmx";
    service.Credentials = CredentialCache.DefaultCredentials;

    //Get child webs
    XmlNode nodes = service.GetWebCollection();
```

```
    //Add child webs to tree
    foreach(XmlNode node in nodes)
    {
        TreeNode child = new TreeNode();
        child.Text = node.Attributes["Title"].Value;
        child.Tag = node.Attributes["Url"].Value;
        parent.Nodes.Add(child);
        fillTree(child);

    }
}
```

Running the Sample

After you have all the code entered, simply run the project. The tree view should return with
a complete listing of all sites and webs in the target installation. If you have trouble, check to
be sure that you are referencing the correct server and that your account has permission to
access the WSS content database.

■ ■ ■

CHAPTER 3

Advanced Web Part Techniques

The basic web part construction technique that we have all learned utilizes the CreateChildControls method to add server controls to web part interfaces. Using this method, we can add any server control that is normally found in the Visual Studio .NET toolbox. Although the basic technique works fine for many web parts and can result in a good user interface, it requires significant attention to detail. Frequently I find that I must run web parts over and over again while making small changes in order to create the desired appearance. I also find that it is difficult to create web parts that go beyond the basic elements of text boxes, lists, and buttons.

In this chapter, I will examine several techniques for improving the look and functionality of your web parts. These techniques will include the use of new controls that you may not have used yet as well as techniques designed specifically to improve your productivity while building web parts. The goal is to present solutions that allow your web parts to go beyond simple interfaces to more compelling functionality.

Before starting, however, I should emphasize that I assume you already know the basics of web part construction. I assume you know and understand how to create properties, strongly name as assembly, and make changes to the web.config file to address code access security. I covered all of these topics thoroughly in my first SharePoint book titled *Microsoft SharePoint: Building Office 2003 Solutions* (Apress, 2004). If you are weak in these areas, you should review them before continuing or you will likely not be successful with these new techniques.

Using the Internet Explorer Web Controls

Although our web parts have access to a wide variety of server controls that ship with Visual Studio .NET, I am frequently frustrated by the absence of more advanced server controls like a good tree control. This frustration, in fact, transcends the creation of web parts; I have the same issue whenever I create ASP.NET applications. Fortunately, Microsoft has created some excellent advanced server controls that can be downloaded separately from Visual Studio .NET. These advanced server controls are known collectively as the Internet Explorer Web Controls. In this section, we'll examine how to use these controls to improve the look and feel of your web parts. I should note that you could certainly create your own advanced controls, but using the Internet Explorer Web Controls makes it easier to standardize the techniques presented in the book.

The Internet Explorer Web Controls consist of the `TreeView`, `Toolbar`, `TabStrip`, and `MultiPage` controls. The `TreeView` control can be used to create an expandable tree that functions similarly to any explorer interface. The `Toolbar` control provides a clickable toolbar similar to that found in standard Microsoft Office products. The `TabStrip` and `MultiPage` controls are used together to create tabbed interfaces. Figure 3-1 shows an example of the `TreeView` control used to create a hierarchical listing of subsites in a web part.

Figure 3-1. *The TreeView control*

Installing the IE Web Controls

The IE Web Controls are packaged for download from Microsoft and ship with a batch utility designed to help compile the controls into a .NET assembly. The problem, however, is that the IE Web Controls were not designed for use with WSS. Therefore, you will not be able to use the default batch build process. Instead, you will have to create our own project in Visual Studio .NET and make some adjustments before the server controls can be used with WSS.

To begin the installation process, download the control set from `www.asp.net/IEWebControls/Download.aspx`. After the download is complete, you will need to execute the downloaded file, which is `IEWebControls.exe`. When the installation routine runs, you will have an opportunity to specify the folder where the control files will be extracted. If you accept the default, then the files will be placed in `\Program Files\IE Web Controls`.

If you open the Windows File Explorer and navigate to the installation directory, you will find the source files for all of the server controls and a batch file named `build.bat`. If you were simply using the IE Web Controls with an ASP.NET application, then you could execute this batch file to build the source files into a .NET assembly. If you want to use the controls in web parts, however, this build process will not create an assembly you can use.

■**Note** Although the assembly created from the batch build process is unusable, you should still execute the batch. This is because the batch also creates a set of images that are used by the `TreeView` control. These images are stored in a directory named `Runtime`.

The primary problem with the default build of the control set is that the .NET assembly constructed by the batch file does not have a strong name. As experienced web part developers know, all web parts must have a strong name in order to be used in a WSS site. Additionally, the security restrictions of the .NET Framework require that all assemblies referenced by a strongly named assembly must also have a strong name. Therefore, the assembly we create for the IE Web Controls must be strongly named. In order to meet this requirement, we will have to create our own project with a strong name.

Follow these steps to create the Visual Studio .NET project:

1. In Visual Studio .NET, select File ➤ New Project from the menu.

2. In the New Project dialog, select Visual C# Projects from the Project Types list.

3. Select Web Control Library from the Templates list.

4. Name the new project **IEWebControls**. Figure 3-2 shows the New Project dialog.

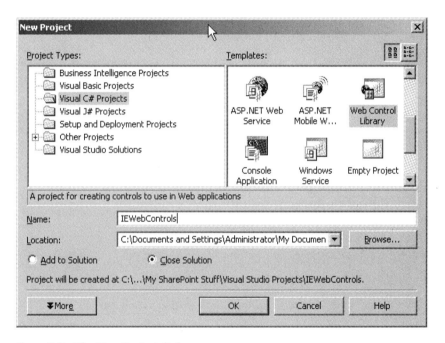

Figure 3-2. *The New Project dialog*

5. Click the OK button to create the new project.

6. After the new project is created, delete the files `AssemblyInfo.cs` and `WebCustomControl1.cs`.

7. In Visual Studio .NET, select Project ➤ Add Existing Item from the menu.

8. In the Add Existing Item dialog, navigate to the folder `\Program Files\IE Web Controls\ src` to reveal the control source files.

9. Select all of the source files in this directory and click the Open button to add them to the project.

10. In the Solution Explorer, right-click the project IEWebControls and select Add ➤ New Folder from the context menu.

11. Name the new folder **Resources**.

12. Right-click the Resources folder and select Add ➤ Add Existing Item from the context menu.

13. In the Add Existing Item dialog, navigate to the folder \Program Files\IE Web Controls\ src\Resources.

14. In the Files of Type list, select All Files to reveal the resource files located in the directory.

15. Select all files in this directory that have either a .bmp or .resources extension and click the Open button to add them to the project.

16. In the Solution Explorer, right-click the project IEWebControls and select Add ➤ New Folder from the context menu.

17. Name the new folder **Design**.

18. Right-click the Design folder and select Add ➤ Add Existing Item from the context menu.

19. In the Add Existing Item dialog, navigate to the folder \Program Files\IE Web Controls\ src\Design.

20. Select all of the files in this directory and click Open to add them to the project.

21. In Visual Studio .NET, select Project ➤ Add Reference.

22. In the Add Reference dialog, select to add references to the following assemblies: System.Data.dll, System.Design.dll, System.Windows.Forms.dll, and System.Xml.dll.

23. In Visual Studio .NET, set the Solution Configuration to **Release**.

24. Select Build ➤ Build Solution from the main menu and verify that the project builds successfully.

Successfully building the IEWebControls project will yield an assembly named IEWebControls.dll. However, this assembly is not yet strongly named. In order to complete the assembly, we must create a key file that can be used to strongly name the assembly. This key file must then be referenced within the project. Finally, we have to rebuild the assembly. Follow these steps to strongly name the assembly:

1. From the Start menu, select All Programs ➤ Microsoft Visual Studio .NET ➤ Visual Studio .NET Tools ➤ Visual Studio .NET 2003 Command Prompt.

2. In the Command Prompt window, create a key file using the strong name tool, as shown in the following command:

```
sn.exe -k c:\keypair.snk
```

3. In the Solution Explorer, open the file `Version.cs`.

4. Add the following attribute to `Version.cs` to reference the key file you created.

   `[assembly:AssemblyKeyFile("c:\\keypair.snk")]`

5. Select Build ➤ Rebuild Solution from the main menu and verify that the project builds successfully.

6. Copy the release version of the assembly named `IEWebControls.dll` into the `\inetpub\wwwroot\bin` directory.

Once you have successfully rebuilt the `IEWebControls` project, it will be ready for use with WSS web parts. All you have to do is reference the strongly named assembly from within your web part. You will then be able to create any of the four server controls and add them to the user interface of a web part. If you wish, you can now install the assembly into the Global Assembly Cache (GAC) to make it available universally.

Using the TreeView Control

The `TreeView` control creates a hierarchical view of information that can be expanded or collapsed by clicking on nodes within the tree. The behavior is similar to any of the explorer-style viewers found in Windows. For Internet Explorer 5.5 or higher, the behavior is driven by Dynamic HTML (DHTML), which means that all of the processing occurs on the client without a need for a round-trip to the server. For earlier browsers, or non-Microsoft browsers, the `TreeView` control executes a post back to the server whenever a node is clicked.

Besides the node expansion behavior, one of the nice things about the `TreeView` control is that it supports the use of images for the nodes. In fact, the `TreeView` control uses images in many different ways to present a professional look and feel. Images of plus and minus signs appear when a node is collapsed or expanded, and images of dotted lines are used to express the relationship between parent and child nodes. Images such as these are standard in a typical explorer view, of course, but they are a little more difficult to achieve in a server control. To support this look and feel, the `TreeView` control utilizes image files that are stored on the web server. In ASP.NET applications this is a simple matter of copying files, but making the images available to web parts is a little more difficult.

Follow these steps to make the tree images available:

1. Open the Windows File Explorer and create a new directory structure with the path `\inetpub\wwwroot\webctrl_client\1_0`.

2. Copy the contents of the directory `\Program Files\IE Web Controls\build\Runtime` to the directory `\inetpub\wwwroot\webctrl_client\1_0`.

3. Open the SharePoint Central Administration site.

4. Select Virtual Server Configuration ➤ Configure Virtual Server Settings.

5. On the Virtual Server List page, select the server where WSS is installed.

6. On the Virtual Server Settings page, select Virtual Server Management ➤ Define Managed Paths.

7. On the Define Managed Paths page, enter **/webctrl_client** in the Add a New Path section.

8. Change the selected Type to Excluded Path.

9. Click the OK button to add the new path to the list of exclusions.

Once the images are available in the correct path, you can create a TreeView control for your web part in the CreateChildControls method using the standard technique. Within your web part project, simply set a reference to the assembly IEWebControls.dll. Then add the following statement to use the namespace in your web part:

```
using Microsoft.Web.UI.WebControls;
```

Using the TreeView control in code is fairly easy. Each node in the tree also contains a collection of nodes. You can use the Add method of any node to put new subnodes in the collection. Each individual node also has a set of properties that you can use to set things like the image that is displayed or associate a hyperlink with the node. Listing 3-1 shows the complete C# code for a simple web part that displays a hierarchical listing of sites beneath the current site.

Listing 3-1. *Using the TreeView Control*

```csharp
using System;
using System.ComponentModel;
using System.Web.UI;
using System.Web.UI.WebControls;
using System.Xml.Serialization;
using Microsoft.SharePoint;
using Microsoft.SharePoint.Utilities;
using Microsoft.SharePoint.WebPartPages;
using Microsoft.SharePoint.WebControls;
using Microsoft.Web.UI.WebControls;

namespace SPSSubSiteTreeView
{

    [DefaultProperty(""),
        ToolboxData("<{0}:Builder runat=server></{0}:Builder>"),
        XmlRoot(Namespace="SPSSubSiteTreeView")]
    public class Builder : Microsoft.SharePoint.WebPartPages.WebPart
    {

        TreeView tree;

        protected override void CreateChildControls()
        {
            tree = new TreeView();
            Controls.Add(tree);
        }
```

```
protected override void RenderWebPart(HtmlTextWriter output)
{
    //get this web
    SPSite site = SPControl.GetContextSite(Context);
    SPWeb web = site.OpenWeb();

    //add tree root
    TreeNode root = new TreeNode();
    root.Text = web.Title;
    root.ImageUrl = "/_layouts/images/globe.gif";
    root.Expanded = true;
    tree.Nodes.Add(root);

    //add children
    addChildNodes(root,web);

    //display tree
    tree.RenderControl(output);
}

private void addChildNodes(TreeNode parentNode, SPWeb parentWeb)
{
    //get child webs
    SPWebCollection webs = parentWeb.GetSubwebsForCurrentUser();

    foreach(SPWeb sub in webs)
    {
        //add to tree
        TreeNode node = new TreeNode();
        node.Text = sub.Title;
        node.ImageUrl = "/_layouts/images/asp16.gif";
        node.NavigateUrl = sub.Url;
        node.Target = "";
        parentNode.Nodes.Add(node);

        //recurse
        addChildNodes(node,sub);
    }
}
}
}
```

If you examine the code in Listing 3-1, you'll see that each node added to the tree is assigned a value for the Text, NavigateUrl, Target, and ImageUrl properties. The Text property is used to provide the caption for the node. The NavigateUrl property is used to specify a location to open when the node is clicked. The Target property is set to an empty string to force the navigation to occur within the same browser, but you could set it to open a new window as well.

The ImageUrl is used to specify an image for the node. In the example, the node uses an image already available from the WSS installation. This is a great technique because WSS provides many images that are already sized appropriately for use with the TreeView control. The URL /_layouts/images corresponds to the directory \Program Files\Common Files\ Microsoft Shared\web server extensions\60\Templates\images. You can use any of the images located in this directory or even place your own images in this directory. Additionally, you can make use of the images not just for the standard image property, but also for images that appear when the node is expanded or selected using the ExpandedImageUrl and SelectedImageUrl properties, respectively.

Using the Toolbar Control

The Toolbar control allows you to create a toolbar for your web parts similar to those found in standard Microsoft Office products. It provides several styles of buttons, including simple push buttons, state buttons, and list buttons. I find this control useful for easily changing options or settings for a web part when a round-trip to the server is required. As an example, Figure 3-3 shows a text editor web part that uses the Toolbar control to alter the font style.

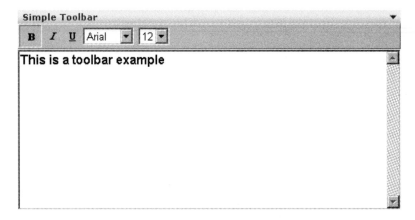

Figure 3-3. *The Toolbar control*

Using the Toolbar control begins by creating an instance in the CreateChildControls method. Just as the TreeView object was a container for node objects, the Toolbar object is a container for button objects. Therefore, you must create an instance of a particular button object and add it to the Items collection of the Toolbar object. The toolbar supports several button styles that allow you to implement different types of functionality. Table 3-1 lists the available button types along with a description.

Table 3-1. *Supported Button Types*

Button Type	Description
ToolbarButton	A simple push button control that fires a server-side event
ToolbarCheckButton	A stateful button that remains depressed when clicked
ToolbarDropDownList	A list control that displays the currently selected item on the toolbar
ToolbarLabel	A simple text control displayed on the toolbar
ToolbarSeparator	A separator used to visually group sets of buttons on the toolbar
ToolbarTextBox	An editable text control displayed on the toolbar

Each of the button types has an appropriate set of properties that allow you to change the appearance or manipulate their contents. Most of these properties are similar to those found in similar stand-alone controls. For example, the SelectedItem property of the ToolbarDropDownList object returns the currently selected list item just as it does in a standard ASP.NET ListBox object. For this reason, you will find that learning how to use each button type is fairly straightforward.

When you interact with any toolbar button, server-side events are generated that are trapped at the toolbar level. For example, clicking any button will cause the ButtonClick event to fire for the Toolbar object. You can then determine which button was clicked by examining the sender object, which contains the ID of the clicked button. It is, therefore, a good idea to assign a unique String value to each button's ID property so that you can detect it in the toolbar events. The following code shows an example of using a Select-Case statement in Visual Basic .NET to determine which button in a toolbar was clicked:

```
Private Sub objToolbar_ButtonClick _
(ByVal sender As Object, ByVal e As System.EventArgs) _
Handles objToolbar.ButtonClick

    Select Case sender.ToString
        Case "Button1"
            .
            .
            .
        Case "Button2"
            .
            .
            .
        Case "Button3"
            .
            .
            .
    End Select

End Sub
```

Once you understand the basics of creating the toolbar, adding buttons, and trapping the events, you can easily add the control to your web parts. Because the control is a server-side control with ViewState support, the toolbar can even be used to maintain state without the need to code web part properties. As an example, Listing 3-2 shows a complete web part written in Visual Basic .NET that implements the text editor displayed in Figure 3-3.

Listing 3-2. *Using the Toolbar Control*

```
Option Explicit On
Option Strict On
Option Compare Text

Imports System
Imports System.ComponentModel
Imports System.Web.UI
Imports System.Web.UI.WebControls
Imports System.Xml.Serialization
Imports Microsoft.SharePoint
Imports Microsoft.SharePoint.Utilities
Imports Microsoft.SharePoint.WebPartPages
Imports Microsoft.Web.UI.WebControls

<DefaultProperty(""), ToolboxData("<{0}:Builder runat=server></{0}:Builder>"),
XmlRoot(Namespace:="SPSSimpleToolbar")> _
Public Class Builder
    Inherits Microsoft.SharePoint.WebPartPages.WebPart

    Private WithEvents objToolbar As Toolbar
    Private objBoldButton As ToolbarCheckButton
    Private objItalicButton As ToolbarCheckButton
    Private objUnderlineButton As ToolbarCheckButton
    Private objNameListButton As New ToolbarDropDownList
    Private objSizeListButton As New ToolbarDropDownList
    Private objText As TextBox

    Protected Overrides Sub CreateChildControls()

        'Create parent toolbar
        objToolbar = New Toolbar
        With objToolbar
            .AutoPostBack = True
            .Width = New Unit(100, UnitType.Percentage)
        End With

        'Create font style buttons
        objBoldButton = New ToolbarCheckButton
        With objBoldButton
            .ImageUrl = "/_layouts/1033/images/bold.gif"
            .ID = "BoldButton"
        End With
        objToolbar.Items.Add(objBoldButton)
```

```
objItalicButton = New ToolbarCheckButton
With objItalicButton
    .ImageUrl = "/_layouts/1033/images/italic.gif"
    .ID = "ItalicButton"
End With
objToolbar.Items.Add(objItalicButton)

objUnderlineButton = New ToolbarCheckButton
With objUnderlineButton
    .ImageUrl = "/_layouts/1033/images/rteundl.gif"
    .ID = "UnderlineButton"
End With
objToolbar.Items.Add(objUnderlineButton)

'Create font name list
objNameListButton = New ToolbarDropDownList
With objNameListButton
    .Items.Add("Arial")
    .Items.Add("Courier")
    .ID = "NameList"
End With
objToolbar.Items.Add(objNameListButton)

'Create font size list
objSizeListButton = New ToolbarDropDownList
With objSizeListButton
    .Items.Add("8")
    .Items.Add("9")
    .Items.Add("10")
    .Items.Add("11")
    .Items.Add("12")
    .ID = "SizeList"
End With
objToolbar.Items.Add(objSizeListButton)

Controls.Add(objToolbar)

'Create TextArea
objText = New TextBox
With objText
    .TextMode = TextBoxMode.MultiLine
    .Width = New Unit(100, UnitType.Percentage)
    .Height = New Unit(200, UnitType.Pixel)
    .Columns = 40
    .Rows = 10
End With

Controls.Add(objText)
```

```
      End Sub

      Protected Overrides Sub RenderWebPart( _
      ByVal output As System.Web.UI.HtmlTextWriter)

        With objText
          .Font.Bold = objBoldButton.Selected
          .Font.Italic = objItalicButton.Selected
          .Font.Underline = objUnderlineButton.Selected
          .Font.Name = objNameListButton.SelectedItem.ToString
          .Font.Size = New FontUnit(CInt(objSizeListButton.SelectedItem.ToString))
        End With

          objToolbar.RenderControl(output)
          objText.RenderControl(output)

      End Sub

End Class
```

Using the TabStrip and MultiPage Controls

The TabStrip control allows you to create a set of tabs displayed either vertically or horizontally. The MultiPage control generates a set of pages that stack on top of each other and can be rearranged like cards in a deck. Although both the TabStrip and MultiPage controls can be used separately, when combined they implement a tabbed dialog metaphor that is useful for presenting complementary information in a limited space. Figure 3-4 shows an example of combining the controls to shows site membership by role.

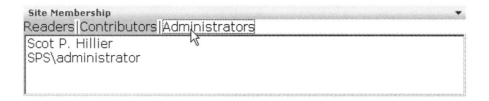

Figure 3-4. *The TabStrip and MultiPage controls*

Both the TabStrip and the MultiPage controls act as collections for the elements they display. The TabStrip control contains a set of Tab objects while the MultiPage control contains a set of PageView objects. Tab objects are added to the Items collection of the TabStrip, and PageView objects are added to the Controls collection of the MultiPage. Additionally, you can add other controls to the PageView object to create an interface for that page. The following Visual Basic .NET code shows how to create a single tab and a single page, and how to add several controls to the new page:

```
Dim objTabStrip As New TabStrip
Dim objTab As New Tab
objTab.Text = "Tab1"
objTabStrip.Items.Add(objTab)

Dim objMultiPage As New MultiPage
Dim objPage As New PageView
With objPage
    .Controls.Add(New TextBox)
    .Controls.Add(New Label)
    .Controls.Add(New ListBox)
End With
objMultiPage.Controls.Add(objPage)
```

Adding controls to the appropriate collection will give you sets to work with, but will not coordinate the tab and page behavior. Ultimately, you want to associate a Tab object with a PageView object so that when a tab is clicked, the appropriate page is displayed. This association is accomplished by assigning an ID to the MultiPage control and referencing that ID from the TabStrip control. The following Visual Basic .NET code shows how to make the association between a TabStrip and a MultiPage control:

```
Dim objTabStrip As New TabStrip
Dim objMultiPage As New MultiPage
objMultiPage.ID = "MyPages"
objTabStrip.TargetID = objMultiPage.ID
```

When the appropriate association is made, the web controls automatically create a one-to-one relationship between Tabs and PageViews. Furthermore, all of the tab and page functionality is implemented through DHTML behaviors, so switching pages by clicking on the tabs is fast and smooth. As an example, Listing 3-3 shows a complete web part written in Visual Basic .NET that uses the TabStrip and MultiPage controls to implement the membership display shown in Figure 3-4.

Listing 3-3. *Using the TabStip and MultiPage Controls*

```
Option Explicit On
Option Strict On
Option Compare Text

Imports System
Imports System.ComponentModel
Imports System.Web.UI
Imports System.Web.UI.WebControls
Imports System.Xml.Serialization
Imports Microsoft.SharePoint
Imports Microsoft.SharePoint.Utilities
Imports Microsoft.SharePoint.WebPartPages
Imports Microsoft.SharePoint.WebControls
Imports Microsoft.Web.UI.WebControls
```

```vbnet
<DefaultProperty(""), ToolboxData("<{0}:Builder runat=server></{0}:Builder>"), _
XmlRoot(Namespace:="SPSTabbedMembers")> _
Public Class Builder
    Inherits Microsoft.SharePoint.WebPartPages.WebPart

    Private WithEvents objTabStrip As TabStrip
    Private WithEvents objMultiPage As MultiPage
    Private lstReaders As ListBox
    Private lstContributors As ListBox
    Private lstAdministrators As ListBox

    Protected Overrides Sub CreateChildControls()

        'TabStrip
        objTabStrip = New TabStrip
        With objTabStrip
            .ID = "MemberTabs"
            .Font.Size = New FontUnit(FontSize.Small)
        End With
        Controls.Add(objTabStrip)

        'MultiPage
        objMultiPage = New MultiPage
        With objMultiPage
            .ID = "MemberPages"
            .Font.Size = New FontUnit(FontSize.Small)
        End With
        objTabStrip.TargetID = objMultiPage.ID
        Controls.Add(objMultiPage)

        'Tabs
        Dim objTab As New Tab
        With objTab
            .Text = "Readers"
        End With
        objTabStrip.Items.Add(objTab)

        Dim objSeparator As New TabSeparator
        With objSeparator
            .Text = "|"
        End With
        objTabStrip.Items.Add(objSeparator)

        objTab = New Tab
        With objTab
            .Text = "Contributors"
        End With
        objTabStrip.Items.Add(objTab)
```

```
objSeparator = New TabSeparator
With objSeparator
    .Text = "|"
End With
objTabStrip.Items.Add(objSeparator)

objTab = New Tab
With objTab
    .Text = "Administrators"
End With
objTabStrip.Items.Add(objTab)

'Pages
lstReaders = New ListBox
With lstReaders
    .Width = New Unit(100, UnitType.Percentage)
    .Font.Size = New FontUnit(FontSize.Small)
End With

Dim objPage As New PageView
With objPage
    .Controls.Add(lstReaders)
End With
objMultiPage.Controls.Add(objPage)

lstContributors = New ListBox
With lstContributors
    .Width = New Unit(100, UnitType.Percentage)
    .Font.Size = New FontUnit(FontSize.Small)
End With

objPage = New PageView
With objPage
    .Controls.Add(lstContributors)
End With
objMultiPage.Controls.Add(objPage)

lstAdministrators = New ListBox
With lstAdministrators
    .Width = New Unit(100, UnitType.Percentage)
    .Font.Size = New FontUnit(FontSize.Small)
End With

objPage = New PageView
With objPage
    .Controls.Add(lstAdministrators)
End With
objMultiPage.Controls.Add(objPage)
```

```
    End Sub

    Protected Overrides Sub RenderWebPart( _
    ByVal output As System.Web.UI.HtmlTextWriter)

        Dim objSite As SPSite = SPControl.GetContextSite(Context)
        Dim objWeb As SPWeb = objSite.OpenWeb

        'Add Readers
        For Each objUser As SPUser In objWeb.Roles.Item("Reader").Users
            lstReaders.Items.Add(objUser.Name)
        Next

        'Add Contributors
        For Each objUser As SPUser In objWeb.Roles.Item("Contributor").Users
            lstContributors.Items.Add(objUser.Name)
        Next

        'Add Administrators
        For Each objUser As SPUser In objWeb.Roles.Item("Administrator").Users
            lstAdministrators.Items.Add(objUser.Name)
        Next

        'Draw controls
        objTabStrip.RenderControl(output)
        objMultiPage.RenderControl(output)

    End Sub

End Class
```

Working with Web Forms User Controls

When building web parts, you can utilize any server control to help create the user interface. These controls can be the standard controls available in Visual Studio .NET, a separate assembly containing controls such as the Internet Explorer Web Controls, or controls you create yourself, called *User Controls*. This last option can be a powerful way to create controls for use in web parts because Visual Studio .NET supports a graphical technique for creating User Controls known as *Web Forms User Controls*. This means that you can develop a methodology for creating web parts using the same drag-and-drop techniques that we use in ASP.NET applications. This approach has the promise of significantly improving your productivity when you're creating web parts.

Working with the User Control Designer

The first thing to note about developing Web Forms User Controls is that they are built in a standard ASP.NET project type. This is an important issue, because ASP.NET applications cannot be developed on a site controlled by WSS due to the managed-path processing of the

ISAPI filter `stsfltr.dll`. Therefore, you have to set up a directory for these projects that is excluded from the set of managed paths in much the same way as we did for the images used by the `TreeView` control earlier in this chapter.

Follow these steps to set up a site for your Web Forms User Controls:

1. Open the Internet Information Services (IIS) Manager.

2. Expand the Web Sites folder until the WSS site is visible.

3. Right-click the WSS site node and select New ➤ Virtual Directory from the context menu.

4. In the Virtual Directory Creation Wizard, click the Next button.

5. On the Virtual Directory Alias screen, name the new directory **WebFormsUserControls** and click the Next button.

6. On the Web Site Content Directory screen, click the Browse button.

7. In the Browse for Folder dialog, create a new folder for the virtual directory at **Inetpub\wwwroot\WebFormsUserControls** and click the OK button.

8. Click the Next button.

9. On the Virtual Directory Access Permissions screen, click the Next button.

10. Click the Finish button to complete the wizard.

11. Select All Programs ➤ Administrative Tools ➤ SharePoint Central Administration.

12. Select Virtual Server Configuration ➤ Configure Virtual Server Settings.

13. On the Virtual Server List page, select the server where WSS is installed.

14. On the Virtual Server Settings page, select Virtual Server Management ➤ Define Managed Paths.

15. On the Define Managed Paths page, enter **/WebFormsUserControls** in the Add a New Path section.

16. Click the Excluded Path option.

17. Click the OK button to add the new path.

Once you have created a directory where you can freely build ASP.NET projects, you are ready to create a Web Forms User Control. The process begins by creating an ASP.NET project in Visual Studio .NET under the new directory. Once the project is opened, you will immediately delete the `Global.asax`, `Web.config`, and `WebForm1.aspx` files. None of these files are needed to create the Web Forms User Control. Once the new project is created, you will then need to add a new Web Forms User Control by using the Project menu.

The Web Forms User Control is a file with an `.ascx` extension. Just like a regular ASP.NET page, the Web Forms User Control consists of a design surface and a code window. Using the design surface, you can create a user interface graphically. Initially, the Web Forms User Control will utilize relative positioning when you drop controls onto the surface. If you want to use absolute positioning, then you must drop a Grid Layout Panel onto the design surface before you begin to create the user interface. Using the code window, you can program the graphical elements and interact with the WSS object model to create the web part functionality.

Depending on the exact functionality of your web part, the productivity gain from this approach can be tremendous. This is especially true if you are working with any server control that has wizards or design tools built into Visual Studio .NET. As a simple example, consider using a DataGrid control to display a DataSet. Our goal is to create a visually appealing display similar to that shown in Figure 3-5.

au_id	au_lname	au_fname	phone	address	city	state	zip	contract
172-32-1176	White	Johnson	408 496-7223	10932 Bigge Rd.	Menlo Park	CA	94025	True
213-46-8915	Green	Marjorie	415 986-7020	309 63rd St. #411	Oakland	CA	94618	True
238-95-7766	Carson	Cheryl	415 548-7723	589 Darwin Ln.	Berkeley	CA	94705	True
267-41-2394	O'Leary	Michael	408 286-2428	22 Cleveland Av. #14	San Jose	CA	95128	True
274-80-9391	Straight	Dean	415 834-2919	5420 College Av.	Oakland	CA	94609	True

Web Forms User Control Host

Figure 3-5. *Records displayed in a web part*

If you were to take the traditional web part development approach, the grid would be entirely constructed using code in the CreateChildControls method. This code would include not only creating the grid, but also coding all of the style changes and adding the grid to the set of user interface elements. Furthermore, you would likely have to run and view the web part several times before you were finally happy with the appearance. The following code shows an example of typical DataGrid programming in a web part:

```
protected override void CreateChildControls()
{

    //Purpose: draw the user interface
    grdOrders = new DataGrid();
    grdOrders.AutoGenerateColumns=true;
    grdOrders.Width=Unit.Percentage(100);
    grdOrders.HeaderStyle.Font.Name = "arial";
    grdOrders.HeaderStyle.Font.Name = "arial";
    grdOrders.HeaderStyle.Font.Bold = true;
    grdOrders.HeaderStyle.ForeColor = System.Drawing.Color.Wheat;
    grdOrders.HeaderStyle.BackColor = System.Drawing.Color.DarkBlue;
    grdOrders.AlternatingItemStyle.BackColor = System.Drawing.Color.LightCyan;
    Controls.Add(grdOrders);

}
```

In contrast to the effort required to create the grid in code, a Web Forms User Control allows us to use the graphical designer associated with the DataGrid control to easily set all of the properties. Once the DataGrid is added to the design surface of the project, you can easily select a color scheme using the Auto Format hyperlink in the Properties window of Visual Studio .NET. In this case, we can achieve the same appearance created in the previous code by simply selecting the Professional 1 style. Figure 3-6 shows the Auto Format dialog with the appropriate style selected.

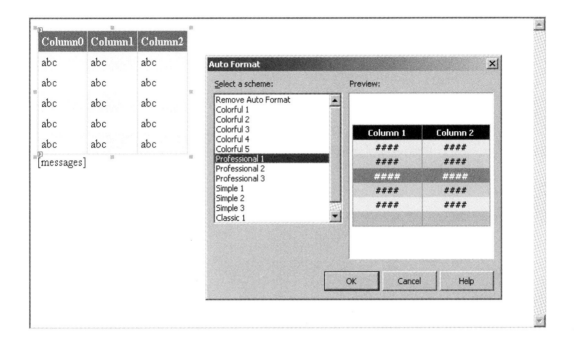

Figure 3-6. *Formatting a DataGrid*

Hosting and Deploying the User Control

While Web Forms User Controls offer an excellent way to graphically create user interfaces, they are not capable of being loaded directly into a WSS site. Instead, they must be hosted by a standard web part that loads the control at runtime. The standard web part provides a placeholder for the Web Forms User Control as well as a mechanism for interacting with properties through the web part framework.

In order to host the Web Forms User Control, you must create a new web part project in Visual Studio .NET and set a reference to the Web Forms User Control project. Once the reference is set, you can load the Web Forms User Control in the CreateChildControls method of the hosting web part. It is then a simple matter to render the interface in the RenderWebPart method. Listing 3-4 shows complete C# code for hosting a DataGrid of records in a Web Forms User Control named SimpleReport.Report.

Listing 3-4. *Hosting a Web Forms User Control*

```
using System;
using System.ComponentModel;
using System.Web.UI;
using System.Web.UI.WebControls;
using System.Xml.Serialization;
using Microsoft.SharePoint;
using Microsoft.SharePoint.Utilities;
using Microsoft.SharePoint.WebPartPages;

namespace SimpleReportHost
{

    [DefaultProperty(""),
    ToolboxData("<{0}:Container runat=server></{0}:Container>"),
    XmlRoot(Namespace="SimpleReportHost")]
    public class Container : Microsoft.SharePoint.WebPartPages.WebPart
    {

        //Holder for User Control
        protected SimpleReport.Report report;

        protected override void CreateChildControls()
        {
            //Load the User Control
            report = (SimpleReport.Report)Page.LoadControl
            ("/WebFormsUserControls/SimpleReport/report.ascx");
            Controls.Add(report);
        }

        protected override void RenderWebPart(HtmlTextWriter output)
        {
            //Render the User Control
            report.RenderControl(output);
        }
    }
}
```

If you are using Web Forms User Controls extensively, it helps to create a generic host web part that you can use for any Web Forms User Control. This makes your development even more efficient because the same web part can be used over and over again to host different solutions. The generic host uses a web part property to specify the path where the Web Forms User Control is located. The loaded control is then cast generically to a UserControl object, which is subsequently rendered. Listing 3-5 shows the complete code for a generic host that you can use with your solutions.

Listing 3-5. *A Generic Web Forms User Control Host*

```
using System;
using System.ComponentModel;
using System.Web.UI;
using System.Web.UI.WebControls;
using System.Xml.Serialization;
using Microsoft.SharePoint;
using Microsoft.SharePoint.Utilities;
using Microsoft.SharePoint.WebPartPages;

using System.Collections;

//Key Points
// 1. Reference System.Collections
// 2. Must have an excluded path for the ASCX files
// 3. Deploy the assembly in the \bin directory

namespace WebFormsUserControlHost
{

    [DefaultProperty("ControlPath"),
    ToolboxData("<{0}:Host runat=server></{0}:Host>"),
    XmlRoot(Namespace="WebFormsUserControlHost")]
    public class Host : Microsoft.SharePoint.WebPartPages.WebPart
    {

        private string path = "";

        [Browsable(true),
            Category("Miscellaneous"),
            DefaultValue(""),
            WebPartStorage(Storage.Shared),
            FriendlyName("Web Forms User Control Path"),
            Description("The URL of the User Control to display.")]
        public string ControlPath
        {
            get
            {
                return path;
            }

            set
            {
                path = value;
            }
        }
```

```
        Label messages = new Label();

        protected override void CreateChildControls()
        {
            try
            {
                Controls.Add(messages);
                Controls.Add(Page.LoadControl(ControlPath));
            }
            catch (Exception x)
            {
                messages.Text = x.Message;
            }
        }

        protected override void RenderWebPart(HtmlTextWriter output)
        {

            IEnumerator controls = Controls.GetEnumerator();
            controls.Reset();
            while (controls.MoveNext())
            {
                try
                {
                    if (!controls.Current.Equals(messages))
                      ((UserControl)controls.Current).RenderControl(output);
                }
                catch (Exception x)
                {
                    messages.Text += x.Message;
                }
            }
            output.Write("<br>");
            messages.RenderControl(output);
        }
    }
}
```

Before compiling the solution for deployment, you should make sure that the Web Forms User Control is strongly named so that it can be called by the host web part. Once you have successfully compiled the solution, you will be left with an assembly for the Web Forms User Control and an assembly for the host web part. Both of these assemblies must then be deployed to the WSS server.

In my opinion, the best practice for deployment is to place both assemblies in the Inetpub\ wwwroot\bin directory of your WSS installation. However, you may always choose to place them in the GAC if you prefer. Be aware that assemblies in the GAC always operate with full trust. Placing the assemblies in the Inetpub\wwwroot\bin directory, on the other hand, allows you to control the trust granted to the assemblies using the web.config file.

Along with the assemblies, you must also deploy the ASCX file that represents the Web Forms User Control interface. This file must be deployed into a directory that is excluded from WSS control. This generally means that you must create this directory on the target WSS server by hand and exclude the path. You can simply follow the steps I presented earlier to create this directory and then copy the ASCX file into that directory.

Understanding the Solution Life Cycle

Just like standard web parts, the Web Forms User Control and host web part participate in a server-side request/response sequence. Because the Web Forms User Control provides user interface functionality and the host web part provides interaction with the web part framework, it is important to understand the life cycle of the solution as a whole and the limitations it imposes. Understanding this life cycle will help you determine where to code the various parts of your solution.

Just like any ASP.NET or web part, the life cycle of the Web Forms User Control solution begins with a call to the OnInit method. While both the Web Forms User Control and the host web part have OnInit methods, at this point the Web Forms User Control has not yet been loaded into the web part. This means that only the OnInit event for the host web part will fire. The web part is subsequently initialized with any property values that were set when the web part was added to the page. In the case of the host web part, this is most likely the property that specifies the path to the Web Forms User Control.

If we were developing a standard web part, we would now concern ourselves with the order of events that fire within the web part. In a standard web part, the ViewState of the web part is populated followed by a call to the OnLoad method. In our Web Forms User Control solution these events still occur, but we are less interested in them. Instead, the next milestone that concerns us is when the Web Forms User Control is loaded.

When the Web Forms User Control is loaded by the host web part, it receives a call to the OnInit method in the same way that the host web part does. This event is then followed by a call to the OnLoad method. The difference, of course, is that these methods are part of the Web Forms User Control and not the host web part. You will find, however, that the Web Forms User Control has complete access to the WSS object model throughout these events, and that you can code the bulk of your functionality directly in the Web Forms User Control even before it is rendered by the host web part.

Once the control is loaded and initialized, the web part renders the user interface. At this point, users may interact with the Web Forms User Control. Handling user interaction is straightforward; you may code the event handlers exactly as you would for any ASP.NET application. For the most part, these events will initiate round-trips to the server, which means that the Web Forms User Control will be torn down and rebuilt just like any ASP.NET application. Figure 3-7 shows a summary of the solution life cycle in a flow chart.

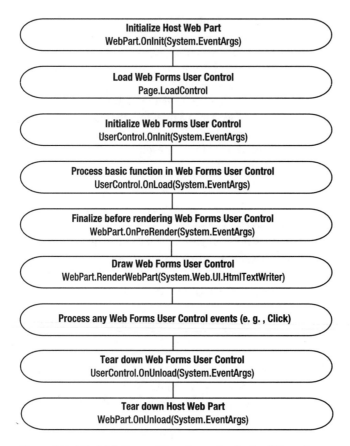

Figure 3-7. *The Web Forms User Control solution life cycle*

Handling Web Part Properties

Web Forms User Controls work well when the web part is essentially acting as a host for the user interface. If, however, you need to communicate between the host web part and the Web Forms User Control, the situation gets a bit more complicated. This issue arises most often when you want to store properties in the web part framework but utilize them in the Web Forms User Control. In this case, you must create properties and methods within the Web Forms User Control that can be accessed by the host web part at runtime.

As an example, let's take the concept I used earlier of displaying a set of records in a grid. I want to use a Web Forms User Control because it is simpler to build the user interface, but I want to store the database connection string information in web part properties so that they will persist and be available to all users of the web part. When the host web part loads the Web Forms User Control, it will then pass the information on so the database query can be made.

I'll start the solution by defining one property and one method in the Web Forms User Control. The property will contain the connection string information, and the method will execute the query. Listing 3-6 shows the complete code for the Web Forms User Control containing the DataGrid.

Listing 3-6. *Creating Properties and Methods in the Web Forms User Control*

```
using System;
using System.Data;
using System.Data.SqlClient;
using System.Drawing;
using System.Web;
using System.Web.UI.WebControls;
using System.Web.UI.HtmlControls;
using System.Web.UI;

public class Report : System.Web.UI.UserControl
{
    protected System.Web.UI.WebControls.DataGrid grid;
    protected System.Web.UI.WebControls.Label messages;
    string m_connection = null;

    public string ConnectionString
    {
        get
        {
            return m_connection;
        }

        set
        {
            m_connection = value;
        }
    }

    public void runQuery()
    {
        try
        {
            SqlConnection con = new SqlConnection(ConnectionString);

            string sqlString = "Select Top 5 * From authors";
            SqlCommand command = new SqlCommand(sqlString,con);

            SqlDataAdapter adapter = new SqlDataAdapter(command);
            DataSet dataset = new DataSet("root");
            adapter.Fill(dataset,"authors");
```

```
            grid.DataSource = dataset;
            grid.DataMember = "authors";
            grid.DataBind();
        }
        catch (Exception x)
        {
            messages.Text = x.Message;
        }


    }
}
```

When I design the host web part, I'll now include four properties that allow the user to set the username, password, database, and server for the database query. Because these properties are all defined as standard web part properties, they will be serialized by the web part framework and persist even if the user closes down the browser.

In order to use the properties, I will load the Web Forms User Control and then set the ConnectionString property using the four properties defined for the host web part. Once the connection string is set, the host web part will call the runQuery method of the Web Forms User Control to produce the grid. Listing 3-7 shows the complete code for the new host web part.

Listing 3-7. *Using Web Part Properties*

```
using System;
using System.ComponentModel;
using System.Web.UI;
using System.Web.UI.WebControls;
using System.Xml.Serialization;
using Microsoft.SharePoint;
using Microsoft.SharePoint.Utilities;
using Microsoft.SharePoint.WebPartPages;

namespace SimpleReportHost
{

    [DefaultProperty(""),
    ToolboxData("<{0}:Container runat=server></{0}:Container>"),
    XmlRoot(Namespace="SimpleReportHost")]
    public class Container : Microsoft.SharePoint.WebPartPages.WebPart
    {

        //Property members
        protected string m_sqlServer;
        protected string m_database;
        protected string m_userName;
        protected string m_password;
```

```csharp
[Browsable(true), Category("Miscellaneous"),
DefaultValue(""),Description("The server where the database resides"),
FriendlyName("SQL Server"),WebPartStorageAttribute(Storage.Shared)]
public string sqlServer
{
    get
    {
        return m_sqlServer;
    }

    set
    {
        m_sqlServer = value;
    }
}

[Browsable(true), Category("Miscellaneous"),
DefaultValue(""),Description("The name of the database"),
FriendlyName("Database"),WebPartStorageAttribute(Storage.Shared)]
public string database
{
    get
    {
        return m_database;
    }

    set
    {
        m_database = value;
    }
}

[Browsable(true), Category("Miscellaneous"),
DefaultValue(""),Description("The account to access the database"),
FriendlyName("Username"),WebPartStorageAttribute(Storage.Shared)]
public string userName
{
    get
    {
        return m_userName;
    }

    set
    {
        m_userName = value;
    }
}
```

```
        [Browsable(true), Category("Miscellaneous"),
        DefaultValue(""),Description("The password for the account"),
        FriendlyName("Password"),WebPartStorageAttribute(Storage.Shared)]
        public string password
        {
            get
            {
                return m_password;
            }

            set
            {
                m_password = value;
            }
        }


        //Holder for User Control
        protected SimpleReport.Report report;

        protected override void CreateChildControls()
        {
            //Load the User Control
            report = (SimpleReport.Report)Page.LoadControl
            ("/WebFormsUserControls/SimpleReport/report.ascx");
            Controls.Add(report);
        }

        protected override void RenderWebPart(HtmlTextWriter output)
        {
            //Run Query
            report.ConnectionString = "User ID=" + userName +
                ";Password=" + password +
                ";Data Source=" + sqlServer +
                ";Initial Catalog=" + database;

            report.runQuery();

            //Render the User Control
            report.RenderControl(output);
        }
    }
}
```

Creating a Custom Project Wizard

If you decide to make a commitment to creating web parts using the graphical techniques outlined in this section, you will find yourself repeatedly creating ASP.NET applications and then modifying them to build the Web Forms User Controls. Because this process is always the same, it makes sense to create a new project type in Visual Studio .NET to support the technique. We can accomplish this by building a Custom Project Wizard that will run in Visual Studio .NET and give us the new project type shown in Figure 3-8.

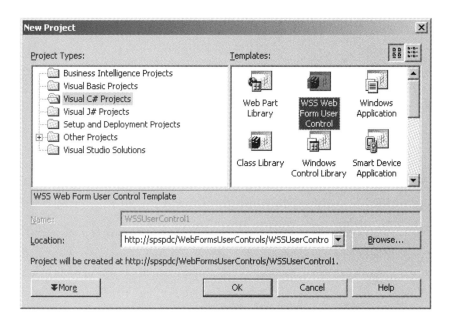

Figure 3-8. *A Web Forms User Control project type*

Understanding VSZ and VSDIR Files

Creating a new project type begins with the creation of a VSZ file. Visual Studio .NET uses VSZ files to contain the initialization information for running wizards that create new projects. For C# projects, these files are located in the directory `\Program Files\Microsoft Visual Studio .NET 2003\VC#\CSharpProjects`. There is a separate `\VBProjects` directory that contains similar information for Visual Basic .NET project types. The following code shows a file I created named `CSharpWebFormUserControl.vsz` designed to initialize a new Web Forms User Control Project:

```
VSWIZARD 7.0
Wizard=VsWizard.VsWizardEngine.7.1
Param="WIZARD_NAME = CSharpWebFormUserControl"
Param="WIZARD_UI = FALSE"
Param="PROJECT_TYPE = CSPROJ"
```

The `VSWIZARD` entry in the file is the version of the template file format and should not be changed. The `Wizard` entry is the name of the Visual Studio .NET wizard assembly that will create the new project. The assembly name in my file is for Visual Studio .NET. The `Param` entries are all parameters that are passed to the project wizard when it launches. The most important of these parameters is the `WIZARD_NAME`, which gives the project type a name that will be associated with other operations later in the process.

Located in the same directory as the VSZ file, you will find files with VSDIR extensions. These files contain information that specifies the icon, text, and other settings that appear in the New Project dialog. The following code shows a file I created named `CSharpWebFormUserControl.vsdir` that supports the VSZ file. The entries are all pipe-delimited and normally appear on a single line in a text file. They appear on multiple lines here to support the page format of this book.

```
CSharpWebFormUserControl.vsz|{FAE04EC1-301F-11d3-BF4B-00C04F79EFBC}
|WSS Web Forms User Control|1|WSS Web Forms User Control Template
|{FAE04EC1-301F-11d3-BF4B-00C04F79EFBC}|4547|1|WSSUserControl1|web
```

The name of the VSDIR file has no significance because the file itself contains all of the information necessary to associate it with the correct project wizard. Additionally, VSDIR files may have multiple entries, so you will not see a one-to-one mapping of VSZ and VSDIR files in Visual Studio .NET. Table 3-2 lists each field in the file along with a description.

Table 3-2. *VSDIR File Entries*

Field	Description
Relative Path	The name of the associated VSZ file
Package GUID	The GUID representing an assembly containing resources for the wizard
Localized Name	The name that appears in the Visual Studio .NET dialog
Sort Priority	A number determining the order in which the project type appears in the dialog
Description	A description of the project type
Icon Resource GUID	The GUID representing an assembly containing icon resources for the wizard
Icon Resource	A reference to an icon resource used to represent the project
Flags	A number specifying options for wizard behavior
Base Name	The name of the project when it is created

The first entry in the file is the relative path to the related VSZ file. Because the VSZ and VSDIR files are in the same directory, this entry contains only the name of the file. The GUID entries in the file refer to an assembly associated with Visual Studio .NET from which we can use strings and icon resources and should not be changed. The icon reference represents a basic project icon that will appear in the New Project dialog.

Programming the Wizard

While the VSZ and VSDIR files are required to initialize the project wizard engine, they do not contain all of the information necessary to create a new project in Visual Studio .NET. In order to successfully create a new project, you must create a script that programs the project wizard engine and provide templates for the files that will make up the project. The script and templates are stored in subdirectories underneath the directory `\Program Files\Microsoft Visual Studio .NET 2003\VC#\VC#Wizards`. In this directory, you will find subdirectories with the same name specified in the VSZ file earlier. In our example, a new directory named `\CSharpWebFormUserControl` was created with additional subdirectories named `\Scripts` and `\Templates`. Each of these directories was then given a subdirectory representing the localized culture under which the wizard will run. Figure 3-9 shows the directory structure in the Windows File Explorer.

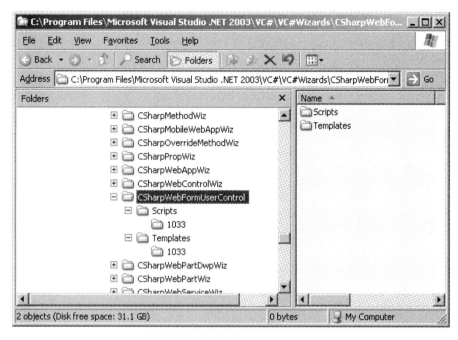

Figure 3-9. *The wizard directory*

The \Templates directory contains all of the files that are to be added to the project when it is created. In my example, there are only two files: AssemblyInfo.cs and WebUserControl.ascx. These files are subsequently listed in the Templates.inf file so that the wizard script can access a single source to retrieve a list of all project files to be added. A template file can be fully coded as is the case for AssemblyInfo.cs, or it can contain tokens that the wizard will fill with information during the project creation process. For example, the following code shows the contents of the WebUserControl.ascx file, which contains tokens necessary to create the Web Forms User Control in the new project:

```
<%@ Control Language="c#"
AutoEventWireup="false" Codebehind="$FILENAME$.cs"
Inherits="$INHERITS$"
TargetSchema="http://schemas.microsoft.com/intellisense/ie5"%>
```

After the templates are defined, the last step is to create a script file that programs the project wizard to create the new project, add the required files, and set the required assembly references. This script is written into a text file named default.js and is stored under the \Scripts directory.

When the project wizard has initialized, it calls the OnFinish function in default.js to create the new project. In this function, the script typically makes a subsequent call to the CreateCSharpProject function to build the basic project. This function and the basic project template are both stored in separate include files that are available to all of the scripts written for the wizard engine. The project files are then added through a call to the `AddFilesToCSharpProject` function. Listing 3-8 shows the code for the `OnFinish` function I used in my project template.

Listing 3-8. *The OnFinish Function*

```
function OnFinish(selProj, selObj)
{
    var oldSuppressUIValue = true;
    try
    {
        oldSuppressUIValue = dte.SuppressUI;

        var strProjectPath = wizard.FindSymbol("PROJECT_PATH");
        var strProjectName = wizard.FindSymbol("PROJECT_NAME");

        var bEmptyProject = 0; //wizard.FindSymbol("EMPTY_PROJECT");

        var proj = CreateCSharpProject(strProjectName, strProjectPath,
        "defaultwebproject.csproj");

        if( !ProjectIsARootWeb( strProjectPath ) )
        {
            wizard.AddSymbol("NOT_ROOT_WEB_APP", true);
        }

        var InfFile = CreateInfFile();
        if (!bEmptyProject && proj)
        {
            AddReferencesForWebForm(proj);

            // add the project properties
            wizard.AddSymbol("DEFAULT_SERVER_SCRIPT", "JavaScript");
            wizard.AddSymbol("DEFAULT_CLIENT_SCRIPT", "JavaScript");

            // add project files
            AddFilesToCSharpProject(proj, strProjectName, strProjectPath,
            InfFile, false);
            SetStartupPage(proj, "WebUserControl1.ascx");
                        CollapseReferencesNode(proj);
                        AddSharePointReferences(proj)
```

```
        }
        proj.Save();
    }
    catch(e)
    {
        if( e.description.length > 0 )
            SetErrorInfo(e);
        return e.number;
    }
    finally
    {
            dte.SuppressUI = oldSuppressUIValue;
            if( InfFile )
            InfFile.Delete();
    }
}
```

After the project is created and the new files are added, you will probably want to add assembly references to the project. This is done through the Add method of the CSharpReferenceManager. Using this object, you can add references to any existing .NET Framework assembly or even load a custom assembly. Listing 3-9 shows a custom function I copied from the standard web part project that adds a reference to Windows SharePoint Services.

Listing 3-9. *Adding References*

```
function AddSharePointReferences(oProj)
{
    var refmanager = GetCSharpReferenceManager(oProj);
    var bExpanded = IsReferencesNodeExpanded(oProj);

    refmanager.Add("System.Xml");

    try
    {
        var ref = refmanager.Add("Microsoft.SharePoint.dll");
        ref.CopyLocal = false;
    }
    catch(e)
    {
        var sharePointRefMissingError =
        "The path to Microsoft.SharePoint.dll was not found.";
        wizard.ReportError(sharePointRefMissingError);
    }
    if(!bExpanded)
        CollapseReferencesNode(oProj);
}
```

Along with all the major work of constructing the project, you will typically find several helper functions included in the script file. These functions can set property values on components, open files for editing, and the like. Listing 3-10 shows the helper functions I included in my project so you can have a complete reference to use in the exercise at the end of this chapter.

Listing 3-10. *Helper Functions*

```
function GetCSharpTargetName(strName, strProjectName)
{
    var strTarget = strName;

    switch (strName)
    {
        case "webusercontrol.ascx":
            strTarget = "WebUserControl1.ascx";
            break;
        case "assemblyinfo.cs":
            strTarget = "AssemblyInfo.cs";
            break;
    }
    return strTarget;
}

function DoOpenFile(strName)
{
    var bOpen = false;

    switch (strName)
    {
        case "WebUserControl1.ascx":
            bOpen = true;
            break;
    }
    return bOpen;
}

function SetFileProperties(oFileItem, strFileName)
{
    if(strFileName == "WebUserControl1.ascx")
    {
        oFileItem.Properties("SubType").Value = "Form";
    }
}
```

Exercise 3-1. Using Advanced Techniques

In this chapter, we examined several techniques for improving your productivity when building web parts. In this exercise, we will tie all of these techniques together by creating a new project type in Visual Studio .NET and using it to create a web part based on Web Forms User

Controls and utilizing the Internet Explorer Web Controls. This web part will display all of the lists contained in a team site using a `TreeView` control.

Prerequisites

Before you begin this exercise, there are several prerequisites that must be met. First, ensure that you have properly built and deployed the assembly `IEWebControls.dll` according to the instructions given earlier in the chapter. The assembly should be strongly named and located in the `Inetpub\wwwroot\bin` directory of your WSS server. Additionally, you should have deployed the `TreeView` control images to the `webctrl_client` directory and excluded this directory from WSS control. Second, you should have created a new virtual directory named `/WebFormsUser-Controls` in accordance with the instructions given earlier in the chapter and this directory should also be excluded from WSS control.

Creating the Custom Project Wizard

This project uses a custom project type to create the base Web Forms User Control interface. In order to use the project type, you will have to create it based on the file listings described earlier in this chapter. Once you create the project type, you can use it for all your web parts.

Follow these steps to create the new project type:

1. Create a new file in Notepad or any text editor.

2. Add the following code to create a VSZ file:

   ```
   VSWIZARD 7.0
   Wizard=VsWizard.VsWizardEngine.7.1
   Param="WIZARD_NAME = CSharpWebFormUserControl"
   Param="WIZARD_UI = FALSE"
   Param="PROJECT_TYPE = CSPROJ"
   ```

3. Save the file as `\Program Files\Microsoft Visual Studio .NET 2003\VC#\CSharpProjects\CSharpWebFormUserControl.vsz`.

4. Create a new file in Notepad or any text editor.

5. Add the following code on a single line to create a VSDIR file:

   ```
   CSharpWebFormUserControl.vsz|{FAE04EC1-301F-11d3-BF4B-00C04F79EFBC}
   |WSS Web Forms User Control|1|WSS Web Forms User Control Template
   |{FAE04EC1-301F-11d3-BF4B-00C04F79EFBC}|4547|1|WSSUserControl1|web
   ```

6. Save the file as `\Program Files\Microsoft Visual Studio .NET 2003\VC#\CSharpProjects\CSharpWebFormUserControl.vsdir`.

7. Create a new directory named `\Program Files\Microsoft Visual Studio .NET 2003\VC#\VC#Wizards\CSharpWebFormUserControl`.

8. Create new subdirectories under this directory named `\Scripts` and `\Templates`.

9. Under the `\Scripts` and `\Templates` directories, create a directory using the integer representation of your localized culture (`\1033` for en-us).

10. Create a new file in Notepad or any text editor.

11. Add the following code on a single line to create a template for the Web Forms User Control file:

```
<%@ Control Language="c#"
AutoEventWireup="false" Codebehind="$FILENAME$.cs"
Inherits="$INHERITS$"
TargetSchema="http://schemas.microsoft.com/intellisense/ie5"%>
```

12. Save the file as `\Program Files\Microsoft Visual Studio .NET 2003\VC#\VC#Wizards\` `CSharpWebFormUserControl\Templates\`*culture*`\webusercontrol.ascx`.

13. Copy the file `assemblyinfo.cs` from the directory `\Program Files\Microsoft Visual` `Studio .NET 2003\VC#\VC#Wizards\CSharpWebAppWiz\Templates\`*culture* to the directory `\Program Files\Microsoft Visual Studio .NET 2003\VC#\VC#Wizards\` `CSharpWebFormUserControl\Templates\`*culture*.

14. Create a new file in Notepad or any text editor.

15. Add the following lines to list all of the files to be added to the new project:

```
assemblyinfo.cs
webusercontrol.ascx
```

16. Save the file as `\Program Files\Microsoft Visual Studio .NET 2003\VC#\VC#Wizards\` `CSharpWebFormUserControl\Templates\`*culture*`\Templates.inf`.

17. Create a new file in Notepad or any text editor.

18. Enter the code from Listings 3-8, 3-9, and 3-10 to create the program script for the wizard.

19. Save the file as `\Program Files\Microsoft Visual Studio .NET 2003\VC#\VC#Wizards\` `CSharpWebFormUserControl\Scripts\`*culture*`\default.js`.

20. Start Visual Studio .NET and select File ➤ New ➤ Project from the menu.

21. In the New Project dialog, open the Visual C# Projects folder.

22. Select the new project type WSS Web Forms User Control.

23. In the Location box, enter the path to the `WebFormsUserControls` virtual directory you created earlier and name the new project **SiteLists**.

24. Click the OK button to create the new project.

Building the Web Forms User Control

Once the new project is created in Visual Studio .NET, you should have a new Web Forms User Control open. Using the design surface, add a `TreeView` control to display information and a `Label` control to display any error messages. Before you can add the `TreeView` control, however, you'll have to retrieve it from the Internet Explorer Web Controls assembly.

Follow these steps to add controls to the design surface:

1. In Visual Studio .NET, right-click the Toolbox and select Add/Remove Items from the context menu.

2. In the Customize Toolbox dialog, click the Browse button and locate the TreeView control associated with the assembly IEWebControls.dll.

3. Click the OK button to add the TreeView control to the Toolbox.

4. Drag a Label control from the Toolbox to the design surface.

5. Press the Enter key to start a new line and drag a TreeView control from the Toolbox to the design surface.

Coding the Web Forms User Control

Once the controls are added to the design surface, then you can code the control. In this example, simply return all of the lists on the host site and display them in the tree. Add the code from Listing 3-11 to create the tree.

Listing 3-11. *Populating the Tree*

```
namespace SiteLists
{
    using System;
    using System.Data;
    using System.Drawing;
    using System.Web;
    using System.Web.UI.WebControls;
    using System.Web.UI.HtmlControls;
    using Microsoft.SharePoint;
    using Microsoft.SharePoint.Utilities;
    using Microsoft.SharePoint.WebPartPages;
    using Microsoft.SharePoint.WebControls;
    using Microsoft.Web.UI.WebControls;

    public class WebUserControl1 : System.Web.UI.UserControl
    {
        protected System.Web.UI.WebControls.Label Label1;
        protected Microsoft.Web.UI.WebControls.TreeView TreeView1;

        private void Page_Load(object sender, System.EventArgs e)
        {
            try
            {

                //get this web
                Label1.Text = "";
                SPSite site = SPControl.GetContextSite(Context);
                SPWeb web = site.OpenWeb();
```

```
//add tree root
TreeNode root = new TreeNode();
root.Text = web.Title;
root.ImageUrl = "/_layouts/images/globe.gif";
root.Expanded = true;
TreeView1.Nodes.Clear();
TreeView1.Nodes.Add(root);

//add documents node
TreeNode docs = new TreeNode();
docs.Text = "Libraries";
docs.ImageUrl = "/_layouts/images/folder16.gif";
root.Nodes.Add(docs);

//add tasks node
TreeNode tasks = new TreeNode();
tasks.Text = "Task Lists";
tasks.ImageUrl = "/_layouts/images/taskpane.gif";
root.Nodes.Add(tasks);

//add others node
TreeNode others = new TreeNode();
others.Text = "Other Lists";
others.ImageUrl = "";
root.Nodes.Add(others);

//add lists to the tree
SPListCollection lists = web.Lists;

foreach (SPList list in lists)
{
    TreeNode node = new TreeNode();

    switch(list.BaseTemplate)
    {
        case SPListTemplateType.DocumentLibrary:
            node.Text = list.Title;
            node.ImageUrl = "/_layouts/images/doc16.gif";
            node.NavigateUrl = list.DefaultViewUrl;
            docs.Nodes.Add(node);
            break;

        case SPListTemplateType.Tasks:
            node.Text = list.Title;
            node.ImageUrl = "/_layouts/images/check.gif";
            node.NavigateUrl = list.DefaultViewUrl;
            tasks.Nodes.Add(node);
            break;
```

```
                    default:
                        node.Text = list.Title;
                        node.ImageUrl = "/_layouts/images/list.gif";
                        node.NavigateUrl = list.DefaultViewUrl;
                        others.Nodes.Add(node);
                        break;

                }
            }
        }
        catch(Exception x)
        {
            Label1.Text = x.Message;
        }
    }
  }
}
```

Building the Host Web Part

After the user interface is completed, you must create a web part to host the Web Forms User Control. This is accomplished by adding a new web part project to the solution and referencing the Web Forms User Control. Once the project is created, you will then write the code to load the user interface.

Follow these steps to create the host web part:

1. In Visual Studio .NET, select File ➤ Add Project ➤ New Project from the main menu.

2. In the Add New Project dialog, open the Visual C# Projects folder and select to create a new Web Part Library project.

3. Name the new project **SiteListsHost** and click the OK button.

4. When the new project is created, select Project ➤ Add Reference from the main menu.

5. In the Add Reference dialog, select the Projects tab.

6. On the Projects tab, select to add a reference to the SiteLists project and click the OK button.

7. Change the name of the file WebPart1.dwp to **Container.dwp**.

8. Open Container.dwp for editing and change the contents to appear like the following:

```xml
<?xml version="1.0" encoding="utf-8"?>
<WebPart xmlns="http://schemas.microsoft.com/WebPart/v2" >
        <Title>Site Lists Host Web Part</Title>
        <Description>A host for the Site Lists</Description>
        <Assembly>SiteListsHost</Assembly>
        <TypeName>SiteListsHost.Container</TypeName>
        <!-- Specify initial values for any additional base class or custom
properties here. -->
</WebPart>
```

9. Change the name of the file WebPart1.cs to **Container.cs**.

10. Open Container.cs for editing and change the code to look like Listing 3-12.

Listing 3-12. *The Host Web Part*

```
using System;
using System.ComponentModel;
using System.Web.UI;
using System.Web.UI.WebControls;
using System.Xml.Serialization;
using Microsoft.SharePoint;
using Microsoft.SharePoint.Utilities;
using Microsoft.SharePoint.WebPartPages;

namespace SiteListsHost
{

    [DefaultProperty(""),
    ToolboxData("<{0}:Container runat=server></{0}:Container>"),
    XmlRoot(Namespace="SiteListsHost")]
    public class Container : Microsoft.SharePoint.WebPartPages.WebPart
    {

        //Holder for User Control
        protected SiteLists.WebUserControl1 tree;

        protected override void CreateChildControls()
        {
            //Load the User Control
            tree =
            (SiteLists.WebUserControl1)Page.LoadControl(
            "/WebFormsUserControls/SiteLists/WebUserControl1.ascx");
            Controls.Add(tree);
        }

        protected override void RenderWebPart(HtmlTextWriter output)
        {
            //Render the User Control
            tree.RenderControl(output);
        }
    }
}
```

Deploying the Web Part

Deploying the web part and Web Forms User Control requires you to ensure that both assemblies are strongly named. Therefore, you should edit the AssemblyInfo files to include a reference to a key pair file. Once this is done, you should be able to successfully build the solution and produce two assemblies. Take both of these assemblies and copy them to the \Inetpub\wwwroot\bin directory. After that, you must edit the web.config file to ensure that the assemblies are marked as safe. These are steps you should be familiar with from other web part deployments, so I will not cover them in detail here. Once these steps are completed, you should now be able to import the DWP file into any team site and see the web part. Figure 3-10 shows the final project.

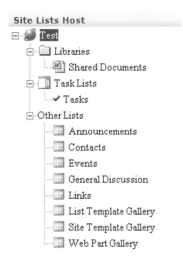

Figure 3-10. *The completed project*

Advanced SharePoint Portal Server Solutions

While many of the techniques and projects I discuss in this book are applicable to both Windows SharePoint Services (WSS) and SharePoint Portal Server (SPS), this chapter is specifically geared toward developers who have deployed SPS as part of their solution and want to customize the portal. SPS provides a number of features that enhance the overall SharePoint infrastructure, including My Site, search, audiences, and profiles. Many of these features are candidates for customization and improvement. In this chapter, I will address the most common issues with SPS development and show you some solutions.

Customizing SharePoint Portal Server Search

If your organization is going to use a SharePoint installation seriously, then a full-strength search engine is critical. Although WSS sites offer a limited search capability, SPS provides a much more robust search mechanism that allows administrators to specify search scopes while giving end users advanced tools to build and execute queries. This enhanced search functionality is one of the primary reasons to deploy SPS alongside WSS sites.

SPS users can take advantage of two different search web parts to build and execute queries. The first web part executes simple keyword queries and the second web part allows an end user to create more complicated queries. When a query is executed using either interface, the results are displayed on the Search.aspx page. Once the results are displayed on the page, you can subsequently use associated command links to group and sort the results. Figure 4-1 shows a typical query result in SPS.

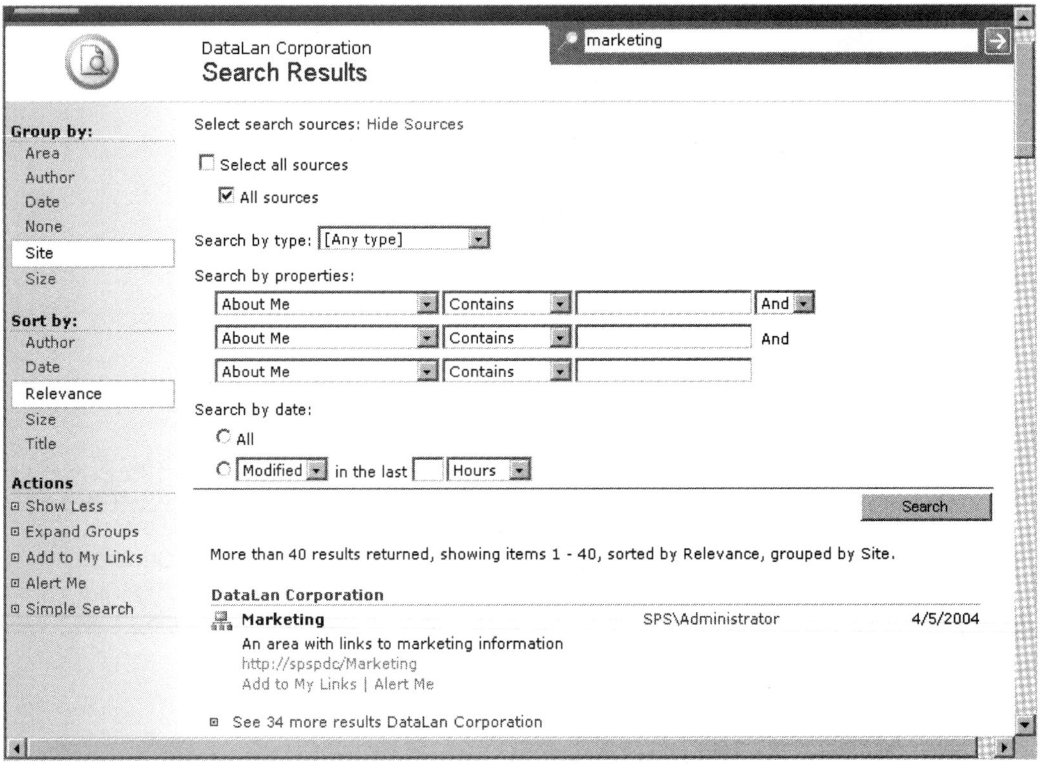

Figure 4-1. *Query results displayed on Search.aspx*

While the standard query functionality and resulting display are fine for general purposes, there are many occasions when you may want to customize the way queries are executed or how the results are displayed. If you are creating a customer extranet, for example, you may not want users to be able to search for other users because this would essentially allow direct access to your customer base. In other cases, you may simply want to make the query more focused or display the results in a compact format.

In this section, I'll present several techniques for customizing search in SPS. These techniques will include ways to build a custom query interface as well as a custom result display. Using these techniques, you will be able to create an appropriate search interface to complement any SPS solution.

Sending Parameters to Search.aspx

Perhaps the simplest way to create a custom search interface is to post queries directly to the Search.aspx page. This technique involves encoding a query into a URL. When the query is posted to the Search.aspx page, the results of the query are displayed in the standard manner.

While the simplicity of this technique makes it attractive, it can theoretically be used to execute complicated queries as well. The problem, however, is that the documentation provided in the SDK is horrible. As of this writing, there is only a single page in the SDK dedicated to this technique. Therefore, we are left alone to figure out by trial and error what can be accomplished. In this section, I'll cover the most useful parameters and help you understand how to use them.

Using Search Keywords

You can specify keyword searches using the k parameter. When you use this parameter alone, the search will be run against all search scopes, and the result will contain all available types such as categories, sites, and documents. You can only specify a single value and wildcards cannot be used. This query will return the same results as if you had typed the keyword into the simple search box. The following code shows how to post the query:

```
http://[server]/Search.aspx?k=[keyword]
```

Specifying Search Scopes

If you would like to narrow the search, you can specify one or more search scopes using the s parameter. Search scopes are specified using the name of the scope as it is defined in the portal administration pages. You can also see the names of the available search scopes using the drop-down list of the simple search box, as shown in Figure 4-2.

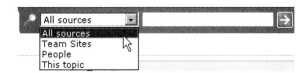

Figure 4-2. *Identifying search scopes*

In my installation, I have created several new search scopes. I have one named Team Sites that includes only WSS team sites. I have also defined one named People for searching only for portal users. Finally, I have one named File System that searches nonportal content. These search scopes make it much easier to return the correct information.

Follow these steps to create a new search scope:

1. Log into SPS as a member of the Administrator Site Group.

2. On the portal home page, click Site Settings.

3. On the Site Settings page, click Search Settings and Indexed Content ➤ Manage Search Scopes.

4. On the Manage Search Scopes page, click New Search Scope.

5. On the Add Search Scope page, name the new scope **Team Sites**.

6. Under the Topics and Areas section, click the option Include No Topic or Area in This Scope.

7. Under the Content Source Groups section, click the option Limit the Scope to the Following Groups of Content Sources.

8. Check the Sites in Site Directory box.

9. Click the OK button.

Once you have defined your search scopes, you can use them when posting queries to Search.aspx. The search you create can use one or more of the defined scopes. As an example, the following query searches for people associated with the Marketing department:

```
http://[server]/Search.aspx?s=People&k=Marketing
```

When you include multiple scopes in the query, the scope names must be separated by the special character set %2c. The names of the scopes must also be encoded, which usually means replacing the spaces with plus (+) signs. As an example, the following query searches for both people and sites that are associated with the Human Resources department:

```
http://[server]/Search.aspx?s=People%2cTeam+Sites&k=Human+Resources
```

Once you are posting queries using the k and s parameters, you have essentially duplicated the functionality of the standard simple search web part. If you look closely, in fact, you'll notice that the simple search web part will reflect the same scope and keyword that you specify in your query. This shows how tightly query posting is integrated with SPS.

Using Advanced Search Types

Just like you can duplicate the behavior of the simple search web part, you can also duplicate the behavior of the advanced search web part. Along with allowing the user to select one or more scopes, the advanced search capability also allows a user to select a search type. The search type specifies what kind of information should be returned from the search and is defined using the tp parameter. This parameter supports the following values: any, announcement, category, contacts, document, discussions, event, listing, person, picture, site, stsitems, and tasks.

When using a search type, you can specify one or more scopes as well as a keyword. When you run a query this way, you'll also notice that the advanced search web part will appear and reflect your settings just as the simple search did previously. As an example, the following query searches all team sites for documents that have the keyword Sales:

```
http://[server]/Search.aspx?s= Team+Sites&tp=Document&k=Sales
```

Using WHERE Clauses

While the keyword search is useful, it is limited by the fact that you can only specify a single keyword. Furthermore, the k parameter doesn't support Boolean algebra or wildcards. In order to add these capabilities to our queries, we will need to specify a WHERE clause using the w parameter. This parameter will allow you to use the conditional statements available from the SQL full-text search language. For example, the following query searches using two keywords:

```
http://[server]/Search.aspx?s=
All+Sources&w=CONTAINS('Microsoft%20AND%20SharePoint')
```

The CONTAINS predicate is a powerful way to customize your queries. Along with Boolean algebra, you can also use it to specify wildcard searches. Be careful with the syntax for wildcard searches because the query expects the wildcard argument to be surrounded by double quotes and then again by single quotes. The following code shows how an asterisk, double quotes, and single quotes are used together to find all items that contain a word beginning with "Micro":

```
http://[server]/Search.aspx?s=All+Sources&w=CONTAINS('"Micro*"')
```

The WHERE clauses you create for your queries can utilize any legal syntax available in the SQL full-text query language. An exhaustive examination of the query syntax is beyond the scope of this book; however, you can access the complete documentation online at http://msdn.microsoft.com/library/en-us/acdata/ac_8_qd_15_3rqg.asp?frame=true.

Using the QueryProvider Class

Although you can support complicated queries by posting to the Search.aspx page, my experience is that this technique is best suited for simple or moderately complex queries. When you really want complete control over query creation and execution, you should utilize the Microsoft.SharePoint.Portal.Search.QueryProvider class. This class will allow you to create custom full-text queries, run them, and return a DataSet object.

Constructing a new QueryProvider object in code requires you to provide the SearchApplicationName for the portal or area to be searched. The SearchApplicationName is a GUID that identifies the portal or area that will be queried by the QueryProvider object. The easiest way to get the SearchApplicationName is to use the Microsoft.SharePoint.Portal.PortalContext object. The PortalContext object allows access to useful information about the portal or area including the SearchApplicationName. The following code shows how to access the PortalContext object and use it to create a new QueryProvider object when a web part loads:

```
protected override void OnLoad(System.EventArgs e)
{
    PortalContext context = PortalApplication.GetContext();
    QueryProvider query = new QueryProvider(context.SearchApplicationName);
}
```

Once the QueryProvider object is created, you may use it to execute a full-text query against the search service. Executing the query is a straightforward process of building a search string and calling the Execute method. This method runs the query and returns a DataSet object, which you can use to display the results. Once again, the challenge is to correctly create the full-text query. Later in this chapter I'll show you how you can create and copy queries using SPS and a custom web part, but for now I've provided a complete function in Listing 4-1 that returns a query string based on a keyword.

Listing 4-1. *Creating a Full-Text Query*

```
private string buildQuery(string keyword)
{
//Create query string from keywords
string queryText =        "SELECT" +
"\"DAV:href\"," +
"\"DAV:displayname\"," +
```

```
"\"DAV:contentclass\"," +
"\"DAV:getlastmodified\"," +
"\"DAV:getcontentlength\"," +
"\"DAV:iscollection\"," +
"\"urn:schemas-microsoft-com:sharepoint:portal:profile:WorkPhone\"," +
"\"urn:schemas-microsoft-com:sharepoint:portal:profile:WorkEmail\"," +
"\"urn:schemas-microsoft-com:sharepoint:portal:profile:Title\"," +
"\"urn:schemas-microsoft-com:sharepoint:portal:profile:Department\"," +
"\"urn:schemas.microsoft.com:fulltextqueryinfo:PictureURL\"," +
"\"urn:schemas-microsoft-com:office:office#Author\"," +
"\"urn:schemas.microsoft.com:fulltextqueryinfo:description\"," +
"\"urn:schemas.microsoft.com:fulltextqueryinfo:rank\"," +
"\"urn:schemas.microsoft.com:fulltextqueryinfo:sitename\"," +
"\"urn:schemas.microsoft.com:fulltextqueryinfo:displaytitle\"," +
"\"urn:schemas-microsoft-com:publishing:Category\"," +
"\"urn:schemas-microsoft-com:office:office#ows_CrawlType\"," +
"\"urn:schemas-microsoft-com:office:office#ows_ListTemplate\"," +
"\"urn:schemas-microsoft-com:office:office#ows_SiteName\"," +
"\"urn:schemas-microsoft-com:office:office#ows_ImageWidth\"," +
"\"urn:schemas-microsoft-com:office:office#ows_ImageHeight\"," +
"\"DAV:getcontenttype\"," +
"\"urn:schemas-microsoft-com:sharepoint:portal:area:Path\"," +
"\"urn:schemas-microsoft-com:sharepoint:portal:area:CategoryUrlNavigation\"," +
"\"urn:schemas-microsoft-com:publishing:CategoryTitle\"," +
"\"urn:schemas.microsoft.com:fulltextqueryinfo:sdid\"," +
"\"urn:schemas-microsoft-com:sharepoint:portal:objectid\"" +
" from " +
"( TABLE Portal_Content..Scope() " +
"UNION ALL TABLE Non_Portal_Content..Scope() ) " +
" where " +
"WITH " +
"(\"DAV:contentclass\":0, " +
"\"urn:schemas.microsoft.com:fulltextqueryinfo:description\":0, " +
"\"urn:schemas.microsoft.com:fulltextqueryinfo:sourcegroup\":0, " +
"\"urn:schemas.microsoft.com:fulltextqueryinfo:cataloggroup\":0, " +
"\"urn:schemas-microsoft-com:office:office#Keywords\":1.0, " +
"\"urn:schemas-microsoft-com:office:office#Title\":0.9, " +
"\"DAV:displayname\":0.9, " +
"\"urn:schemas-microsoft-com:publishing:Category\":0.8, " +
"\"urn:schemas-microsoft-com:office:office#Subject\":0.8, " +
"\"urn:schemas-microsoft-com:office:office#Author\":0.7, " +
"\"urn:schemas-microsoft-com:office:office#Description\":0.5, " +
"\"urn:schemas-microsoft-com:sharepoint:portal:profile:PreferredName\":0.2, " +
"contents:0.1,*:0.05) AS #WeightedProps " +
"((\"urn:schemas-microsoft-com:publishing:HomeBestBetKeywords\"" +
"= some array ['" + keyword + "'] " +
" RANK BY COERCION(absolute, 999)) " +
```

```
"OR (FREETEXT(" +
"\"urn:schemas-microsoft-com:sharepoint:portal:profile:PreferredName\", '" +
keyword + "') " +
"OR CONTAINS('\"" + keyword + "\"') " +
"RANK BY COERCION(multiply, 0.01)) " +
"OR FREETEXT(#WeightedProps, '" + keyword + "') ) " +
"ORDER BY \"urn:schemas.microsoft.com:fulltextqueryinfo:rank\" DESC";

return queryText;
}
```

Once you have a good way for building a full-text query, it is relatively easy to create a web part that uses the query to return results. If you use the function in Listing 4-1, then you will be returning just about every column you may be interested in. You can then pick which columns to display. As always, the simplest thing to do is bind the results to a DataGrid control. Listing 4-2 shows a complete web part that uses a keyword to return a hyperlink and description for each matching item.

Listing 4-2. *A QueryProvider Web Part*

```
using System;
using System.ComponentModel;
using System.Web.UI;
using System.Web.UI.WebControls;
using System.Xml.Serialization;
using Microsoft.SharePoint;
using Microsoft.SharePoint.Portal;
using Microsoft.SharePoint.Utilities;
using Microsoft.SharePoint.WebPartPages;
using Microsoft.SharePoint.WebControls;
using Microsoft.SharePoint.Portal.Search;
using System.Data;
using System.Data.SqlClient;

namespace SPSQueryProvider
{
    [DefaultProperty(""),
    ToolboxData("<{0}:Search runat=server></{0}:Search>"),
    XmlRoot(Namespace="SPSQueryProvider")]
    public class Search : Microsoft.SharePoint.WebPartPages.WebPart
    {

        //GUI elements
        TextBox keywords;
        Button search;
        DataGrid grid;
        Label messages;
```

```csharp
//Search objects
PortalContext context;
QueryProvider query;
DataSet results;

protected override void OnLoad(System.EventArgs e)
{
    try
    {
        //Retrieve context for search
        context = PortalApplication.GetContext();
        query = new QueryProvider(context.SearchApplicationName);
    }
    catch
    {
        context=null;
        query=null;
    }
}

protected override void CreateChildControls()
{
    //Build GUI
    keywords = new TextBox();
    Controls.Add(keywords);

    search = new Button();
    search.Text = "Search";
    search.Click += new EventHandler(search_Click);
    Controls.Add(search);

    grid = new DataGrid();
    grid.AutoGenerateColumns = false;
    grid.GridLines = GridLines.None;
    Controls.Add(grid);

    HyperLinkColumn linkColumn = new HyperLinkColumn();
    linkColumn.DataNavigateUrlField = "DAV:href";
    linkColumn.DataTextField =
    "urn:schemas.microsoft.com:fulltextqueryinfo:displaytitle";
    linkColumn.HeaderText = "Title";
    grid.Columns.Add(linkColumn);

    boundColumn = new BoundColumn();
    boundColumn.DataField =
    "urn:schemas.microsoft.com:fulltextqueryinfo:description";
    boundColumn.HeaderText = "Description";
    grid.Columns.Add(boundColumn);
```

```
        messages = new Label();
        Controls.Add(messages);

    }

    protected override void RenderWebPart(HtmlTextWriter output)
    {
        try
        {
            //Bind results
            grid.DataSource = results;
            grid.DataBind();
        }
        catch(Exception x)
        {
            messages.Text += x.Message;
        }

        //Display GUI
        output.Write("<TABLE BORDER=0>");
        output.Write("<TR>");
        output.Write("<TD>");
        keywords.RenderControl(output);
        output.Write("</TD>");
        output.Write("</TR>");
        output.Write("<TR>");
        output.Write("<TD>");
        search.RenderControl(output);
        output.Write("</TD>");
        output.Write("</TR>");
        output.Write("<TR>");
        output.Write("<TD>");
        grid.RenderControl(output);
        output.Write("</TD>");
        output.Write("</TR>");
        output.Write("<TR>");
        output.Write("<TD>");
        messages.RenderControl(output);
        output.Write("</TD>");
        output.Write("</TR>");
        output.Write("</TABLE>");
    }

    private void search_Click(object sender, EventArgs e)
    {
        try
```

```
        {
            //Execute Query
            results = query.Execute(buildQuery());
        }
        catch(Exception x)
        {
            messages.Text += x.Message;
        }
    }

    }
}
```

Customizing Search Results

Using the QueryProvider class to execute a query and display results gives you complete control over the searching process, but it also requires you to handle every aspect of displaying, sorting, and grouping the results. This means that you are unable to use the standard sorting and grouping functionality found in the action list on Search.aspx. These actions offer significant functionality that you will have to develop yourself when you use a QueryProvider class. In many cases, what we want is a way to customize how results are displayed, but still utilize the action links shown in Figure 4-3.

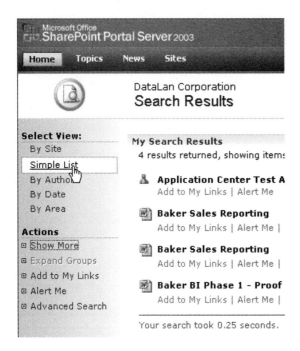

Figure 4-3. *Sorting and grouping links*

The search results that normally appear on Search.aspx are created by the web part
Microsoft.SharePoint.Portal.WebControls.SearchResults while the action links are generated by the web part Microsoft.SharePoint.Portal.WebControls.SearchResultManagement. In
order to create our own custom result set that can interact with the SearchResultManagement
web part, we must inherit from the SearchResults web part. While it is certainly unusual to
inherit directly from web parts in SPS, this approach is what ensures that the resulting web part
will interact correctly with the SearchResultManagement web part.

In order to inherit from the SearchResults web part, you create a web part project as normal, but instead of inheriting from Microsoft.SharePoint.WebPartPages.WebPart, the project
inherits from Microsoft.SharePoint.Portal.WebControls.SearchResults. Once you inherit
from the SearchResults web part, you can override any event in the web part life cycle to customize the presentation of the results. As a simple exercise to get started, you can create a web
part that inherits from SearchResults but makes no changes to the output. Listing 4-3 shows
the code for such a web part. You should note the call to base.RenderWebPart, which displays
the search results in the Search.aspx page.

Listing 4-3. *Inheriting from SearchResults*

```
using System;
using System.ComponentModel;
using System.Web.UI;
using System.Web.UI.WebControls;
using System.Xml.Serialization;
using Microsoft.SharePoint;
using Microsoft.SharePoint.Utilities;
using Microsoft.SharePoint.WebPartPages;

namespace MySearchResults
{

    [DefaultProperty(""),
    ToolboxData("<{0}:ResultSet runat=server></{0}:ResultSet>"),
    XmlRoot(Namespace="MySearchResults")]
    public class ResultSet :
    Microsoft.SharePoint.Portal.WebControls.SearchResults
    {

        protected override void RenderWebPart(HtmlTextWriter output)
        {
            base.RenderWebPart(output);
        }
    }
}
```

Once you create the web part, you must give it a strong name, place it in the \bin directory, and register it as safe in the web.config file. Then you are ready to add it to the Search.aspx page. Unlike most pages, however, the Search.aspx page does not have an explicit edit command available in the actions list. Instead, you must manually place the page in edit mode by navigating to the following URL in the browser:

```
http://[server]/Search.aspx?Mode=Edit&PageView=Shared
```

Once the page enters edit mode, you should see the familiar Modify Shared Page menu in the upper-right corner. You can now use this menu to import the new web part. After importing the new web part and running a search, you will see the new web part displaying the same results as the standard implementation of the SearchResults web part. At this point, you could go to the Web Parts Maintenance page and close the original SearchResults web part, leaving only your custom web part on the page. The Web Parts Maintenance page can be reached by appending ?contents=1 to any page, as shown in this example:

```
http://[server]/[sitename]/default.aspx?contents=1
```

Note When working with web parts on Search.aspx, you might find it helpful to add a Links web part to the page that contains a link placing the page in edit mode. You may also want to add a link to the Web Parts Maintenance page, which can be useful for removing malfunctioning web parts during testing.

Although we have created our own web part that shows results, you may notice that it does not yet respond to the sorting and grouping links. This is because the connection between our custom SearchResults web part and the SearchResultManagement web part has not yet been established. We can connect the web parts by setting the TargetResultListID property of the SearchResultManagement web part to the same value as the ResultListID property of our custom web part. Both of these properties are accessible through the web part properties pane and are located under the Miscellaneous section. However, you will not be able to access the properties for the SearchResultManagement web part in SPS. Instead, open Search.aspx in Microsoft FrontPage and set the properties to the same value. Figure 4-4 shows the properties pane for each of the web parts.

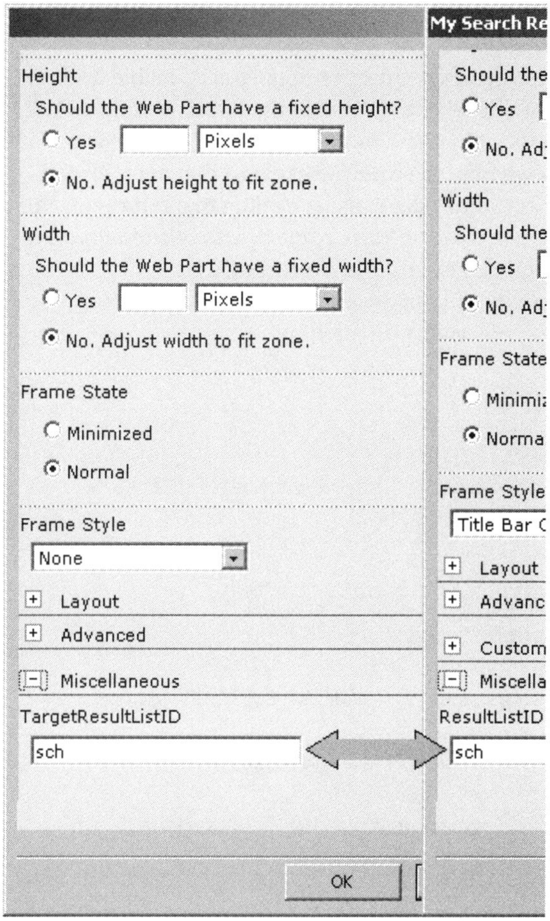

Figure 4-4. *Connecting the web parts in Microsoft FrontPage*

Modifying the Query Behavior

At this point, we have done little more than reproduce the functionality of the original SearchResults web part, but we have created a project that will now allow us to override that functionality in several ways. The first changes we can make involve how the query is processed before the results are displayed. It turns out that the SearchResults web part does more than just display the query results—it actually processes the query as well.

The SearchResults web part maintains a template for creating queries. The template is made up of four parts that are saved as properties of the web part. These properties are QueryTemplateSelectPart, QueryTemplateFromPart, QueryTemplateWherePart, and QueryTemplateOrderByPart. These templates are used to generate a full-text query string when the GenerateQueryString method is called. This query string is then executed to produce the result set.

The template information, query creation, and execution behavior are contained within the parent SearchResults class. If we want to change the query, therefore, we have to override the GenerateQueryString method and modify the query templates. Once we modify the templates, the result set will be based on our new query.

One of the most popular reasons for modifying the query templates is to enable wildcard searching in SPS. This will allow you to put an asterisk after a term in the search box. By default, the query templates do not support wildcards, but we can modify the QueryTemplateWherePart to include this functionality. The templates we want to modify use tokens that are replaced when the query is created, so we have to specify the change using a token that represents the query parameter. The query parameter token is the term keywordinput with two underscores at the beginning and the end. Listing 4-4 shows an example of overriding the GenerateQueryString method to add wildcard functionality to the search. Simply adding this code to the code from Listing 4-3 will enable wildcard searching.

Listing 4-4. *Incorporating Wildcard Searches*

```
protected override string GenerateQueryString(string
strKeyword,System.Collections.ArrayList rgScopeList,string strWhereAndPart,

out string strSavedQuery)
{
    //Add wildcard functionality to the query
    string wherePart = base.QueryTemplateWherePart;
    string firstPart =
        wherePart.Substring(0,wherePart.LastIndexOf("RANK BY COERCION"));
    string lastPart =
        wherePart.Substring(wherePart.LastIndexOf("RANK BY COERCION"));
    wherePart =
        firstPart + " OR CONTAINS('\"%__keywordinput__%\"') " + lastPart;
    base.QueryTemplateWherePart = wherePart;

    //Run query
    string query =
        base.GenerateQueryString(strKeyword,rgScopeList,
                                strWhereAndPart,out strSavedQuery);
    strSavedQuery = query;
    return query;
}
```

Generating Custom Displays

While the standard result display is useful in most situations, you may want to change the way the results are shown in Search.aspx. In this case, we want to override the rendering behavior of the parent base class and create a custom look. This look may be as simple as binding the results to a DataGrid, or it may be as specialized as using a TreeView control to group results in a compact format. In any case, we must intercept the query results and process them on our own.

Intercepting the query results is accomplished by overriding the `IssueQuery` method. The `IssueQuery` method executes the query that was created in the `GenerateQueryString` method and returns a `DataSet`. Once we have intercepted the `DataSet`, we can produce a custom look for the results. Listing 4-5 shows how to override the `IssueQuery` method.

Listing 4-5. *Intercepting Query Results*

```
DataSet results;

protected override object IssueQuery(string strQuery, int startRowIndex,
int endRowIndex)
{
    results =(System.Data.DataSet)
        base.IssueQuery (strQuery, startRowIndex, endRowIndex);
    return results;
}
```

If you choose to create your own results page, then you will not have to call the `RenderWebPart` method of the base class. Instead, you just simply process the results yourself. Most of the time this means overriding the `CreateChildControls` method to add a `DataGrid` or `TreeView` to the page and then processing the `DataSet` to fill the appropriate control. Finally, you should note that creating your own custom display will divorce your web part from the `SearchResultManagement` web part. If you create your own display, be sure to remove the `SearchResultManagement` web part from the `Search.aspx` page.

Customizing SharePoint Portal Server Navigation

One of the complaints I hear regularly about SPS is that the system of topics, areas, and sites is confusing and difficult to navigate. This confusion is caused by several factors that are unique to the way in which SPS was designed and built by Microsoft. Therefore, it is important to understand the design philosophy behind SPS before we can attempt to improve its navigation system.

Technical people tend to think in highly organized hierarchies represented by tree views. This structured approach is valuable when analyzing and solving engineering problems, but often leads to a rigid user interface design. This thinking is so strong that developers initially assume that topics, areas, and sites must have a hierarchical relationship. Therefore, every developer I talk to about SPS navigation wants a hierarchical tree view for navigation similar to the one shown in Figure 4-5.

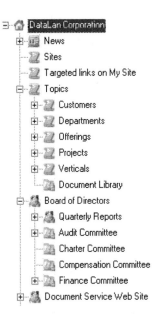

Figure 4-5. *A hierarchy of topics, areas, and sites*

The problem with the monolithic tree view approach to SPS navigation is that the relationship between SPS and WSS is not hierarchical. SPS is, in fact, a site collection and is, therefore, a peer with every other WSS site collection. This means that there is no effective way to create a true hierarchical view of all topics, areas, and sites.

The challenge becomes even greater when you realize that each time a new site collection is created, the author is given the opportunity to select multiple SPS areas that will link to the new site. This means that a hierarchical view of the entire SharePoint infrastructure would contain the same site listed in multiple branches of the tree. Furthermore, it is impossible to know which branch was navigated to arrive at the site. An attempt to create such a view results in a tree similar to the one shown in Figure 4-6, where the Board of Directors site is shown under eight different branches of the tree.

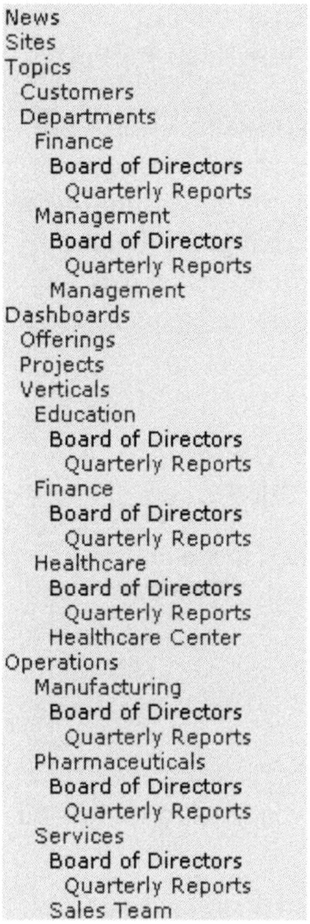

```
News
Sites
Topics
  Customers
  Departments
    Finance
      Board of Directors
        Quarterly Reports
      Management
        Board of Directors
          Quarterly Reports
          Management
Dashboards
  Offerings
  Projects
  Verticals
    Education
      Board of Directors
        Quarterly Reports
    Finance
      Board of Directors
        Quarterly Reports
    Healthcare
      Board of Directors
        Quarterly Reports
      Healthcare Center
Operations
  Manufacturing
    Board of Directors
      Quarterly Reports
  Pharmaceuticals
    Board of Directors
      Quarterly Reports
  Services
    Board of Directors
      Quarterly Reports
    Sales Team
```

Figure 4-6. *A hierarchy with the same site in multiple branches*

Once you encounter the problem of multiple listings for the same site, you begin to understand why Microsoft designed SPS navigation as it did. Furthermore, the realization demands a rethinking of the relationship between SPS and WSS that will bring clarity to developers and end users. This is why I prefer to think of SPS like a Google engine on steroids.

Changing your SPS paradigm from a strict hierarchy to a Google-like search environment is useful because it implies separation between SPS and WSS. Additionally, it is a paradigm that end users understand. No one thinks of the Google search engine as having a hierarchical relationship with the sites that it aggregates. End users know that Google provides links to sites of interest, but that Google itself is not part of those sites. Once you click a link on the Google site, you leave Google and go to the target site. This is the true relationship between SPS and WSS. The issue is how best to reflect this to the end user.

Using Themes to Differentiate Functionality

Perhaps the simplest way to help end users understand the difference between SPS and WSS is to use different themes for each. The themes can be similar in appearance in order to suggest a relationship, but different enough to indicate that the relationship is casual and not strictly hierarchical. WSS ships with several predefined themes that work well for this purpose. For example, you might use the default theme for SPS and choose the Compass theme for all of your WSS sites. This is easily accomplished for WSS sites by selecting Site Settings ➤ Apply Theme to Site.

Unfortunately, it is not possible to use this same technique to change the SPS theme. Once again, this is because of the design choices made by Microsoft. It turns out that sub areas underneath the portal home are specialized versions of WSS sites that do not fit into the existing theme management framework. There is no link available under Site Settings to change the theme for any area in SPS. If you alternately try to change the theme in FrontPage, the operation fails and you are told that the theme is read-only. Fortunately, we can utilize a workaround to make use of the existing theme set.

Follow these steps to change the SPS theme:

1. Open the Windows File Explorer and navigate to \Program Files\Common Files\Microsoft Shared\web server extensions\60\TEMPLATE\THEMES.

2. Copy all of the subfolders, which contain the various WSS themes, to the folder \Program Files\Common Files\Microsoft Shared\web server extensions\60\TEMPLATE\LAYOUTS*culture*\STYLES.

3. Log into SPS as a portal administrator.

4. Select Site Settings from the portal home page.

5. On the Site Settings page, select General Settings ➤ Change Portal Site Properties and SharePoint Site Creation Settings.

6. In the Custom Cascading Style Sheet section, type the address of the new style sheet in the following form:

   /_layouts/[culture]/styles/[theme folder]/theme.css

7. Click the OK button to apply the new style.

Using Tree Views Effectively

While there is no way to use a hierarchical tree view to show the entire SharePoint infrastructure, that does not mean that tree views have no place in the navigation system. The key to using tree views effectively is to limit their scope so that the displayed information is meaningful to the end user. This will require us to adopt a slightly different approach for areas than we use for sites.

When displaying a tree view in SPS areas, it is best to show the complete hierarchy of topics and areas as well as the site listings contained in each area. This provides a reasonable view of the portal structure down to the site collection level. Limiting the hierarchy to these elements makes it manageable and provides good navigation information to the end user. Figure 4-7 shows a typical tree view in SPS that replaces the standard topic navigation system.

Figure 4-7. *A tree view showing topics, areas, and listings*

The `Microsoft.SharePoint.Portal.SiteData.AreaManager` and `Area` classes are used to build the hierarchical view, which is contained inside a `TreeView` control. For each area, the tree also shows links from the `Listings` collection associated with the area. Because opening a new window can also be an effective way to signal the differences between SPS and WSS, an option on the web part allows you to either navigate directly to a clicked link or open it in a new window.

When presenting the same tree view on a WSS site, I have chosen to expand the tree branch that contains the area where the user originally clicked the site link. This gives the user a sense of continuity. I have also added the site collection hierarchy as a left-justified branch in the tree. Figure 4-8 shows the web part in a WSS site. You will build this web part in its entirety in an exercise at the end of this chapter.

Figure 4-8. *A tree view on a WSS site*

Using Breadcrumb Navigation

Another popular navigation alternative is *breadcrumb* navigation. Breadcrumb navigation uses the same principles as tree view navigation, except it only shows a single branch of the tree. Breadcrumbs are excellent for showing a simplified navigation trail using little screen real estate. Each breadcrumb in the trail is a hyperlink so users can easily return to previously visited pages. Figure 4-9 shows a typical breadcrumb display on a WSS site.

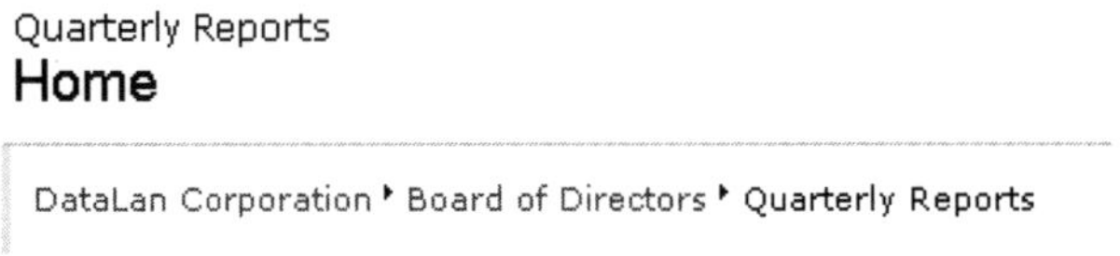

Quarterly Reports
Home

DataLan Corporation ▸ Board of Directors ▸ Quarterly Reports

Figure 4-9. *A breadcrumb navigation web part*

In order to start building the breadcrumb trail, we need to first get a reference to the current web. The trail is then built by recursing backwards through the parent webs until a complete tree branch is created. Listing 4-6 shows how this is done for WSS site collections.

Listing 4-6. *Building a Breadcrumb Trail for a Site Collection*

```
Private strTrail As String = ""

Protected Overrides Sub RenderWebPart( _
ByVal output As System.Web.UI.HtmlTextWriter)

    Try

        Dim objWeb As SPWeb = SPControl.GetContextWeb(Context)
        strTrail = objWeb.Title
        BuildTrail(objWeb)
        output.Write(strTrail)

    Catch x As Exception
        strTrail += "<p>" & x.Message & "</p><br>"
    End Try

End Sub

Private Sub BuildTrail(ByVal objWeb As SPWeb)

    Try
```

```
            If objWeb.IsRootWeb = False Then
                'Show the Parent Web
                strTrail = _
                "<a href='" & objWeb.ParentWeb.Url & "'>" _
                & objWeb.ParentWeb.Title _
                & "</a><img src='/_layouts/images/blk_rgt.gif'>" & strTrail

                'Recurse
                BuildTrail(objWeb.ParentWeb)
            End If

        Catch x As Exception
            strTrail += "<p>" & x.Message & "</p><br>"
        End Try

End Sub
```

Creating a breadcrumb trail is fairly simple if you are only interested in showing the current site collection. If you want to link back to the areas in SPS, however, you face the same problem as with the tree view navigation; the user could have come from any of several areas to arrive at the current site. In order to solve this, I use the `Page.Request.UrlReferrer.AbsolutePath` property to identify the area that referred the user to the current page. This is done by checking it against the collection of areas in SPS until a match is found. Listing 4-7 shows the Visual Basic .NET code for finding an area based on a referring URL.

Listing 4-7. *Finding an Area by URL*

```
Private Function GetAreaByURL( _
ByVal strURL As String, ByVal objAreas As AreaCollection) As Area

    Try

        Dim objReturnArea As Area = Nothing

        'Find the Area matching the given URL
        For Each objSubArea As Area In objAreas
            If objSubArea.AreaTemplate = "SPSTOPIC" AndAlso _
            strURL.IndexOf(objSubArea.WebUrl) = 0 Then
                objReturnArea = objSubArea
                Exit For
            Else
                Dim objSubSubArea = GetAreaByURL(strURL, objSubArea.Areas)
                If Not (objSubSubArea Is Nothing) Then
                    objReturnArea = objSubSubArea
                    Exit For
                End If
            End If
        Next
```

```
        Return objReturnArea

    Catch x As Exception
        Return Nothing
    End Try

End Function
```

Handling Performance Issues

The web parts I have presented in this section all share a common potential performance issue. Because these parts must traverse large parts of the SharePoint site structure, they can easily create performance bottlenecks that can lead to slow page loading or even page time-outs. Therefore, this is a good place to discuss some general techniques for improving web part performance. In particular, I will look at two approaches for improving performance: asynchronous data retrieval and data caching.

Understanding Asynchronous Data Retrieval

Whenever pages are loaded that contain web parts, SharePoint uses a single thread to load the page and process the web parts. This means that the time to load a page is increased as the sum of all the data-retrieval processes increase. If you build web parts that require a lot of processing—like filling a tree control with sites—this delay could become unacceptable. One way to mitigate this problem is to build your web parts so that they perform all data-retrieval operations on a separate thread. This type of asynchronous data retrieval is supported directly in the web part framework through the GetRequiresData and GetData methods.

The GetRequiresData method is called during the web part life cycle, and determines whether or not asynchronous data retrieval will be implemented. Normally, this method returns False, which means that none of the standard web parts implement asynchronous data retrieval. You may, however, override this method and return True, which will signal your intention to use asynchronous data retrieval. The following code shows how this is done:

```
public override bool GetRequiresData()
{
    return true;
}
```

If the GetRequiresData method returns True, then the web part framework will call the GetData method. The GetData method is used to register a callback method, which ultimately will perform the data retrieval on a different thread. Therefore, you must first define a callback method that conforms to the type System.Threading.WaitCallback. The function signature for this type has no return value and takes a single argument of type object. The argument is used to pass any data you want to the callback method. The following code shows an example callback method to build a simple list of subsites. Note how the object data type is cast to the correct data type before it is used for retrieval.

```
public void buildTree(object data)
{
    //get child webs
    SPWeb web = (SPWeb)data;
    SPWebCollection webs = web.Webs;

    foreach(SPWeb subweb in webs)
    {
        tree += "<p>" + subweb.Title + "</p>";
    }
}
```

Registering the callback method is accomplished using the `RegisterWorkItemCallback` method. This method is called from the `GetData` method, where the arguments are created and passed to the callback method. The following code shows an example using the callback method I showed earlier:

```
public override void GetData()
{
    SPSite site = SPControl.GetContextSite(Context);
    SPWeb web = site.OpenWeb();
    tree = "<p>" + web.Title + "</p>";
    RegisterWorkItemCallback(new WaitCallback(buildTree),web);
}
```

When callback methods are used to retrieve data, the web part framework will track their work and wait for them to complete before trying to render the web part. The timeout for asynchronous data retrieval is controlled by the `WebPartWorkItem` element in the `web.config` file and is set to 7 seconds by default. If an asynchronous data-retrieval operation takes longer than this time, the `RenderWorkItemTimeout` method is called. Using this method, you can create a simple HTML message to indicate that the web part has timed out. The following code shows an example:

```
protected override void RenderWorkItemTimeout(HtmlTextWriter writer)
{
    writer.Write("<p>Web part timed out</p>");
}
```

Understanding Data Caching

While asynchronous data retrieval may lead to somewhat improved performance in multi-processor machines, data caching will typically yield even bigger performance improvements. When you create web parts, you can make use of either the SharePoint or ASP.NET cache. The cache that is utilized is determined by the value of the `Storage` attribute of the `WebPartCache` element in the `web.config` file. This element is set to `CacheObject` by default, which utilizes the ASP.NET cache. Setting this attribute to `Database` utilizes the SharePoint database as a cache.

The `PartCacheWrite` method is used to write data to the cache and the `PartCacheRead` method is used to read data from the cache. Typically, a web part will read from the cache and check to see if the return value is `null`. If the value is `null`, then the web part will process normally and write the results to the cache for future use. The `PartCacheInvalidate` method is used to clear the cache, which functions to force a refresh of the data. Listing 4-8 shows a complete web part that creates a simple HTML list of subsites while using the cache to improve performance.

Listing 4-8. *Caching Web Part Data*

```
namespace SPSCacheTreeView
{

    [DefaultProperty(""),
        ToolboxData("<{0}:Builder runat=server></{0}:Builder>"),
        XmlRoot(Namespace="SPSCacheTreeView")]
    public class Builder : Microsoft.SharePoint.WebPartPages.WebPart
    {

        string tree;
        int i = 0;
        LinkButton button;

        public void buildTree()
        {
            SPSite site = SPControl.GetContextSite(Context);
            SPWeb web = site.OpenWeb();
            tree = web.Title + "<br>";
            i++;
            addChildWebs(web);
            i--;
          PartCacheWrite(Storage.Shared,"tree", tree, TimeSpan.FromSeconds(10));
        }

        public void addChildWebs(SPWeb parent)
        {
            try
            {

                //get child webs
                SPWebCollection webs = parent.Webs;

                foreach(SPWeb subweb in webs)
                {
                    //add to tree
                    tree += subweb.Title.PadLeft(subweb.Title.Length + i,
                        "-".ToCharArray()[0]) + "<br>";
                    i++;
                    addChildWebs(subweb);
                    i--;
```

```
                }
            }
            catch(Exception x)
            {
                tree += "<p>" + x.Message + "</p>";
            }
        }

        protected override void CreateChildControls()
        {
            button = new LinkButton();
            button.Text = "Refresh";
            button.Click +=new EventHandler(Refresh);
            Controls.Add(button);
        }

        protected override void RenderWebPart(HtmlTextWriter output)
        {
            //display tree
            if(PartCacheRead(Storage.Shared,"tree") == null) buildTree();

            output.Write("<br>");
            output.Write(tree);
            button.RenderControl(output);
        }

        private void Refresh(object sender, EventArgs e)
        {
            PartCacheInvalidate(Storage.Shared, "tree");
        }
    }
}
```

Improving Presentation with Audiences

If you have used SPS in any way, then you have undoubtedly experienced the use of *audiences* to target content. To review briefly, audiences are groups of users that are interested in the same information. These groups can be based on almost any relationship, such as department, team membership, or job role. SPS allows you to specify audience membership based on profile attributes. The important thing to remember about audiences is that they are used for presentation only and have no ability to secure information. Figure 4-10 shows a classic use of audiences to drive the Links for You web part that appears on the SPS home page.

Figure 4-10. *Using audiences to target content*

While audiences are useful for determining when links and web parts should be displayed, we may also want to make use of them within web parts that we create. Using audiences in this way allows your web part to render targeted content, which can significantly improve the end user experience. This strategy also allows you to introduce audience functionality into WSS sites, where it is normally not available.

The entry point for all audience-based functionality is the `Microsoft.SharePoint.Portal.Audience.AudienceManager` class. This class allows you to retrieve audience definitions for the current user or for the entire portal. You can also perform several administrative functions such as adding new audiences to the portal, but our focus will be on using the existing audience definitions.

When you create web parts that access audience information, you will quite often be concerned with identifying the audience membership of the current user. This will allow your web part to determine the appropriate content for targeting. You can easily return a collection of audiences to which the current user belongs by calling the `GetUserAudienceIDs` method of the `AudienceManager` class.

The `GetUserAudienceIDs` method returns an `ArrayList` of `AudienceNameID` objects. The `AudienceNameID` objects can be used to access the GUID for the audience and the name of the audience and to determine if the audience is currently valid. Listing 4-9 shows a complete web part that lists the audiences to which the current user belongs.

Listing 4-9. *Listing Audience Membership*

```
using System;
using System.ComponentModel;
using System.Web.UI;
using System.Web.UI.WebControls;
using System.Xml.Serialization;
using Microsoft.SharePoint;
using Microsoft.SharePoint.Utilities;
```

```csharp
using Microsoft.SharePoint.WebPartPages;
using Microsoft.SharePoint.Portal;
using Microsoft.SharePoint.Portal.Audience;
using System.Collections;

namespace SPSMyAudiences
{

    [DefaultProperty(""),
        ToolboxData("<{0}:Membership runat=server></{0}:Membership>"),
        XmlRoot(Namespace="SPSMyAudiences")]
    public class Membership : Microsoft.SharePoint.WebPartPages.WebPart
    {

        protected override void RenderWebPart(HtmlTextWriter output)
        {

            try
            {
                //Get the portal context
                SPSite portal =
                new SPSite(Page.Request.Url.GetLeftPart(UriPartial.Authority));
                PortalContext context = PortalApplication.GetContext(portal.ID);

                //Get the list of audiences for the user
                AudienceManager manager = new AudienceManager(context);
                ArrayList audienceIDList = manager.GetUserAudienceIDs();

                if(audienceIDList != null)
                {
                    IEnumerator audienceNameIDs = audienceIDList.GetEnumerator();

                    output.Write("<div class=\"ms-sectionheader\">");
                    while(audienceNameIDs.MoveNext())
                    {
                        output.Write(
                          ((AudienceNameID)audienceNameIDs.Current).AudienceName
                          + "<br>");
                    }
                    output.Write("</div>");
                }
            }

            catch (Exception x)
            {
                output.Write("<p>" + x.Message + "</p>");
            }
        }
    }
}
```

Along with determining the membership for the current user, you will often want to retrieve the complete set of audiences for the portal. This information is useful for assigning targeted content to individual audiences. You can either use the information within the web part to change the display, or you can use it in a tool part to target the entire web part. At the end of this chapter, you will find an exercise that uses such information internally to display list items organized by audience. For this discussion, we'll look at using audience information to target an entire web part on a WSS site. This functionality will reproduce the audience targeting capabilities found in SPS, but not normally available in WSS. Figure 4-11 shows a typical web part property in SPS used to target audiences.

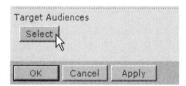

Figure 4-11. *Targeting a web part in SPS*

In order to re-create the audience targeting functionality found in SPS, we must construct a custom tool part. Custom tool parts are similar to web parts, but they are intended to be displayed in the properties pane and not in the site itself. This allows us to create complex interfaces for setting web part properties. Because I covered tool part creation in detail in my first book, *Microsoft SharePoint: Building Office 2003 Solutions*, I'm going to assume some familiarity with the concept and cover just the highlights. In our example, we will create a tool part that lists all of the available audiences and allows an administrator to select the ones to associate with the web part. We will then use the information to allow only users who are members of the selected audiences to see the web part.

As I noted, tool parts are similar to web parts in their construction and support nearly the same life-cycle events. This means that the code we write will be similar to any web part. Listing 4-10 shows the basics of our tool part, which fills a list with the set of all available audiences in SPS.

Listing 4-10. *Listing Audiences in a Tool Part*

```
public class AudienceTool : ToolPart
{
    //variables
    protected ListBox audienceList;
    protected TextBox audienceString;
    protected TextBox cancelString;

    protected override void OnLoad(EventArgs e)
    {
        //Get the portal context
        SPSite portal =
        new SPSite(Page.Request.Url.GetLeftPart(UriPartial.Authority));
        PortalContext context = PortalApplication.GetContext(portal.ID);
```

```
        //Get the list of audiences
        AudienceManager manager = new AudienceManager(context);

        EnsureChildControls();
        if (audienceList.Items.Count==0)
        {
            Container webpart = (Container)this.ParentToolPane.SelectedWebPart;
            audienceString.Text = webpart.Audiences;
            cancelString.Text = webpart.Audiences;

            //Fill the ListBox
            foreach(Audience audience in manager.Audiences)
            {
                audienceList.Items.Add(audience.AudienceName);
            }
        }
    }

    protected override void CreateChildControls()
    {
            audienceList = new ListBox();
            audienceList.SelectionMode = ListSelectionMode.Multiple;
            Controls.Add(audienceList);

            audienceString = new TextBox();
            Controls.Add(audienceString);

            cancelString = new TextBox();
            cancelString.Visible=false;
            Controls.Add(cancelString);

    }

    protected override void RenderToolPart(HtmlTextWriter output)
    {
            //Draw list
            audienceList.RenderControl(output);
            output.Write("<br>");
            audienceString.RenderControl(output);
            output.Write("<br>");
            cancelString.RenderControl(output);
    }
}
```

The main difference between tool parts and web parts is that tool parts must respond when the user clicks the OK, Apply, or Cancel button in the properties pane. In our design, the tool part will then build a semicolon-delimited string that contains the selected audiences and pass it to the parent web part. The parent web part can then parse the string and determine if the current user is a member of the designated audiences.

Our tool part will receive a call to the ApplyChanges function whenever the OK or Apply button is clicked. The CancelChanges function is called when the Cancel button is clicked. The SyncChanges function is called after any operation in order to synchronize the web part with the tool part. In our example, we are assuming that the tool part is being used by a web part named Container. Listing 4-11 shows the code for setting the Audience property of the web part based on the selections made in the tool part.

Listing 4-11. *Setting the Web Part Property*

```
public override void ApplyChanges()
{
    //Build audience list
    EnsureChildControls();
    cancelString.Text = audienceString.Text;
    audienceString.Text="";

    foreach(ListItem item in audienceList.Items)
    {
        if(item.Selected==true)
            audienceString.Text += item.Text + ";";
    }

    //Update web part property
    Container webpart = (Container)ParentToolPane.SelectedWebPart;
    webpart.Audiences = audienceString.Text;

}

public override void SyncChanges()
{
    //Update web part property
    EnsureChildControls();
    Container webpart = (Container)this.ParentToolPane.SelectedWebPart;
    audienceString.Text = webpart.Audiences;
    cancelString.Text = webpart.Audiences;
}

public override void CancelChanges()
{
    EnsureChildControls();
    audienceString.Text = cancelString.Text;
    Container webpart = (Container)ParentToolPane.SelectedWebPart;
    webpart.Audiences = cancelString.Text;
}
```

Once the tool part is complete, it is associated with the parent web part by overriding the GetToolParts function. We can then use the audience information for targeting the web part.

For this example, the Container web part is a page viewer that creates a Frameset element for viewing another web page. Listing 4-12 shows how this web part uses the information from the tool part to decide whether to show the targeted web page.

Listing 4-12. *Targeting a Web Page*

```
[DefaultProperty("URL"),
ToolboxData("<{0}:Container runat=server></{0}:Container>"),
XmlRoot(Namespace="SPSPageView")]
public class Container : Microsoft.SharePoint.WebPartPages.WebPart
{
    //NOTE: URL and PageHeight property code not shown
    protected String m_audiences="All portal users;";

    [Browsable(false),Category("Miscellaneous"),
    DefaultValue("All portal users;"),
    WebPartStorage(Storage.Shared),
    FriendlyName("Audiences"),Description("The selected audiences.")]
    public string  Audiences
    {
        get
        {
            return m_audiences;
        }

        set
        {
            m_audiences = value;
        }
    }

    public override ToolPart[] GetToolParts()
    {
        WebPartToolPart webPartToolPart = new WebPartToolPart();
        CustomPropertyToolPart customToolPart = new CustomPropertyToolPart();
        AudienceTool audienceTool = new AudienceTool();

        ToolPart[] toolParts = new ToolPart[3]
        {webPartToolPart,customToolPart,audienceTool};
        return toolParts;
     }

    protected override void RenderWebPart(HtmlTextWriter output)
    {
        //Get the portal context
        SPSite portal =
        new SPSite(Page.Request.Url.GetLeftPart(UriPartial.Authority));
        PortalContext context = PortalApplication.GetContext(portal.ID);
```

```
//Get the list of audiences for the user
AudienceManager manager = new AudienceManager(context);
ArrayList audienceIDList = manager.GetUserAudienceIDs();

//Get the list of authorized audiences
String [] audiences = Audiences.Split(";".ToCharArray());
Boolean authorized = false;

//Check the lists
if(audienceIDList != null)
{
    IEnumerator audienceNameIDs = audienceIDList.GetEnumerator();

    while(audienceNameIDs.MoveNext())
    {
        for(int i=audiences.GetLowerBound(0);
        i<=audiences.GetUpperBound(0);i++)
        {
            if(audiences[i]==
            ((AudienceNameID)audienceNameIDs.Current).AudienceName)
            authorized=true;
        }
    }
}

//Draw web part
if(authorized==true)
    output.Write("<div><iframe height='"
    + PageHeight + "' width='100%' src='" + URL + "'></iframe></div>");
    }
}
```

Exercise 4-1. Tree View Navigation

Many developers and end users find that the default navigation system associated with SPS provides them with insufficient information and capabilities to effectively navigate a SharePoint installation. They would prefer a more inclusive explorer that allows them to better understand the SharePoint topics, areas, and sites without having to leave the current page. In this exercise, you will build a tree view web part with improved navigation capabilities.

Prerequisites

Before beginning this exercise, be sure that you have properly built and deployed the assembly IEWebControls.dll according to the instructions given in Chapter 3. The assembly should be strongly named and located in the Inetpub\wwwroot\bin directory of your WSS server. This exercise also assumes that you have SPS installed as part of your SharePoint infrastructure.

Starting the Project

This exercise will use the TreeView web control presented in Chapter 3. For simplification, however, we will use standard web part development techniques as opposed to the Web Forms User Control techniques described in Chapter 3. Therefore, you will use the standard web part template for this project.

Follow these steps to start the project:

1. In Visual Studio .NET, select File ➤ New ➤ Project from the menu.

2. In the New Project dialog, select the Visual Basic Projects folder in the Project Types list.

3. In the Templates list, select Web Part Library.

4. Name the project **SPSTreeNav** and click the OK button.

5. In the Solution Explorer, rename WebPart1.vb to **SPSTreeNav.vb**.

6. In the Solution Explorer, rename WebPart1.dwp to **SPSTreeNav.dwp**.

7. Open the file Manifest.xml for editing in Visual Studio .NET.

8. In the DwpFiles section, change the web part description filename to **SPSTreeNav.dwp**.

9. Save and close the file.

10. Open the file SPSTreeNav.dwp for editing in Visual Studio .NET.

11. Change the file contents to appear as shown in Listing 4-13.

12. Save and close the file.

Listing 4-13. *The Web Part Description File*

```
<?xml version="1.0" encoding="utf-8"?>
<WebPart xmlns="http://schemas.microsoft.com/WebPart/v2" >
    <Title>Tree Navigation</Title>
    <Description>Collapsable Treeview Navigation control</Description>
    <Assembly>SPSTreeNav</Assembly>
    <TypeName>SPSTreeNav.Lister</TypeName>
    <FrameType>None</FrameType>
</WebPart>
```

Coding the Web Part

Once the project is started, you are ready to code the web part. The code for the web part is moderately complex primarily due to the recursion required to build the tree. Before you get started on the code, however, you will need to set some references and specify imported libraries.

Follow these steps to add references and libraries:

1. In Visual Studio .NET, select Project ➤ Add Reference from the menu.

2. In the Add Reference dialog, click the Browse button and locate the IEWebControls.dll assembly.

3. Click the OK button to add these references to the project.

4. Open `SPSTreeNav.vb` for editing in Visual Studio. NET.

5. Add the following `Imports` statements to the top of the file:

```
Imports Microsoft.SharePoint.WebControls
Imports Microsoft.SharePoint.Portal
Imports Microsoft.SharePoint.Portal.Topology
Imports Microsoft.SharePoint.Portal.SiteData
```

6. Change the name of the class to **Lister** and the default property to **WSSMode** so that your code looks like Listing 4-14.

Listing 4-14. *The Web Part Code*

```
Imports System
Imports System.ComponentModel
Imports System.Web.UI
Imports System.Web.UI.WebControls
Imports System.Xml.Serialization
Imports Microsoft.SharePoint
Imports Microsoft.SharePoint.Utilities
Imports Microsoft.SharePoint.WebPartPages
Imports Microsoft.Web.UI.WebControls
Imports Microsoft.SharePoint.Portal
Imports Microsoft.SharePoint.Portal.Topology
Imports Microsoft.SharePoint.Portal.SiteData
Imports System.Web
Imports Microsoft.SharePoint.WebControls

<DefaultProperty("WSSMode"), ToolboxData("<{0}:Lister _
runat=server></{0}:Lister>"), XmlRoot(Namespace:="SPSTreeNav")> _
Public Class Lister
    Inherits Microsoft.SharePoint.WebPartPages.WebPart

    Protected Overrides Sub RenderWebPart( _
    ByVal output As System.Web.UI.HtmlTextWriter)

    End Sub

End Class
```

Coding the Properties

The web part uses several properties to customize its look and behavior. The most important of these properties is the `WSSMode` property. This property determines what branch on the tree expands automatically. When set to `False`, the default, the tree expands to show the area that the end user is currently viewing. When set to `True`, the tree expands to show the area from which the user just navigated. The web part is set to `False` when placed on an area and `True` when placed on a WSS site.

The other properties of the web part control the background color and font style for the tree. These properties are useful in helping to match the look of the web part to the current site theme. There is also a property you can set to specify whether a new window is opened when a user clicks on a node in the tree. Add the code from Listing 4-15 to your web part to code the properties.

Listing 4-15. *The Web Part Properties*

```
'Member Variables
Private objTree As TreeView
Private lblMessages As Label
Private objCurrentWeb As SPWeb
Private m_WSSMode As Boolean = False
Private m_Red As Integer = 234
Private m_Green As Integer = 234
Private m_Blue As Integer = 234
Private m_FontName As String = "arial"
Private m_FontSize As String = "9pt"
Private m_NewWindow As Boolean = False


<Browsable(True), Category("Tree View"), DefaultValue(False), _
WebPartStorage(Storage.Shared), FriendlyName("WSSMode"), Description( _
"Sets the display mode of the tree.")> _
Property WSSMode() As Boolean
    Get
        Return m_WSSMode
    End Get

    Set(ByVal Value As Boolean)
        m_WSSMode = Value
    End Set
End Property

<Browsable(True), Category("Tree View"), DefaultValue(234), _
WebPartStorage(Storage.Shared), FriendlyName("Background Red"), Description( _
"Red portion of RGB background color.")> _
Property Red() As Integer
    Get
        Return m_Red
    End Get

    Set(ByVal Value As Integer)
        m_Red = Value
    End Set
End Property
```

```vb
<Browsable(True), Category("Tree View"), DefaultValue(234), _
WebPartStorage(Storage.Shared), FriendlyName("Background Green"), _
Description("Green portion of RGB background color.")> _
Property Green() As Integer
    Get
        Return m_Green
    End Get

    Set(ByVal Value As Integer)
        m_Green = Value
    End Set
End Property

<Browsable(True), Category("Tree View"), DefaultValue(234), _
WebPartStorage(Storage.Shared), FriendlyName("Background Blue"), _
Description("Blue portion of RGB background color.")> _
Property Blue() As Integer
    Get
        Return m_Blue
    End Get

    Set(ByVal Value As Integer)
        m_Blue = Value
    End Set
End Property

<Browsable(True), Category("Tree View"), DefaultValue("arial"), _
WebPartStorage(Storage.Shared), FriendlyName("Font Name"), Description( _
"Name of the display font.")> _
Property FontName() As String
    Get
        Return m_FontName
    End Get

    Set(ByVal Value As String)
        m_FontName = Value
    End Set
End Property

<Browsable(True), Category("Tree View"), DefaultValue("9pt"), _
WebPartStorage(Storage.Shared), FriendlyName("Font Size"), Description( _
"Size of the display font.")> _
Property FontSize() As String
    Get
        Return m_FontSize
    End Get
```

```
        Set(ByVal Value As String)
            m_FontSize = Value
        End Set
End Property


<Browsable(True), Category("Tree View"), DefaultValue(False), _
WebPartStorage(Storage.Shared), FriendlyName("New Window"), _
Description( _
"Determines iF a new window is opened when a listing link is clicked.")> _
Property NewWindow() As Boolean
    Get
        Return m_NewWindow
    End Get

    Set(ByVal Value As Boolean)
        m_NewWindow = Value
    End Set
End Property
```

Creating the Child Controls

Creating the set of child controls for the web part is straightforward. Along with the TreeView, the web part also contains a Label control, which is used to display any error messages that occur during processing. Add the code from Listing 4-16 to create the child controls.

Listing 4-16. *Creating the Child Controls*

```
Protected Overrides Sub CreateChildControls()
    'Add Tree
    objTree = New TreeView
    objTree.BackColor = System.Drawing.Color.FromArgb(Red, Green, Blue)
    objTree.DefaultStyle.Add("font-family", FontName)
    objTree.DefaultStyle.Add("font-size", FontSize)
    Controls.Add(objTree)

    'Add message label
    lblMessages = New Label
    Controls.Add(lblMessages)
End Sub
```

Adding Areas and Listings

Whenever the tree displays an area, it must also list the associated subareas and listings. Because we cannot predict how many listings and subareas will be underneath the current area, we must write a function that is called recursively until all of the child information is collected.

Along with building the tree, we also want to make a decision as to whether or not the branch we are building should be expanded. This process is based on the value of the WSSMode property as I described previously. Along with expanding the appropriate branch, the web part also makes the key nodes bold so that they stand out to the end user. Add the code from Listing 4-17 to build the areas and listings into the tree.

Listing 4-17. *Adding Areas and Listings*

```
Private Function AddSubAreasAndListings( _
ByVal objParentNode As TreeNode, ByVal objParentArea As Area) As Boolean

    Try

        Dim blnReturn As Boolean = False

        'Add the subareas under the parent area
        For Each objSubArea As Area In objParentArea.Areas
            If objSubArea.AreaTemplate = "SPSTOPIC" Then
                Dim objAreaNode As New TreeNode
                With objAreaNode
                    .Text = objSubArea.Title
                    .NavigateUrl = _
                    System.Web.HttpUtility.UrlPathEncode(objSubArea.WebUrl)
                    .ImageUrl = "/_layouts/images/cat.gif"
                    If WSSMode = False _
                    AndAlso Page.Request.Url.AbsolutePath.IndexOf( _
                    HttpUtility.UrlPathEncode(objSubArea.WebUrl)) = 0 Then
                        objAreaNode.Expanded = True
                        objAreaNode.DefaultStyle.Add("font-weight", "bold")
                        blnReturn = True
                    ElseIf WSSMode = True _
                    AndAlso Page.Request.UrlReferrer.AbsolutePath.IndexOf( _
                    HttpUtility.UrlPathEncode(objSubArea.WebUrl)) = 0 Then
                        objAreaNode.Expanded = True
                        objAreaNode.DefaultStyle.Add("font-weight", "bold")
                        blnReturn = True
                    End If

                End With
                objParentNode.Nodes.Add(objAreaNode)

                'Recursively add additional sub areas and listings
                If AddSubAreasAndListings(objAreaNode, objSubArea) = True Then
                    objAreaNode.Expanded = True
                    blnReturn = True
                End If
            End If
        Next
```

```
            'Add the portal listings for this area
            For Each objListing As AreaListing In objParentArea.Listings
                If objListing.Type = ListingType.Site _
                Or objListing.Type = ListingType.TeamSite Then
                    Dim objListingNode As New TreeNode
                    With objListingNode
                        .Text = objListing.Title
                        .NavigateUrl = objListing.URL
                        .ImageUrl = "/_layouts/images/link.gif"
                        If NewWindow = True Then .Target = "_BLANK"
                    End With
                    objParentNode.Nodes.Add(objListingNode)
                End If
            Next

            Return blnReturn

        Catch x As Exception
            lblMessages.Text += x.Message
        End Try

End Function
```

Add Sites and Subsites

Just like we want to add areas and listings to the tree, we also want to add sites and subsites. Unlike areas, however, sites are only added if the tree is in WSSMode. This means that the sites should not appear on an area page, but only when the tree is on a team site. Add the code from Listing 4-18 to put the sites and subsites in the tree.

Listing 4-18. *Adding Sites and Subsites*

```
Private Sub AddSubSites( _
ByVal objParentNode As TreeNode, ByVal objParentWeb As SPWeb)

    Try

        Dim objWebs As SPWebCollection = objParentWeb.GetSubwebsForCurrentUser()

        For Each objWeb As SPWeb In objWebs

            'Add Node
            Dim objNode As New TreeNode
            With objNode
                .Text = objWeb.Title
                .ImageUrl = "/_layouts/images/asp16.gif"
                .NavigateUrl = objWeb.Url
            End With
            objParentNode.Nodes.Add(objNode)
```

```
                'Recurse sub nodes
                AddSubSites(objNode, objWeb)

        Next

    Catch x As Exception
        lblMessages.Text += x.Message
    End Try

End Sub
```

Rendering the Web Part

Once all of the helper functions are coded, you are ready to render the web part. The tree is built by first creating the portal home as the root and then adding areas, listings, sites, and subsites as appropriate. Add the code from Listing 4-19 to render the web part.

Listing 4-19. *Rendering the Web Part*

```
Protected Overrides Sub RenderWebPart( _
ByVal output As System.Web.UI.HtmlTextWriter)
    Try

        'Get portal home Area
        Dim objPortalSite As New _
        SPSite(Page.Request.Url.GetLeftPart(UriPartial.Authority))
        Dim objContext As PortalContext = _
        PortalApplication.GetContext(objPortalSite.ID)
        Dim PortalGuid As Guid = _
        AreaManager.GetSystemAreaGuid(objContext, SystemArea.Home)
        Dim objPortalArea As Area = AreaManager.GetArea(objContext, PortalGuid)

        'Add the portal home Area to the tree
        Dim objPortalNode As New TreeNode
        With objPortalNode
            .Text = objPortalArea.Title
            .NavigateUrl = objPortalArea.WebUrl
            .ImageUrl = "/_layouts/images/sphomesm.gif"
            .Expanded = True
        End With
        objTree.Nodes.Add(objPortalNode)

        'Add subareas and listings
        If AddSubAreasAndListings(objPortalNode, objPortalArea) = True Then
            objPortalNode.Expanded = True
        End If
```

```
        'Add the WSS Site Collection to the tree
        If WSSMode = True Then

            'Get this web
            Dim objSite As SPSite = SPControl.GetContextSite(Context)
            Dim objSiteWeb As SPWeb = objSite.OpenWeb()

            'Add it to tree
            Dim objSiteNode As New TreeNode
            With objSiteNode
                .Text = objSiteWeb.Title
                .NavigateUrl = objSiteWeb.Url
                .ImageUrl = "/_layouts/images/globe.gif"
                .DefaultStyle.Add("font-weight", "bold")
                .Expanded = True
            End With
            objPortalNode.Nodes.Add(objSiteNode)

            'Add subsites
            AddSubSites(objSiteNode, objSiteWeb)

        End If

    Catch x As Exception
        lblMessages.Text += x.Message
    End Try

    'Draw Controls
    objTree.RenderControl(output)
    lblMessages.RenderControl(output)

End Sub
```

Deploying the Web Part

Deploying the web part requires a strongly named assembly. Therefore, you should edit the AssemblyInfo file to include a reference to a key pair file. Once this is done, you should be able to build the solution. Copy the built assembly to the \Inetpub\wwwroot\bin directory and edit the web.config file to mark the assembly as safe. These are steps you should be familiar with from other web part deployments, so I will not cover them in detail here. Once the assembly is deployed, you can use it on any page as normal, but if you want to deploy it in place of the standard navigation tree, then you must perform some special steps.

Follow these steps to replace the standard navigation tree:

1. In Microsoft FrontPage 2003, select File ➤ Open Site from the menu.

2. In the Open Site dialog, type the URL of the SPS home page and click the Open button.

3. When the site opens, select View ➤ Folders from the menu.

4. Each area in your SPS installation will appear as a folder in FrontPage. Select one of the areas and double-click it.

5. When the area folder opens, double-click the `default.aspx` file to edit the page.

6. In Design View, right-click the standard navigation tree and select Cut from the context menu. Be sure to completely remove all pieces of the standard navigation tree.

7. Select View ➤ Task Pane to open the FrontPage Task Pane.

8. In the Task Pane, select Web Parts from the drop-down menu.

9. Click the New Web Part Zone button located on the Task Pane.

10. Select File ➤ Save from the menu to save the changes.

11. Close Microsoft FrontPage.

12. Return to SPS and use the standard techniques to place the new tree navigation web part in the zone you created in FrontPage.

Exercise 4-2. Grouping List Items by Audience

Audience functionality is a great way to target content at end users. Unfortunately, audiences are associated with SPS and cannot normally be used with WSS sites. What's more, SPS usually limits audience functionality to targeting the entire web part. In this exercise, we'll overcome these limitations by creating a web part that can consume any list on a site and target the individual list items to selected audiences.

Starting the Project

This exercise makes use of a connected web part to consume a list on a WSS site and target the content. Because I covered connected web parts in detail in my first book, *Microsoft SharePoint: Building Office 2003 Solutions*, I will assume some familiarity with the concept and focus instead on the audience aspects of the project.

Follow these steps to start the project:

1. In Visual Studio .NET, select File ➤ New ➤ Project from the menu.

2. In the New Project dialog, select the Visual C# Projects folder in the Project Types list.

3. In the Templates list, select Web Part Library.

4. Name the project **SPSListByAudience** and click the OK button.

5. In the Solution Explorer, rename `WebPart1.cs` to **SPSListByAudience.cs**.

6. In the Solution Explorer, rename `WebPart1.dwp` to **SPSListByAudience.dwp**.

7. Open the file `Manifest.xml` for editing in Visual Studio .NET.

8. In the `DwpFiles` section, change the web part description filename to **SPSListByAudience.dwp**.

   9. Save and close the file.

   10. Open the file SPSListByAudience.dwp for editing in Visual Studio .NET.

   11. Change the file contents to appear as shown in Listing 4-20.

   12. Save and close the file.

Listing 4-20. *The Web Part Description File*

```xml
<?xml version="1.0" encoding="utf-8"?>
<WebPart xmlns="http://schemas.microsoft.com/WebPart/v2" >
    <Title>Display List By Audience</Title>
    <Description>Displays a connected list by Audience</Description>
    <Assembly>SPSListByAudience</Assembly>
    <TypeName>SPSListByAudience.Grouper</TypeName>
</WebPart>
```

Coding the Web Part

Once the project is started, you are ready to create the web part. The coding for this project is complex because of the functionality required to implement the web part connections. Before we start on the connections, however, you must set references to some key libraries.

Follow these steps to add references and libraries:

   1. In Visual Studio .NET, select Project ➤ Add Reference from the menu.

   2. In the Add Reference dialog, choose Microsoft.SharePoint.Portal.dll and System.Data from the Component Name list and click the Select button.

   3. Click the OK button to add these references to the project.

   4. Open SPSListByAudience.cs for editing in Visual Studio .NET.

   5. Add the following using statements to the top of the file:

```csharp
using Microsoft.SharePoint.Portal;
using Microsoft.SharePoint.Portal.Audience;
using Microsoft.SharePoint.WebPartPages.Communication;
using System.Security;
using System.Data;
using System.Collections;
```

   6. Change the name of the class to **Grouper** and clear the default property so that your code looks like Listing 4-21.

Listing 4-21. *The Initial Web Part Code*

```csharp
using Microsoft.SharePoint.Portal;
using Microsoft.SharePoint.Portal.Audience;
using Microsoft.SharePoint.WebPartPages.Communication;
using System.Security;
```

```
using System.Data;
using System.Collections;
using System;
using System.ComponentModel;
using System.Web.UI;
using System.Web.UI.WebControls;
using System.Xml.Serialization;
using Microsoft.SharePoint;
using Microsoft.SharePoint.Utilities;
using Microsoft.SharePoint.WebPartPages;

namespace SPSListByAudience
{

    [DefaultProperty(""),
        ToolboxData("<{0}:Grouper runat=server></{0}:Grouper>"),
        XmlRoot(Namespace="SPSListByAudience")]
    public class Grouper :
    Microsoft.SharePoint.WebPartPages.WebPart,
    Microsoft.SharePoint.WebPartPages.Communication.IListConsumer
    {
    }
}
```

Creating the Child Controls

This project uses an HTML table to render the consumed list grouped by audience; however, it also uses a simple Label control to display any error messages that might occur. Therefore, we must code a CreateChildControls function within the Grouper class. Add the code from Listing 4-22 to create the message label.

Listing 4-22. *Creating the Child Controls*

```
//member variables
protected DataTable list;
protected String [] displayNames;
protected Label messages;
protected Boolean isConnected;
protected int colSpan;

protected override void CreateChildControls()
{
    messages = new Label();
    Controls.Add(messages);
}
```

Coding the Web Part Connection

The Grouper class implements the IListConsumer interface so that it can connect to any list on a WSS site. Therefore, we must code the appropriate connection life cycle for the web part. As I stated earlier, I am not going to focus on the mechanics of connecting web parts because that is beyond the scope of this chapter. The most important thing to know about this code is that the consumed list is passed to the Grouper class when the ListReady function is called by the web part infrastructure. Add the code from Listing 4-23 to implement the web part connection.

Listing 4-23. *Connecting the Web Part to a List*

```
public override void EnsureInterfaces()
{
    try
    {
        RegisterInterface("AudienceGrouper",
        "IListConsumer",
        WebPart.LimitOneConnection,
        ConnectionRunAt.Server,
        this,"","Get a list from...",
        "Receives a list for grouping.");
    }

    catch(SecurityException e)
    {
        messages.Text += "<p>" + e.Message + "</p>";
    }
}

public override ConnectionRunAt CanRunAt()
{
    return ConnectionRunAt.Server;
}

public override void PartCommunicationConnect(string interfaceName,
    WebPart connectedPart, string connectedInterfaceName, ConnectionRunAt runAt)
{
    if(runAt==ConnectionRunAt.Server)
    {
        EnsureChildControls();
        if(interfaceName=="AudienceGrouper")isConnected=true;
    }
}
```

```
public void ListProviderInit(object sender,
ListProviderInitEventArgs listProviderInitEventArgs)
{
    //Get the display names of the fields
    displayNames = listProviderInitEventArgs.FieldDisplayList;
    colSpan = displayNames.GetLength(0);
}

public void PartialListReady(object sender,
PartialListReadyEventArgs partialListReadyEventArgs)
{
    // Nothing to do
}

public void ListReady(object sender, ListReadyEventArgs listReadyEventArgs)
{
    list = listReadyEventArgs.List;
}
```

Rendering the Web Part

Once the list has been passed to the Grouper class, we are free to render it in any way that we want. Our web part assumes that one of the fields passed in from the consumed list is named "Audience". Our web part uses this value to filter and group the individual list items by audience. This technique is better than creating a separate list view based on the Audience field because we will only show list items that correspond to the audiences associated with the current user. This is a nice way to simplify lists and target the individual items to the appropriate users. Add the code in Listing 4-24 to render the consumed list.

Listing 4-24. *Rendering the List*

```
protected override void RenderWebPart(HtmlTextWriter output)
{
    try
    {
        if(isConnected==true)
        {

            //Write out the column display names
            output.Write("<table border=0 width=\"100%\">");
            output.Write(" <tr>");
            for(int i=displayNames.GetLowerBound(0);
            i<=displayNames.GetUpperBound(0);i++)
            {
                if(displayNames[i]!="Audience")
                output.Write("      <th>" + displayNames[i] + "</th>");
            }
```

```
//Get the portal context
SPSite portal =
new SPSite(Page.Request.Url.GetLeftPart(UriPartial.Authority));
PortalContext context = PortalApplication.GetContext(portal.ID);

//Get the list of audiences for the user
AudienceManager manager = new AudienceManager(context);
ArrayList audienceIDList = manager.GetUserAudienceIDs();

if(audienceIDList != null)
{
    IEnumerator audienceNameIDs = audienceIDList.GetEnumerator();

    while(audienceNameIDs.MoveNext())
    {

        //Get the set of items for this audience
        String audienceName =
            ((AudienceNameID)audienceNameIDs.Current).AudienceName;
        DataView dataView = new DataView(list,
            "Audience='" + audienceName + "'",
            "",DataViewRowState.CurrentRows);

        if (dataView.Count!=0)
        {
            //Write out the audience name
            output.Write(
                "   <tr><td class=\"ms-sectionheader\" colspan=\""
                + colSpan.ToString() + "\">" + audienceName
                + "</td></tr>");

            //Write out the rows
            foreach (DataRowView rowView in dataView)
            {
                output.Write("   <tr>");

                //Write out columns
                IEnumerator columns
                    = rowView.Row.ItemArray.GetEnumerator();
                 while(columns.MoveNext())
                {
                    if(columns.Current.ToString()!=audienceName)
                    output.Write("      <td>"
                        + columns.Current.ToString() + "</td>");
                }
```

```
                            output.Write("    </tr>");
                    }


                }
            }
        }

        //close the table
        output.Write("</table>");
    }
    else
    {
        messages.Text += "<p>Connect this web part to a list.</p>";
    }

    //Show messages
    messages.RenderControl(output);

    }
    catch(Exception x)
    {
        output.Write("<p>" + x.Message + "</p>");
    }
}
```

Deploying the Web Part

Follow all the normal steps necessary to build and deploy the web part. Once it's deployed, you can add it to a page. If successful, the web part should display a message asking you to connect it to a list. You can connect the web part to any list that is displayed on the same page. In order to work successfully, the connected list must have a custom field named "Audience". Figure 4-12 shows an example of the web part connected to a standard document library.

Follow these steps to connect a list:

1. Navigate to any WSS site as a member of the Administrators Site Group.

2. On the site, click the Create link.

3. On the Create page, select the option to create a new Document Library.

4. Follow the steps necessary to create the library. When complete, click the Modify Settings and Columns link.

5. On the Customize page, select to add a new column named **Audience**.

6. Make the new column a single line of text with a default value of **All portal users**, and make the column part of the default view.

7. Add several documents to the library.

8. Return to the site home page and add the new Document Library to the home page as a web part.

9. Select a view for the web part that contains the new Audience column.

10. Connect the new Document Library to the Grouper web part.

Shared Documents By Audience				▼
Type	**Name**	**Modified**	**Modified By**	**Checked Out To**
All portal users				
doc	Baker BI Phase 1 - Proof Addendum.doc	2004-08-07 10:45:39	SPS\administrator	
doc	Baker Sales Reporting Addendum - Final.doc	2004-08-07 10:45:39	SPS\administrator	
doc	Baker Sales Reporting Addendum.doc	2004-08-07 10:45:39	SPS\administrator	
Delivery				
doc	Baker PSP - Scope Definition.doc	2004-08-07 11:22:50	SPS\administrator	
Sales				
doc	Baker CSR Migration.doc	2004-08-07 11:22:37	SPS\administrator	
doc	Baker PSP Revenue Cycle Phase 1.doc	2004-08-07 11:23:03	SPS\administrator	

Figure 4-12. *The completed project*

CHAPTER 5

■■■

The Information Bridge Framework

Beginning with the concept of dynamic data exchange (DDE), Microsoft recognized the value of linking Office documents with data contained in line-of-business (LOB) systems. Over the years, this concept has evolved through Object Linking and Embedding (OLE), automation, and the Component Object Model (COM). With the release of Office XP and then Office 2003, this concept expanded again to include solutions based on "smart" technologies that provided more direct interfaces to LOB systems using Office documents. These smart technologies include smart tags, smart documents, and research services.

Smart tag solutions recognize keywords in documents and present a menu directly in the document that can be used to access related information. Smart documents take advantage of the new XML-based structure of Office documents to present related information based on the document section currently being edited. Research services allow users to perform searches against LOB systems using the Office task pane.

In my previous book, I discussed smart documents and research services at length and used them to create solutions that complemented Windows SharePoint Services (WSS); therefore, I am assuming some knowledge of these solutions right from the start. While these solutions are powerful ways to improve the productivity of information workers, currently they are not widely used because they are often highly specialized and can take significant effort to create.

Encouraging widespread use of smart technologies is becoming extremely important to Microsoft as a means of maintaining control over the desktop and selling more Office 2003 licenses. Therefore, Microsoft has a vested interest in making these solutions easier to create and more reusable across a wide variety of business scenarios. This is where the Microsoft Office Information Bridge Framework (IBF) comes into play. IBF is a framework for creating solutions based on smart technologies. With it, Microsoft hopes to drive an increase in productivity that is tied directly to the use of Office 2003.

Utilizing the IBF framework results in solutions that are nearly identical to the custom solutions you can build yourself without IBF. The big difference is that IBF solution components are reusable in other scenarios and are easier to modify as end-user needs change. The drawback, however, is that IBF has a steep learning curve that can easily be frustrating in the beginning. In fact, IBF is so broad and deep that someone could easily write an entire book on the subject. My objective in this chapter is to give you a firm foundation and a significant leg up on that steep learning curve. When you complete this chapter, you should be able to create basic IBF solutions on your own. Figure 5-1 shows a typical IBF solution using a smart tag to recognize a company name and then displaying details in the task pane of Microsoft Word.

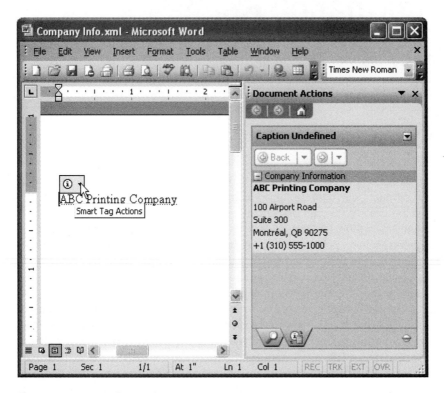

Figure 5-1. *A typical IBF solution*

Understanding Key IBF Concepts

The most important thing to understand about IBF is that it enables the creation of smart solutions based on metadata. The heart of IBF is an XML metadata set that describes how an Office document interacts with a LOB system and displays data in the task pane. This meta-data approach is intended to eliminate the coding necessary to connect documents with data stores and user interfaces. Instead, the connections are described in XML metadata, and IBF builds the connection when the solution executes.

In order to facilitate the interaction between Office and LOB systems, IBF utilizes a server-side component and a client-side component. The server-side component stores the solution metadata in a SQL Server database and exposes it through a set of web services. The client side reads the metadata and uses it to establish the connection between smart technologies in the Office document and LOB systems. Figure 5-2 shows a drawing of the complete IBF architecture.

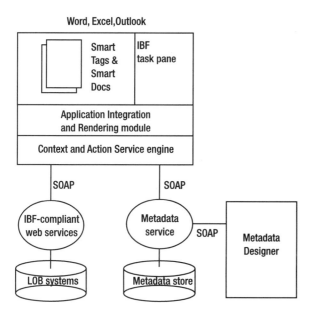

Figure 5-2. *The IBF architecture*

Understanding IBF-Compliant Web Services

IBF solutions access LOB systems through web services. Therefore, every LOB system that will participate in an IBF solution must be wrapped in a web service. Additionally, the methods defined for these web services must be carefully designed and coded to present an interface and provide data in formats expected by IBF. For the most part, this means that web services must accept parameters and return data as serializable XML.

The XML data sent into a web service by IBF is called a *reference*. References are generally specific instances of some business element such as a customer name or an account number. You can think of a reference as a parameter passed into a web service method except that it goes beyond a simple value and is represented through serializable XML describing the parameter. The exact XML that describes the parameter is defined by an input schema, which will be stored in the IBF metadata. The following code is a typical IBF reference passed to a web service:

```
<Customer xmlns="schemas-datalan-com"><LastName>Smith</LastName></Customer>
```

A web service method returns information about an *entity*. An entity is a business item that has meaning to the end user of the solution. Typical entities include items such as customer, invoice, or product. You can think of an entity almost like a table in SQL Server. Entities are most often defined in a web service as a serializable class and have a corresponding metadata definition in IBF.

The entity information returned from a web service is known as a *view* in IBF. A view provides information about an entity; for example, a customer view would likely include an address and a phone number. Other views may include multiple instances of an entity, as in a product catalog or customer contact list. Additionally, entities can have multiple views defined in IBF metadata. Views in IBF can be thought of exactly like views from a SQL Server database. The following code shows a typical view in XML:

```
<Products xmlns="CatalogService">
    <GetProductsResult>
      <Product>
        <Name xmlns="ProductData">Tiger Tank</Name>
        <Description xmlns="ProductData">Plastic model</Description>
      </Product >
      <Product >
        <Name xmlns="ProductData">Olive Drab</Name>
        <Description xmlns="ProductData">Acrylic paint</Description>
      </Product >
    </GetProductsResult>
  </Products>
```

While IBF solutions often focus on reading data from LOB systems, they are not strictly limited to retrieving data. Web services in IBF may define Get, Put, or Act methods. Get methods return views for an entity as I described earlier. Put methods are used to update LOB systems and typically involve simple operations like updating a phone number. Act methods are the most complicated and involve initiating a business activity such as an approval workflow or e-mail notification.

Understanding Metadata and the Metadata Service

Much of an IBF solution revolves around the creation of solution metadata. As I explained earlier, metadata is nothing more than XML that is used by IBF to bind the elements of a solution together. When you're building and debugging an IBF solution, this metadata is maintained in an XML file in Visual Studio. When the IBF solution is deployed, however, the metadata is written to a SQL Server database that is available to all Office applications that will use the solution. The database, which is exposed to clients through a web service, is known as the *metadata service*. The metadata service serves as both a repository of metadata and a security boundary to prevent unauthorized users from executing the solution.

Although the concept of metadata is simple, the structure of metadata in an IBF solution is not trivial, and this is what causes the learning curve to be so steep. Later in the chapter, I will define key metadata elements and show you how to properly configure them in an IBF solution. You will find, however, that the XML used by IBF can become quite complicated and borders on indecipherable at times. Fortunately, IBF provides us with several tools to generate and manage metadata, including a new Visual Studio .NET project type that provides a *metadata explorer* for viewing and managing metadata. Figure 5-3 shows a typical metadata explorer in Visual Studio .NET.

Understanding the Context and Action Service Engine

The Context and Action Service (CAS) engine is a client-side component that communicates with the metadata service and IBF-compliant web services. The CAS engine serves two functions. The first is to request metadata from the metadata service in response to user activity.

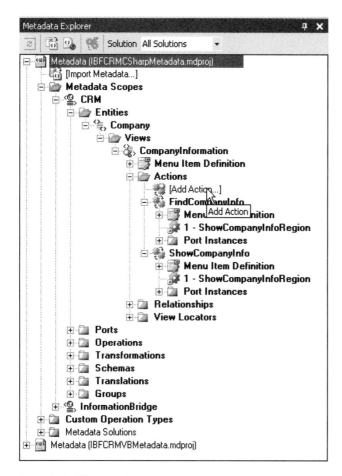

Figure 5-3. *The metadata explorer*

These actions can include typing a term that is recognized by a smart tag, navigating to a specific field in a smart document, or initiating a search. When the CAS engine retrieves metadata from the metadata service, it caches the metadata on the client to avoid unnecessary calls to the metadata service and to permit solutions to run offline. The second function is to execute the solution by calling IBF-compliant web services and to return entity views.

Understanding the Application Integration and Rendering Module

The Application Integration and Rendering (AIR) module is a client-side component that connects the CAS engine with the host Office application. User activities occurring in an Office document are routed to the CAS engine by the AIR module. Entity view information returned by the CAS engine is routed to the AIR module, which displays data in the task pane of the Office application. Figure 5-4 shows the IBF task pane with search results information displayed.

Figure 5-4. *The IBF task pane*

Understanding the Role of Smart Technologies

When developers created smart solutions in the past, they would have to write code that recognized a term in a document and responded by generating a data view in the task pane. In an IBF solution, smart tags and smart documents are integrated into Office when the developer creates an XML reference and passes it to the AIR module. IBF then handles accessing the LOB systems and generating the data view in the task pane. The result is a solution that requires much less custom coding. Figure 5-5 shows the steps involved in a typical IBF solution where a round-trip is made from an Office document to the metadata service.

Creating a Development Environment

Installing IBF and creating a development environment requires many steps. As of this writing, the files required to successfully install, develop, and deploy IBF solutions are located in different places on the Microsoft web site. In order to successfully install IBF, you will have to download several files, unzip them, and run the installation programs. The best place to start is at the home page for IBF located at http://msdn.microsoft.com/office/understanding/ibframework/default.aspx. On this page, you will find links to information, technical articles, and downloads. The main download page can be accessed from the IBF home and is located at www.microsoft.com/downloads/details.aspx?FamilyId=2833D4A7-9856-4E25-B7D6-E0C68872AF83&displaylang=en.

   On the download page, you will find links to several components and tools. For a basic installation of IBF, you will need to download the main installation files and the IBF Resource

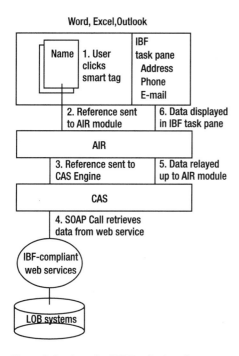

Figure 5-5. *A typical IBF solution flow*

Kit. The links to these items are shown in Table 5-1. The downloaded files are all self-executing zip files. You should run each one of the downloaded packages and extract the contents to separate folders. The extracted files will be used during the IBF installation process.

■**Note** I recommend selecting the default installation paths because it makes the setup process much easier in the later steps.

Table 5-1. *Key IBF Installation Files*

Name	Description	Location
MOIBF1.0.exe	Main installation file pack	http://www.microsoft.com/downloads/ details.aspx?familyid=2833d4a7-9856- 4e25-b7d6-e0c68872af83&displaylang=en
MOIBF1.0_ResKit_ Documentation1.0.exe	Resource Kit documentation	http://www.microsoft.com/downloads/ details.aspx?familyid=5ACA5705-4A5C- 406B-BAD7-05EBB069B71E&displaylang=en
MOIBF1.0_ResKit_ Commons1.0.exe	Resource Kit common components	http://www.microsoft.com/downloads/ details.aspx?FamilyId=324CAD02-2A25- 4F62-86E1-1FEA1DAEF6CE&displaylang=en

(Continues)

Table 5-1. *Key IBF Installation Files (Continued)*

Name	Description	Location
MOIBF1.0_ResKit_Tools_Cache1.0.exe	CAS Cache tool	http://www.microsoft.com/downloads/details.aspx?FamilyId=324CAD02-2A25-4F62-86E1-1FEA1DAEF6CE&displaylang=en
MOIBF1.0_ResKit_Tools_DSReg1.0.exe	Registration tool for Operation Assemblies	http://www.microsoft.com/downloads/details.aspx?FamilyId=324CAD02-2A25-4F62-86E1-1FEA1DAEF6CE&displaylang=en
MOIBF1.0_ResKit_Tools_WSDL1.0.exe	WSDL to metadata tool	http://www.microsoft.com/downloads/details.aspx?FamilyId=324CAD02-2A25-4F62-86E1-1FEA1DAEF6CE&displaylang=en
MOIBF1.0_ResKit_Tools_EPReg1.0.exe	Creates IBF entry points for smart tags	http://www.microsoft.com/downloads/details.aspx?FamilyId=324CAD02-2A25-4F62-86E1-1FEA1DAEF6CE&displaylang=en

Performing the Server Installation

The first thing to note about the server installation is that you do not need it for developing and debugging solutions. The server installation is only required for deployment. Additionally, the IBF server installation will only run on Windows 2003 Server. Before beginning the server installation, you should ensure that the target server is running Internet Information Server and that the Microsoft .NET Framework is installed. You should also have access to a SQL Server installation where the metadata can be stored.

■**Note** I recommend selecting the default installation ports for the metadata service because it makes the setup and development process much easier.

Follow these steps to install the IBF server:

1. On the Windows 2003 Server, select Start ➤ Run and navigate to the IBF server installation package named Microsoft.InformationBridge.Framework.Server1.0.msi.

2. Click the OK button to start the installation.

3. After accepting the license agreement, you will arrive at the Configure Database screen. Enter the name of the SQL Server installation where the IBF database will be installed.

4. Accept the default name for the database and select either Windows Authentication or SQL Server Authentication based on your credentials.

5. Click the Next button.

6. On the Installation Options screen, select the default options and click the Next button.

7. On the Configure Your Server screen, examine the default port numbers for the Read and Write service. Make sure that these ports are not used by any existing web site on the server.

8. Click the Next button and complete the installation.

Once the web services are installed on the server, you can access them with the browser to verify that they are running. If you did not change the default installation ports, then the address for the Read service will be `http://server:8081/IBFReadService.asmx` and the address for the Write service will be `http://server:8082/IBFWriteService.asmx`. If you access the services using Internet Explorer, you will initially get the message "Server Error in '/' Application". This message is expected and means the services are installed. If you wish to interact with the web services and not see the expected error, you can accomplish this by modifying the `web.config` file.

Follow these steps to modify the `web.config` file for IBF:

1. Open the Windows File Explorer and navigate to the directory `\Inetpub\IBFReadService`.

2. In the `\IBFReadService` directory, open the `web.config` file for editing in Visual Studio .NET.

3. Modify the <Web Services> section so that it appears as follows:

```
<webServices>
    <protocols>
        <!-- <remove name="Documentation"/> -->
    </protocols>
</webServices>
```

4. Save `web.config` and close Visual Studio .NET.

5. Select Start ➤ Administrative Tools ➤ Internet Information Services (IIS) Manager.

6. In the IIS Manager, right-click the local computer and select All Tasks ➤ Restart IIS from the context menu.

7. Once IIS restarts, navigate to the Read service in the browser. You should now see the page shown in Figure 5-6.

8. Repeat the above steps for the Write service.

Performing the Client Installation

The client installation in this section is designed to set up an environment that you can use for creating and debugging IBF solutions in this chapter. While it is possible to install both the client and the server on the same Windows 2003 server, you may want to set up a separate Windows XP client for development. A separate Windows XP client will allow you to create IBF solutions without connectivity with a server.

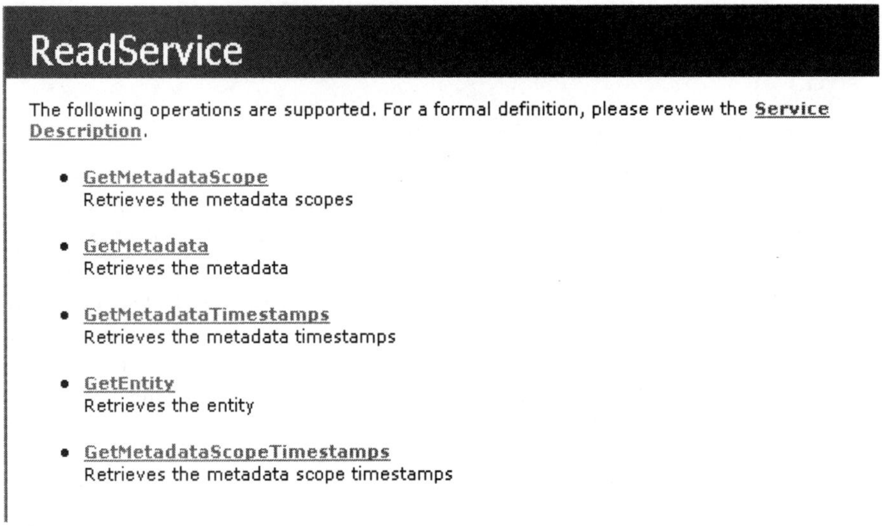

ReadService

The following operations are supported. For a formal definition, please review the **Service Description**.

- **GetMetadataScope**
  Retrieves the metadata scopes

- **GetMetadata**
  Retrieves the metadata

- **GetMetadataTimestamps**
  Retrieves the metadata timestamps

- **GetEntity**
  Retrieves the entity

- **GetMetadataScopeTimestamps**
  Retrieves the metadata scope timestamps

Figure 5-6. *Displaying the IBF service in a browser*

■**Caution** The IBF debugging environment is dependent on Visual C++; therefore, you must install Visual C++ as part of Visual Studio .NET or the debugging engine will not start.

Installing the Primary Interop Assemblies

Before you can install IBF on the client, you must install the primary Interop assemblies (PIA) for Office. The PIA act as a layer that allows the .NET assemblies of IBF to communicate with the COM-based architecture of Office. These assemblies must be installed for both the development environment and any client that will use the deployed solution. As of this writing, IBF only supports Word, Outlook, and Excel so you only have to install the PIA for these products.

To install required programmability support:

1. Place the Microsoft Office 2003 setup disk in the drive.

2. When prompted by the setup routine, choose to perform a Custom Install if Office is not already installed; otherwise choose Add or Remove Features.

3. Click the Next button.

4. On the Custom Setup screen, check the Choose Advanced Customization of Applications option.

5. Click the Next button.

6. On the Advance Customization screen, expand the tree and choose to install .NET Programmability Support for Word, Excel, and Outlook.

7. Expand the tree for Office Tools and choose to install Smart Tag .NET Programmability Support. Figure 5-7 shows the selections.

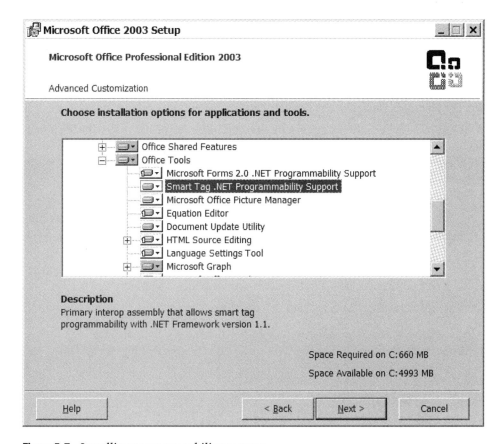

Figure 5-7. *Installing programmability support*

8. Click the Next button for a clean installation or the Update button if this is an update to an existing installation.

9. If this is a clean installation, review the installation options and click the Install button.

Installing the IBF Client

After the PIA are installed, you are ready to perform the IBF client installation. The IBF client consists of the CAS engine and AIR module. During the installation, you will be asked to provide the web address of the IBF Read service. Therefore, you should make a note of its location before beginning.

Follow these steps to install IBF on the client:

1. Select Start ➤ Run and navigate to the IBF client installation package named `Microsoft.InformationBridge.Framework.Client1.0.msi`.

2. Click the OK button to start the installation.

3. After accepting the license agreement, you will arrive at the Installation Options screen. Enter the server name and the port number for the IBF Read service and check the Validate Metadata Service Location box.

4. Click the Next button and complete the installation.

Installing the Metadata Designer and Resource Kit

Once you have verified that the IBF services are running correctly, you can install the Metadata Designer project type and Resource Kit. The Metadata Designer project type allows you to create a new metadata project in Visual Studio .NET that uses the metadata explorer. The Resource Kit tools are used throughout the IBF development process to speed common tasks.

To install the components, follow these steps:

1. Select Start ➤ Run and navigate to the appropriate installation packages one at a time to install the following: `Microsoft.InformationBridge.MetadataDesigner1.0.msi`, `MOIBF1.0_ResKit_Common1.0.msi`, `MOIBF1.0_ResKit_Tool_Cache1.0.msi`, `MOIBF1.0_ResKit_Tool_DSReg1.0.msi`, `MOIBF1.0_ResKit_Tool_EPReg1.0.msi`, and `MOIBF1.0_ResKit_Tool_WSDL1.0.msi`.

2. In Microsoft Visual Studio .NET, select File ➤ Open Solution.

3. In the Open Solution dialog, select the solution located at `\Program Files\ Microsoft Information Bridge\1.0\Resource Kit\1.0\Tools\EPReg\epreg.sln`.

4. Click the OK button to open the EPReg solution.

5. Select Build ➤ Rebuild epreg.

6. Select File ➤ Open Solution from the menu.

7. In the Open Solution dialog, select the solution located at `\Program Files\ Microsoft Information Bridge\1.0\Resource Kit\1.0\Tools\DSReg\dsreg.sln`.

8. Click the OK button to open the DSReg solution.

9. Select Build ➤ Rebuild dsreg.

10. Close Visual Studio .NET.

Configuring Microsoft Outlook

Microsoft Outlook is a little different from Word or Excel in that it does not directly support a task pane. IBF works with Outlook because the AIR module generates a stand-alone task pane that floats above Outlook. Additionally, smart tags are only available in Outlook when Word is designated as the default e-mail editor. Therefore, you have to configure Outlook to work properly with IBF.

Follow these steps to configure Outlook:

1. Select Tools ➤ Options from the Microsoft Outlook menu.

2. In the Options dialog, select the Mail Format tab.

3. In the Message Format section, select HTML from the Compose in This Message Format drop-down list.

4. Check the Use Microsoft Office Word 2003 to Edit E-mail Messages option.

5. Click the OK button to save the changes.

▨**Note** If you are using Windows XP, service pack 2, then you must perform the following steps in order to make smart tags visible in Microsoft Outlook.

---

6. Select Start ➤ Run.

7. In the Open dialog, type **regedit** to start the Registry Editor.

8. Locate the following key and select it:

   HKEY_CURRENT_USER\Software\Microsoft\Office\11.0\Outlook\Security

9. Select Edit ➤ New ➤ Key from the menu.

10. Create a new key named **RenderedIEBehaviors**.

11. Select the new key.

12. Select Edit ➤ New ➤ DWORD Value from the menu.

13. Create a new DWORD Value named **#default#ieooui**.

14. Set the value of the new entry to **1**.

Building IBF Solutions

Creating solutions in IBF—especially your first one—is not simple. In fact, you may find yourself wondering why you should use IBF as you are struggling to get the solution to work. Keep in mind, however, that an IBF solution is not intended to be created by a single individual. Microsoft's intention is that tasks such as web service development, metadata development, and smart tag development are distributed among different people. This approach is supposed to help organizations create and use smart solutions because one person does not have to know all of the different technologies required in such a solution. In this section, however, we will learn to develop IBF solutions single-handedly. Later, you can decide how to divide tasks among your team.

The basic process for creating an IBF solution involves four phases. First, you must develop the IBF-compliant web services that will wrap your LOB systems. Second, you must develop the user interface that will appear in the IBF task pane when information is displayed. Third, you must develop the metadata that binds the Office document, IBF task pane, and web services together.

Designing an IBF Solution

Before beginning to code an IBF solution, you must consider the business scenario under which the solution will be used. Remember that the starting point for IBF solutions is an Office document. Therefore, you have to think about what types of information may be present in the document that can function as a starting point for an IBF solution. For example, a customer service representative may receive an e-mail referencing an invoice number in the body. This invoice number could be recognized by a smart tag and offer a way to look up the details of the invoice through IBF. Another scenario might be a sales person filling out a product order. When the salesperson places the document cursor into the product number field, suggestions could be generated by IBF and appear in the task pane.

At the simplest level, this is what an IBF solution is all about. An Office document contains a keyword or special field that functions as an input and IBF responds with related data. When users subsequently insert information from the IBF task pane into the document, this new information can also act as a starting point for IBF.

The data that acts as an input to IBF, like invoice number, is a specific example of a *reference* in IBF. The data that is returned into the IBF task pane is a *view* of an entity in IBF. The process of using the data to return a view is known as an *operation* in IBF. The user interaction, such as clicking a smart tag menu, is called an *action* in IBF. Identifying the types of entities, views, actions, operations, and references that are appropriate for your solution should be done before you begin any solution development.

As a simple example, consider a scenario in which you want to recognize customer names in documents and return their contact information such as address and phone number. In this case, I'll identify a single entity called customer. The operation for this scenario is GetContactInfo. The view of the entity will be address and main phone number. The reference will be the customer name, and the action that initiates the operation will be a smart tag associated with the customer name in a document.

One of the nice things about an IBF solution is that you can start small and grow. I could start with the simple scenario described above and then later add another view of the customer that could return specific sales opportunities or associated invoices. This type of iterative approach will allow you to get partial solutions up and running faster. You can make subsequent changes as the solution is reviewed by business users. This rapid iterative development is the true value of a metadata-based solution.

Building IBF-Compliant Web Services

Once you have identified the entities, views, actions, operations, and references for your solution, you can begin to build web services that define these elements. You should start by creating a new web service project in Visual Studio .NET. You can create this in either C# or Visual Basic .NET, but you must use an attribute to define a namespace for the web service. IBF expects the web services you create to specifically define namespaces to which they belong.

This is not difficult to do because you can make up any name you want for the namespace and simply reference it using a WebService attribute on the class. The following code shows examples in both C# and Visual Basic .NET:

```
//C# Web Services class
[WebService(Namespace="CustomerService")]
public class WebServiceClass : System.Web.Services.WebService

'VB.NET web services class
<WebService(Namespace:="CustomerService")> _
Public Class WebServiceClass
    Inherits System.Web.Services.WebService
```

After you define the web services class, you should define the entities and references that you want to use with the web service. You can simply think of the references as the parameters that will be passed into the methods of the web service and the entities as forming the basis for the view returned from the web service. The key to defining these elements is to use the XmlRoot attribute on the classes so that they will be serialized properly. Listing 5-1 shows how I defined the reference for the company name in Visual Basic .NET.

Listing 5-1. *An IBF Reference Class*

```
'Name Reference
<XmlRoot(Namespace:="CustomerData", IsNullable:=False)> _
Public Class CompanyName

    Dim m_Name As String

    Public Property Name() As String
        Get
            Return m_Name
        End Get
        Set(ByVal Value As String)
            m_Name = Value
        End Set
    End Property

End Class
```

Notice that the namespace I assigned to the reference class is different from the namespace I assigned to the web service class. This is an important distinction because it allows you to easily identify data elements in the IBF metadata. Also, don't confuse the namespace of the .NET assembly with the XML namespace of the serialized data. All of the classes in the project can belong to the same assembly namespace. Just be sure to separate the entities and references into a separate XML namespace. Listing 5-2 shows a company entity defined in C# and belonging to the same namespace as the reference shown earlier.

Listing 5-2. *An IBF Entity Class*

```
//Company Entity
[XmlRoot(Namespace="CustomerData",IsNullable=false)]
public class Company
{
    String name;
    string address1;
    string address2;
    string city;
    string state;
    string zip;
    string phone;

    public string Name
    {
        get{return name;}
        set{name = value;}
    }

    public string Address1
    {
        get{return address1;}
        set{address1 = value;}
    }

    public string Address2
    {
        get{return address2;}
        set{address2 = value;}
    }

    public string City
    {
        get{return city;}
        set{city = value;}
    }

    public string State
    {
        get{return state;}
        set{state = value;}
    }
```

```
    public string Zip
    {
        get{return zip;}
        set{zip = value;}
    }

    public string Phone
    {
        get{return phone;}
        set{phone = value;}
    }
}
```

Once the references and entities are defined, you can then create the web methods that will return views of the entity. For the most part, writing the code to implement the method is straightforward and you may use any approach allowed in typical web service programming. The key to writing IBF-compliant web methods is to serialize the input and output of the function. This involves using attributes on the method definitions similar to those used on the class definitions. For example, if you want to return a company entity using a specific company name as a reference, Listing 5-3 shows how to create the appropriate web method in both C# and Visual Basic .NET.

Listing 5-3. *IBF-Compliant Web Methods*

```
//IBF-Compliant C# WebMethod
[WebMethod]
[return:XmlElement(ElementName="Company",Namespace="CustomerData")]
public Company GetCompany(
    [XmlElement(ElementName="CompanyName",Namespace="CustomerData")]
    CompanyName reference)

'IBF-Compliant VB.NET WebMethod
<WebMethod()> _
Public Function GetCompany( _
    <XmlElement(ElementName:="CompanyName", Namespace:="CustomerData")> _
    ByVal objReference As CompanyName) _
    As <XmlElement(ElementName:="Company", Namespace:="CustomerData")> Company
```

Notice that the applied attributes used to guarantee the input and output data match the expected schema as defined by the reference and entity. This synchronization between the class definitions and the method definitions is critical to success with IBF. Using the schemas correctly will also allow you to return sets of entities as a view. For example, Listing 5-4 shows how you might return a set of companies as an XML array.

Listing 5-4. *Returning a Set of Entities as a View*

```
//Returning an XmlArray in C#
[WebMethod]
[return:XmlArray]
public Company [] GetCompanies(
    [XmlElement(ElementName="CompanyName",Namespace="CustomerData")]
    CompanyName reference)

'Returning an XmlArray in VB.NET
    <WebMethod()> _
    Public Function GetCompanies( _
    <XmlElement(ElementName:="CompanyName", Namespace:="CustomerData")> ByVal _
    objReference As CompanyName) As <XmlArray()> Company()
```

As I stated earlier, implementing the web methods you define is done using standard
.NET coding techniques for accessing databases, calling SharePoint web services, or any
other data store. When accessing these systems, however, you should be sure to utilize the
Microsoft Single Sign-On (SSO) service in your code. SSO is a service that stores credential
sets for individual users and then makes them available programmatically. I will not cover
SSO here because I covered it in detail in my first book; however, it should be considered an
essential part of an IBF solution. For simplicity, I will use hard-coded database access strings
in this chapter. Listing 5-5 shows an example web method in C# that takes a company name
as an argument and returns a set of related customer entities.

Listing 5-5. *A Complete IBF-Compliant Web Method*

```
[WebMethod]
[return:XmlArray]
public Customer [] GetCustomers(
    [XmlElement(ElementName="CompanyName",Namespace="CustomerData")]
    CompanyName reference)
    {
    try
    {
      //Build query
      string sql =
      "SELECT dbo.Contact.Last_Name + ', ' + dbo.Contact.First_Name AS Name, " +
      "dbo.Contact.Job_Title AS Title, dbo.Contact.Phone, dbo.Contact.Email " +
      "FROM dbo.Contact INNER JOIN dbo.Company " +
      "ON dbo.Contact.Company_Id = dbo.Company.Company_Id " +
      "WHERE (dbo.Company.Company_Name = '" + reference.Name + "')";

      string conn =
      "Password=;User ID=sa;Initial Catalog=MyDatabase;Data Source=(local);";
```

```
    //Execute query
    SqlDataAdapter adapter = new SqlDataAdapter(sql,conn);
    DataSet root = new DataSet("root");
    adapter.Fill(root,"results");
    DataTable results = root.Tables["results"];

    //Build array for results
    Customer [] customers = new Customer[results.Rows.Count];
    int i=0;

    //Populate array
    foreach(DataRow row in results.Rows)
    {
        customers[i] = new Customer();
        customers[i].Name = row.ItemArray[0].ToString();
        customers[i].Title = row.ItemArray[1].ToString();
        customers[i].Phone = row.ItemArray[2].ToString();
        customers[i].Email = row.ItemArray[3].ToString();
        i++;
    }

    //Return results
    return customers;
}

catch(Exception x)
{
    Customer [] error = new Customer[1];
    error[0] = new Customer();
    error[0].Name = "Error";
    error[0].Title = x.Message;
    return error;
}
}
```

Once you have completed your web services, references, and entities, you should view the web services in the browser and verify that the input and output schemas make sense. I have found it easy to make typographical errors in the function signatures that cause problems later when you are creating IBF metadata. Unfortunately, the complex nature of the inputs to most of your web methods will preclude testing them directly in the browser; therefore, I recommend that you create test methods that allow you to enter simple values to test the web methods. Listing 5-6 shows a simple test method that I used to test the function in Listing 5-5.

Listing 5-6. *A Simple Test Method*

```
[WebMethod][return:XmlArray]
public Customer [] TestGetCustomers(string reference)
{
    CompanyName companyName = new CompanyName();
    companyName.Name=reference;
    return GetCustomers(companyName);
}
```

After you have verified that your web services function correctly, you should comment out the test methods. Commenting out the test methods ensures that they are not translated into metadata later. Also, commenting out the code allows you to keep the test methods in place if you need to troubleshoot the web methods later.

Building User Interfaces

While IBF-compliant web services act as the source of information for an IBF solution, the data they return is not formatted for view by a business user. In order to display the data, the XML returned from the web services must be parsed and loaded into controls that are hosted in the Office task pane. As an IBF solution developer, you must create a user interface that is compatible with the task pane and can present returned data to the user.

When you install the client component of IBF, a specialized task pane is installed that can interact with the AIR module. This task pane consists of several display elements that are available to you when building solutions. The most important of these elements are the collapsible regions. Regions are areas within the task pane that display information. In order to utilize a region for display, you must create custom user controls that are referenced in metadata and loaded by IBF at runtime. Much like creating IBF-compliant web services, IBF-compliant user controls are created in the normal way with just a few modifications.

Building a user interface for the task pane begins by creating a new Windows Control Library project in Visual Studio .NET. Once the new project is created, you must then set a reference to the two libraries that are exposed by IBF, which are `Microsoft.InformationBridge.Framework.Interfaces` and `Microsoft.InformationBridge.Framework.UI.Interop`. Additionally, you'll want to add a namespace for `System.Xml` because you will be parsing XML for display in the user interface. Once these references are made, you'll want to add the namespaces to your project, as shown in the following code:

```
//Add IBF References and Namespaces in C#
using Microsoft.InformationBridge.Framework.Interfaces;
using Microsoft.InformationBridge.Framework.UI.Interop;
using System.Xml;

'Add IBF References and Namespaces in VB.NET
Imports Microsoft.InformationBridge.Framework.Interfaces
Imports Microsoft.InformationBridge.Framework.UI.Interop
Imports System.Xml
```

Once the appropriate references are set, we can proceed to make the user control IBF compliant. This is accomplished by inheriting the interface Microsoft.InformationBridge.Framework.Interfaces.IRegion. The IRegion interface implements four properties that allow the user control to interact with the task pane. These properties are Data, HostProxy, HostType, and VisualStyle. Listing 5-7 shows how to implement the IRegion interface in C#.

Listing 5-7. *The IRegion Interface*

```csharp
public class CompanyControl : UserControl,IRegion
{

    private IRegionFrameProxy frameProxy;
    private FrameType frameType;
    private IVisualStyles visualStyles;
    private XmlNode data;

    public IRegionFrameProxy HostProxy
    {
        get{return frameProxy;}
        set{frameProxy = value;}
    }

    public System.Xml.XmlNode Data
    {
        set{data = value;}
    }

    public Microsoft.InformationBridge.Framework.Interfaces.FrameType HostType
    {
        get{return frameType;}
        set{frameType = value;}
    }

    public IVisualStyles VisualStyle
    {
        get{return visualStyles;}
        set{visualStyles = value;}
    }
}
```

Understanding the Data Property

The most important of all of the properties in IRegion is Data. In fact, you do not have to implement any of the other properties for a basic IBF solution. Data is a write-only property that receives an XmlNode containing the data returned from the IBF-compliant web service. The schema of this data exactly matches the return schema from the web service. Once you receive this data, you can parse it and put it in the constituent controls that make up your user control. The easiest way to do this is to simply process the XML directly in the property. Listing 5-8 shows a Visual Basic .NET example of processing the XML to place the returned values in labels.

Listing 5-8. *Processing XML for Display*

```
Public WriteOnly Property Data() As System.Xml.XmlNode Implements _
Microsoft.InformationBridge.Framework.Interfaces.IRegion.Data

    Set(ByVal Value As System.Xml.XmlNode)

        'Save XML input
        Dim objData As XmlNode = Value

        'Display values
        If objData("Name") Is Nothing Then
            lblName.Text = String.Empty
        Else
            lblName.Text = objData("Name").InnerText
        End If
        If objData("Address1") Is Nothing Then
            lblAddress1.Text = String.Empty
        Else
            lblAddress1.Text = objData("Address1").InnerText
        End If
        If objData("Address2") Is Nothing Then
            lblAddress2.Text = String.Empty
        Else
            lblAddress2.Text = objData("Address2").InnerText
        End If
        If objData("City") Is Nothing Then
            lblCityStateZip.Text = String.Empty
        Else
            lblCityStateZip.Text = objData("City").InnerText
        End If
        If Not (objData("State") Is Nothing) Then
            lblCityStateZip.Text += ", " & objData("State").InnerText
        End If
        If Not (objData("Zip") Is Nothing) Then
            lblCityStateZip.Text += " " & objData("Zip").InnerText
        End If
    End Set
End Property
```

When laying out the controls that make up the user interface, be aware that IBF will always respect the height of your user control, but not the width. This means that whatever height you set for the user control will be fixed when it is displayed in the task pane, but the width will be affected when a user resizes the pane. For this reason, you should make use of the Dock and Anchor properties to control the appearance of the constituent controls that make up the user interface. If necessary, you should even utilize the Resize event to ensure that the control always looks good.

Understanding the HostProxy and HostType Properties

The HostProxy and HostType properties are used to interact with the IBF task pane and the hosting Office application. The HostType property allows you to determine what is hosting your region while the HostProxy property allows you to communicate with that host. For the most part you can ignore the HostType property, but the HostProxy property has several uses.

The HostProxy property allows you to interact directly with the IBF task pane so that you can perform tasks such as adding custom menus. Additionally, it enables you to access the object model of the hosting Office application so that you can programmatically insert content or execute macros. These functions are beyond the scope of this chapter and not necessary for most basic IBF solutions.

Understanding the VisualStyle Property

The VisualStyle property is used to detect changes in the style settings in Windows and apply them to your user control. The code to respond to style changes is straightforward and nearly the same in every solution. Listing 5-9 shows how to capture style changes and apply them to a user control using C#.

Listing 5-9. *Applying Style Changes*

```
public IVisualStyles VisualStyle
{
    get{return visualStyles;}
    set
    {
        //Save the styles
        visualStyles = value;

        //Set the styles
        if(visualStyles!=null)
        {
            visualStyles_UserPreferencesChanged(null,null);
            visualStyles.UserPreferencesChanged += new
                Microsoft.Win32.UserPreferenceChangedEventHandler
                (visualStyles_UserPreferencesChanged);
        }
    }
}
```

```
private void visualStyles_UserPreferencesChanged(object sender,
    Microsoft.Win32.UserPreferenceChangedEventArgs e)
{
    if(visualStyles!=null)
    {
        //Get styles
        Color backColor = visualStyles.GetColor(Colors.RegionBackColor);
        Color foreColor = visualStyles.GetColor(Colors.RegionHeaderText);
        Font boldFont = visualStyles.GetFont(Fonts.DefaultFontBold);
        Font defaultFont = visualStyles.GetFont(Fonts.DefaultFont);

        //Set styles
        BackColor = backColor;

        foreach(Control control in Controls)
        {
            control.BackColor = backColor;
            control.ForeColor = foreColor;

            if(control.Name=="lblName")
                control.Font = boldFont;
            else
                control.Font = defaultFont;
        }
    }
}
```

Building IBF Metadata

While building web services and user controls are familiar tasks that must be modified for use with IBF, creating IBF metadata is a new and unique effort that requires careful attention to complete successfully. IBF metadata is nothing more than XML, but the number and variety of elements involved can be overwhelming. Microsoft has provided some projects and tools to help us create metadata, but we will occasionally have to edit the data directly in order to build a solution.

After you have completed building all of the web services and user controls required for your solution, it is time to make a new metadata project. This new project type becomes available in Visual Studio .NET after you install the package Microsoft.InformationBridge.MetadataDesigner1.0.msi. Because the project is simply used to edit XML metadata, there is no language requirement; the same project type is used for both C# and Visual Basic .NET solutions. Figure 5-8 shows the Add New Project dialog with the metadata project selected.

When you create a new metadata project, the metadata explorer appears inside of Visual Studio .NET. The purpose of the metadata explorer is to give you a simplified and organized view of the IBF metadata. Additionally, the metadata explorer acts as a launching point for various dialogs that help you create valid IBF metadata. Figure 5-9 shows the metadata explorer after a new metadata project is created.

Add New Project

Project Types:

- Visual Basic Projects
- Visual C# Projects
- Visual J# Projects
- Visual C++ Projects
- Information Bridge Metadata Projects
- Setup and Deployment Projects
- Other Projects

Templates:

Metadata

Metadata Project

Name: MetadataProject1

Location: C:\Documents and Settings\administrator\My Documents\Visual Stu   Browse...

Project will be created at C:\...\My Documents\Visual Studio Projects\IBFCRM\MetadataProject1.

OK   Cancel   Help

Figure 5-8. *Starting a metadata project*

Metadata Explorer

- Metadata (MetadataProject1.mdproj)
  - [Import Metadata...]
  - Metadata Scopes
  - Custom Operation Types
    - [Add Custom Operation Type...]
  - Metadata Solutions
    - [Add Solution...]

Figure 5-9. *The metadata explorer*

When you first start a metadata project, a new XML file named MSIBFMetadata.xml is created for the solution. You can examine the content of this file directly in Visual Studio .NET because it is exposed in the solution explorer under the folder named Current Metadata. Initially the metadata file is nearly empty, but it will contain many elements before the solution is complete. The following code shows the contents when a new project is created:

```
<?xml version="1.0" encoding="utf-8"?>
<Metadata Version="1.0.0.0"
xmlns=http://schemas.microsoft.com/InformationBridge/2004/Metadata
xmlns:xsi="http://www.w3.org/2001/XMLSchema-instance" />
```

Describing Web Services in Metadata

There are several ways to edit the metadata for an IBF solution. You can edit it directly in Visual Studio .NET, double-click one of the add commands in the metadata explorer, or import metadata. You'll almost always begin your project by importing metadata that describes the web services you created earlier. IBF uses metadata to describe the web services so that they may be mapped to references, entities, views, and operations. While it is theoretically possible to enter this information directly into the XML file, you will always make use of the WSDL to Metadata tool that comes with the Resource Kit to define the necessary metadata.

The WSDL to Metadata tool is contained in the package `MOIBF1.0_ResKit_Tool_WSDL1.0.exe`. Once installed, the tool can be run from the executable `Microsoft.InformationBridge.Tools.WsdlToMetadata.exe`. If you accepted the default installation path, then this tool is located at `\Program Files\Microsoft Information Bridge\ 1.0\Resource Kit\1.0\Tools\WsdlToMetadata`.

Typically, you will simply run the WSDL to Metadata tool directly from its installation directory. The tool is a simple form that asks you to provide the location of the WSDL file for the target web service, the name of a Metadata scope, and a version number. Figure 5-10 shows the WSDL to Metadata tool with values entered.

Figure 5-10. *The WSDL to Metadata tool*

When you enter the WSDL file location, you can use either a URL or a file path. The simplest thing to do is to use the URL of the target web service with the query string `?WSDL` appended to the end. The Metadata scope is like a namespace for IBF and can be any text you want, but you should use a name that is representative of your solution in general such as "Finance" or "Sales". The Metadata scope version can also be any text, but you should enter a true version number. Checking the Embed Schemas option causes the schema information for the web service to be saved in the metadata. You should leave this box checked. Checking the Wrap Methods option causes the tool to look for methods that are wrapped in different namespaces. We will not design any web services that have wrapped methods; however, you can leave this box checked just the same.

Once the appropriate values are entered in the tool, clicking the Generate Metadata button causes the WSDL to Metadata tool to create an XML file with metadata describing the web service. The XML file is created outside of the metadata project in Visual Studio .NET and will be placed into the same directory from which the tool was run. Once the metadata is generated, you can import it into the metadata project by double-clicking the node labeled [Import Metadata...] located in the metadata explorer.

Once the metadata is imported into the project, you can examine it using the metadata explorer or by opening the XML file directly. You will notice immediately that the metadata describing the web service is extensive and far from human readable. Despite this fact, there are a few things to note about this initial metadata.

First, you can observe that a new Metadata scope has been defined in the metadata explorer using the name you entered in the WSDL to Metadata tool. Metadata scopes serve as organizational containers for metadata and can simply be thought of as a namespace that contains other elements. Each scope can contain entities, ports, operations, transformations, schemas, translations, and groups. Defining these elements are the essential tasks of creating the metadata project. The WSDL to Metadata tool defines some of these entries, but not all of them. Figure 5-11 shows the metadata explorer with typical web service metadata visible.

The first elements defined by the web service metadata are *ports*. Ports are connections between IBF and an external resource. This external resource can be a web service, user control, XML file, or other resource that IBF needs to bind with at runtime. At this point, the WSDL to Metadata tool has defined ports that describe the inputs and outputs of the web methods along with the protocol that supports communicating with them.

The second elements defined by the web service metadata are *operations*. Operations are the actual web methods that can be called by IBF. In the metadata explorer, you will see an entry for each web method you defined on your web service. Operations are executed by IBF to retrieve data from LOB systems.

The final elements defined by the web service metadata are *schemas*. Schemas define the references that are sent into the web service and the entities that are returned. Schemas institute a form of sophisticated type checking that guarantees the data sent to the web services conforms to the expected type.

Importing Search Metadata

After you import the web service metadata, you will want to immediately import the predefined search metadata. The search metadata describes the predefined functionality of the Search tab in the IBF task pane. You import this metadata by double-clicking the [Import Metadata...] node in the metadata explorer and locating the file `Microsoft.InformationBridge.Framework.UI.Search.Metadata.xml`, which can be found in the Resource Kit documentation package `MOIBF1.0_ResKit_Documentation1.0.exe`. This predefined metadata describes a new Metadata scope named "Information Bridge". This scope contains ports, operations, and schemas, as well as entities, transformations, and translations.

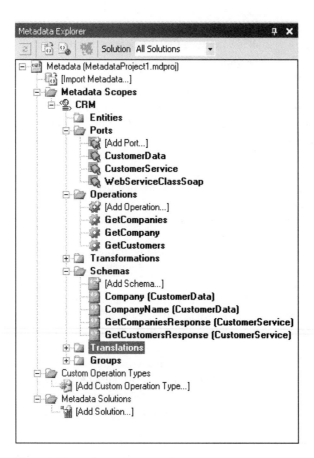

Figure 5-11. *Web service metadata*

■**Caution** The `Microsoft.InformationBridge.Framework.UI.Search.Metadata.xml` file has a stray line break at the top of the file that may prevent it from loading. If you have a problem, open the file and remove the line break manually.

I have already discussed entities, ports, operations, and schemas. We will examine them in more detail and use these elements extensively in the exercise at the end of the chapter. Therefore, I won't describe them again here.

In addition to the elements we have already discussed, the search metadata also defines several *transformations*. Transformations are used to change XML data from one format to another. This is accomplished when, for example, data needs to be transformed within IBF from the schema created by the web service to the schema needed by the user control for display. Transformations are not necessary in many simple IBF solutions, as we will see later.

The last elements described by the search metadata are *translations*. Translations are used by IBF to localize strings for display. Again, many simple IBF solutions do not require translations. However, the search metadata defines these elements so that IBF can be localized as required.

Defining Entities and Views

Once you have imported your web services metadata and the search metadata, the easy part is over. Now you must define the entities and views that IBF will display. The reason that this task is so difficult is that there are no automated tools to help you. Entities and views must be defined by hand directly in the XML metadata.

To get started, you must open the metadata directly in Visual Studio .NET. Because you have already imported a significant amount of metadata, the file is going to be large and confusing. The good news, however, is that you only have to add a small amount of information to successfully define an entity and a view. Listing 5-10 shows a complete entity and view definition that we can use for our discussion.

Listing 5-10. *Entity and View Metadata*

```
<?xml version="1.0" encoding="utf-8"?>
<Metadata Version="1.0.0.0"
xmlns="http://schemas.microsoft.com/InformationBridge/2004/Metadata">
  <MetadataScopes xmlns:xsd=http://www.w3.org/2001/XMLSchema
  xmlns:xsi="http://www.w3.org/2001/XMLSchema-instance">
    <MetadataScope Name="CRM" Version="1.0">
      <Entities>
        <Entity Name="Company"
            DefaultReferenceSchemaName="Company (CustomerData)">
          <Views>
            <View Name="CompanyInformation" IsList="false">
              <MenuItemDefinition MenuType="0">
              </MenuItemDefinition>
              <ViewLocators>
                <ViewLocator ReferenceSchemaName="CompanyName (CustomerData)">
                  <OperationInstance OperationName="GetCompany" Index="0">
                    <TransformationInstances>
                      <TransformationInstance Index="1"
                          InputOperationIndex="-1001">
                      </TransformationInstance>
                    </TransformationInstances>
                  </OperationInstance>
                </ViewLocator>
              </ViewLocators>
            </View>
          </Views>
        </Entity>
      </Entities>
```

When you define an entity and view in IBF, you place the elements directly beneath the MetadataScope element, which will already be defined by the web service metadata you imported previously. The `Entity` element defines a business item for which you want to display information, and I have presented examples of this concept several times throughout the chapter. In this example, I have defined "Company" as an entity. My solution will recognize the company names of customers using a smart tag and invoke IBF to show details about the company. Table 5-2 lists the attributes of the `Entity` element.

Table 5-2. *The Entity Element*

Attribute	Required	Description
Comments	No	Comment text about the entity.
DefaultReferenceSchemaName	No	The name of a schema representing the default reference to the entity.
DefaultViewName	No	The name of the default view for this entity.
Name	Yes	A unique identifier for the entity.

As I discussed earlier in the chapter, entities can have multiple views defined by `View` elements. A view is simply the set of information defined for display in the task pane. In this case, I have defined a single view named "CompanyInformation", which will display the address and main phone number of the selected company. Table 5-3 lists the attributes of the `View` element.

Table 5-3. *The View Element*

Attribute	Required	Description
Comments	No	Comment text about the view.
IsList	Yes	Indicates whether this view contains an item or a list of items. This attribute is for informational purposes only and has no effect on IBF behavior.
Name	Yes	A unique identifier for the view.
SchemaName	No	The name of the schema that defines the data for the view.

The `ViewLocator` element associates an input reference schema with a view. The `ReferenceSchemaName` attribute is the only attribute and contains the name of the schema that defines the input argument. This schema name is typically created by the WSDL to Metadata tool and can be found in the schemas folder of the metadata explorer. The `OperationInstance` element contains the name of the web method to call that generates the view. Table 5-4 lists the attributes of the `OperationInstance` element.

Table 5-4. *The OperationInstance Element*

Attribute	Required	Description
OperationName	Yes	The name of the operation. This is typically a web method name.
Index	Yes	The execution order of the operation when multiple operations are defined.
OperationMetadataSolutionName	No	The name of a metadata solution used to group elements together. This attribute has no effect on IBF behavior.

The TransformationInstance defines a transformation to perform on the operation. A transformation changes the form of the data before the operation is called. In many cases, data does not need to be transformed to successfully execute an operation. Table 5-5 lists the attributes of the TransformationInstance element.

Table 5-5. *The TransformationInstance Element*

Attribute	Required	Description
Index	Yes	The order in which the transformation is applied when multiple transformation are defined.
InputOperationIndex	Yes	An index specifying the input schema for the transformation. Using the value -1001 causes IBF to use the DefaultReferenceSchemaName defined for the entity.
InputOperationOutputSchemaIndex	No	Defines the index of the output schema for the operation.
TransformationMetadataSolutionName	No	The name of a metadata solution used to group elements together. This attribute has no effect on IBF behavior.
TransformationName	No	The name of the transformation to be applied. If this attribute is not supplied, then the output schema is the same as the input schema and no transformation takes place.

Defining entities and views can be difficult until you begin to better understand the metadata. When designing your first solutions, follow the example format shown here and the data used in the exercise at the end of the chapter. Microsoft has also provided a detailed help file with the metadata project that is integrated with Visual Studio .NET. Use this file to study the elements carefully as you build solutions. The better you understand the metadata, the more likely you are to be successful with IBF.

Understanding How IBF Uses Metadata

Once the entity is defined, you will need to create additional metadata that defines the expected user actions and the sequence of events that result in the display of information in the task pane. This sequence of events is known as an IBF *pipeline*. The key to understanding this process is to understand how IBF responds to user activity and the steps involved in a typical IBF pipeline.

All IBF pipelines begin with a user action in an Office document such as clicking a smart tag menu. When this action occurs, special XML data is sent from Office to the CAS engine. This data contains all of the information necessary to tell IBF what entity and view to display. The data sent to IBF, however, is not in the proper form to act as an input to the associated web service. Therefore, IBF applies a transformation to format the data correctly.

After the transformation, IBF routes the data to the web service method designated in the OperationInstance element to produce the desired view. The web service then returns data in the form designated by the web service. The output schema returned by the web service, however, may not be appropriate to send directly to the user control for display in the task pane. Therefore, the data is transformed again and sent to the task pane for display. Figure 5-12 shows a flowchart representation of the IBF pipeline.

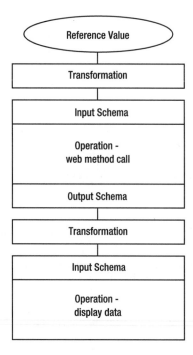

Figure 5-12. *The IBF pipeline*

Defining the pipeline sequence is a little easier than defining entities and views because the metadata explorer provides dialog boxes that help you through the process. In a typical solution, you must define additional ports that describe the user controls used for displaying the data, additional operations to display data, and any required transformations. Finally, you will define an action that initiates the flow of events through the pipeline. After a pipeline is defined in the metadata project, you can test it directly in Visual Studio .NET.

Once you are happy with the solution pipeline, you can deploy it directly from Visual Studio .NET to the metadata service. Once the metadata is deployed, any client with the CAS engine installed can access the solution. All that is left is to define a component—like a smart tag—that will initiate the pipeline.

Deploying IBF Solutions

After you build and debug your IBF solution, you will want to make it available to other Office 2003 clients on the network. To start this process, you should publish the metadata to the meta-data server. Do this by right-clicking the Metadata scope and selecting Publish Metadata from the context menu. Next, you must install the Office PIAs, Smart Tag support, and the IBF client on each machine that will use your IBF solution.

Along with the client installation, you must also make any assemblies associated with your solution available and trusted. Typically, this involves the assemblies you used for the user inter-face. These assemblies must be given a strong name and made available to all clients. Further-more, the assemblies must operate with full trust on the client. I use a shared file location to make the assemblies available and a CASPOL batch file for trusting assemblies in the shared directory. For an enterprise rollout, you will want to make use of group policies to simplify deployment. The following code is a typical CASPOL batch file design to trust assemblies that are stored in a mapped network drive designated with the letter F:

```
cd C:\WINDOWS\Microsoft.NET\Framework\v1.1.4322
caspol.exe -polchgprompt off -user -addgroup 1 -allcode Nothing➡
    -name "IBF_Solutions" -user -addgroup IBF_Solutions➡
    -url "file://F/IBF Assemblies/*"➡
    FullTrust -name "IBF Solutions"
caspol.exe -polchgprompt on
Pause
```

Finally, you must give end users permission to use your IBF solution through the Authorization Manager. The Authorization Manager is a Windows 2003 utility that is used to provide role-based access to various applications. IBF uses its own special store for managing permissions. Each Metadata scope you define will appear in the Authorization Manager. Using this utility, you can define access to the operations contained in the metadata.

Follow these steps to open the Authorization Manager:

1. Log into the server where IBF is installed as an administrator.

2. Select Start ➤ Run.

3. In the Open dialog, type **azman.msc** and click the OK button.

4. Connect to the IBF data store located at \Inetpub\azRoles\ Microsoft.InformationBridgeRoles.xml.

Understanding Smart Tags

Although you can test pipelines in a metadata project without a smart tag, you will need to build one in order to deploy most solutions. Building smart tags is a separate topic, which could easily comprise its own chapter. In this chapter, however, we will focus on the steps necessary to create an IBF-compliant smart tag that can initiate a pipeline.

Before you begin creating smart tags, you should download and install the Microsoft Office 2003 Smart Tag SDK. The SDK is located at www.microsoft.com/downloads/ details.aspx?FamilyID=c6189658-d915-4140-908a-9a0114953721&displaylang=en. Installing the SDK will install tools and examples that can help you successfully write smart tags.

Building Smart Tags

The first thing to understand about building smart tags is that they consist of two major components: a recognizer and an action handler. The recognizer identifies key terms in a document and marks them with a smart tag. The action handler defines what happens when the end user selects an item from the smart tag menu. Although you can write your own action handler for IBF-compliant smart tags, it is not necessary because IBF defines a default handler already. Therefore, all you really need to do is create an IBF-compliant recognizer.

Creating a recognizer begins with a new Class Library project in Visual Studio .NET. A recognizer is built from a class that implements both the IRecognizer and IRecognizer2 interfaces, which are members of the `Microsoft.Office.Interop.SmartTag` namespace. In order to use this namespace, you will have to set a reference to the COM library Microsoft Smart Tags 2.0 Type Library.

The recognizer interfaces consist of several functions that must be coded to make the smart tag operate correctly. Fortunately, many of these functions require trivial coding for a simple IBF-compliant recognizer. In this section, I'll focus on the key functions. In the exercise at the end of this chapter, you will build and deploy a complete IBF-compliant recognizer.

When a recognizer is first loaded by an Office application, the `SmartTagInitialize` function is called. In this function, the recognizer executes any code necessary to prepare it to recognize key terms. This typically means loading the key terms in some fashion such as a local XML file. Listing 5-11 shows an example in Visual Basic .NET that simply loads hard-coded terms into an array.

Listing 5-11. *Initializing a Smart Tag*

```
Private intTerms As Integer
Private strTerms(30) As String

Public Sub SmartTagInitialize(ByVal ApplicationName As String) Implements _
Microsoft.Office.Interop.SmartTag.ISmartTagRecognizer2.SmartTagInitialize
    strTerms(1) = "Vancouver Print & Copy"
    strTerms(2) = "Southwestern Publishing Company"
    strTerms(3) = "Kirkland Photocopier Sales"
    strTerms(4) = "LA Office Surplus"
    strTerms(5) = "Las Vegas Hotel & Casino"
    strTerms(6) = "Last Chance Printing"
    strTerms(7) = "Long Beach Copy Center"
    strTerms(8) = "Long Island Office Supplies"
    strTerms(9) = "MacDonald & Associates"
    strTerms(10) = "mComputer Plus"
    intTerms = 10
End Sub
```

All smart tags have a formal name associated with them. These names always take the form SchemaName#TagName. When you write your own custom smart tags, you can use any name that you want. When you write a simple IBF-compliant recognizer, however, you must use the predefined smart tag name provided by Microsoft. Using this name is what connects your recognizer to the default IBF action handler. Listing 5-12 shows how to implement the `SmartTagName` property in Visual Basic .NET and return the predefined IBF smart tag name.

Listing 5-12. *Returning the Smart Tag Name*

```
Public ReadOnly Property SmartTagName(ByVal SmartTagID As Integer) As String _

Implements Microsoft.Office.Interop.SmartTag.ISmartTagRecognizer.SmartTagName
    Get
        Return "http://schemas.microsoft.com/InformationBridge/2004#reference"
    End Get
End Property
```

Once your smart tag is loaded by the host Office application, initialized with a set of terms, and connected to the default IBF action handler, the `Recognize2` function is called to allow your smart tag to compare the current document text with the list of key terms. In this function, you can use almost any technique to identify terms that match. Once you identify a match, however, you must insert the appropriate IBF context string into the tag in order to initiate an IBF pipeline.

IBF context strings contain many of the metadata elements we discussed earlier. The exact format of this string is dictated by the designers of IBF and can be cryptic to say the least. I have found the best way to get an IBF context string is to save a Word document that contains an IBF tag as XML in the WordML format. Once it's saved as XML, you can open the file in Visual Studio .NET and copy the smart tag information. Listing 5-13 shows an example of the WordML associated with an IBF-compliant smart tag.

Listing 5-13. *An IBF Smart Tag Contained in WordML*

```
<st1:reference data="&lt;?xml version=&quot;1.0&quot;
encoding=&quot;utf-16&quot;?&gt;&#xA;&lt;ContextInformation
xmlns:xsd=&quot;http://www.w3.org/2001/XMLSchema&quot;
xmlns:xsi=&quot;http://www.w3.org/2001/XMLSchema-instance&quot;
MetadataScopeName=&quot;CRM&quot; EntityName=&quot;Company&quot;
ViewName=&quot;CompanyInformation&quot; ReferenceSchemaName=&quot;
Company (CustomerData)&quot;
xmlns=&quot;http://schemas.microsoft.com/InformationBridge/2004/
ContextInformation&quot;&gt;&#xA;  &lt;Reference&gt;&#xA;    &lt;
CompanyName xmlns=&quot;CustomerData&quot;
d2p1:MetadataScopeName=&quot;CRM&quot; d2p1:EntityName=&quot;Company&quot;
d2p1:ViewName=&quot;CompanyInformation&quot;
d2p1:ReferenceSchemaName=&quot;Company (CustomerData)&quot;
xmlns:d2p1=&quot;http://schemas.microsoft.com/InformationBridge/2004&quot;
&gt;&#xA&lt;Name&gt;ABC Printing Company&lt;/Name&gt;&#xA;
&lt;/CompanyName&gt;&#xA;&lt;/Reference&gt;&#xA;&lt;/ContextInformation&gt;"
title="ABC Printing Company" description="No Description was defined."
w:st="on">
<w:r><w:t>ABC Printing Company</w:t></w:r>
</st1:reference>
```

In order to convert the WordML string into something you can use in code, you must replace the `&quot;` token with a quote, the `&lt` token with a less-than symbol, and the `&gt` token with a greater-than symbol, and then delete every occurrence of the `&#xA;` token. Once this is accomplished, you will have to massage the string a bit to make it compliant with your programming language choice. You'll also need to replace the specific tag value with a token that will act as a placeholder for a new value. Listing 5-14 shows a valid IBF context string in Visual Basic .NET created from the WordML in Listing 5-13. Note the value of the `Name` element has been replaced with the token `{0}`.

Listing 5-14. *A Valid IBF Context String*

```
"<?xml version=""1.0"" encoding=""utf-16""?>" & _
"<ContextInformation xmlns:xsd=""http://www.w3.org/2001/XMLSchema""" & _
" xmlns:xsi=""http://www.w3.org/2001/XMLSchema-instance""" & _
" MetadataScopeName=""CRM"" EntityName=""Company"" " & _
"ViewName=""CompanyInformation""" & _
" ReferenceSchemaName=""CompanyName (CustomerData)"" " & _
"xmlns=""" & _
"http://schemas.microsoft.com/InformationBridge/2004/" & _
" ContextInformation"">" & _
"<Reference><CompanyName xmlns=""CustomerData""" & _
" d2p1:MetadataScopeName=""CRM"" d2p1:EntityName=""Company""" & _
" d2p1:ViewName=""CompanyInformation""" & _
" d2p1:ReferenceSchemaName=""CompanyName (CustomerData)"" " & _
"xmlns:d2p1=""http://schemas.microsoft.com/InformationBridge/2004"">" & _
"<Name>{0}</Name></CompanyName></Reference></ContextInformation>"
```

Inserting the IBF context string into the smart tag is reasonably straightforward. IBF expects you to place the context string into a special property named data. When you have done this, IBF will show a default menu item, Show Details, that calls the default IBF action handler and passes the context string. This will run your IBF pipeline and display data in the task pane. Listing 5-15 shows the Visual Basic .NET code that is used to insert the context string in the smart tag.

Listing 5-15. *Putting the Context String in the Smart Tag*

```
For Each objMatch As Match In objMatches

    Dim strMatchedTerm As String = objMatch.Groups("term").Value
    Dim intTagLength As Integer = strTerms(i).Length
    Dim intIndexOfMatch As Integer = _
       Text.ToUpper(CultureInfo.CurrentCulture).IndexOf( _
       strTerms(i).ToUpper(CultureInfo.CurrentCulture), _
       objMatch.Index, objMatch.Length)

    'Context string to invoke IBF
    Dim strContextString As String = _
       String.Format(COMPANY_CONTEXT_XML, strTerms(i))

    'Format the strings
    Dim strTermFormatted As String = _
       HttpUtility.HtmlEncode(strTerms(i))
    Dim strContext As String = _
       String.Format(CultureInfo.CurrentCulture, _
       strContextString, strTermFormatted)
```

```
'Write the tag
Dim objPropertyBag As ISmartTagProperties = _
  RecognizerSite2.GetNewPropertyBag()
objPropertyBag.Write("data", strContext)
RecognizerSite2.CommitSmartTag( _
  "http://schemas.microsoft.com/InformationBridge/2004#reference", _
  intIndexOfMatch + 1, intTagLength, objPropertyBag)
```

Next

Deploying Smart Tags

Once you have created an IBF-compliant recognizer, you can deploy it for use with Microsoft Office. Because smart tags were originally COM-based solutions, you must still register the recognizer in the system registry before Office can use it. This involves writing the assembly name into the key `HKEY_LOCAL_MACHINE\Software\Microsoft\Office\Common\Smart Tag\Recognizers`. In the exercise at the end of the chapter, you will create a REG file to properly register a smart tag recognizer.

Along with registration, smart tags must also be trusted by the .NET Framework. Smart tags created in Visual Studio .NET can bypass the traditional Office security model and make use of the Visual Studio Tools for Office (VSTO) security model, which utilizes the .NET Framework. In the exercise at the end of the chapter, you will create a BAT file to trust an assembly containing a recognizer.

Exercise 5-1. Creating IBF Solutions

IBF is an integration accelerator intended to be used by corporate IT staffs and Microsoft Solution Providers to speed the development of smart documents within the Office 2003 system. Because it is an integration accelerator and not a full commercial product, the technology assumes significant expertise on the part of the developer. When building IBF solutions, you will build web services, custom user controls, XML files, and schemas. In this exercise, I take you through the basics of building an IBF solution that you can subsequently modify to use with your own business systems.

Prerequisites

This exercise assumes that you are developing the IBF solution on a Windows XP Professional client with access to a SQL Server installation that contains the pubs database. This exercise also assumes that you have performed the appropriate client installation procedures described earlier in this chapter and that the Metadata Designer project type is available.

Creating the Web Service

The first step in creating an IBF solution is to build web services that access the line-of-business systems that will provide the data for the solution. Web services intended for use with IBF must have certain characteristics so that metadata can be created that will describe the service to IBF. While many of the steps in this process will be familiar to any developer who has previously created a web service, several details are specific to IBF.

Follow these steps to create a web service:

1. In Visual Studio .NET, select File ➤ New ➤ Blank Solution from the menu.

2. In the New Project dialog, name the new solution **IBF Pubs**.

3. Click the OK button to create the new solution.

4. When the new solution is created, select File ➤ Add Project ➤ New Project from the menu.

5. In the Add New Project dialog, select Visual C# Projects from the Project Types list.

6. Select ASP.NET Web Service from the Templates list.

7. Name the new web service project **IBFPubsService**.

8. Click the OK button to add the new project to the solution.

9. Open the file `Service1.asmx` for editing.

10. Decorate the `Service1` class with the following attribute to designate the XML namespace to which the service belongs:

    ```
    [WebService(Namespace="PubsService")]
    ```

11. Add using directives for the `System.Xml.Serialization` and the `System.Data.SqlClient` namespaces to the web service class. Listing 5-16 shows the code as it should appear with the comments removed for simplicity.

Listing 5-16. *The Initial Web Service Code*

```
using System;
using System.Collections;
using System.ComponentModel;
using System.Data;
using System.Diagnostics;
using System.Web;
using System.Web.Services;
using System.Xml.Serialization;
using System.Data.SqlClient;

namespace IBFPubsService
{
    [WebService(Namespace="PubsService")]
    public class Service1 : System.Web.Services.WebService
    {
        public Service1()
        {
            InitializeComponent();
        }
```

```
        #region Component Designer generated code

        private IContainer components = null;

        private void InitializeComponent()
        {
        }

        protected override void Dispose( bool disposing )
        {
            if(disposing && components != null)
            {
                components.Dispose();
            }
            base.Dispose(disposing);
        }

        #endregion

    }
}
```

Defining the Data Elements

Once the basic web service is created, you must create classes that represent the data elements to be used by the web service and IBF. These classes should belong to the same XML
namespace, which should be different than the namespace to which the web service belongs.
In this exercise, we will use the last name of an author to return the titles and publishers for
related books. Add the code from Listing 5-17 to define the data classes for these elements.

Listing 5-17. *Data Elements*

```
//Author element
[XmlRoot(Namespace="PubsData",IsNullable=false)]
public class Author
{
    string lastName;

    public string LastName
    {
        get{return lastName;}
        set{lastName = value;}
    }
}
```

```
//Book element
[XmlRoot(Namespace="PubsData",IsNullable=false)]
public class Book
{
    string title;
    string publisher;

    public string Title
    {
        get{return title;}
        set{title = value;}
    }

    public string Publisher
    {
        get{return publisher;}
        set{publisher = value;}
    }
}
```

Defining the Web Methods

After the data elements are defined, you can use them as inputs and outputs for methods in the web service. In this exercise, we want to pass in an Author element and return an array of corresponding Book elements. We use serialization attributes to clearly define the format of the incoming and outgoing XML. Add the code from Listing 5-18 to define the web method.

Listing 5-18. *Returning a Set of Books*

```
[WebMethod]
[return:XmlArray]
public Book [] GetBooks(
    [XmlElement(ElementName="Author",Namespace="PubsData")]
    Author author)
{
    try
    {
        //Build query
        string sql =
          "SELECT dbo.titles.title, dbo.publishers.pub_name AS Publisher "
          + "FROM dbo.publishers INNER JOIN "
          + "dbo.titles ON dbo.publishers.pub_id = dbo.titles.pub_id "
          + "INNER JOIN "
          + "dbo.titleauthor ON dbo.titles.title_id = dbo.titleauthor.title_id "
          + "INNER JOIN "
          + "dbo.authors ON dbo.titleauthor.au_id = dbo.authors.au_id "
          + "WHERE (dbo.authors.au_lname = '" + author.LastName + "')";
```

```
        string conn =
            "Password=;User ID=sa;Initial Catalog=pubs;Data Source=(local);";

        //Execute query
        SqlDataAdapter adapter = new SqlDataAdapter(sql,conn);
        DataSet root = new DataSet("root");
        adapter.Fill(root,"details");
        DataTable details = root.Tables["details"];

        //Build array for results
        Book [] books = new Book[details.Rows.Count];
        int i=0;

        //Populate array
        foreach(DataRow row in details.Rows)
        {
            books[i] = new Book();
            books[i].Title = row.ItemArray[0].ToString();
            books[i].Publisher = row.ItemArray[1].ToString();
            i++;
        }

        //Return results
        return books;
    }

    catch(Exception x)
    {
        Book [] errorsBook = new Book[1];
        errorsBook[0] = new Book();
        errorsBook[0].Title = "Error";
        errorsBook[0].Publisher = x.Message;
        return errorsBook;
    }
}
```

Testing the Web Service

Once you have finished coding, you can build and test the web service. Because the web service deals with complex object data types, you will not be able to perform a functional test at this point; however, you can verify the function signature to ensure the input and output definitions are correct. Select Debug ➤ Start from the menu and then click on the GetBooks method in the browser. You should see the sample SOAP request shown in Listing 5-19.

Listing 5-19. *Sample SOAP Request*

```
POST /IBFPubsService/Service1.asmx HTTP/1.1
Host: localhost
Content-Type: text/xml; charset=utf-8
Content-Length: length
SOAPAction: "PubsService/GetBooks"

<?xml version="1.0" encoding="utf-8"?>
<soap:Envelope xmlns:xsi=http://www.w3.org/2001/XMLSchema-instance
xmlns:xsd=http://www.w3.org/2001/XMLSchema
xmlns:soap="http://schemas.xmlsoap.org/soap/envelope/">
  <soap:Body>
    <GetBooks xmlns="PubsService">
      <Author xmlns="PubsData">
        <LastName>string</LastName>
      </Author>
    </GetBooks>
  </soap:Body>
</soap:Envelope>
HTTP/1.1 200 OK
Content-Type: text/xml; charset=utf-8
Content-Length: length

<?xml version="1.0" encoding="utf-8"?>
<soap:Envelope xmlns:xsi=http://www.w3.org/2001/XMLSchema-instance
xmlns:xsd=http://www.w3.org/2001/XMLSchema
xmlns:soap="http://schemas.xmlsoap.org/soap/envelope/">
  <soap:Body>
    <GetBooksResponse xmlns="PubsService">
      <GetBooksResult>
        <Book>
          <Title xmlns="PubsData">string</Title>
          <Publisher xmlns="PubsData">string</Publisher>
        </Book>
        <Book>
          <Title xmlns="PubsData">string</Title>
          <Publisher xmlns="PubsData">string</Publisher>
        </Book>
      </GetBooksResult>
    </GetBooksResponse>
  </soap:Body>
</soap:Envelope>
```

Generating the Web Service Metadata

Once the web service is completed, you need to generate the metadata that describes the service. Creating the metadata is done using the WSDL tool that you installed earlier.

The WSDL tool takes the URL for the web service WSDL as an input and generates an XML file as the output. Later in the exercise, you will import this metadata into the Metadata Designer to describe the web service to IBF.

Follow these steps to generate metadata for the web service:

1. Open the Windows File Explorer and navigate to the directory where the WSDL tool is installed. If you accepted the default installation, the tool should be located at `\Program Files\Microsoft Information Bridge\1.0\Resource Kit\1.0\Tools\ WsdlToMetadata\Microsoft.InformationBridge.Tools.WsdlToMetadata.exe`.

2. Run the WSDL tool from its current location.

3. In the WSDL file location box, enter the URL for your web service's WSDL (e.g., `http://localhost/IBFPubsService/Service1.asmx?WSDL`).

4. In the Metadata Scope box, enter **PubsScope**.

5. In the Metadata Scope Version box, enter **1.0**.

6. Click the Generate Metadata button, and the WSDL tool will create a file named `Service1Metadata.xml` located in the same directory from where you ran the WSDL tool.

Creating the User Interface

IBF utilizes custom Windows Controls to create regions within the Office task pane to display information. In this exercise, you will create a region to display the book information returned from the web service. This information will be displayed based on an author name that appears in a smart tag that you will create later in the exercise.

Follow these steps to create the user interface:

1. Select File ➤ Add Project ➤ New Project from the menu.

2. In the Add New Project dialog, select Visual C# Projects from the Project Types list.

3. Select Windows Control Library from the Templates list.

4. Name the new project **IBFPubsUI**.

5. Click the OK button to add the new project to the solution.

6. When the new project is created, add a `Label` control to the design surface of the custom control.

7. Select Project ➤ Add Reference from the menu in Visual Studio .NET.

8. In the Add Reference dialog, select to add references to the Microsoft Information Bridge Framework Interfaces and Microsoft Information Bridge Framework UI Interop libraries.

9. Click the OK button to add the references.

Once the references are added, you must implement the interface that allows the control to appear in the task pane. This is the Microsoft.InformationBridge.Framework.Interfaces.IRegion interface. The IRegion interface implements four properties that allow your control to interact with data from IBF and the hosting task pane. In this exercise, you will only need to implement the Data property. This is the property that receives the XML data from IBF. Listing 5-20 shows the interface code for the user control. After you have coded the control, build the assembly.

Listing 5-20. *Coding the User Interface*

```
//Implement this interface
public Microsoft.InformationBridge.Framework.Interfaces.IRegionFrameProxy
 HostProxy
{
    set
    {
    }
}

public System.Xml.XmlNode Data
{
    set
    {
        try
        {
            label1.Text="";

            XmlNode books = (XmlNode)value;
            foreach (XmlNode book in books.ChildNodes)
            {
                foreach(XmlNode info in book.ChildNodes)
                {
                    label1.Text += info.InnerText + "\n";
                }
            }
        }
        catch(Exception x)
        {
            label1.Text = x.Message;
        }
    }
}

public Microsoft.InformationBridge.Framework.Interfaces.FrameType
 HostType
```

```
{
    set
    {
    }
}

public Microsoft.InformationBridge.Framework.Interfaces.IVisualStyles
 VisualStyle
{
    set
    {
    }
}
```

Creating the Metadata Project

The heart of any IBF solution is the metadata project. The metadata project binds the web services, user interface, and Office task pane together to form a complete solution. The first time you create a solution, you will undoubtedly find the process cryptic and hard to follow. The key, however, is to develop a strong understanding of the metadata elements and how they are used by IBF.

Follow these steps to create the metadata project:

1. Select File ➤ Add Project ➤ New Project from the menu

2. In the Add New Project dialog, select Information Bridge Metadata Projects from the Project Types list.

3. Select Metadata from the Templates list.

4. Name the new project **IBFPubsMetadata**.

5. Click the OK button to add the new project to the solution.

6. When the new project is created, right-click the project in the solution explorer and select Set As StartUp Project from the context menu.

Importing Metadata

Once the metadata project is created, you can import the web service metadata you created earlier. The web service metadata describes the input and output data schemas as well as the available web methods. This binds the data layer to IBF. Additionally, you will import some predefined metadata that contains several operations that are specific to the task pane.

Follow these steps to import the metadata:

1. In the metadata explorer, double-click [Import Metadata...].

2. In the Import Metadata dialog, select the File option.

3. Click the Browse button and navigate to the Service1Metadata.xml file you created earlier.

4. Click the OK button to import the metadata for your web service.

5. In the metadata explorer, double-click [Import Metadata...].

6. In the Import Metadata dialog, select the File option.

7. Click the Browse button and navigate to the file
   `Microsoft.InformationBridge.Framework.UI.Search.Metadata.xml`
   located in the Resource Kit documentation files you installed earlier.

8. Click the OK button to import the metadata.

Adding a Blank Schema

IBF uses schemas to define the data as it moves through the pipeline. By importing the web
service metadata, IBF already knows about the schemas defining inputs and outputs for our
web methods. We also need schemas, however, to control the way data is transformed for
display in the task pane. In this exercise, however, we will simply use a blank schema that
won't transform the data, but will satisfy the IBF requirement to have a schema.

Follow these steps to add the required schema:

1. In the metadata explorer, navigate to Metadata Scopes ➤ PubsScope ➤ Schemas.

2. Notice that the schema folder already contains definitions for the `Author` element and
   the array of `Book` elements that will be returned from the web service.

3. Double-click the node labeled [Add Schema...].

4. In the Add Schema dialog, type **BlankSchema** in the Name box.

5. Select Schema String from the drop-down list.

6. Click the OK button to create the new schema.

Creating the Entity

Now that we have defined the basic metadata, we can move on to define an `Entity`. Entities represent business items in the IBF metadata. Typical entities include customer, invoice, employee,
etc. Essentially any noun can be considered a candidate `Entity`. In turn, entities have `Views`
associated with them. `Views` define a data set that gives information about the `Entity`.

Creating entities in IBF is the most difficult and error-prone step in the process. This is
primarily because you must edit the metadata by hand in this step. Although the metadata
project has significant intelligence built into the XML file, it is not foolproof. Errors in this
process can keep your IBF solution from functioning.

Earlier in the chapter, I covered the key elements in the metadata file, so I will not repeat
the information here; however, you should note that the `ReferenceSchemaName` attribute is set
to the definition of the `Author` element and the `OperationName` attribute is set to the `GetBooks`
method.

In this project, you must open the `MSIBFMetadata.xml` file located in the solution explorer
under the `IBFPubsMetadata` project and edit the file by hand in Visual Studio .NET. Save the file
after you edit it. When prompted, choose to merge the new metadata with the current metadata.
Listing 5-21 shows a portion of the `MSIBFMetadata.xml` file with the `Entity` definition included.

Listing 5-21. *Defining the Entity*

```xml
<?xml version="1.0" encoding="utf-8"?>
<Metadata Version="1.0.0.0"
xmlns="http://schemas.microsoft.com/InformationBridge/2004/Metadata">
  <MetadataScopes xmlns:xsd=http://www.w3.org/2001/XMLSchema
  xmlns:xsi="http://www.w3.org/2001/XMLSchema-instance">
    <MetadataScope Name="PubsScope" Version="1.0">
      <Entities>
        <Entity Name="Library">
          <Views>
            <View Name="BasicView" IsList="false">
              <MenuItemDefinition MenuType="0">
              </MenuItemDefinition>
              <ViewLocators>
                <ViewLocator ReferenceSchemaName="Author (PubsData)">
                  <OperationInstance OperationName="GetBooks" Index="0">
                    <TransformationInstances>
                      <TransformationInstance Index="1" InputOperationIndex="-1"
                          InputOperationOutputSchemaIndex="1">
                      </TransformationInstance>
                    </TransformationInstances>
                  </OperationInstance>
                </ViewLocator>
              </ViewLocators>
            </View>
          </Views>
        </Entity>
      </Entities>
```

Adding Ports

IBF uses ports to connect to external resources like web services and .NET assemblies. In this project, you will use ports to allow IBF to connect with the user interface you built earlier. This process will require one port that references the .NET assembly you created and another port that defines the control class defined within the assembly.

Follow these steps to define the required ports:

1. In the metadata explorer, navigate to Metadata Scopes ➤ PubsScope ➤ Ports.

2. Double-click the [Add Port..] node.

3. In the Add Port dialog, enter **IBFPubsUIPortAssembly** in the Name box.

4. Select Port Assembly from the Type drop-down list.

5. Click the Browse button and navigate to the assembly IBFPubsUI.dll.

6. Click OK to define the new port.

7. Double-click the [Add Port...] node.

8. In the Add Port dialog, enter **IBFPubsUIPortFile** in the Name box.

9. Select Port File Xml from the Type drop-down list.

10. Select the Enter XML Port Data to Save in the Metadata option.

11. Select **RegionUserControl.xsl** from the XML Template drop-down list.

12. Click the Insert button.

13. In the XSL code that appears, locate the `msibf:RegionProperties` element.

14. Modify this element to appear as shown here:

```
<msibf:RegionProperties RegionName="LibraryRegion"
Caption="Books" Description="Book Information"
TypeName="IBFPubsUI.UserControl1" ShowAs="ExpandedRegion">
```

15. When you have modified the XSL, click the OK button.

Adding an Operation

Your IBF solution already has several operations defined, including those associated with the web service you built earlier. In this section, you will define an operation to display your user control in the Office task pane. For this operation, you will use a blank input and output schema because we do not need any input and output definitions as part of this operation.

Follow these steps to define an operation:

1. In the metadata explorer, navigate to Metadata Scopes ➤ PubsScope ➤ Operations.

2. Double-click the node [Add Operation...].

3. In the Add Operation dialog, enter **ShowLibrary** in the Name box.

4. Select Library from the Entity drop-down list.

5. Select MSIBF.UI.ShowRegion from the Type drop-down list.

6. Select BlankSchema from the Input Schema drop-down list.

7. Select BlankSchema from the Output Schema drop-down list.

8. Select IBFPubsUIPortAssembly from the Port drop-down list.

9. Click the OK button to create the operation.

Adding a Transformation

In the previous step, you defined an operation to load the assembly containing your user control. This operation needs to be transformed so that the assembly will emit an instance of the control class it contains. For this transformation, we will use a blank input and output schema because we do not need any input and output definitions as part of this transformation.

Follow these steps to define a transformation:

1. In the metadata explorer, navigate to Metadata Scopes ➤ PubsScope ➤ Transformations.

2. Double-click the node [Add Transformation...].

3. In the Add Transformation dialog, enter **ShowLibraryTransform** in the Name box.

4. Select TransformationXsl from the Type drop-down list.

5. Select BlankSchema from the Input Schema drop-down list.

6. Select BlankSchema from the Output Schema drop-down list.

7. Select IBFPubsUIPortFile from the Port drop-down list.

8. Click the OK button to create the transformation.

Adding an Action

An action defines something that happens when a user interacts with an entity. Actions contain one or more operations that define the sequence of events that can occur for each user interaction. In this project, you will define a simple action that will execute the ShowLibrary operation to display the books associated with an author. Because there is only one operation in our action, the action may seem redundant. Keep in mind, however, that actions can contain multiple operations.

Follow these steps to create a new action:

1. In the metadata explorer, navigate to Metadata Scopes ➤ PubScopes ➤ Entities ➤ Library ➤ Views ➤ BasicView ➤ Actions.

2. Double click the node [Add Action...].

3. In the Add Action dialog, enter **ShowLibraryNow** in the Name box.

4. Select EnterContext from the Type drop-down list.

5. Select Author (PubsData) from the Parameters Schema drop-down list.

6. Click the OK button to create the new action.

7. When the ShowLibraryNow action appears in the metadata explorer, double-click it to open its associated design canvas.

8. Using the Toolbox, drag the ShowLibrary operation onto the design canvas. This associates the operation with the action.

9. On the design canvas, right-click the operation and select Properties from the pop-up menu.

10. In the Properties window, click the ellipsis next to the TransformationInstances property.

11. Select View Data from the Input Operation Name drop-down list.

12. Select ShowLibraryTransform from the Transformation Name drop-down list.

13. Click the OK button.

14. Select File ➤ Save All from the menu in Visual Studio .NET.

Adding a Search Capability

IBF makes it easy to add a search capability to your solutions. Using metadata, you can connect the predefined search capabilities of IBF with an action. In this section, you will create a search pane that accepts an argument and calls the action you have already created.

Follow these steps to add a search:

1. Open the MSIBFMetadata.xml file in Visual Studio .NET for editing.

2. Select Edit ➤ Find and Replace ➤ Find from the menu.

3. In the Find dialog, enter the term **<SearchTypes>**—be sure to include the brackets—and click the Find Next button.

4. Locate the SearchTypes element in the metadata. This element will be empty because no search solutions have yet been defined.

5. Add the code from Listing 5-22 to set up a search type for this solution.

Listing 5-22. *Describing a Search Type*

```
<SearchType Name="BookSearch" Caption="Find Books" ActionName="ShowLibraryNow"
  Target="SearchRegion" MetadataScopeName="PubsScope" EntityName="Library"
  ViewName="BasicView" ReferenceSchemaName="Author (PubsData)">
    <InputReferenceInstance Namespaces="n=&quot;PubsData&quot;">
        <Author xmlns="PubsData">
            <LastName>
            </LastName>
        </Author>
    </InputReferenceInstance>
    <SearchCriteria>
        <SearchCriterion Caption="Book Titles" Name="Titles"
          Type="text" Required="true" XPath="//n:LastName">
        </SearchCriterion>
    </SearchCriteria>
</SearchType>
```

Testing the Solution

Once the solution is merged and saved, you can test it in Visual Studio .NET. During debugging, IBF uses the project metadata locally and does not require access to the IBF Read service. This allows you to easily build and debug without having to deploy the solution.

Follow these steps to test your solution:

1. In the metadata explorer, right-click the ShowLibraryNow action and select Build Solution and Execute Action from the context menu.

2. In the Build and Execute Action dialog, enter the following XML into the Reference box:

```
<Author xmlns="PubsData"><LastName>green</LastName></Author>
```

3. Select Author (PubsData) from the View Locator Schema drop-down list.

4. Click the OK button to run the solution. You should see the task pane shown in Figure 5-13.

5. Once the task pane appears, select Copy Smart Tag from the drop-down menu.

6. Close the task pane to stop the project.

7. Open Microsoft Word and paste the smart tag into a new blank document.

8. Save the document as **IBFTest.xml** and close Word.

9. Locate the file you just saved and open it inside Visual Studio .NET for editing.

10. Select Edit ➤ Find and Replace ➤ Replace from the menu in Visual Studio .NET.

11. In the Replace dialog, enter **Caption Undefined** in the Find what box and **Green** in the Replace with box.

12. Click the Replace All button.

13. Save and close the file.

14. Select Debug ➤ Start from the menu in Visual Studio .NET to start your solution in Microsoft Word.

15. When Microsoft Word appears, select File ➤ Open from the menu.

16. Open the file IBFTest.xml and notice the smart tag now shows the Author name *Green*.

17. Hover over the keyword to make the smart tag appear.

18. Select Show Details from the Smart Tag drop-down menu.

19. The task pane in Word should now show the list of books associated with the author *Green*.

20. Click on the Search tab and enter the name **Green**.

21. Click the green arrow to perform the search.

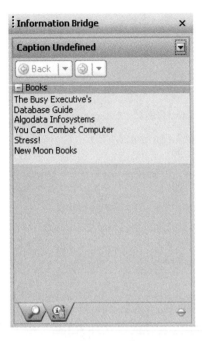

Figure 5-13. *The IBF task pane*

Exercise 5-2. Creating a Smart Tag Recognizer

Smart tags are often used as starting points to initiate IBF pipelines. In this exercise, you will build a smart tag recognizer that works with the IBF pipeline you built in Exercise 5-1. This smart tag will recognize author names when you type them into a document and call the default IBF action handler to initiate the pipeline. Before you begin this exercise, be sure that you have completed Exercise 5-1 and that you have installed the Smart Tag SDK.

Starting the Project

Smart tags are built using standard .NET class libraries. The classes in the library implement interfaces that allow them to interact with Office applications. Therefore, most of the development effort involves writing code to implement the interfaces.

Follow these steps to get started:

1. Open the solution you created in Exercise 5-1 in Visual Studio .NET.

2. When the new solution is open, select File ➤ Add Project ➤ New Project from the menu.

3. In the Add New Project dialog, select Visual C# Projects from the Project Types list.

4. Select Class Library from the Templates list.

5. Name the new web service project **IBFPubsSmartTag**.

6. Click the OK button to add the new project to the solution.

7. From the menu, select Project ➤ Add Reference and add a reference to the System.Web and System.Windows.Forms namespaces.

8. In the Add Reference dialog, click the COM tab.

9. In the COM tab, double-click the library titled "Microsoft Smart Tags 2.0 Type Library".

10. Click the OK button to add the reference to the project.

11. Open the file Class1.cs for editing.

12. Change the name of the class to **AuthorRecognizer**.

13. Add namespace references and inherit interfaces to make your initial code equivalent to Listing 5-23.

Listing 5-23. *The Initial Project Code*

```
using System;
using System.Web;
using System.Windows.Forms;
using System.Threading;
using System.Globalization;
using System.Text.RegularExpressions;
using Microsoft.Office.Interop.SmartTag;

namespace IBFPubsSmartTag
{

    public class AuthorRecognizer: ISmartTagRecognizer, ISmartTagRecognizer2
    {
    }
}
```

Initializing the Recognizer

When the recognizer is first loaded, it must initialize all of the variables necessary to perform recognition. In this example, you will use a simple array to recognize author names. You will also initialize a context string that has all the information necessary to initiate an IBF pipeline except that the author name has been replaced by a token so that the actual value may be inserted later. Add the code from Listing 5-24 to initialize the recognizer.

Listing 5-24. *Initializing the Recognizer*

```
int numTerms;
string[] terms = new string[30];

private const string AUTHOR_CONTEXT_XML =
    "<?xml version=\"1.0\" encoding=\"utf-16\"?>" +
    "<ContextInformation xmlns:xsd=\"http://www.w3.org/2001/XMLSchema\" " +
    "xmlns:xsi=\"http://www.w3.org/2001/XMLSchema-instance\" " +
    "MetadataScopeName=\"Pubs\" EntityName=\"Library\" ViewName=\"BasicView\" " +
    "ReferenceSchemaName=\"Author (PubsData)\" " +
    "xmlns=" +
 "\"http://schemas.microsoft.com/InformationBridge/2004/ContextInformation\">" +
    "<Reference>" +
    "<Author xmlns=\"PubsData\" d2p1:MetadataScopeName=\"Pubs\" " +
    "d2p1:EntityName=\"Library\" d2p1:ViewName=\"BasicView\" " +
    "d2p1:ReferenceSchemaName=\"Author (PubsData)\" " +
    "xmlns:d2p1=\"http://schemas.microsoft.com/InformationBridge/2004\">" +
    "<LastName>{0}</LastName></Author></Reference></ContextInformation>";

public void SmartTagInitialize(string ApplicationName)
{
    try
    {
        terms[1] = "White";
        terms[2] = "Green";
        terms[3] = "Carson";
        terms[4] = "O'Leary";
        terms[5] = "Straight";
        terms[6] = "Smith";
        terms[7] = "Bennet";
        terms[8] = "Dull";
        terms[9] = "Gringlesby";
        terms[10] = "Locksley";
        terms[11] = "Blotchet-Halls";
        terms[12] = "Yokomoto";
        terms[13] = "del Castillo";
        terms[14] = "DeFrance";
        terms[15] = "Stringer";
        terms[16] = "MacFeather";
        terms[17] = "Karsen";
        terms[18] = "Panteley";
        terms[19] = "Hunter";
        terms[20] = "McBadden";
        terms[21] = "Ringer";
```

```
        numTerms = 21;
    }
    catch (System.Exception x)
    {
        MessageBox.Show (x.ToString());
    }
}
```

Recognizing Terms

After initialization, the recognizer is called to examine the document for key terms. When a term is recognized, the context string is filled with the author name and placed into the smart tag using the data property. Add the code from Listing 5-25 to recognize terms and build the smart tag.

Listing 5-25. *Recognizing Key Terms*

```
public void Recognize2(string Text, IF_TYPE DataType, int LocaleID,
ISmartTagRecognizerSite2 RecognizerSite2, string ApplicationName,
ISmartTagTokenList TokenList)
{
    try
    {
        // Set the culture info for string comparisions
        Thread.CurrentThread.CurrentCulture = new CultureInfo(LocaleID);

        for(int i=1; i<=numTerms; i++)
        {
            //Look for the term in the Text
            string expression = @"(\W|^)*(?<term>" + terms[i] + @")(\W|$)";
            Regex regex = new Regex(expression, RegexOptions.IgnoreCase);
            MatchCollection matches = regex.Matches(Text);

            //Process each match in the Text
            foreach (Match match in matches)
            {
                string matchedTerm = match.Groups["term"].Value;
                int indexOfMatch =
                  Text.ToUpper(CultureInfo.CurrentCulture).IndexOf(
                  terms[i].ToUpper(CultureInfo.CurrentCulture),
                  match.Index, match.Length);

                //Length will always be the length of the term.
                int tagLength = terms[i].Length;
```

```
                    //Context string to invoke IBF
                    string contextString =
                      string.Format(AUTHOR_CONTEXT_XML,terms[i]);

                    //Format the strings
                    string termFormatted = HttpUtility.HtmlEncode(terms[i]);
                    string context = string.Format(
                      CultureInfo.CurrentCulture, contextString, termFormatted);

                    //Write the tag
                    ISmartTagProperties propertyBag =
                      RecognizerSite2.GetNewPropertyBag();
                    propertyBag.Write("data", context);
                    RecognizerSite2.CommitSmartTag(
                    "http://schemas.microsoft.com/InformationBridge/2004#reference",
                    indexOfMatch+1, tagLength, propertyBag);
                    }
                }
            }
    catch(Exception x)
    {
        MessageBox.Show(x.Message);
    }
}
```

Finishing the Recognizer

The recognizer must implement several other functions to be complete. The most important of these remaining functions returns the name of the smart tag using the predefined IBF name. Add the code from Listing 5-26 to complete the smart tag.

Listing 5-26. *Completing the Smart Tag*

```
public string ProgId
{
    get{return "IBFPubsSmartTag.AuthorRecognizer";}
}

public string get_Name(int LocaleID)
{
    return "Author Recognizer";
}

public string get_Desc(int LocaleID)
{
    return "Author Recognizer recognizes last names in documents";
}
```

```
public string get_SmartTagName(int SmartTagID)
{
    if (SmartTagID==1)
    {
        return "http://schemas.microsoft.com/InformationBridge/2004#reference";
    }
    return "";
}

public int SmartTagCount
{
    get
    {
    return 1;
    }
}

public string get_SmartTagDownloadURL(int SmartTagID)
{
    return "";
}

public void Recognize(string Text, IF_TYPE DataType, int LocaleID,
  ISmartTagRecognizerSite RecognizerSite)
{
    // Not using this because using Recognize2 method instead.
}

public void DisplayPropertyPage(int SmartTagID, int LocaleID)
{
    // Not implemented
}

public bool get_PropertyPage(int SmartTagID, int LocaleID)
{
    return false;
}
```

Deploying the Smart Tag

Once the smart tag is completed, you should compile it. In order to get the tag to run in Office, you must register it and grant it full trust. You register the recognizer by creating a REG file and grant trust by creating a BAT file.

Follow these steps to deploy the smart tag:

1. Start Notepad or any text editor.

2. Create a text file with the following registry commands. Replace the [Path] token with the path to your solution.

```
Windows Registry Editor Version 5.00
```

[HKEY_LOCAL_MACHINE\Software\Microsoft\Office\Common\➥
```
Smart Tag\Recognizers\IBFPubsSmartTag.AuthorRecognizer]➥
"Filename"="C:\\[Path]\\IBF Pubs\\IBFPubsSmartTag➥
\\bin\\Debug\\IBFPubsSmartTag.dll"
"Managed"=dword:00000001
```

3. Save the file as **Register.reg**.

4. Execute `Register.reg` to register the recognizer.

5. Start a new file in the text editor.

6. Create a text file with the following batch file commands that use the `caspol` utility to grant full trust to your recognizer assembly. Replace the [Drive] token with your system drive letter and the [Path] token with the path to your project.

```
cd [Drive]:\WINDOWS\Microsoft.NET\Framework\v1.1.4322
caspol.exe -polchgprompt off -user -addgroup 1 -allcode Nothing➥
    -name "SmartTag_Author" -user -addgroup SmartTag_Author➥
    -url "file://[Path]/IBF Pubs/IBFPubsSmartTag/bin/*"➥
    FullTrust -name "Author Tag"
caspol.exe -polchgprompt on
Pause
```

7. Save the file as **Trust.bat**.

8. Execute `Trust.bat` to grant full trust to your assembly.

9. In Visual Studio .NET, select Debug ➤ Start to run the IBF solution.

10. Microsoft Word will start automatically and load your smart tag. Type a recognized term and verify that a smart tag appears.

11. Select Show Details from the Smart Tag menu and verify the correct data appears in the IBF task pane.

CHAPTER 6

■■■

The Business Scorecards Accelerator

Enterprise Performance Management (EPM) embodies the processes and tools necessary to measure organizational performance. EPM is a deep and wide subject with several approaches that typically go well beyond the traditional measurements of revenue and profitability. The Business Scorecards Accelerator (BSA) is a framework for EPM based on the balanced scorecard methodology developed by Robert Kaplan and David Norton. This methodology presents corporate performance metrics using a simple scorecard that rolls up measurements into an assessment of an organization's performance in four key areas. These areas—financial, customer, internal business processes, and learning and growth—are designed to help an organization understand its current performance as well as the actions required to improve future performance. Figure 6-1 shows a typical balanced scorecard.

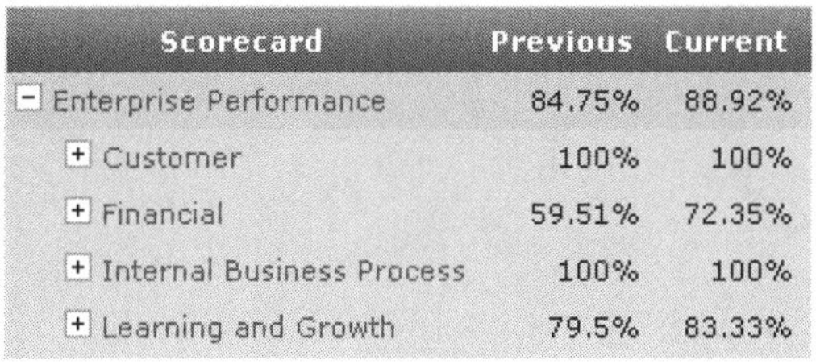

Scorecard	Previous	Current
⊟ Enterprise Performance	84.75%	88.92%
⊞ Customer	100%	100%
⊞ Financial	59.51%	72.35%
⊞ Internal Business Process	100%	100%
⊞ Learning and Growth	79.5%	83.33%

Figure 6-1. *A balanced scorecard*

Although balanced scorecards focus on four key areas, the concept of a scorecard can contain information from any number of areas. If we create scorecards that do not comply with all of the requirements for a balanced scorecard, then we are said to have created a *business scorecard*. This is an important distinction because BSA is capable of creating both balanced scorecards and business scorecards. We can, therefore, look at BSA as a generalized scorecard tool for measuring organizational performance.

Understanding BSA Data Sources

All scorecards built with BSA use *cubes* as the data source. Cubes are specialized data structures that are optimized for reading through multiple indexes. The optimized reading performance and multiple indexes allow BSA to rapidly access measures contained in the cube and display them in a scorecard. In this section, I'll provide an overview of relational databases, data warehouses, and cubes necessary to get you going with BSA.

Understanding Data Warehouses

Creating a cube always begins with understanding the data found in your organization's line of business (LOB) systems. These LOB systems utilize relational databases to store information, and this is a concept that is well understood. If you are reading this book, you have probably written many applications that use relational databases. The key point of emphasis here, however, is that these relational databases are designed for optimal data storage. Figure 6-2 shows a classic relational database diagram from a customer relationship management (CRM) system representing the relationships between an organization's sales opportunities, customer companies, customer contacts, and the organization's employee working the deal.

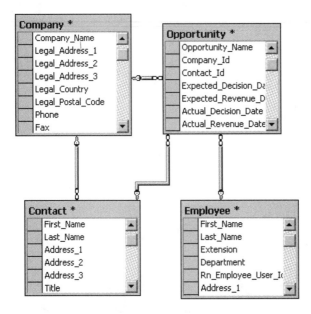

Figure 6-2. *A relational database diagram*

Although relational databases are designed mainly for optimal storage, the vast majority of organizations regularly use them directly as enterprise reporting sources. Initially, this seems to make sense. Reporting systems such as SQL Reporting Services can connect directly to the databases and run reports, and the available data is always up to date because the report is run directly against the transactional system. Invariably, however, challenges arise with this approach for several reasons.

Because relational databases are not optimized for reporting, running enterprise reports against transactional systems can have a significant performance impact. In fact, the performance degradation can be so great that it affects the internal processes of the organization. Then people start to complain about the system.

IT generally reacts to this situation by scheduling enterprise reports to run at night. This seems like a good idea because the information workers can use the system by day and the enterprise reporting infrastructure can use the system by night. This solution may work initially, but as reporting needs grow so does the processing time required for the reports. In many cases, this leads to a situation in which reports are still running when the workday begins.

The solution to the reporting problem rests in creating a *data warehouse*. A data warehouse is a separate database created from one or many LOB systems that is optimized for enterprise reporting. Although data warehouses can be quite complicated and incorporate many data sources, the concept is pretty simple. While relational databases are optimized for storage with no repeating data, data warehouses purposely repeat data to make it easier to generate reports. Furthermore, because the data warehouse is separate from the LOB system, reports can be run any time of the day.

The process of creating a data warehouse begins by moving data from target LOB systems into a new database called a *staging area*. The purpose of the staging area is to join data from different LOB systems into a single set of tables and to reconcile the data from the various systems. Reconciling the data—or *cleansing* the data—is required because different LOB systems may have different formats, conflicting data, or incorrect values. The process of moving the data from the LOB systems to the staging area is known as extract, transform, and load (ETL). Several commercial ETL tools are available on the market with significant feature sets designed to solve data cleansing problems while data is staged. Microsoft is behind in this area of development and offers only Data Transformation Services (DTS), which is available in SQL Server.

Once the data is cleaned, it is then moved from the staging area into the data warehouse. The value of the data warehouse rests in its table structure. Instead of a relational structure, data warehouses utilize a *fact table*. A fact table can be thought of as a view that joins many relational tables together to focus on a certain area. For example, if we wanted to run reports about the sales opportunities shown in Figure 6-2, we might create a fact table of opportunities that joins together the four tables in a single view. This fact table would contain the value of every sales opportunity as a row along with the primary keys for the other tables of interest. Figure 6-3 shows such a fact table.

The primary keys contained in a fact table are said to be the *dimensions* of the table, while the values contained in the fact table are called *measures*. Dimensions are used to create views of the measures in your reports. The fact table shown in Figure 6-3, for example, would allow us to create a report that shows sales opportunity dollar values by employee. This report is a classic sales pipeline used by all sales organizations.

In a data warehouse, the dimensions in the fact table are joined to tables that contain the actual values for the dimensions. This database structure results in a centralized fact table joined with many dimension tables. The resulting structure is called a *star schema* because the database diagram resembles a star. Figure 6-4 shows a star schema for the fact table presented in Figure 6-3.

	OpportunityFactID	Opportunity_Id	Employee_Id	Company_Id	Contact_Id	Territory_Id	Estimated_Total
▶	1	<Binary>	<Binary>	<Binary>	<Binary>	<Binary>	175914
	2	<Binary>	<Binary>	<Binary>	<Binary>	<Binary>	0
	3	<Binary>	<Binary>	<Binary>	<Binary>	<Binary>	1950000
	4	<Binary>	<Binary>	<Binary>	<Binary>	<Binary>	1875000
	5	<Binary>	<Binary>	<Binary>	<Binary>	<Binary>	262500
	6	<Binary>	<Binary>	<Binary>	<Binary>	<Binary>	290000
	7	<Binary>	<Binary>	<Binary>	<Binary>	<Binary>	350000
	8	<Binary>	<Binary>	<Binary>	<Binary>	<Binary>	700000
	9	<Binary>	<Binary>	<Binary>	<Binary>	<Binary>	190000
	10	<Binary>	<Binary>	<Binary>	<Binary>	<Binary>	71250
	11	<Binary>	<Binary>	<Binary>	<Binary>	<Binary>	2047500
	12	<Binary>	<Binary>	<Binary>	<Binary>	<Binary>	1365000
	13	<Binary>	<Binary>	<Binary>	<Binary>	<Binary>	1050000
	14	<Binary>	<Binary>	<Binary>	<Binary>	<Binary>	2047500
	15	<Binary>	<Binary>	<Binary>	<Binary>	<Binary>	713037.5
	16	<Binary>	<Binary>	<Binary>	<Binary>	<Binary>	1422645
	17	<Binary>	<Binary>	<Binary>	<Binary>	<Binary>	1426075
	18	<Binary>	<Binary>	<Binary>	<Binary>	<Binary>	148000
	19	<Binary>	<Binary>	<Binary>	<Binary>	<Binary>	1397095
	20	<Binary>	<Binary>	<Binary>	<Binary>	<Binary>	697095
	21	<Binary>	<Binary>	<Binary>	<Binary>	<Binary>	1225000

Figure 6-3. *A fact table*

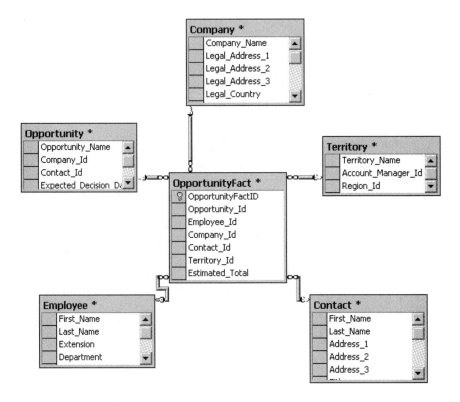

Figure 6-4. *A star schema*

Understanding Cubes

A data warehouse is an excellent structure for use with enterprise reporting tools like SQL Reporting Services; however, reporting represents only one part of an organization's business intelligence needs. Along with classic reporting, organizations need a way for information workers and senior management to analyze performance data. Analysis involves more than just static reporting because it allows people to answer questions by dynamically manipulating performance data.

As an example, consider what happens when an executive receives a report that quarterly earnings have dropped by 20 percent. The natural reaction is to ask why earnings are down. If an organization has no analysis capability, the IT department is left writing report after report trying to create a view of the data that will provide an answer. With the analysis capability embodied in a cube, data may be directly manipulated to provide different views without writing a single report.

A cube is built using the star schema of the data warehouse as a starting point. SQL Analysis Services, which is part of the SQL Server product family, transforms the data warehouse into a cube. Just like a data warehouse, the cube will have facts, measures, and dimensions. The difference between the data warehouse and the cube is that the cube will be optimized for analysis so that different views can be created on the fly without running a new report. Figure 6-5 shows a cube based on the star schema shown in Figure 6-4.

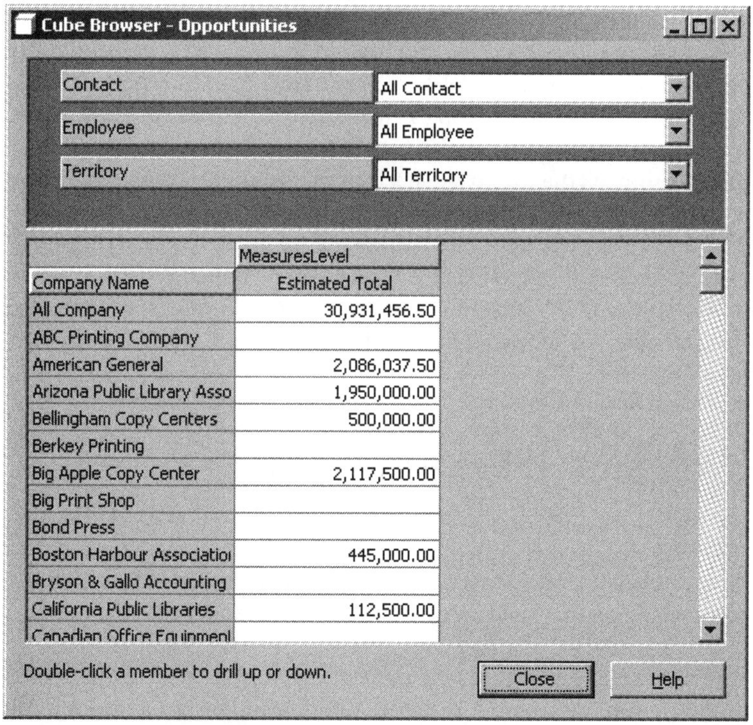

Company Name	MeasuresLevel
	Estimated Total
All Company	30,931,456.50
ABC Printing Company	
American General	2,086,037.50
Arizona Public Library Asso	1,950,000.00
Bellingham Copy Centers	500,000.00
Berkey Printing	
Big Apple Copy Center	2,117,500.00
Big Print Shop	
Bond Press	
Boston Harbour Associatio	445,000.00
Bryson & Gallo Accounting	
California Public Libraries	112,500.00
Canadian Office Equipment	

Figure 6-5. *Analyzing a cube*

Understanding Business Scorecards

Business scorecards are a particular mechanism for displaying cube data designed to support decision making at the executive level. In business scorecard language, the data points in a cube are called *measures*. From an organizational perspective, not all measures in a cube are of equal importance. Typically, organizations focus on just a few measurements that they believe will better help them understand and improve their performance. The most important measures are referred to as *key performance indicators (KPI)*.

BSA integrates with corporate data at the KPI level. In a scorecard, KPIs are compared to target goals and presented as a percentage. Converting all KPIs into a percentage of a goal helps to normalize their presentation so that they are easier to understand. Additionally, converting KPIs to percentage values allows them to be combined with other KPIs to create a rolled-up view of performance. Rolling up KPIs in scorecards is done through a weighted average that results in an aggregate value called an *objective*.

Objectives are important because they begin to translate the raw numeric values of measures into strategic metrics that indicate the performance of the organization. As an example, a company might have an objective to grow the business. This objective could be a combination of profitability and the number of new customer accounts opened. The profitability KPI measures the immediate growth, but the new customer accounts KPI measures what the growth will be in the future. This roll-up could be further enhanced by weighting the KPIs. Perhaps the organization wants immediate profitability to be weighted twice as much as new customer accounts. The resulting percentage indicates how well the company is growing.

Just as KPIs can be rolled up, objectives can be rolled up into *perspectives*. Perspectives are the highest level aggregation in a scorecard. If you were creating a balanced scorecard, then the perspectives are mandated by the methodology to be financial, customer, internal business processes, and learning and growth. If you are creating a generalized scorecard, however, the perspectives can be anything you want.

Along with aggregating measures all the way to perspectives, scorecards can also implement special groupings that focus attention on certain performance aspects. These special groupings are known as *themes* and *initiatives*. Themes and initiatives are used to group objectives together. This allows a scorecard to present an aggregate value that is not normally seen in a perspective. This grouping might exist only for a period of time during which the organization is focused on a particular theme or initiative. Figure 6-6 shows a typical scorecard containing many of the elements discussed in this section.

Creating a Development Environment

All of the scorecards built with BSA require SQL Analysis Services as the data source. Additionally, SQL Analysis Services requires service pack 2 (SP2) to run on Windows 2003 Server. Although the order is not technically important, you should install SQL Analysis Services and SP2 prior to installing BSA so that your installation process is in sync with the process described in this chapter. All of the examples and exercises used in this chapter assume that you have established a development environment with access to WSS or SPS, SQL Server, Analysis Services, Office Web Components (OWC), and Microsoft Visio 2003. The following sections will help you create the required environment.

Scorecard	Previous	Current	Target	Status
⊟ Enterprise Performance	84.75%	88.92%		◯
⊟ Customer	100%	100%		◯
⊟ Increase Customer Loyalty	100%	100%		▉▉▉▉
Issues	15	20	10	◯
Response Time	42	30	24	◯
⊟ Financial	59.51%	72.35%		◯
⊟ Increase Sales	59.51%	72.35%		▉▉▉
New Customers	12	10	15	△
Profit	32,000	51,000	48,000	◯
Revenue	280,000	320,000	450,000	△
⊟ Internal Business Process	100%	100%		◯
⊟ Improve Efficiency	100%	100%		▉▉▉▉
Defects	7	5	3	◯
⊟ Learning and Growth	79.5%	83.33%		◯
⊟ Become a top employer	79.5%	83.33%		▉▉▉▉
Certifications	22	30	25	◯
Retention	39	36	48	◯

Figure 6-6. *A business scorecard*

Installing Core Files

Although BSA relies on several other products for a complete solution, the base installation is relatively straightforward. Before you begin, however, you will need to download the BSA installation package. This package is located at www.microsoft.com/downloads/ details.aspx?FamilyId=3C4A9762-646B-41BD-9D42-5765B262624B&displaylang=en. Once you download and save the package MOBSASetup.msi, you are ready to begin installation.

■Caution If you completed the exercises in Chapter 1, then you will have defined a site template in the file WEBTEMPDL.xml that uses an ID of 10001. The BSA installation creates a template with this exact identifier, which will cause errors if both solutions are on the same server.

Follow these steps to install the core files:

1. Log in as an administrator on the server where SharePoint is installed and run MOBSASetup.msi.

2. Work through the first few screens of the installation wizard until you arrive at the Select Installation Type screen. In this screen, be sure that the Complete option is selected.

3. Work your way through the next few screens, which will verify installation prerequisites and the location of the web.config file. A standard installation of WSS or SPS should require no changes to these screens.

4. On the Scorecard Development Site Screen, enter the username and e-mail address for the person who will be the owner of the BSA development site.

5. On the Database Login Information screen, verify that the suggested values are appropriate for your installation of SQL Server.

6. On the Database Access Information screen, verify that the suggested application pool account is in fact the account running your installation of WSS or SPS.

7. Complete the installation wizard.

8. When the installation is complete, select Start ➤ All Programs ➤ Microsoft Office Business Scorecard Accelerator ➤ Scorecard Development Site. If your installation was successful, you should see the development site shown in Figure 6-7.

Figure 6-7. *The BSA development site*

Configuring the Scorecard Web Service

Although BSA is set up to create scorecards displayed in WSS or SPS, you may want to use the same functionality to create scorecards that are displayed using other front-ends such as ASP.NET or Microsoft Excel. BSA supports this type of custom development through the Scorecard Web Service (SWS). SWS exposes an application interface that gives programmatic access to much of the BSA functionality. SWS is installed as part of the core BSA installation, but it is not enabled by default.

Follow these steps to configure SWS:

1. Select Start ➤ Administrative Tools ➤ Internet Information Services (IIS) Manager.

2. In the IIS Manager, click the Web Service Extensions folder.

3. Ensure that ASP.NET is marked as Allowed.

4. Expand the Web Sites folder.

5. Right-click the Microsoft Business Scorecards Web Service node and select Properties from the context menu.

6. Click on the Home Directory tab.

7. In the Application Pool drop-down list, select the name of the application pool used by your SharePoint installation. This pool will also be used by SWS.

8. Click on the Directory Security tab.

9. In the Authentication and Access Control box, click the Edit button.

10. Verify that the only authentication method selected is Integrated Windows Authentication and click the OK button.

11. In the Properties dialog, click OK to save your changes.

12. Right-click the Microsoft Business Scorecards Web Service node and select Open from the context menu.

13. Open the `web.config` file in any text editor.

14. Locate the `appSettings` section and verify that the connection string is correct and that the `ConnectionPerUser` property is set to `False`. The following code shows an example:

```
<appSettings>
    <add key="Scorecard.ConnectionString" value="Integrated Security=SSPI;
    Initial Catalog=BusinessScorecards; Data Source=(local)"/>
    <add key="Scorecard.ConnectionPerUser" value="False"/>
</appSettings>
```

15. Save and close `web.config`.

16. In the IIS Manager, right-click the Microsoft Business Scorecards Web Service node and select Start from the context menu.

17. Verify the service is running correctly by right-clicking `ScorecardManagerService.asmx` and selecting Browse from the menu. You should see the page shown in Figure 6-8.

Creating a Test Scorecard Site Collection

When you install the core BSA files, a site is created to allow the development of scorecards; however, the development site is not used to display scorecards to end users. Scorecards can be displayed in any site collection once they are defined in the development site. In this chapter, we will create a site collection where we can display the scorecards we build. In a true business scenario, you will likely use existing WSS sites to display scorecards.

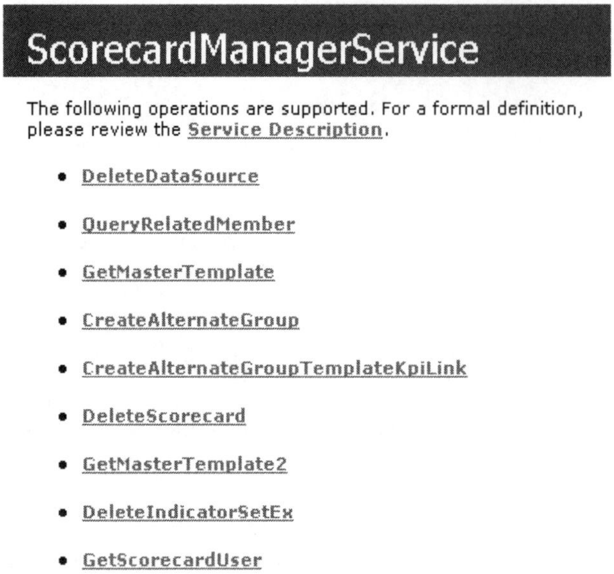

ScorecardManagerService

The following operations are supported. For a formal definition, please review the Service Description.

- DeleteDataSource
- QueryRelatedMember
- GetMasterTemplate
- CreateAlternateGroup
- CreateAlternateGroupTemplateKpiLink
- DeleteScorecard
- GetMasterTemplate2
- DeleteIndicatorSetEx
- GetScorecardUser

Figure 6-8. *The Scorecard Web Service description*

Follow these steps to create a test scorecard site:

1. Select Start ➤ All Programs ➤ Administrative Tools ➤ SharePoint Central Administration.

2. On the Central Administration page, select Virtual Server Configuration ➤ Create a Top-Level Web Site.

3. On the Virtual Server List page, select the virtual server where BSA is installed.

4. On the Create Top-level Web Site page, name the site **TestScorecards** and fill in the owner information.

5. Click the OK button to create the new site.

6. On the Top-Level Site Successfully Created page, click the Template Selection Page link.

7. On the Template Selection Page, select Blank Site and click the OK button to create the site.

8. When the new site appears, click the Create link.

9. On the Create page, click Document Library.

10. On the New Document Library page, name the Document Library **Scorecards**.

11. Select Web Part Page from the Document Template drop-down list.

12. Press Create to add the new Document Library.

13. After the new Document Library is created, click Site Settings.

14. On the Site Settings page, select Administration ➤ Go to Site Administration.

15. On the Top-Level Site Administration page, select Site Collection Galleries ➤ Manage Web Part gallery.

16. On the Web Part Gallery page, click Upload Web Part.

17. On the Upload Web Part page, click the Upload Multiple Files link.

18. Navigate to `\Program Files\Microsoft Office Business Scorecards Accelerator\ WebParts`.

19. Select to upload all of the web part description files (DWP) located in the directory.

20. Click Save and Close.

Installing Client Components

Clients using BSA features require several components to be installed on their machine. Business analysts who will create strategy maps require the full-client version of Microsoft Visio 2003. Anyone, including analysts with Visio installed, wanting to read strategy maps must have the Visio viewer installed. Additionally, OWC is used by BSA to display pivotal tables for analysis functions. These functions allow users to perform deeper analysis of scorecards and KPIs.

OWC and the Visio viewer are available as downloads from the Microsoft site. The OWC installation is contained in the package `owc11.exe` located at `www.microsoft.com/downloads/ details.aspx?familyid=7287252C-402E-4F72-97A5-E0FD290D4B76&displaylang=en`. The Visio viewer is contained in the package `vviewer.exe` located at `www.microsoft.com/downloads/ details.aspx?FamilyId=3FB3BD5C-FED1-46CF-BD53-DA23635AB2DF&displaylang=en`. All three of the installations—Visio, Visio viewer, and OWC—are straightforward and require no special considerations.

Creating Business Scorecards

Business scorecards are created by defining KPIs and then mapping them to measures within a cube. With the exception of creating the cube itself, all scorecard development is accomplished in the scorecard development site, which is created when you install BSA. In this section, I will cover the steps necessary to create a scorecard using the scorecard development site.

Defining Cubes and Sources

Once you have installed SQL Analysis Services, you are ready to make cubes to support your scorecards. All of the work to build a cube is accomplished using the Analysis Manager, which is accessible by selecting Start ➤ All Programs ➤ Microsoft SQL Server ➤ Analysis Services ➤ Analysis Manager. Exercise 6-1 at the end of the chapter takes you through the process of building a cube in detail so I will just summarize the steps here.

When you first run the Analysis Manager, you will notice that it already has a set of demo cubes installed called FoodMart 2000. If you expand the tree under this project, you will see that it consists of folders named Data Sources, Cubes, Shared Dimensions, Mining Models, and Database Roles. Every project you create will have the same folder structure, and this structure is actually maintained inside of a SQL Server database created by Analysis Manager. While Analysis Manager gives you complete control over the creation of your cubes, it also provides a set of wizards that make it easy to get started.

Once a new project database is created, you must create a data link that references the data warehouse where your star schema is located. This step is accomplished by right-clicking the Data Sources folder and selecting New Data Source from the context menu, which brings up a Data Link dialog.

After the data link is established, you can add the dimensions from the warehouse to your cube project. Do this by right-clicking the Shared Dimensions folder and selecting New Dimension ➤ Wizard. Using the wizard, you can select the dimension tables that map to your fact table.

Once you have defined all of the dimensions, you can use another wizard to build the cube itself. This is done by right-clicking the Cubes folder and selecting New Cube ➤ Wizard. In the wizard, you will associate the fact table with the dimensions. When you have completed the wizard, you can reference it in BSA from the Scorecard Data Sources page on the scorecard development site.

Defining Scorecard Elements

Scorecard elements such as perspectives, objectives, and KPIs are used as a structure to display and evaluate cube measures. BSA allows you to define these elements in the scorecard development site by clicking on the Scorecard Elements link in the Scorecard Modules list. Scorecard elements defined in BSA are independent of the cube used as the scorecard data source. This means that the scorecard elements you define can be generalized elements that may be mapped to more than one data source.

BSA provides a folder structure that allows you to define scorecard elements for balanced scorecards as well as general business scorecards. For example, you can create the classic balanced scorecard perspectives—financial, customer, internal business processes, and learning and growth—and reuse these for any scorecard you create. You could then define objectives such as "increase revenue" or "improve customer satisfaction" that can be grouped under the perspectives. Finally, you can create KPIs such as "profit" or "support issues" that will map to specific cube measures.

When you create scorecard elements, you can specify a weight for the element. This weighting affects the roll-up average performed by the scorecard. You can also associate documents with the elements through URLs that reference WSS Document Libraries. These documents might include related reports or perhaps a business plan that is pertinent to the scorecard element.

In addition to the quantitative roll-ups presented in a scorecard, you can select a graphical indicator for each element. The graphic shown in the scorecard is based on the number of *levels* that you select for the display. Selecting a level simply specifies how many steps exist between the data points in an element. If, for example, you select three levels, then the scorecard will always use a red, yellow, and green graphic that resembles a stoplight. If you select four or more levels for the element, then the scorecard shows a sliding gauge graphic.

Defining a Scorecard

Once the scorecard elements are defined, then you can use them to define a scorecard. Defining a scorecard is done by selecting the Scorecard Builder link in the Scorecard Modules list. The Scorecard Builder section allows you to group KPIs, objectives, and perspectives into a logical hierarchy that will make up the scorecard. This is a straightforward process of grouping the scorecard elements that you created earlier. Figure 6-9 shows a balanced scorecard definition in the Scorecard Builder.

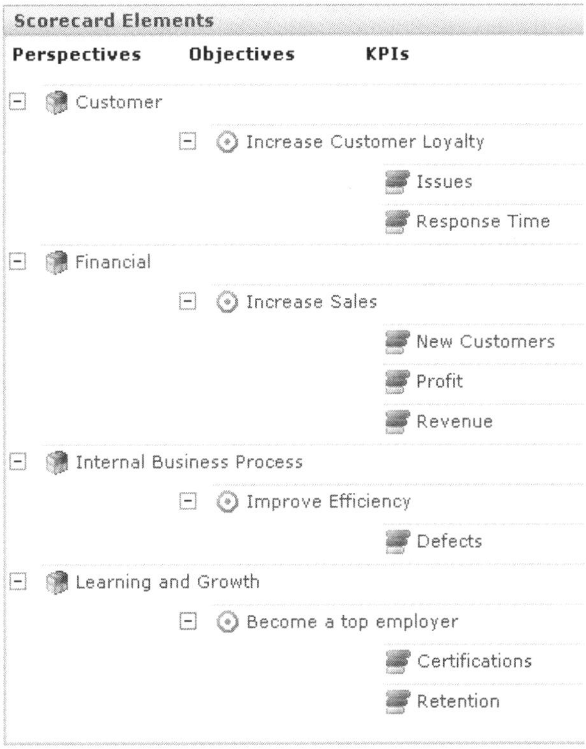

Figure 6-9. *The Scorecard Builder*

Along with grouping the KPIs, objectives, and perspectives, you may also want to adjust the *banding* associated with the KPIs. Banding is used by BSA to determine when a graphical indicator changes color or position. The default three-level banding, for example, uses 0–50 percent for red, 51–75 percent for yellow, and 76–100 percent for green. You can adjust these values to present the graphic that is appropriate for your card.

Mapping the Scorecard

Once the scorecard is defined, it must be mapped to a cube data source. The data sources were defined earlier, so all you have to do is associate the cube measures with the scorecard KPIs. This task is accomplished on the Scorecard Data Sources page. On this page, clicking the Scorecards link will show a list of all the scorecards you have defined. You can then select a scorecard and choose Map Scorecard from the menu. Figure 6-10 shows the menu item selected for a scorecard.

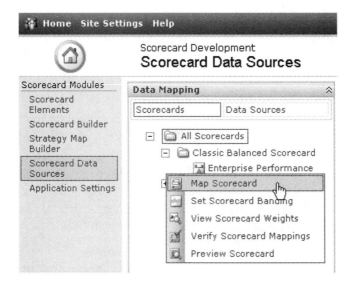

Figure 6-10. *Mapping a scorecard*

When you map a KPI to a measure, you must specify the source for the actual value and the target value. The data for these values can be specific entries you type in or can come from a cube measure or an MDX formula. MDX is the language used to query cubes. Writing these formulas will allow you greater control over how data is mapped to a KPI. You might, for example, use MDX to filter out certain values that could skew the scorecard in an unacceptable manner.

Defining a Strategy Map

Strategy maps are another way of viewing scorecard elements that can help analysts to create scorecards that better reflect business goals. Strategy maps are a particular feature of the balanced scorecard methodology and are not strictly required to create scorecards with BSA. BSA supports using strategy maps to create scorecard elements as well as using scorecard elements to create strategy maps. Whether or not you use strategy maps will depend on how strongly your organization has adopted the balanced scorecard methodology.

You create strategy maps on the Strategy Map Builder page. If your scorecard is already defined, then you can choose the scorecard and select Create Strategy Map from the menu. All you need to do is give the new map a name and BSA will create a strategy map based on the scorecard definition. Figure 6-11 shows a typical strategy map.

If you compare the strategy map in Figure 6-11 to the scorecard definition shown in Figure 6-9, you'll see how the strategy map relates to the scorecard. Once the strategy map is created, you can open it in Microsoft Visio and edit it. These edits can then be used to create scorecard elements.

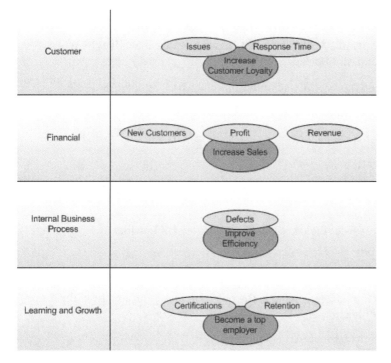

Figure 6-11. *A strategy map*

Managing Scorecard Security

Once scorecards are created, BSA allows you to specify whether they are available for public view or just for certain users. You can set the security levels for a scorecard on the Application Settings page by selecting Administration ➤ Manage Users for Scorecard Views. Using this page, you can designate a scorecard as private and select the users who have permission to view it.

Exercise 6-1. Creating a Simple Cube

BSA uses cubes as data sources to generate scorecards. Cubes in turn are created using SQL Analysis Services and use SQL databases as inputs. Typically, the database used as the basis for a cube is created with fact tables, measures, and dimensions in a star schema. In this exercise, however, you will create a cube based on the pubs database that ships with SQL Server. While this database is not designed with a star schema, we can use several of the related tables to show the basics of creating cubes.

Creating a New Database

Before you can build a cube, you must create a new database to hold the data sources, cubes, and dimensions that support cube creation. In this section you will create the new database and designate the data source for the cube. Once this basic structure is available, you can move on to define dimensions and build a cube.

Follow these steps to set up a new database:

1. Select Start ➤ All Programs ➤ Microsoft SQL Server ➤ Analysis Services ➤ Analysis Manager to start Analysis Manager.

2. In Analysis Manager, expand the tree until your analysis server node is visible.

3. Right-click the server name and select New Database from the context menu.

4. In the Database dialog, name the new database **PubsMart** and click the OK button.

5. Expand the PubsMart folder.

6. Right-click the Data Sources folder and select New Data Source from the context menu.

7. In the Data Link Properties dialog, select Microsoft OLE DB Provider for SQL Server from the Provider list.

8. Click the Next button.

9. Select the name of the SQL Server where the pubs database is located from the drop-down list on the Connection tab.

10. Enter appropriate credentials to access the database.

■Note If you use SQL Authentication for the database credentials, you must check the Allow Saving Password box or the connection will fail later in the exercise.

---

11. Select Pubs from the drop-down list on the Connection tab.

12. Click the OK button.

Creating Dimensions

The dimensions of a cube act as the categories by which information is sorted and grouped for display. A cube can have any number of dimensions such as time, geography, customer, or business unit. Additionally, dimensions can have multiple levels such as when geography is divided into country, region, and province. In this example, you will be creating a cube that views book sales information by title, publisher, and store.

Follow these steps to define the cube dimensions:

1. Right-click the Shared Dimensions folder and select New Dimension ➤ Wizard from the context menu.

2. When the Dimension Wizard starts, click the Next button.

3. On the Choose How You Want to Create the Dimension screen, select the Snowflake Schema: Multiple, Related Dimension Tables option and click the Next button.

4. On the Select the Dimension Tables screen, double-click the `titles` and `publishers` tables.

5. Click the Next button.

6. On the Create and Edit Joins screen, click the Next button.

7. On the Select the Levels for Your Dimension screen, select the `pub_name` field.

8. Click the Next button.

9. On the Specify the Member Key Columns screen, select `"dbo"."publishers".pub_id"` from the Member Key Column drop-down list and click the Next button.

10. On the Select Advanced Options screen, click the Next button.

11. On the Finish the Dimension Wizard screen, name the new dimension **Publishers** and click the Finish button.

12. When the Dimension Editor opens, select File ➤ Exit from the menu.

13. Right-click the Shared Dimensions folder and select New Dimension ➤ Wizard from the context menu.

14. When the Dimension Wizard starts, click the Next button.

15. On the Choose How You Want to Create the Dimension screen, select the Star Schema: A Single Dimension Table option and click the Next button.

16. On the Select the Dimension Table screen, double-click `stores` and click the Next button.

17. On the Select the Levels for Your Dimension screen, double-click the `stor_name` field.

18. On the Specify the Member Key Columns screen, select `"dbo"."stores"."stor_id"` from the Member Key Column drop-down list and click the Next button.

19. On the Select Advanced Options screen, click the Next button.

20. On the Finish the Dimension Wizard screen, name the new dimension **Stores** and click the Finish button.

21. When the Dimension Editor opens, select File ➤ Exit from the menu.

22. Right-click the Shared Dimensions folder and select New Dimension ➤ Wizard from the pop-up menu.

23. When the Dimension Wizard starts, click the Next button.

24. On the Choose How You Want to Create the Dimension screen, select the Star Schema: A Single Dimension Table option and click the Next button.

25. On the Select the Dimension Table screen, double-click `titles` and click the Next button.

26. On the Select the Dimension Type screen, select Standard Dimension and click the Next button.

27. On the Select the Levels for Your Dimension screen, double-click the `title` field and click the Next button.

28. On the Specify the Member Key Columns screen, select `"dbo"."titles"."title_id"` from the Member Key Column drop-down list and click the Next button.

29. On the Select Advanced Options screen, click the Next button.

30. On the Finish the Dimension Wizard screen, name the new dimension **Titles** and click the Finish button.

31. When the Dimension Editor opens, select File ➤ Exit from the menu.

Creating a New Cube

Once the dimensions are created, you can use them along with a fact table as the basis for a cube. In this exercise, you will use the `sales` table from the pubs database as a fact table. The dimensions you defined earlier will then provide different views of the sales information.

Follow these steps to create the Sales cube:

1. Right-click the Cubes folder and select New Cube ➤ Wizard from the context menu.

2. On the Welcome screen, click the Next button.

3. On the Select a Fact Table from a Data Source screen, select the `sales` table.

4. Click the Next button.

5. On the Select the Numeric Columns That Define Your Measures screen, double-click the `qty` field to make this field a measure in the cube.

6. Click the Next button.

7. On the Select Dimension for Your Cube screen, double-click the `Publishers`, `Titles`, and `Stores` dimensions you created earlier.

8. Click the Next button.

9. On the Finish the Cube screen, name the cube **Sales** and click the Finish button. The Cube Editor will open as shown in Figure 6-12.

10. Select File ➤ Save from the Cube Editor to save the cube.

11. Select Tools ➤ Design Storage from the Cube Editor.

12. When the Storage Design Wizard starts, click the Next button.

13. On the Select the Type of Data Storage screen, select MOLAP, which will save the data as a multidimensional cube, and click the Next button.

14. On the Set Aggregation Options screen, select the option Until I Click Stop and click the Start button.

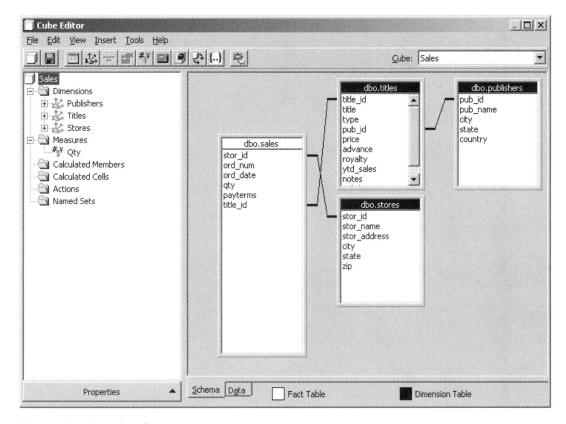

Figure 6-12. *The Cube Editor*

15. When the aggregation design process is complete, click the Next button.

16. On the Finish the Storage Design Wizard screen, select the option Process Now and click the Finish button.

17. When the processing is completed, close the Process window.

18. In the Cube Editor, select File ➤ Exit.

19. In Analysis Manager, right-click the Sales cube and select Browse Data from the context menu. You should see the cube data shown in Figure 6-13.

Exercise 6-2. Creating a Balanced Scorecard

After you have created cubes to contain measures, you can move on to create scorecards with BSA. In this exercise, you will use the scorecard development site to create a basic scorecard. This exercise will use the cube from Exercise 6-1 as a data source, so be sure to complete that exercise before beginning this one.

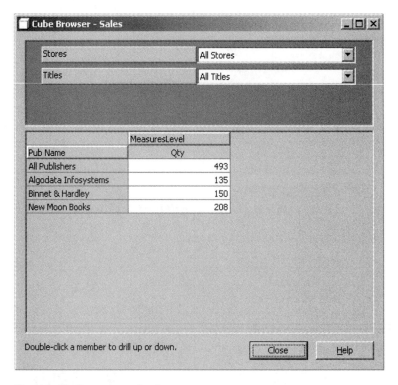

Figure 6-13. *Browsing cube data*

Defining Scorecard Elements

Scorecard elements are used as the framework for displaying measures and rolling them up. The rolled-up values are used to indicate the performance of an organization against an objective. In this exercise, you will create a perspective, objective, and KPI.

Follow these steps to create the scorecard elements:

1. Open the Scorecard Development Site by selecting Start ➤ All Programs ➤ Microsoft Office Business Scorecards Accelerator ➤ Scorecard Development Site.

2. Click on the Scorecard Elements link in the Scorecard Modules list.

3. On the Scorecard Elements page, expand the Balanced Scorecard Elements folder.

4. Hover over the Perspectives folder until a downward-facing triangle appears.

5. Click the downward-facing triangle and select Create Perspective from the drop-down menu.

6. Name the new perspective **Stores** and click the OK button.

7. Hover over the Objectives folder until a downward-facing triangle appears.

8. Click the downward-facing triangle and select Create Objective from the drop-down menu.

9. Name the new objective **Increase Sales**.

10. Select the Stores perspective from the Perspective for Objective drop-down list.

11. Click the OK button.

12. Hover over the KPIs (All Scorecards) folder until a downward-facing triangle appears.

13. Click the downward-facing triangle and select Create KPI from the drop-down menu.

14. Name the new KPI **Units Sold**.

15. Select Quarterly from the Frequency of Data drop-down list.

16. Enter **100** in the KPI Current Model Value text box.

17. Enter **50** in the KPI Previous Model Value text box.

18. Enter **200** in the Target Model Value text box.

19. Click the OK button.

Defining a Scorecard

Once the scorecard elements are defined, you can use them to create a scorecard. The scorecard relates the perspectives, objectives, and KPIs. In this exercise, you will create a scorecard that shows sales performance for book titles.

Follow these steps to define the scorecard:

1. Click on the Scorecard Builder link in the Scorecard Modules list.

2. Hover over the All Scorecards folder until a downward-facing triangle appears.

3. Click the downward-facing triangle and select Create Folder from the drop-down menu.

4. In the pop-up dialog, name the new folder **Exercise 6-2** and click the OK button.

5. Hover over the Exercise 6-2 folder until a downward-facing triangle appears.

6. Click the downward-facing triangle and select Create Scorecard from the drop-down menu.

7. Name the new scorecard **Titles** and click the OK button.

8. Hover over the Titles scorecard node until a downward-facing triangle appears.

9. Click the downward-facing triangle and select Add Perspective from the drop-down menu.

10. On the pop-up dialog, check the Stores perspective and click the OK button.

11. In the Scorecards Elements section, hover over the Stores perspective until a downward-facing triangle appears.

12. Click the downward-facing triangle and select Add Objective from the drop-down menu.

13. In the pop-up dialog, check the Increase Sales objective and click the OK button.

14. In the Scorecards Elements section, hover over the Increase Sales objective until a downward-facing triangle appears.

15. Click the downward-facing triangle and select Add KPI from the drop-down menu.

16. In the pop-up dialog, check the Units Sold KPI option and click the OK button.

17. Hover over the Titles scorecard node until a downward-facing triangle appears.

18. Click the downward-facing triangle and select Preview Scorecard from the drop-down menu. You should see the scorecard preview shown in Figure 6-14.

Scorecard	Previous	Current	Target
⊟ Titles	16.67%	33.33%	
⊟ Stores	16.67%	33.33%	
⊟ Increase Sales	16.67%	33.33%	
Units Sold	50	100	200

Figure 6-14. *Scorecard preview*

Creating a Strategy Map

A strategy map is a visual representation of a scorecard. While strategy maps are not required to create scorecards in BSA, some analysts like to use them as a tool for mapping scorecards to business strategy. In this exercise, you'll build a simple strategy map from a scorecard definition.

Follow these steps to build a strategy map:

1. Click on the Strategy Map Builder link in the Scorecard Modules list.

2. Hover over the Titles scorecard node until a downward-facing triangle appears.

3. Click the downward-facing triangle and select Create Strategy Map from the drop-down menu.

4. Name the new strategy map **Sales Strategy** and click the OK button. You should see the strategy map preview shown in Figure 6-15.

Mapping the Scorecard

Once the scorecard is created, you can map the KPIs to measures. When mapping the scorecard, you must provide mappings for the actual and target values. In this exercise, you will map the actual display to a cube measure and the target display to a fixed value.

Follow these steps to map the scorecard:

1. Click on the Scorecard Data Sources link in the Scorecard Modules list.

2. In the Data Mapping section, click the Data Sources link.

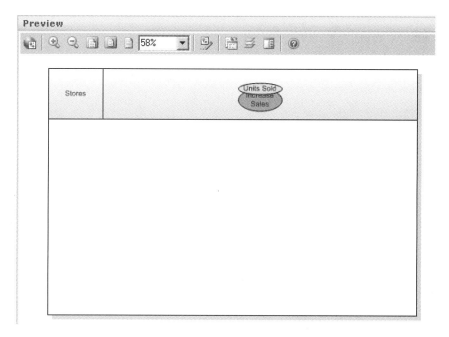

Figure 6-15. *Strategy map preview*

3. Hover over the All Data Sources folder until a downward-facing triangle appears.

4. Click the downward-facing triangle and select Create Data Source from the drop-down menu.

5. Name the new data source **Analysis Services**.

6. In the Server Name text box, enter the name of the server where you created the cube in Exercise 6-1 and click the Connect button.

7. Select PubsMart from the Database Name drop-down list and click the Test Connection button.

8. After the connection is verified, click the OK button.

9. In the Data Mapping section, click the Scorecards link.

10. Expand the tree and hover over the Titles scorecard node until a downward-facing triangle appears.

11. Click the downward-facing triangle and select Map Scorecard from the drop-down menu.

12. In the Select Data Source drop-down list, select Analysis Services.

13. In the Select Cube drop-down list, select Sales.

14. In the Actual Information drop-down list, select Cube Measure. The Qty field should appear automatically.

15. In the Target Information drop-down list, select Single Value.

16. Enter a target value of **500** for the scorecard.

17. Click the OK button.

Viewing the Scorecard

Once the mapping is complete, the scorecard is ready for use. BSA provides several web parts that provide different views of the scorecard. In this exercise, you will display the scorecard using a web part that provides a standard view.

Follow these steps to display the scorecard:

1. Navigate to the home page of the Test Scorecards site collection you created earlier in this chapter.

2. From the home page, click the Create link.

3. On the Create page, select to create a Web Part Page.

4. Name the new page **BookSales** and click the Create button.

5. Drag the Scorecard Standard View web part from the web part pane and drop it into a zone.

6. Click the downward-facing triangle on the web part and select Modify Shared Web Part from the drop-down menu.

7. Select Titles from the Scorecard drop-down list in the properties list and click the OK button. You should see the scorecard shown in Figure 6-16.

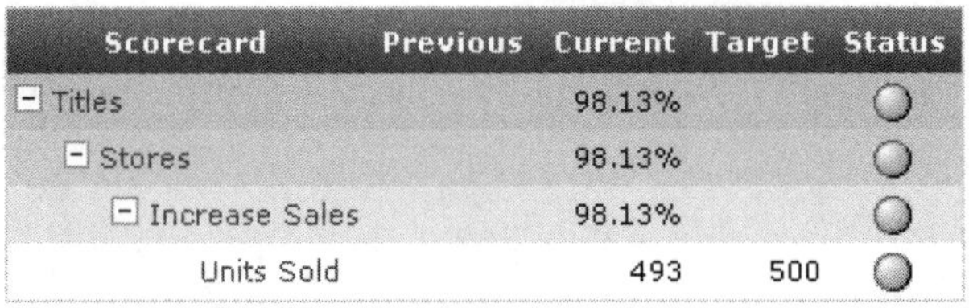

Scorecard	Previous	Current	Target	Status
⊟ Titles		98.13%		○
⊟ Stores		98.13%		○
⊟ Increase Sales		98.13%		○
Units Sold		493	500	○

Figure 6-16. *The final scorecard*

■■■

CHAPTER 7

SharePoint and BizTalk Server 2004

Microsoft BizTalk Server (BTS) 2004 is an application integration platform that allows you to interconnect different systems whether those systems are part of the same infrastructure or shared between business partners. This capability is of particular interest to SharePoint developers because Windows SharePoint Services (WSS) provides very little native support for business process automation and Enterprise Application Integration (EAI). Even a process as simple as approving a vacation request cannot easily be created in WSS. In this chapter, I'll show how you can use a combination of BTS, WSS, and Microsoft Office 2003 to interconnect systems and add business processes to your SharePoint solutions.

The latest version of BTS contains many different components that go beyond simple message processing. Some of these components are designed to facilitate automated processes between trading partners or improve the productivity of information workers. My goal in this chapter is to introduce the basic message processing functionality that is central to BTS and show how it can be integrated with SharePoint.

Understanding BizTalk Server Architecture

Although BTS consists of many different components, conceptually it is a simple product. At the highest level, BTS receives data from one application, processes the data, and delivers the resulting data to another application. Therefore, BTS must provide a mechanism to send and receive data from multiple systems using different protocols along with a processing engine. Figure 7-1 shows an architectural diagram of BTS.

Understanding BTS Adapters

Because BTS must be capable of interacting with many different systems that utilize a wide variety of protocols, the input and output interfaces of the BTS engine must be generalized. This generalization is accomplished through the use of *adapters*. Adapters exist to send and receive data using any number of standard protocols as well as some specialized ones—including an adapter that integrates with WSS libraries. Table 7-1 lists the available standard and custom BTS adapters.

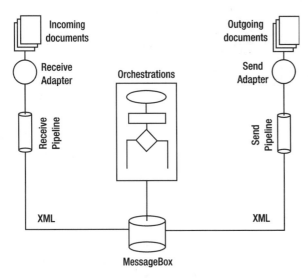

Figure 7-1. *The BizTalk Server architecture*

Table 7-1. *BTS Adapters*

Adapter	Description
FILE	Supports the exchange of information through standard file directories
HTTP	Supports the exchange of information by exposing URLs as locations for sending or receiving data
FTP	Supports the exchange of information through FTP servers
Base EDI	Supports the exchange of information through the standard Electronic Data Interchange format
SOAP	Supports the exchange of information by exposing web services for sending and receiving data
MSMQT	Supports the exchange of information through the Microsoft Message Queuing (MSMQ) protocol
SMTP	Supports the exchange of information using standard e-mail addresses for sending and receiving data
SQL	Supports the exchange of information through SQL Server databases
WSSLib	Supports the exchange of information through WSS libraries

When creating BTS solutions, a process may be connected to different systems by selecting different send and receive adapters. You could, for example, receive InfoPath documents from a WSS Document Library and deliver them to a partner through a web service. Because adapters are managed administratively, they may be easily changed to allow the same process to interact with different systems. Thus, BTS solutions are more easily reused than custom solutions built from scratch.

Understanding BTS Pipelines

One of the key points to understand about BTS is that it only works with XML messages internally. This means that documents must be converted to an XML message before BTS can execute a process. Reverse conversion may also be required after the BTS process runs to transform the internal XML message into a format expected by the receiving system. The processing that occurs before and after a BTS process executes is accomplished by a *pipeline*.

BTS provides some default pipelines that you can use to send and receive messages that are already in the proper XML format. Additionally, pipelines for interacting with WSS libraries are available. If you want to go further, however, you can create your own custom pipeline that will allow you to send and receive messages in virtually any format. In the exercise at the end of the chapter, you will create a custom pipeline to work with InfoPath forms.

Understanding Orchestrations

After a message is received through the adapter and processed through the pipeline, it is dropped into the *MessageBox*. The MessageBox is a SQL Server database that stores the message. BTS then directs the message to a business process called an *orchestration*. The orchestration is responsible for implementing the business rules, transforming the message, and delivering it to the outgoing send pipeline.

Orchestrations are the heart of BTS. While adapters and pipelines provide connectivity to other systems, orchestrations provide the business process automation that adds value to the solution. In an orchestration, you can make decisions based on data in the XML message, alter the data, and define parallel paths, loops, and other constructs that are necessary to implement a business process. Orchestrations are created in BTS solutions using graphical tools that mimic flow chart diagrams. Orchestrations can either be created directly in Visual Studio .NET or using the Orchestration Designer for Business Analysts, which is an add-in to Microsoft Visio.

Setting up a Development Environment

Before we begin to investigate how BTS works with WSS, we must create a suitable development environment. Ultimately, setting up BTS will depend on your particular needs, but I want to present a basic single-server setup that you can use to work all of the examples and the exercise in this chapter. Therefore, I will assume that you have a Windows 2003 Server available with WSS and Microsoft Visual Studio .NET already installed.

In addition to SQL Server, you can also install SQL Analysis Services. Along with the Office Web Components (OWC), Analysis Services is used by BTS to support some advanced analysis. While Analysis Services is not required for the BTS solutions in this chapter, using some of the advanced components of BTS will make it necessary. If you completed the Business Scorecard Accelerator exercises from the previous chapter, you already have Analysis Services installed and configured.

■**Caution** While the Business Scorecards Accelerator (BSA) only requires service pack 2 for Analysis Services, BTS requires service pack 3a.

Installing the Required Updates

Before you can install BTS, you must install several updates to SQL Server and XML Services. These updates are available from the Microsoft site. Download and install the updates in the order listed in Table 7-2.

■**Note** You will be prompted to reboot after installing some of the updates. For simplicity, you can perform all the updates and reboot the server one time at the end.

Table 7-2. *Required Updates*

Filename	Description	Location
sql2kasp3.exe	SQL Analysis Services, SP3a	http://www.microsoft.com/ sql/downloads/2000/sp3.asp
owc11.exe	Office Web Components	http://www.microsoft.com/downloads/ details.aspx?familyid=7287252C-402E- 4F72-97A5-E0FD290D4B76&displaylang=en
msxml.msi	XML Core Services MSXML 4.0, SP2	http://go.microsoft.com/fwlink/ ?LinkId=22826
msxml3*xxx*.msi	XML Parser MSXML 3.0, SP4, where *xxx* is a region designation	http://go.microsoft.com/fwlink/ ?LinkId=22827
sqlxml.msi	XML Support for SQL Server SQLXML 3.0, SP2	http://go.microsoft.com/fwlink/ ?LinkId=22830
SQL2000-KB810185- 8.00.0878-*xxx*.exe	Update Q831950 for SQL Server, where *xxx* is a region designation.	http://go.microsoft.com/fwlink/ ?LinkId=22840

Installing BizTalk Server 2004

Once the updates are applied, installing the core BTS files is straightforward; however, the server configuration that follows the installation is not. During the configuration process, you will have to create several Active Directory groups and will be presented with many options. Therefore, I find it best to perform the installation as a domain administrator. In this section, I'll assume that you have the required privileges.

Creating Required Groups

Before beginning the installation process, you should create the required groups. I am going to keep this process simple by assuming that you have administrator privileges and that you will run all BTS services under this account. Obviously, this type of configuration is inappropriate for production, but it will allow you to get up and running quickly.

■**Note** I recommend creating stand-alone environments using VMware or Microsoft Virtual Server sessions for this chapter. This configuration allows complete control over domain resources without causing issues for other developers on the corporate network. If you are not yet using these products to create development environments, I highly recommend you investigate them.

Follow these steps to create the required BTS groups:

1. Log into the primary domain controller as a domain administrator.

2. Select Start ➤ Administrative Tools ➤ Active Directory Users and Computers.

3. Create the new groups defined in Table 7-3.

4. Add your user account to each of the new groups.

Table 7-3. *Required Groups*

Group Name	Description
BizTalk BAS Administrators	Administrators of Business Activity Services
BizTalk BAS Managers	A group that can configure Business Activity Services
BizTalk BAS Users	Users of Business Activity Services
BizTalk BAS Web Services Group	Accounts under which Business Activity Services run
EDI Subsystem Users	Users of the Electronic Document Interchange system
BizTalk Application Users	Users of BizTalk services
BizTalk Server Administrators	The main administration group for BTS
SSO Administrators	Administrators of the Single Sign-On system
SSO Affiliate Administrators	Administrators of affiliate applications
BizTalk Isolated Host Users	Users of BizTalk services that are deployed as web services

Installing the Server Software

After the required updates are installed, you can insert the BTS CD and begin the server installation process. Generally, you can perform a complete installation of BTS unless you have previously installed the Microsoft Single Sign-On service as part of a SharePoint Portal Server installation. In this case, you should perform a custom installation and remove the Enterprise Single Sign-On and Enterprise Single Sign-On Administration components before proceeding.

The installation process will begin by installing several required prerequisites after which you will have to reboot. Following the server reboot, the BTS files will be installed. When the installation is complete, you will be prompted to configure BTS.

■**Note** If you have to exit the Configuration Wizard for any reason, you can always run it again from the location \Program Files Microsoft BizTalk Server 2004\ConfigFramework.exe.

Follow these steps to configure BTS:

1. After BTS is installed, ensure that the box is checked to run the Configuration Wizard and click the Finish button.

2. On the Welcome screen, click the Next button.

3. On the Configuration Options screen, accept the default settings and click the Next button.

4. On the second Configuration Options screen, accept the default settings and click the Next button. If you do not have Analysis Services installed, uncheck the items that require it.

5. On the Windows Accounts screen, you will see a listing of groups that match the groups you created earlier. Note that many of these groups will have information icons next to them indicating that they are improperly configured. Figure 7-2 shows the Windows Accounts screen.

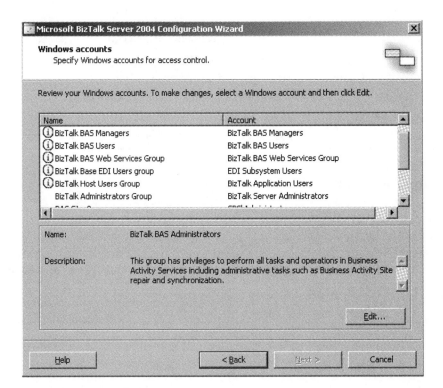

Figure 7-2. *The Windows Accounts screen*

6. Double-click each of the groups in the Windows Accounts list and enter the fully qualified name of the group you created earlier. Generally, this simply means that you must
prefix the existing group name with your domain name. Figure 7-3 shows an example
of this configuration.

▪**Note** Although some groups may not have an exclamation point icon next to them, you should configure
them anyway. This will ensure that the Configuration Wizard properly recognizes the groups you have created.

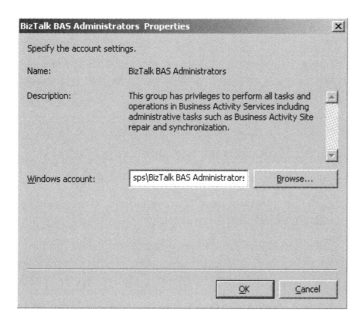

Figure 7-3. *Group properties*

7. After you have configured each group, click the Next button.

8. On the Addresses screen, ensure that the Configuration Wizard has a valid WSS location where it can create the Business Activity Services site and click the Next button.

9. On the Configuration Property Values screen, accept the default values and click the
Next button.

10. On the Web Sites screen, select the web site to use for the Human Workflow Services
web service and click the Next button.

▪**Note** If you select a site that is extended with Windows SharePoint Services, the Configuration Wizard will
automatically exclude the HWS paths from WSS.

---

11. On the Database Configurations screen, accept the default settings and click the Next button.

12. On the Windows Service Configurations screen, you will see a list of BizTalk services that must be associated with a Windows account. Although a production deployment would require special accounts with limited permissions, you can simply assign your own account to each of these services.

■**Note** If you assign an administrator account to these services, you will receive a warning. For the purposes of creating a simplified development environment, you can ignore this warning.

■**Caution** You should use a fully qualified reference to the account to ensure a trouble-free configuration (e. g., sps.local\administrator). Make sure this is a complete LDAP reference and not an old-style NETBIOS reference like sps\administrator.

---

13. When you have finished configuring the accounts, click the Next button.

14. On the BizTalk Messaging screen, accept the defaults and click the Next button.

15. On the Windows SharePoint Services Site Configuration screen, change the Site e-mail setting to your e-mail address and click the Next button.

16. On the Summary screen, click the Next button to complete the configuration.

Installing the WSS Adapter

One of the primary ways that BTS integrates with WSS is through a special adapter. This adapter allows BTS to receive XML documents from a WSS library, process them, and post them to another library. The WSS Adapter is not part of the base BTS installation so you must download the zip file package named BTS2004SharePointAdap.zip from www.gotdotnet.com/Community/Workspaces/viewuploads.aspx?id=0d1aa85c-cf8d-497e-84f4-3ffec8db115f before you can install it.

After you download the package, extract the zip file. Within this zip file, you will find a document describing the adapter and a self-extracting zip file named WSSAdapter.exe. When you unpack these files, you will find three more self-extracting zip files named WSSAdapterCode.exe, WSSAdapterSamples.exe, and WSSAdapterDeploy.exe. WSSAdapterDeploy.exe is used to install the adapter.

Follow these steps to install the adapter:

1. Double-click the file WSSAdapterDeploy.exe.

2. When prompted, unzip the files to the default location.

3. Open the Windows File Explorer and navigate to the file SharePointAdapter.reg located at \Program Files\Microsoft BizTalk Server 2004\SDK\Samples\Adapters\SharePoint\SharePoint Adapter.

4. Double-click the REG file to register the adapter for use.

5. Select Start ➤ All Programs ➤ Microsoft BizTalk Server 2004 ➤ BizTalk Server Administration to open the administration console.

6. In the BizTalk Server Administration Console, expand the Microsoft BizTalk Server 2004 node and click on the Adapters folder.

7. Right-click the Adapters folder and select New ➤ Adapter from the pop-up menu.

8. In the Add Adapter dialog, type **WSSLib** into the Name field.

9. Select WSSLib from the Adapter drop-down list.

10. Type **BizTalk Adapter for SharePoint Libraries** into the Comment field.

11. Click the OK button to close the dialog.

12. Select Start ➤ Administrative Tools ➤ Services to open the Services applet.

13. In the Services applet, restart the BizTalk Service BizTalk Group: BizTalkServerApplication service.

14. Copy the file `WSSDocLibServices.asmx` located at `\Program Files\Microsoft BizTalk Server 2004\SDK\Samples\Adapters\SharePoint\SharePoint WebServices\ WSSWebServices` to the SharePoint server folder `\Program Files\Common Files\ Microsoft Shared\web server extensions\60\ISAPI`.

15. Copy the file `WSSWebServices.dll` located at `\Program Files\Microsoft BizTalk Server 2004\SDK\Samples\Adapters\SharePoint\SharePoint WebServices\ WSSWebServices` to the SharePoint server folder `\Program Files\Common Files\ Microsoft Shared\web server extensions\60\ISAPI\bin`.

16. Verify the web service is properly installed by browsing to the URL `http://server name/_vti_bin/WSSDocLibService.asmx`. Figure 7-4 shows the web service displayed in the browser.

Creating a Test BizTalk Site Collection

Because BTS uses XML files as a primary input, InfoPath forms stored in a Document Library are an excellent way to initiate BTS processes. These forms can be used to initiate batch processes that do not require human interaction or approval processes in which several people view the same form. In this section, you'll create a new site collection that you can use with the examples in this chapter.

Follow these steps to create a test BTS site:

1. Select Start ➤ All Programs ➤ Administrative Tools ➤ SharePoint Central Administration.

2. On the Central Administration page, select Virtual Server Configuration ➤ Create a top-level Web site.

3. On the Virtual Server List page, select the virtual server where WSS is installed.

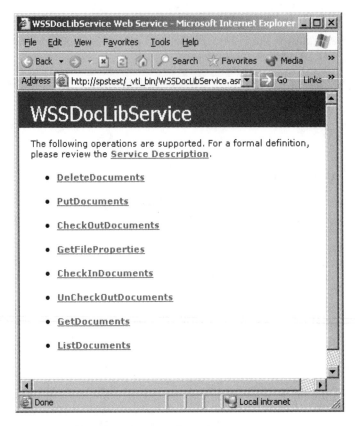

Figure 7-4. *The WSS Adapter web service*

4. On the Create Top-Level Web Site page, name the site **TestBizTalk** and fill in the owner information.

5. Click the OK button to create the new site.

6. On the Top-Level Site Successfully Created page, click the Open the Template Selection Page link.

7. On the Template Selection Page, select Blank Site and click the OK button to create the site.

Creating BizTalk Server Solutions

Creating BTS solutions is done directly in Visual Studio. NET. If you performed a complete installation, the development support components will be installed, which makes several new project types available in Visual Studio .NET. For most projects, you can simply use the Empty BizTalk Server Project shown in Figure 7-5. In this section, I'll take you through the fundamental tasks necessary to create and deploy a BTS solution that integrates with WSS.

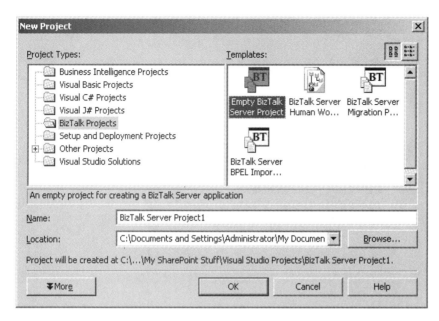

Figure 7-5. *The Empty BizTalk Server Project*

Working with Message Schemas

The first step in creating a BTS solution is to define the message schemas that represent the inputs and outputs of the orchestration. Remember that BTS uses only XML messages internally, and it expects these messages to be well defined. Therefore, you must begin by creating the schemas that define the messages. In a basic BTS solution, you will typically need to define at least one schema for the input message and another for the output message.

You can add a new schema directly to a BTS solution by selecting Project ➤ Add New Item from the main menu in Visual Studio .NET The schema item is available as one of the selection in the New Item dialog. Once the new schema is added to the project, the BizTalk Editor starts. The BizTalk Editor is a schema-editing tool that creates schemas that are fully compliant with the XML Schema definition language (XSD).

When you are creating solutions that integrate WSS and BTS, you will quite often use InfoPath forms to create and view XML. InfoPath is an ideal tool for BTS solutions because it stores data natively in XML and is also fully compliant with XSD. This means that you can either create InfoPath forms from BTS schemas or you can create BTS schemas from InfoPath forms.

Creating an InfoPath form from a BTS schema is done in InfoPath by choosing to design a form based on an existing schema. This is one of the options when you select Design a Form ➤ New from XML Document or Schema. Once the schema is opened, you will be able to drag the nodes onto the design surface and create a form. The final form will then be able to function as an input message to a BTS orchestration.

Importing a schema from an InfoPath form into a BTS solution is also fairly simple. Whenever you create a new InfoPath form, it is saved as an XSN file. While the XSN file appears to be unique to InfoPath, it is actually a cabinet file that contains all of the components in the form. One of those components is the form schema. Therefore, it is a simple matter to open the XSN file in a tool like WinZip and remove the schema file. Once you have the schema as a separate file, you can add it to your BTS project. Figure 7-6 shows a typical XSN file opened in WinZip.

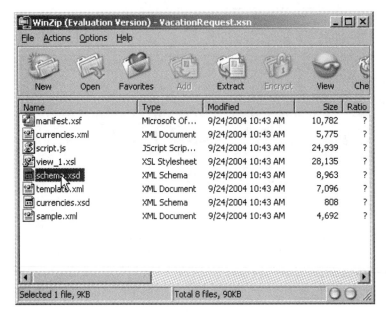

Figure 7-6. *An InfoPath XSN file open in WinZip*

■**Caution** Take care to ensure that you give all of your schemas globally unique names to avoid conflicts with other deployed schemas. The best practice is to adopt a strict naming standard that guarantees uniqueness. I use the format Schema_[verb]_[noun] (e.g., Schema_Request_Vacation.xsd).

Creating Schema Maps

Almost without exception you will find that most of the information in the input message is also contained in the output message. Therefore, you will want to transfer the data from the input message to the output message at some point in your orchestration. Additionally, you will find that the transferred data may need to be transformed as it moves from the input message to the output message. For example, you may need to change the format of currency from U.S. dollars to Japanese yen, or add a date/time stamp indicating when the data was processed. These types of relationships and transformations are accomplished using a schema map.

Schema maps in BTS are fully compliant with the Extensible Stylesheet Language Transformation (XSLT) specification and can be added to a BTS solution using the New Item dialog. When a new map is added to the project, the BizTalk Mapper opens in Visual Studio .NET. The BizTalk Mapper is a graphical tool used to define the relationships and transformations between schema nodes. When creating the new map, you specify a source and destination schema for which you want to define a relationship.

Transferring data from the input message to the output message is a simple matter of dragging from the source schema node to the destination schema node. Complex transformations between nodes are accomplished by using *functoids*. Functoids are transformation function blocks that you may insert between two nodes. BTS provides a number of predefined functoids that are accessible from the toolbox in Visual Studio .NET. Table 7-4 lists the categories of available functoids.

Table 7-4. *BizTalk Mapper Functoid Categories*

Category	Description
Advanced functoids	These functoids represent advanced functionality such as scripting.
Conversion functoids	These functoids are used to convert numeric and character data types.
Cumulative functoids	These functoids are used to operate on values that appear multiple times.
Database functoids	These functoids are used to retrieve data from a database.
Date/Time functoids	These functoids are used to add date/time information to a message.
Logical functoids	These functoids represent logical operations such as Boolean math and comparison operators.
Mathematical functoids	The functoids are used to perform mathematical operations.
Scientific functoids	These functoids are used to perform scientific functions such as logarithms.
String functoids	These functoids are used to perform string manipulations.

Using a functoid in a map is done by dragging the functoid from the toolbox onto the mapping grid, which is a gray area located between the two schemas. Once the functoid is dropped on the mapping grid, you can connect nodes from the source and destination schema to complete the transformation. As an example, consider a vacation request form with fields representing your current balance, requested vacation, and new balance. The current balance and requested vacation fields could map directly from the input to the output message, but the new balance could be calculated with a subtraction functoid. Figure 7-7 shows how the transformation might appear in the BizTalk Mapper.

Promoting Schema Properties

After you have created the schemas and defined the relationships between them, you must decide which schema fields will be promoted. By default, all data contained in an XML message is private to the message. Promotion represents a change in variable scope that makes a field available to the entire BizTalk orchestration. Therefore, you will want to promote fields that will be used for branching decisions or will be directly manipulated by the BTS orchestration.

As an example, consider a message representing a requisition for copier paper. An end user fills out an InfoPath form requesting ten reams of paper. This form is submitted to a BTS orchestration for automatic review and approval. This process determines if the request should be approved based on several factors, including the Quantity field of the incoming message. It responds by updating the Status field of the outgoing message to indicate approval or rejection. In this case, the Quantity field of the input schema and the Status field of the output schema must be promoted.

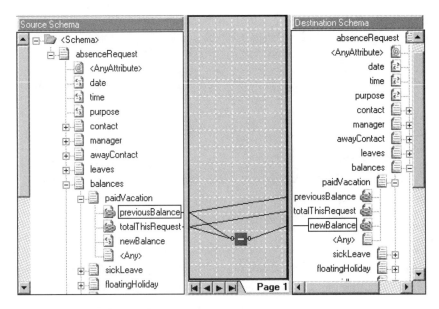

Figure 7-7. *Using functoids in a map*

You can promote any field by right clicking it in the schema editor and selecting Promote ➤ Quick Promotion. When you promote a field, a new schema is added to the project that contains the information describing the promoted fields. Additionally, you can review and change the schema promotions at any time by right-clicking a schema node and selecting Promote ➤ Show Promotions from the context menu.

Validating Schemas and Maps

After you create schemas, maps, and promotions, you can validate them in Visual Studio. NET. To validate a schema, simply right-click it in the solution explorer and select Validate Schema from the context menu. The results of the validation will appear in the Output Window.

While validating the schema, you may also want to create a message instance based on the schema that you can use for debugging. This is done by specifying a filename for the message in the schema properties and then generating a message instance. You can access the Properties dialog by right-clicking the schema file in the solution explorer and selecting Properties from the context menu. Figure 7-8 shows the Properties dialog for a schema file.

The Output Instance Filename property is used to specify the complete path and filename for an XML file that will contain a valid instance generated from the schema. This property is initially blank, and you can specify any filename you want because it will be generated later. I recommend generating this file directly into the solution directory for your project and giving it a meaningful name such as Instance_Input.xml. Once you have specified the filename and location, you can close the Properties dialog, right-click the schema in the solution explorer, and select Generate Instance from the context menu. This will create the file.

Once the file is created, you can open the Properties dialog again and reference this file from the Input Instance Filename property. Once you reference the instance, be sure to validate it by right-clicking the schema in the solution explorer and selecting Validate Instance.

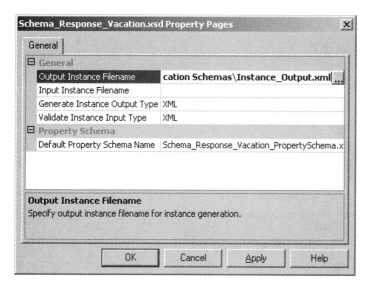

Figure 7-8. *Schema properties*

The validated instance can now be used to validate any maps that you created earlier. Simply right-click an associated map in the solution explorer and select Validate Map from the context menu, then select Test Map. You should be sure that you have successfully validated and tested the schemas and maps before continuing to develop your BTS solution—this will save you a lot of trouble later.

Developing Orchestrations

After the messages are defined, you will need to design the orchestration that acts on them. Orchestrations are added to a BTS solution using the New Item dialog and are designed graphically using a set of shapes available in the toolbox. These shapes can be connected to form a flowchart that defines the processing for a message. Table 7-5 lists the available shapes and describes them. Following the table, I'll describe the most common shapes and how to use them.

Table 7-5. *Orchestration Shapes*

Shape	Description
Call Orchestration	Allows an orchestration to call another orchestration synchronously
Call Rules	Allows an orchestration to call an externally defined Business Rule
Compensate	Allows an orchestration to execute compensating code when errors occur
Construct Message	Allows an orchestration to create a new message instance
Decide	Allows an orchestration to make branching decisions in the process flow
Delay	Allows an orchestration to wait for a specified period of time
Expression	Allows an orchestration to make variable assignments or call .NET functions

(Continues)

Table 7-5. *Orchestration Shapes (Continued)*

Shape	Description
Group	Groups operations together in the orchestration designer for convenience
Listen	Allows an orchestration to wait for a message to be received
Loop	Allows an orchestration to loop until a set of conditions is met
Message Assignment	Allows an orchestration to assign values to promoted schema fields
Parallel Actions	Allows an orchestration to execute multiple actions in parallel
Port	Allows an orchestration to connect to external systems for sending and receiving messages
Receive	Allows an orchestration to receive a new message instance from a port
Role Link	Allows an orchestration to define a collection of ports that interact with the same system
Scope	Allows an orchestration to specify a boundary that groups operations into a single transaction
Send	Allows an orchestration to send a message instance using a port
Start Orchestration	Allows an orchestration to call another orchestration asynchronously
Suspend	Allows an orchestration to suspend operation while waiting for an error condition to be cleared
Terminate	Allows an orchestration to immediately stop when an error occurs
Throw Exception	Allows an orchestration to raise an error during processing
Transform	Allows an orchestration to map an existing message instance into a new message instance

While the message schemas define the structure of XML messages and the orchestration defines the process, we still need to define a variable capable of referencing a message instance as it moves through the orchestration. These message variables allow us to interact with the fields that were promoted earlier in the schemas. You can create the message variables using the Orchestration Explorer, which is a window available in Visual Studio .NET by selecting View ➤ Other Windows ➤ Orchestration View from the menu.

The Orchestration View contains a summary view of key elements in the orchestration including message variables. By right-clicking the Messages folder and selecting New Message, you can create message variables. The message variables are then associated with a message schema through the Message Type property. Figure 7-9 shows the Orchestration View window with some message variables defined.

Understanding Port Shapes

Ports are used in all BTS orchestrations because they connect the orchestration to other systems and processes. Ports are defined by dragging the port shape from the toolbox and dropping it onto the Port Surface portion of the orchestration designer. The port shape may be dropped onto any part of either the left or right Port Surface. These areas exist simply to organize the shapes and have no impact on their functionality.

When you drop a port shape onto the Port Surface, the Port Configuration Wizard starts automatically. When configuring the port, you must associate it with a port type. Ports types

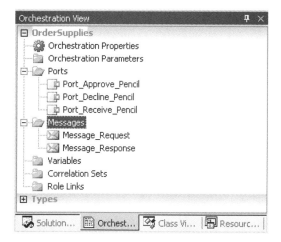

Figure 7-9. *The Orchestration View*

are categories you can use to organize the ports you define in a project. Many different ports can have the same port type. Along with the type, you must also configure the communication pattern, access restrictions, direction of communication, and binding information.

The communication pattern for the port can be either One-Way or Request-Response. The One-Way pattern means that you intend to either send or receive messages on the port. The Request-Response pattern specifies that you intend to both send and receive messages on the port. The pattern choice is determined by your overall design and how you want to communicate with external systems.

Defining access restrictions changes the scope for the port. You can select to make the port private, limit it to just the current project, or make it publicly available. For most situations, you will make the port publicly available. Don't forget that you can limit the users who have access to the solution by controlling their membership in the appropriate Active Directory groups that you set up during installation.

Defining the direction of communication specifies whether the port will be sending messages, receiving messages, or both. If the communication pattern is set to One-Way, then you must select to either send or receive on the port. If the communication pattern is set to Request-Response, then you will send and receive messages on the port.

Once all of the port properties are specified, you can choose to either immediately bind the port using the wizard or bind the port later using administrative tools. For the most part, you will find it easier to bind the port at a later time. This is especially true when connecting to WSS Document Libraries because the Port Configuration Wizard is not aware of the WSSLib adapter.

Understanding the Receive and Send Shapes

Receive and Send shapes are used as interfaces to connect ports with an orchestration. Incoming messages received by a port are sent to a Receive shape for initial processing, and outgoing messages are finalized by a Send shape and sent to a port for delivery. After dragging a Receive or Send shape onto the orchestration design surface, you must specify the types of messages that can be processed using the Message property. This property will contain a list of the message variables defined in the project.

Along with specifying the message variables handled by each shape, you must also connect the shape to an appropriate port. Connecting a Send or Receive shape to a Port shape is done by dragging the green connector icon from one shape and dropping it on the other. A green line connecting the shapes then indicates the connection. Figure 7-10 shows a simple example of an orchestration that connects Send and Receive shapes to ports without any processing.

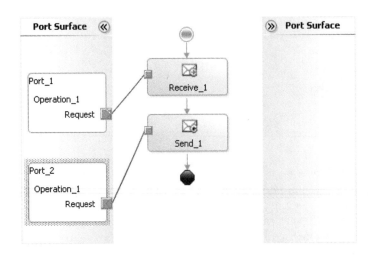

Figure 7-10. *Send and Receive shapes*

By default, Receive shapes do not accept messages automatically. If you want a Receive shape to automatically process messages sent from an associated port, you must set the Activate property to True. If you do not have at least one Receive shape in your orchestration with the Activate property set to True, then the orchestration can only be started by another orchestration. This means that your BTS solution as a whole must have at least one Receive shape activated in at least one orchestration.

After a Receive shape is set to be active, you can specify a filter to screen out messages sent from the port. This filtering mechanism allows you to determine if an incoming message should be processed. For example, you might be using the same WSS Document Library to handle both new and processed InfoPath forms. In this case, you might have a Status field that indicates whether or not the form has been processed already. Define the filter for a Receive shape by right-clicking the shape and selecting Edit Filter Expression from the context menu. In the Filter Expression dialog, you can build a filter based on the promotions you made in the message schemas.

Understanding Flow Control Shapes

Once you have used Port, Send, and Receive shapes to connect with external systems, you will want to define the processing for messages. BTS supports several different flow control shapes that you can use to make decisions, branch, and loop. The most common of these shapes are the Decide, Loop, and Parallel Actions shape.

The Decide shape is used to build an if-then-else statement in the process. When you drag the shape onto the orchestration surface, two branches are created. You can then use the Expression property to create a line of code that specifies the rule that defines success. Writing expressions is a common task in orchestrations and generally involves the use of promoted schema fields. Although the expression coding is not overly difficult, it is somewhat unique to BTS.

Writing an expression begins by typing the name of a message variable followed by an open parenthesis. When you type the parenthesis, IntelliSense will then present a list of promoted fields that you can select. You can then add the closing parenthesis and use a comparison operator to finish the rule definition. The following code shows a message variable named Message_1 with a promoted field named Purpose that must be set to the String "Pleasure" for the rule to be successful. Note that conditional statements do not have semicolons at the end.

```
Message_1(Vacation_Schemas.PropertySchema.purpose)== "Pleasure"
```

The Loop shape is used to build a while loop statement that executes until a condition is met. To define the actions within the loop, you simply drag additional shapes into the body of the loop. The conditional expression that terminates the loop is defined using the same approach I discussed for the Decide shape.

The Parallel Actions shape is used to execute parallel processing branches simultaneously. To define the actions within the branches, you simply drag shapes into each branch. Any shapes that appear after the Parallel Actions shape will not execute until all actions in both branches are complete.

Understanding Message Construction

When you first begin to create BTS orchestrations, you will naturally want to read incoming messages, make processing decisions, and then change the data in the message. However, BTS does not want you to make data changes to the incoming messages. Instead, BTS expects you to create a new outgoing message based on the incoming message. This concept of making a new message is called *message construction*.

The Construct Message shape is used to construct a new message in the orchestration. After you drag a Construct Message shape onto the orchestration design surface, you specify the types of messages the shape can construct using the Messages Constructed property. Once the message types are specified, you can construct a new message using the Transform shape.

The Transform shape allows you to use a schema map to create a new message from an existing message. In most cases, you'll be creating an outgoing message from an existing incoming message. Using the Map Name property of the Transform shape, you can map one message to another. This will create a new message instance using the message variable you defined for that instance.

Once the new message instance exists, you can use the Message Assignment shape to change the value of any promoted field in the new message. Figure 7-11 shows a Transform and Message Assignment shape used inside a Construct Message shape. The Message Assignment shape has an Expression property that you can use to assign a new value to the promoted field. The following code shows a message variable named Message_2 with a property named newBalance set to a value of 100. Note that a semicolon is required when making an assignment in code.

```
Message_2(Vacation_Schemas.Schema_PropertySchema.newBalance)=100;
```

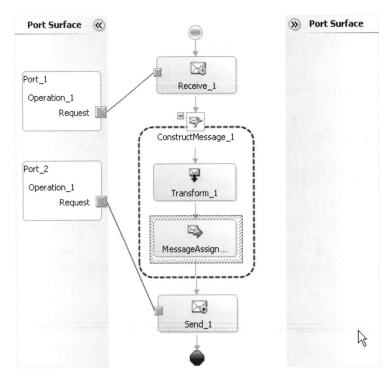

Figure 7-11. *Constructing a new message*

Deploying Orchestrations

Once the schema and orchestrations are completed, they must be deployed to the BizTalk Server Configuration Database and the Global Assembly Cache (GAC) before the solution can be used. As with all assemblies installed in the GAC, you must give your assemblies strong names before they are deployed. If you have a development environment with both Visual Studio .NET and BTS on the same machine, you can simply select Build ➤ Deploy Solution from the Visual Studio .NET menu. For any other deployment, however, you must use the BizTalk Deployment Wizard.

The BizTalk Deployment Wizard allows you to install your assemblies to a specific BizTalk Server Configuration Database. Additionally, you can specify whether or not to install your assemblies in the GAC. This same wizard can also be used to remove assemblies from a BizTalk Server Configuration Database. The wizard is a graphical tool that provides essentially the same functionality as the command-line utility BTSDeploy.

Configuring Ports

After the schema and orchestration assemblies are deployed, the ports must be configured administratively if they have not already been properly configured using the Port Configuration Wizard. In particular, if your ports are connecting to WSS Document Libraries, they will always require administrative configuration. Ports are configured using the BizTalk Explorer, which is available in Visual Studio .NET by selecting View ➤ BizTalk Explorer from the main menu. Figure 7-12 shows the BizTalk Explorer open in Visual Studio .NET.

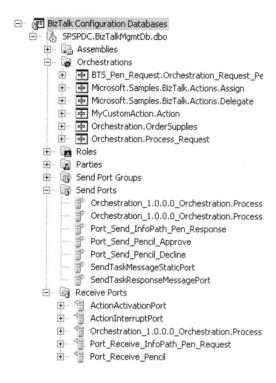

Figure 7-12. *The BizTalk Explorer*

In the BizTalk Explorer, you can right-click either the Receive Ports or Send Ports folder and select to create a new port. For receive ports, you must also create a Receive location underneath the port. As part of the port configuration, you must then select a transport type for the port. Our focus in this chapter is on the WSSLib transport, which allows BizTalk to communicate with WSS Document Libraries.

When configuring a Receive location based on the WSSLib transport, you must specify the address of the Document Library that will be polled by BTS for new documents. You must also select a pipeline for processing the documents. When using the WSSLib transport, you should select the standard SharePoint pipeline named `Microsoft.BizTalk.KwTpm.StsDefaultPipelines.StsReceivePipeline`. Along with these fundamental properties, there are several additional properties you can set to configure the WSSLib transport. Table 7-6 lists these properties and describes them.

Table 7-6. *WSSLib Transport Properties for Receive Locations*

Property	Description
Archive Folder Name	The location where documents should be archived. This property may be blank or refer to a valid WSS Document Library.
Error Threshold	The number of errors tolerated before the Receive location is disabled.
Polling Interval	The number of seconds to wait between checking for new documents.
Site Address URL	The WSS site where new documents can be found.
Site Folder Name	The WSS Document Library where new documents can be found.
View Name	The name of the view associated with the Document Library to use when looking for new documents. If blank, the default view is used.

When configuring a send port for the WSSLib transport, you must set several of the same properties as you do for a Receive location. Send ports, however, have some additional properties. For example, you can choose to have a send port set column values in the library where the processed document is sent. Table 7-7 lists the properties associated with send ports using the WSSLib transport.

Table 7-7. *WSSLib Transport Properties for Send Ports*

Property	Description
Base	This is the name to use for the sent file. This can be a literal or an XPATH expression. Additionally, you can use the token %GUID% to insert the message identifier as part of the name.
Extension	The file extension to use with the sent document.
Namespace	The namespace to use with the sent document.
Overwrite	Set to True if documents with the same name should be overwritten.
Site Address URL	The WSS site where documents are sent.
Site Folder Name	The WSS Document Library where documents are sent.
Property *n* Name	The name of a column in the document library to set.
Property *n* Source	The value of the property as a literal or an XPATH expression.
Property *n* Source Namespace	The namespace to use with the property.

Binding, Enlisting, and Starting an Orchestration

Once the send and receive ports are properly configured, they must be bound to the orchestration. Once again, this is accomplished using the BizTalk Explorer. In the BizTalk Explorer, you will find all of the deployed orchestrations listed under the Orchestrations folder. The binding process starts when you right-click an orchestration and select Bind from the context menu. Binding an orchestration allows you to select the ports that the orchestration will use.

Once the orchestration is bound to the appropriate ports, it must be enlisted. Enlisting an orchestration allows BTS to properly configure the environment in which the orchestration will run. This configuration establishes the communication necessary to properly connect the ports and orchestrations with the associated external systems. Enlisting an orchestration can also be done directly in the BizTalk Explorer by right-clicking the orchestration and selecting Enlist from the context menu. Additionally, you can enlist orchestrations using the BizTalk Server Administration console.

The final step in deploying the BTS solution is to start the orchestration. Once the orchestration starts, message processing will begin. You can start an orchestration using the BizTalk Explorer or the BizTalk Administration Console. When you start the orchestration, BTS will automatically start any dependencies, such as ports.

Exercise 7-1. Using the WSS Adapter

The WSS Adapter allows BTS to exchange messages with SharePoint Document Libraries. Because BTS messages are actually XML documents, InfoPath forms are a natural way to accept input from an information worker that can be processed by a BTS orchestration. In this exercise, you will create a set of InfoPath forms that can be used to request ballpoint pens from the office manager. BTS will process the form and automatically approve or reject the request.

Creating the Message Schemas

BTS relies on XML schemas to define the messages that are processed by an orchestration. These schemas define the incoming messages as well as any outgoing messages. Additionally, you can define transforms that relate one schema to another. In this section, you will create a new BTS project and build the schemas that define the pen request and the automated response.

Follow these steps to create the schemas:

1. In Visual Studio.NET, select File ➤ New ➤ Project from the menu.

2. In the New Project dialog, click the BizTalk Projects folder in the Project Types list.

3. In the Templates list, select Empty BizTalk Server Project.

4. Name the new project **BTS Pen Request**.

5. Click the OK button to create the new project.

6. When the new project is created, select Project ➤ Add New Item from the menu.

7. In the Add New Item dialog, select Schema from the Templates list.

8. Name the new Schema **Schema_Request_Pen**.

9. Click the Open button to open the schema in the BizTalk Schema Editor.

10. In the schema tree, right-click the Root node and select Rename from the context menu.

11. Rename the node as **Request**.

12. Right-click the Request node and select Insert Schema Node ➤ Child Field Element.

13. Name the new field **Date**.

14. Right-click the Request node and select Insert Schema Node ➤ Child Field Element.

15. Name the new field **Quantity**.

16. Save the schema. Figure 7-13 shows the final schema.

Figure 7-13. *The Schema_Request_Pen schema*

17. Select Project ➤ Add New Item from the menu.

18. In the Add New Item dialog, select Schema from the Templates list.

19. Name the new schema **Schema_Response_Pen**.

20. Click the Open button to open the schema in the BizTalk Schema Editor.

21. In the schema tree, right-click the Root node and select Rename from the context menu.

22. Rename the node as **Response**.

23. Right-click the Response node and select Insert Schema Node ➤ Child Field Element.

24. Name the new field **Date**.

25. Right-click the Response node and select Insert Schema Node ➤ Child Field Element.

26. Name the new field **Quantity**.

27. Right-click the Response node and select Insert Schema Node ➤ Child Field Element.

28. Name the new field **Status**.

29. Save the schema. Figure 7-14 shows the final schema.

Figure 7-14. *The Schema_Response_Pen schema*

Promoting Schema Properties

Once the basic schemas are created, you will want to promote the schema node that must be accessed by BTS during processing. Promoting a schema node makes it appear like a property of any message based on that schema. In this way, you can access the field from a BTS orchestration.

Follow these steps to promote properties:

1. In the solution explorer, right-click the file Schema_Request_Pen.xsd and select Properties from the context menu.

2. In the Property Page dialog, change the name for the Default Property Schema Name to **Schema_Request_Pen_Property.xsd**.

3. Click the OK button to close the Property Page dialog.

4. In the solution explorer, double-click the file Schema_Request_Pen.xsd to open it in the BizTalk Schema Editor.

5. Expand the schema tree.

6. Right-click the Quantity node and select Promote ➤ Quick Promotion. When prompted to create a property schema, click the OK button.

7. Save and close the schema.

8. In the solution explorer, right-click the file Schema_Response_Pen.xsd and select Properties from the context menu.

9. In the Property Page dialog, change the name for the Default Property Schema Name to **Schema_Response_Pen_Property.xsd**.

10. Click the OK button to close the Property Page dialog.

11. In the solution explorer, double-click the file Schema_Response_Pen.xsd to open it in the BizTalk Schema Editor.

12. Expand the schema tree.

13. Right-click the Status node and select Promote ➤ Quick Promotion. When prompted to create a property schema, click the OK button.

14. Save and close the schema.

Validating Schemas

Once the promotions are made, then you can validate the schemas before using them in an orchestration. Validation is accomplished by generating a set of test messages that conform to your schemas and then checking them.

Follow these steps to validate your schemas:

1. In the solution explorer, right-click the file Schema_Request_Pen.xsd and select Validate Schema from the context menu.

2. In the solution explorer, right-click the file Schema_Request_Pen.xsd and select Properties from the context menu.

3. Click in the Output Instance Filename box and then click the ellipsis.

4. In the Select Output File dialog, navigate to the folder containing your project and then type **Instance_Request.xml** in the File Name box.

5. Click the OK button to close the Property Page dialog.

6. In the solution explorer, right-click the file `Schema_Request_Pen.xsd` and select Generate Instance from the context menu to create a test message based on the schema.

7. In the solution explorer, right-click the file `Schema_Request_Pen.xsd` and select Properties from the context menu.

8. Click in the Input Instance Filename box and then click the ellipsis.

9. In the Select Input File, navigate to the folder containing your project and select the `Instance_Request.xml` file.

10. Click the Open button to use this message for testing.

11. Click the OK button to close the Property Page dialog.

12. In the solution explorer, right-click the file `Schema_Request_Pen.xsd` and select Validate Instance from the context menu.

13. In the solution explorer, right-click the file `Schema_Response_Pen.xsd` and select Validate Schema from the context menu.

14. In the solution explorer, right-click the file `Schema_Response_Pen.xsd` and select Properties from the context menu.

15. Click in the Output Instance Filename box and then click the ellipsis.

16. In the Select Output File dialog, navigate to the folder containing your project and then type **Instance_Response.xml** in the File Name box.

17. Click the OK button to close the Property Page dialog.

18. In the solution explorer, right-click the file `Schema_Response_Pen.xsd` and select Generate Instance from the context menu to create a test message based on the schema.

19. In the solution explorer, right-click the file `Schema_Response_Pen.xsd` and select Properties from the context menu.

20. Click in the Input Instance Filename box and then click the ellipsis.

21. In the Select Input File, navigate to the folder containing your project and select the `Instance_Response.xml` file.

22. Click the Open button to use this message for testing.

23. Click the OK button to close the Property Page dialog.

24. In the solution explorer, right-click the file `Schema_Response_Pen.xsd` and select Validate Instance from the context menu.

Creating a Schema Map

In most BTS processes, there is a relationship between the input schema and the output schema. In this exercise, the response schema is a superset of the request schema. The response schema adds a Status field to the existing Date and Quantity fields of the request schema. Because there is a relationship between the two schemas, we can create a map that acts as a transformation to convert the incoming request schema to a response schema.

Follow these steps to create the schema map:

1. In Visual Studio .NET, select Project ➤ Add New Item from the main menu.

2. In the Add New Item dialog, select Map from the Templates list.

3. Name the new map **Map_Request_Response.btm**.

4. Click the Open button to open the BizTalk Mapper.

5. In the BizTalk Mapper, click the Open Source Schema link.

6. In the BizTalk Type Picker dialog, expand the Schemas folder, select BTS_Pen_Request.Schema_Request_Pen, and click the OK button.

7. In the BizTalk Mapper, click the Open Destination Schema link.

8. In the BizTalk Type Picker dialog, expand the Schemas folder, select BTS_Pen_Request.Schema_Response_Pen, and click the OK button.

9. In the BizTalk Mapper, expand both schemas so you can see all the nodes.

10. Drag the Date node from the Request schema and drop it on the Date node in the Response schema.

11. Drag the Quantity node from the Request schema and drop it on the Quantity node in the Response schema.

12. Select View ➤ Toolbox from the main menu.

13. In the Visual Studio .NET toolbox, click the Date/Time Functoids palette.

14. Drag the Date and Time functoid from the Date/Time Functoids palette onto the grid between the schemas in the Mapper.

15. Drag a line from the Date/Time functoid to the Status node in the Response schema to initialize this node with the current data and time.

16. Save the map.

17. In the solution explorer, right-click the file Map_Request_Response.btm and select Validate Map from the context menu. Figure 7-15 shows how the final map should appear.

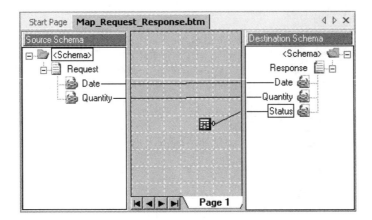

Figure 7-15. *The schema map*

Building the InfoPath Forms

Once the schemas for the process are defined, you must create a set of InfoPath forms that conform to these schemas. Using the schemas as a basis for the InfoPath forms allows you to create rich documents that can be stored in WSS Document Libraries and subsequently processed by a BTS orchestration. In this section, you will create InfoPath form templates and publish them to WSS libraries.

Creating the WSS Site

During the BTS installation process described earlier, you created a test site for use with this chapter. For this exercise, you will create a subsite under the master site for processing the InfoPath forms. This site will be empty except for the form libraries, which will be added when the InfoPath forms are published.

Follow these steps to create the WSS subsite:

1. Navigate to the TestBizTalk site you created earlier.

2. On the home page, click the Create link.

3. On the Create page, click the Sites and Workspaces link to create a new subsite.

4. Name the new subsite **Pen Request** and give it an appropriate URL.

5. Click the Create button.

6. On the Template Selection page, select to create a Blank Site and click the OK button.

Creating the Request Form

The pen request form is an InfoPath form based on the Schema_Request_Pen.xsd schema. You will create this form by referencing the schema and using the form development tools in InfoPath. Once the form is created, it will be published to the WSS site.

Follow these steps to create the pen request form:

1. In Microsoft InfoPath 2003, select File ➤ Design a Form.

2. In the Design a Form task pane, click the New from XML Document or Schema link.

3. In the Data Source Setup Wizard, select the XML Schema or XML Data File option and click the Next button.

4. On the next screen, click the Browse button.

5. In the Open dialog, navigate to the Schema_Request_Pen.xsd file and select it.

6. Click the Open button.

7. In the Data Source Setup Wizard, click the Next button and then click the Finish button.

8. In the InfoPath task pane, click the Layout link.

9. In the Layout task pane, double-click the Table with Title layout in the Insert Layout Tables list.

10. When the table is added to the form, click the area marked Click to Add Title.

11. Change the table title to **Pen Request**.

12. Click in the content area of the form to prepare to add fields.

13. In the InfoPath task pane, click the Data Source link.

14. In the Data Source task pane, right-click the Date node and select More from the context menu.

15. In the Select a Control dialog box, double-click the Date Picker control.

16. In the Data Source task pane, right-click the Quantity node and select Text Box from the context menu.

17. Once the fields are added to the form, select File ➤ Publish from the main menu.

18. When the Publishing Wizard starts, click the Next button.

19. On the next screen, select to publish the form to a SharePoint Form Library and click the Next button.

20. On the next screen, select to create a new form library and click the Next button.

21. On the next screen, enter the address of the subsite you created earlier for this project and click the Next button.

22. On the next screen, name the new form library **Submitted** and click the Next button.

23. On the next screen, click the Add button.

24. Add the Date and Quantity fields as column names to the SharePoint site.

25. Click the Finish button to publish the form.

26. Click the Close button to complete the wizard.

Creating the Response Form

The response form is used to show the results of the processed request. The difference between the two forms is that the response form has a Status field indicating whether or not the request was approved. This decision is made inside the BTS orchestration when the request form is processed.

Follow these steps to create the response form:

1. In Microsoft InfoPath 2003, select File ➤ Design a Form.

2. In the Design a Form task pane, click the New from XML Document or Schema link.

3. In the Data Source Setup Wizard, select the XML Schema or XML Data File option and click the Next button.

4. On the next screen, click the Browse button.

5. In the Open dialog, navigate to the Schema_Response_Pen.xsd file and select it.

6. Click the Open button.

7. In the Data Source Setup Wizard, click the Next button and then click the Finish button.

8. In the InfoPath task pane, click the Layout link.

9. In the Layout task pane, double-click the Table with Title layout in the Insert Layout Tables list.

10. When the table is added to the form, click the area marked Click to Add Title.

11. Change the table title to **Pen Request**.

12. Click in the content area of the form to prepare to add fields.

13. In the InfoPath task pane, click the Data Source link.

14. In the Data Source task pane, right-click the Date node and select More from the context menu.

15. In the Select a Control dialog box, double-click the Date Picker control.

16. In the Data Source task pane, right-click the Quantity node and select Text Box from the context menu.

17. In the Data Source task pane, right-click the Status node and select Text Box from the context menu.

18. Once the fields are added to the form, select File ➤ Publish from the main menu.

19. When the Publishing Wizard starts, click the Next button.

20. On the next screen, select to publish the form to a SharePoint Form Library and click the Next button.

21. On the next screen, select to create a new form library and click the Next button.

22. On the next screen, enter the address of the subsite you created earlier for this project and click the Next button.

23. On the next screen, name the new form library **Processed** and click the Next button.

24. On the next screen, click the Add button.

25. Add the Date, Quantity, and Status fields as column names to the SharePoint site.

26. Click the Finish button to publish the form.

27. Click the Close button to complete the wizard.

Creating the Orchestration

Once the schemas and forms are created, you can use them to create messages that are processed in a BTS orchestration. In this exercise, you will create an orchestration that checks the incoming pen request and sets the status based on a business rule. If the request is for less than six pens, it will be approved. If the request is for more than five pens, it will be rejected.

Follow these steps to create the orchestration:

1. In Visual Studio .NET, select Project ➤ Add New Item.

2. In the Add New Item dialog, select BizTalk Orchestration from the Templates list.

3. Name the new file **Orchestration_Request_Pen.odx**.

4. Click the Open button to add the new orchestration.

5. Drag a Receive shape from the toolbox onto the orchestration design surface and drop it on the area marked Drop a Shape from the Toolbox Here.

6. In the Properties window, change the name of the shape to **Receive_Request_Pen**.

7. Change the Activate property to True.

8. Drag a Decide shape from the toolbox onto the orchestration design surface and drop it directly beneath the Receive shape.

9. In the Properties window, change the name of the shape to **Decide_Quantity**.

10. Select the Rule_1 shape on the orchestration design surface.

11. In the Properties window, change the name of the shape to **Rule_Reject**.

12. Drag a Transform shape from the toolbox and drop it directly beneath the Rule_Reject shape on the area marked Drop a Shape from the Toolbox Here.

13. Select the ConstructMessage_1 shape on the orchestration design surface.

14. In the Properties window, change the name of the shape to **Construct_Response_Rejected**.

15. Select the Transform_1 shape on the orchestration design surface.

16. In the Properties window, change the name of this shape to
Transform_Response_Rejected.

17. Drag a Message Assignment shape from the toolbox and drop it directly beneath the
`Transform_Response_Rejected` shape, but inside of the `Construct_Response_Rejected`
shape.

18. In the Properties window, change the name of this shape to **Assign_Status_Rejected**.

19. Drag a Send shape from the toolbox and drop it directly beneath the
`Construct_Response_Rejected` shape.

20. In the Properties window, change the name of this shape to **Send_Response_Rejected**.

21. Drag a Transform shape from the toolbox and drop it directly beneath the `Else` shape
on the area marked Drop a Shape from the Toolbox Here.

22. Select the `ConstructMessage_1` shape on the orchestration design surface.

23. In the Properties window, change the name of the shape to
Construct_Response_Approved.

24. Select the `Transform_1` shape on the orchestration design surface.

25. In the Properties window, change the name of this shape to
Transform_Response_Approved.

26. Drag a Message Assignment shape from the toolbox and drop it directly beneath the
`Transform_Response_Approved` shape, but inside of the `Construct_Response_Approved`
shape.

27. In the Properties window, change the name of this shape to **Assign_Status_Approved**.

28. Drag a Send shape from the toolbox and drop it directly beneath the
`Construct_Response_Approved` shape.

29. In the Properties window, change the name of this shape to
Send_Response_Approved.

30. Save your work. Figure 7-16 shows what the completed orchestration should look like.

Configuring the Orchestration

Arranging shapes on the orchestration design surface is only the beginning of the steps
required to create and deploy an orchestration. Each of the shapes requires some configuration that is based on the message types processed by the orchestration. In this section, you
will create variables to hold the messages processed by the orchestration and use these variables to configure the orchestration shapes.

Follow these steps to configure the orchestration:

1. With the orchestration open in Visual Studio .NET, you should see the Orchestration
View open with a view of the orchestration elements in your project.

2. In the Orchestration View, right-click the Messages folder and select New Message
from the context menu.

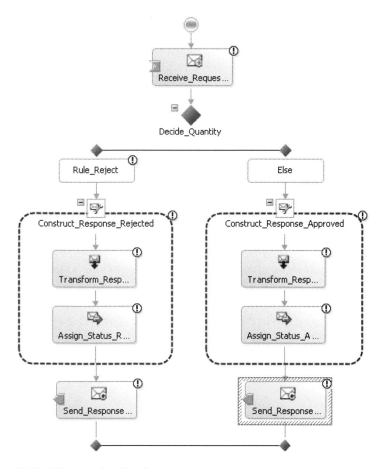

Figure 7-16. *The completed orchestration*

3. In the Properties window, change the name of the new message to **Message_Request_Pen**.

4. In the Message Type drop-down list, expand the Schemas node and select `BTS_Pen_Request.Schema_Request_Pen` to define the type for the new message variable.

5. In the Orchestration View, right-click the Messages folder and select New Message from the context menu.

6. In the Properties window, change the name of the new message to **Message_Response_Pen**.

7. In the Message Type drop-down list, expand the Schemas node and select `BTS_Pen_Request.Schema_Response_Pen` to define the type for the new message variable.

8. On the orchestration design surface, select the `Construct_Response_Rejected` shape.

9. In the Properties window, select `Message_Response_Pen` from the Messages Constructed drop-down list.

10. On the orchestration design surface, select the `Transform_Response_Rejected` shape.

11. In the Properties window, click the ellipsis associated with the `Map  Name` property.

12. In the Transform Configuration dialog, select the Existing Map option.

13. In the Fully Qualified Map Name drop-down list, select `BTS_Pen_Request.Map_Request_Response`.

14. In the Transform list, select the Source item.

15. In the Variable Name field, select `Message_Request_Pen`.

16. In the Transform list, select the Destination item.

17. In the Variable Name field, select `Message_Response_Pen`.

18. Click the OK button to save the changes.

19. On the orchestration design surface, select the `Assign_Status_Rejected` shape.

20. In the Properties window, click the ellipsis associated with the `Expression` property.

21. In the BizTalk Expression Editor, type the following code to set the `Status` field of the message:

```
Message_Response_Pen(BTS_Pen_Request.Schema_Response_Pen_Property.Status)= ➡
"Rejected";
```

22. Click the OK button to save the code.

23. On the orchestration design surface, select the `Rule_Reject` shape.

24. In the Properties window, click the ellipsis associated with the `Expression` property.

25. In the BizTalk Expression Editor, type the following code to check the value of the `Quantity` field:

```
System.Int32.Parse(Message_Request_Pen➡
(BTS_Pen_Request.Schema_Request_Pen_Property.Quantity))>5
```

26. Click the OK button to save the code.

27. On the orchestration design surface, select the `Construct_Response_Approved` shape.

28. In the Properties window, select `Message_Response_Pen` from the Messages Constructed drop-down list.

29. On the orchestration design surface, select the `Transform_Response_Approved` shape.

30. In the Properties window, click the ellipsis associated with the `Map  Name` property.

31. In the Transform Configuration dialog, select the Existing Map option.

32. In the Fully Qualified Map Name drop-down list, select `BTS_Pen_Request.Map_Request_Response`.

33. In the Transform list, select the Source item.

34. In the `Variable Name` field, select `Message_Request_Pen`.

35. In the Transform list, select the Destination item.

36. In the `Variable Name` field, select `Message_Response_Pen`.

37. Click the OK button to save the changes.

38. On the orchestration design surface, select the `Assign_Status_Approved` shape.

39. In the Properties window, click the ellipsis associated with the `Expression` property.

40. In the BizTalk Expression Editor, type the following code to set the `Status` field of the message:

    ```
    Message_Response_Pen(BTS_Pen_Request.Schema_Response_Pen_Property.Status)=➡
    "Approved";
    ```

41. Click the OK button to save the code.

Creating Orchestration Ports

Ports allow a BTS orchestration to exchange documents with an external system. Ports can use several different protocols to interact with file systems, web systems, e-mail, and databases. The ports for this exercise will facilitate connecting the orchestration to your WSS Document Libraries.

Follow these steps to create the ports:

1. In Visual Studio .NET, drag a port shape from the toolbox and drop it on the Port Surface area. The Port Configuration Wizard will start automatically.

2. In the Port Configuration Wizard, click the Next button.

3. Name the new port **Port_Receive_Pen_Request** and click the Next button.

4. In the Port Type Name box, type **PortType_Receive_Pen_Request**.

5. On the Select a Port Type screen, set the Communication Pattern to One-Way and the Access Restrictions to Public – No Limit.

6. Click the Next button.

7. On the Port Binding screen, set the Port Direction of Communication to I'll Always Be Receiving Messages on This Port.

8. Set the Port Binding to Specify Later and click the Next button.

9. Click the Finish button to complete the wizard.

10. On the Port Surface, select the `Operation_1` shape.

11. In the Properties window, change the name of the shape to **Operation_Receive**.

12. On the Port Surface, select the `Request` operation within the port.

13. In the Properties window, drop the list associated with the `Message Type` property, expand the Schemas node, and select `BTS_Pen_Request.Schema_Request_Pen`.

14. On the orchestration design surface, select the `Receive_Request_Pen` shape.

15. In the Properties window, select `Message_Request_Pen` from the drop-down list associated with the `Message` property.

16. Drag a line from the `Port_Receive_Pen_Request` shape to the `Receive_Request_Pen` shape.

17. Drag a port shape from the toolbox and drop it on the Port Surface area. The Port Configuration Wizard will start automatically.

18. In the Port Configuration Wizard, click the Next button.

19. Name the new port **Port_Send_Pen_Response** and click the Next button.

20. In the Port Type Name box, type **PortType_Send_Pen_Response**.

21. On the Select a Port Type screen, set the Communication Pattern to One-Way and the Access Restrictions to Public – No Limit.

22. Click the Next button.

23. On the Port Binding screen, set the Port Direction of Communication to I'll Always Be Sending Messages on This Port.

24. Set the Port Binding to Specify Later and click the Next button.

25. Click the Finish button to complete the wizard.

26. On the Port Surface, select the `Operation_1` shape.

27. In the Properties window, change the name of the shape to **Operation_Send**.

28. On the Port Surface, select the `Request` operation within the port.

29. In the Properties window, change the name to `Response`.

30. Drop the list associated with the `Message Type` property, expand the Schemas node, and select `BTS_Pen_Request.Schema_Response_Pen`.

31. On the orchestration design surface, select the `Send_Response_Rejected` shape.

32. In the Properties window, select `Message_Response_Pen` from the drop-down list associated with the `Message` property.

33. Drag a line from the `Send_Response_Rejected` shape to the `Port_Send_Pen_Response` shape.

34. On the orchestration design surface, select the `Send_Response_Approved` shape.

35. In the Properties window, select `Message_Response_Pen` from the drop-down list associated with the `Message` property.

36. Drag a line from the `Send_Response_Approved` shape to the `Port_Send_Pen_Response` shape. Figure 7-17 shows the orchestration with the configured ports.

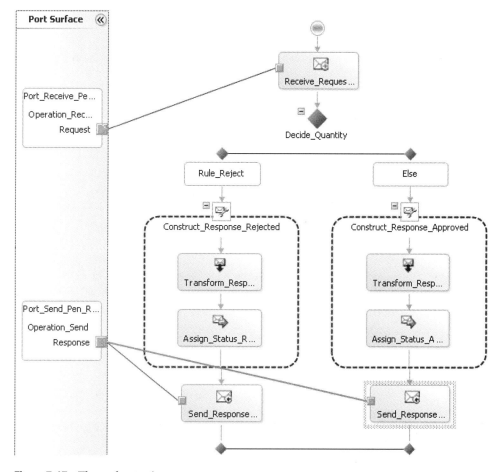

Figure 7-17. *The orchestration ports*

Creating the Send Pipeline

Pipelines allow you to manipulate XML messages so that they may be transformed into useable documents. In this exercise, we need to transform the outgoing XML message so that it can be opened with the appropriate InfoPath form. This will allow you to review the processing results directly in InfoPath.

Follow these steps to create a new pipeline:

1. In Visual Studio .NET, select Project ➤ Add New Item from the main menu.

2. In the Add New Item dialog, select to add a new Send Pipeline.

3. Name the new pipeline **Pipeline_Send_Pen_Response.btp** and click the Open button.

4. In the Pipeline Designer, drag an XML Assembler shape from the toolbox and drop it on the Assemble stage.

5. In the Properties Window, set the `Add Processing Instructions` property to **Create New**.

6. Leave Visual Studio .NET and navigate to the Processed Document Library you created earlier.

7. In the library, click the Fill Out This Form link to see an instance of the response form.

8. Fill in the form with any information and save it to your desktop.

9. Open the saved file in Visual Studio .NET for editing.

10. In Visual Studio .NET, carefully locate the two processing instructions marked by the `<?mso?>` tag. The following code shows an example:

```
<?mso-infoPathSolution solutionVersion="1.0.0.1" productVersion="11.0.5531"
PIVersion="1.0.0.0"
href=http://spspdc/sites/TestBizTalk/PenRequest/Processed/Forms/template.xsn
language="en-us" ?>
<?mso-application progid="InfoPath.Document"?>
```

11. Copy the two entries from the file and paste them into the `Add Processing Instructions Text` property of the XML Assembler in the pipeline. This will associate the outgoing XML with the InfoPath form template in the Processed library.

12. Save your project.

Building and Deploying the Solution

Once the project is saved, you are ready to build and deploy the solution. In order to deploy the solution, you will need to provide strong names for the assemblies. I am assuming that you either have an existing key or know how to generate a key pair since we have used many strongly named assemblies throughout this book.

Follow these steps to build and deploy the solution:

1. In the solution explorer, right-click the BTS Pen Request project and select Properties from the context menu.

2. In the Property Pages dialog, select the Assembly node underneath the Common Properties folder.

3. Click on the Assembly Key File field and enter the complete path to the key file you will use for this project.

4. Click the OK button to save your changes.

5. In Visual Studio .NET, select Deployment from the Configuration drop-down list on the main toolbar.

6. Select Build ➤ Build Solution to compile the project.

7. Once the project has compiled successfully, select Build ➤ Deploy Solution to deploy the project to BizTalk Server 2004.

Configuring the Send and Receive Ports

Because the WSS Adapter is a custom adapter, it cannot be directly configured in the orchestration project. Instead the ports must be configured after the project is deployed. In this section, you will connect the ports to the Document Libraries that you created earlier.

Follow these steps to configure the send and receive ports:

1. In Visual Studio .NET, select View ➤ BizTalk Explorer from the main menu.

2. In the BizTalk Explorer, right-click the BizTalk Configuration Databases node and select Refresh from the context menu.

3. Expand the tree until the Receive Ports folder is visible.

4. Right-click the Receive Ports folder and select Add Receive Port from the context menu.

5. In the Create New Receive Port dialog, specify One-Way Port as the port type and click the OK button.

6. In the One-Way Receive Port Properties dialog, enter **Port_Receive_InfoPath_Pen_Request** as the Name and click the OK button.

7. In the BizTalk Explorer, locate the new port and expand the node to reveal the Receive Locations folder.

8. Right-click the Receive Locations folder and select Add Receive Location from the context menu.

9. In the Receive Location Properties dialog, type **Receive_Location_Submitted_Library** as the Name.

10. Select WSSLib from the drop-down list associated with the Transport Type property.

11. Click the ellipsis associated with the Address (URI) property.

12. In the WSSLib Transport Properties dialog, set the Site Address URL property to point to the subsite you created earlier for this exercise.

13. Set the Site Folder Name property to **Submitted**.

14. Click OK to save your changes

15. In the Receive Location Properties dialog, select BizTalkServerApplication from the drop-down list associated with the Receive Handler property.

16. Select Microsoft.BizTalk.KwTpm.StsDefaultPipelines.StsReceivePipeline from the drop-down list associated with the Receive Pipeline property.

17. Click OK to close the dialog and save your changes.

18. Right-click the Send Ports folder and select Add Send Port from the context menu.

19. In the Create New Send Port dialog, specify Static One-Way Port as the port type and click the OK button.

20. In the Static One-Way Send Port Properties dialog, name the port
    Port_Send_InfoPath_Pen_Response.

21. Select WSSLib from the drop-down list associated with the `Transport Type` property.

22. Click the ellipsis associated with the `Address (URI)` property.

23. In the WSSLib Transport Properties dialog, enter **Response_%GUID%** in the `Base`
    property.

24. Set the `Site Address URL` property to point to the subsite you created earlier for this
    exercise.

25. Set the `Site Folder Name` property to **Processed**.

26. Click the OK button to save your changes.

27. In the Static One-Way Send Port Properties dialog, click on the Send folder.

28. Select `BTS_Pen_Request.Pipeline_Send_Pen_Respone` from the drop-down list associ-
    ated with the `Send Pipeline` property.

29. Click OK to close the dialog and save your changes.

Binding and Starting the Orchestration

Once the ports are properly configured, they must be bound to the orchestration you
deployed earlier. Once they are bound to the orchestration, you can enlist the orchestration
and start it. Once started, the solution will begin polling the Document Library looking for
new InfoPath forms.

Follow these steps to bind and start the orchestration:

1. In the BizTalk Explorer, expand the Orchestrations folder and locate the
   `BTS_Pen_Request.Orchestration_Request_Pen` project.

2. Right-click the `BTS_Pen_Request.Orchestration_Request_Pen` project and select Bind
   from the context menu.

3. In the Port Bindings Properties dialog, select `Port_Receive_InfoPath_Pen_Request`
   from the drop-down list associated with the `Port_Receive_Pen_Request` port.

4. Select `Port_Send_InfoPath_Pen_Response` from the drop-down list associated with the
   `Port_Send_Pen_Response` port.

5. Click the Host node underneath the Configurations folder.

6. Select `BizTalkServerApplication` from the drop-down list associated with the `Host`
   property.

7. Click the OK button to save the bindings.

8. Right-click the `BTS_Pen_Request.Orchestration_Request_Pen` orchestration and select
   Enlist from the context menu.

9. Right-click the BTS_Pen_Request.Orchestration_Request_Pen orchestration and select Start from the context menu.

10. In the Express Start dialog, accept the default settings and click the OK button.

Testing the Solution

Once the solution is deployed and running, you are ready to test it. To test the solution, simply navigate to the Submitted library on the subsite you created for this exercise. Fill out a new InfoPath form and save it to the library. Shortly after saving the form, your BTS orchestration should pick up the form and process it. If everything is working right, the processed form will appear in the Processed library.

If you have trouble getting the project to work, remember that the WSS Adapter runs under the security context of the account running the BizTalk service. This service must have rights to the WSS libraries you are accessing. Additionally, you can check for messages in the Event Log. BTS does a good job of giving reasonably descriptive messages when processing errors occur.

CHAPTER 8

SharePoint and Microsoft Content Management Server

Almost without exception every organization now has an Internet presence as well as some form of internal intranet. For the most part, these sites are built using a combination of static HTML pages and dynamic technology like Active Server Pages (ASP). The problem for these organizations, however, is that the business content displayed in the web pages is hopelessly bound to the technology that implements the page. This means that either the business people must learn to use technical tools or the technical people must learn to understand the business content. More often than not, the result is that any change to a web page is handled by the IT department in response to a business request. Furthermore, these change requests often receive low priority within IT departments that are routinely struggling to keep up with their current workload.

Microsoft Content Management Server (MCMS) is a system for authoring, publishing, and managing web pages, and its main purpose is to separate the business content on those pages from the technology that creates the pages. This means that technical people can focus on providing and maintaining a site structure while business people can focus on creating content. The site structure is created by defining a set of page templates using ASP.NET. These templates consist of controls and placeholders for content. The content is stored in a database and dynamically added to the templates in response to a page request.

While MCMS is intended for use with both public web sites and intranets, organizations that use Windows SharePoint Services (WSS) and SharePoint Portal Server (SPS) have not historically had the option of using MCMS. Because WSS and SPS pages are maintained inside a SQL Server database, they do not fit the MCMS paradigm of template pages with content stored in the MCMS database. We can, however, utilize the CMS Connector for SharePoint Technologies (CST), which allows the two systems to share information in a way that complements both. Using CST, we can access MCMS content from WSS sites and access WSS resources from MCMS sites. In this chapter, I will examine the basics of content management with MCMS and how CST works to provide a bridge with WSS sites.

Understanding MCMS Architecture

The MCMS architecture is based on the principal of creating web pages dynamically using predefined templates with content placeholders. Interestingly, the manner in which MCMS builds and delivers a web page is similar to the same process in WSS. Therefore, anyone familiar with

WSS architecture will find it easy to grasp the fundamentals of MCMS. Figure 8-1 shows a drawing of the basic MCMS architecture. The biggest difference between the two is that WSS maintains entire pages within its database, while MCMS uses external templates and only stores content in the database.

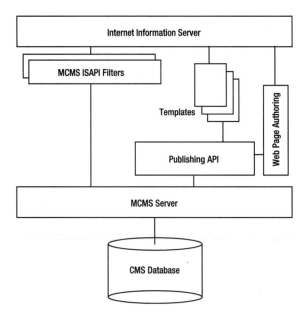

Figure 8-1. *MCMS architecture*

Just like WSS, MCMS relies on ISAPI filters to intercept HTTP page requests from clients and process them. The filter then examines the intercepted request to see if it corresponds to a page in an MCMS *channel*, which defines a virtual web site hierarchy controlled by MCMS. If it does, then the request is modified to reference the ASP.NET template that corresponds to the requested page. Because a single MCMS template can be used to render many different pages, the request is also modified to include a reference to the specific page content to render. MCMS then processes the combination of the ASP.NET template and the designated content to produce the requested page.

The MCMS database, which contains the page content, consists of several dozen tables and is not intended to be accessed directly. Instead, access to content in the database is always done through the Publishing API (PAPI) and managed by the MCMS server. When pages are created in MCMS, authoring tools are used to write content into the database through PAPI. Content is subsequently read out of the database during the rendering process.

Creating a Development Environment

There are obviously many combinations and configurations for both WSS and MCMS. For the purpose of this chapter, I will assume that you have a development environment consisting of a single Windows 2003 server that will host WSS, SPS, and MCMS. The sample data provided by Microsoft assumes this configuration, and so do the exercises in this chapter. Additionally, I am starting with the assumption that you have already installed—or know how to install—WSS, SPS, Visual Studio .NET, and Microsoft Office 2003. Before starting the MCMS installation process, you should download service pack 1a for MCMS and CST. Table 8-1 lists the addresses for the required software.

■**Note** If you do not have SPS available, you can still utilize many parts of this chapter. All of the search capabilities discussed in this chapter, however, require SPS.

Table 8-1. *Required Downloads*

Package	Description	Location
MCMS_2002_SP1a.exe	MCMS Service Pack 1	http://www.microsoft.com/ downloads/details.aspx? FamilyId=62049D3F-24D7-4463-A924-550E5DC34095&displaylang=en
McmsConnectorForSharePointTech.exe	CMS Connector for SharePoint Technologies	http://www.microsoft.com/ downloads/details.aspx? FamilyId=6E9925C4-91DA-404A-86DD-78D51BCF0A51&displaylang=en

Creating Web Sites

The configuration described in this section will install MCMS on the same virtual server as your existing WSS installation; however, you will need to create an additional web site to host the Server Configuration Application (SCA), which can be used to manage MCMS sites. Additionally, you may need to make changes to the Site Application Pool Identity in order to ensure that the MCMS can properly integrate with the SPS search capability.

Follow these steps to create a new web site:

1. Log in as an administrator and select Start ➤ All Programs ➤ Administrative Tools ➤ Internet Information Services (IIS) Manager on the Windows 2003 server where MCMS is to be installed.

2. Right-click the Web Sites folder and select New ➤ Web Site from the context menu to start the Web Site Creation Wizard.

3. On the Welcome screen, click the Next button.

4. On the Web Site Description screen, name the new web site **SCA** and click the Next button.

5. On the IP Address and Port Settings screen, set the TCP port to **8080** and click the Next button.

6. On the Web Site Home Directory screen, uncheck the option to allow anonymous access and click the Browse button.

7. In the Browse for Folder dialog, select the \Inetpub directory and click the Make New Folder button.

8. Name the new folder **SCA** and click the OK button.

9. Click the Next button.

10. On the Web Site Access Permissions screen, click the Next button.

11. Click the Finish button to complete the wizard.

12. Expand the Application Pools folder.

13. Right-click the application pool under which your SPS installation is running and select Properties from the context menu.

14. In the Properties dialog, click the Identity tab.

15. Change the pool identity to a domain account that has rights to perform searches in your SPS installation.

16. Click the OK button to save your changes.

17. Right-click the server icon and select All Tasks ➤ Restart IIS from the context menu.

18. In the Stop/Start/Restart dialog, select Restart Internet Services from the drop-down list.

19. Click the OK button to restart IIS.

Setting the Upload Limits

Windows 2003 Server allows you to configure the upload limits for any site. By default, the limits are too small for use with MCMS. Therefore, you will have to adjust them manually by making changes to the IIS metabase. The IIS metabase is contained in the file MetaBase.xml, which must be edited by hand.

Follow these steps to set the upload limits:

1. Select Start ➤ All Programs ➤ Administrative Tools ➤ Internet Information Services (IIS) Manager on the Windows 2003 Server where MCMS is to be installed.

2. In the IIS Manager, open the Web Sites folder.

3. Select View ➤ Detail from the menu.

4. Record the value of the Identifier column for the default web site. Figure 8-2 shows an example.

5. In the IIS Manager, right-click the server icon and select All Tasks ➤ Restart IIS from the context menu.

6. In the Stop/Start/Restart dialog, select Stop Internet Services from the drop-down list and click the OK button.

7. Open the Windows File Explorer and navigate to the directory \Windows\system32\ inetsrv.

8. Open the file `MetaBase.xml` in Visual Studio .NET for editing.

9. In Visual Studio .NET, select Edit ➤ Find and Replace ➤ Find from the main menu.

10. In the Find dialog, type **<MBProperty>** in the Find What field and click the Find Next button.

11. Directly underneath the `<MBProperty>` tag, insert the following code to define the upload limits. Be sure to use your identifier in the `Location` and `AppRoot` attributes.

```
<IIsWebDirectory   Location ="/LM/W3SVC/identifier/ROOT/NR/System/ResUpload"
AppFriendlyName="ResUpload"
AppIsolated="2"
AppRoot="/LM/W3SVC/identifier/Root/NR/System/ResUpload"
AspMaxRequestEntityAllowed="51200000"
  >
</IIsWebDirectory>
```

12. Save and close the file.

13. In the IIS Manager, right-click the server icon and select All Tasks ➤ Restart IIS from the context menu.

14. In the Stop/Start/Restart dialog, select Start Internet Services from the drop-down list and click the OK button.

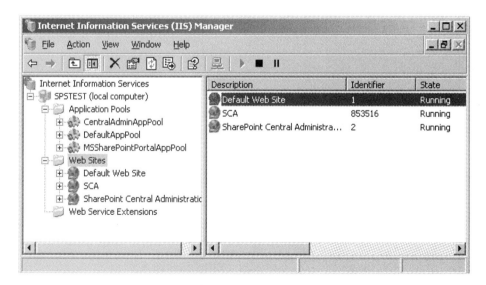

Figure 8-2. *Recording the site identifier*

Creating MCMS Accounts

MCMS installation requires you to create two accounts before you begin. One account is for the MCMS system itself. This account will read and write to the MCMS database. The other account is for the MCMS administrator. The first account is required, but you could use an existing account for the MCMS administrator if you want.

Follow these steps to create the MCMS accounts:

■**Note** The following procedure assumes that you are creating local accounts on the server. It is possible, however, to use domain accounts.

---

1. Select Start ➤ Administrative Tools ➤ Computer Management.

2. In the Computer Management Console, expand the Local Users and Groups node.

3. Right-click the Users folder and select New User from the context menu.

4. In the New User dialog, type **CMSSystem** into the User Name field.

5. Uncheck the User Must Change Password at Next Logon box.

6. Check the User Cannot Change Password and Password Never Expires boxes.

7. Enter a password for the account and click the Create button.

8. In the New User dialog, type **CMSAdmin** into the User Name field.

9. Uncheck the User Must Change Password at Next Logon box.

10. Check the User Cannot Change Password and Password Never Expires boxes.

11. Enter a password for the account and click the Create button.

12. Right-click the CMSAdmin user and select Properties from the context menu.

13. In the Properties dialog, select the Member Of tab.

14. On the Member Of tab, click the Add button.

15. In the Select Group dialog, type **administrators** and click the Check Names button.

16. Click the OK button on each dialog to close it.

Creating a MCMS Database

Before beginning the MCMS installation, you should create a new blank database. This database will be used by MCMS and configured during the installation process. Creating the database ahead of time saves several steps in the installation process.

Follow these steps to create a MCMS database:

1. Log in as an administrator and select Start ➤ All Programs ➤ Microsoft SQL Server ➤ Enterprise Manager from the server where SQL Server 2000 is installed.

2. In the Enterprise Manager, expand the tree until the Databases folder is visible.

3. Right-click the Database folder and select New Database from the context menu.

4. In the Database properties dialog, name the new database **MCMS** and click the OK button.

Installing Content Management Server

Installing MCMS on a Windows 2003 Server and integrating it with SharePoint is a cumbersome process. Because MCMS was originally released before Windows 2003 and WSS were available, you must perform several manual tasks in order to properly configure the installation. This section will walk you through the process and will lead to success if you have the configuration I specified at the beginning of this chapter. If you have a different configuration, then you should read the documentation for service pack 1 and CST for installation guidance.

Installing the Web Controls

MCMS requires the IE Web Controls to be installed before installing the core files. You can find the IE Web Controls in the WebControls folder of the MCMS installation disk. Simply execute the file IEWebControls.msi to install the controls.

■**Note** If you previously installed the IE Web Controls in Chapter 3, you must still run the setup described here to ensure the controls are properly installed in the GAC.

Installing the Core Server Files

After you have completed preparing for the installation, you can install the core MCMS files. While you can install the MCMS software, you cannot yet install Site Manager, Site Stager, or support for Visual Studio .NET. These options are only available after you install service pack 1, which must be done after the core files are installed.

Follow these steps to install the core MCMS files:

1. Log in as an administrator on the server where MCMS will be installed, start the MCMS installation, and select Install Components from the splash screen.

2. On the next screen, select Install MCMS Components, which will initiate a series of checks to make sure your server meets the prerequisites for installation.

3. After the checks are complete, you will see a Welcome screen. Click the Next button to continue.

4. After accepting the license agreement and clicking the Next button, you will see the Custom Setup screen.

5. On the Custom Setup screen, select to install only the CMS Server component.

6. Click the Next button.

7. On the Disk Cache Folder screen, accept the default settings and click the Next button.

8. On the Ready to Install the Program screen, uncheck the Launch Database Configuration Application (DCA) after Installation Is Completed box. Service pack 1 must be installed before the DCA is run.

9. Click the Install button to begin installation.

10. When the installation is complete, click the Finish button and exit the installation utility.

Installing Service Pack 1

Service pack 1 will upgrade the core MCMS installation so that it will run properly on Windows 2003 Server. It will also install several files that allow the Site Stager, Site Manager, and developer tools to work correctly. This is why additional components must be installed after service pack 1.

Follow these steps to install service pack 1:

1. Select Start ➤ Control Panel ➤ Add or Remove Programs.

2. In the Add or Remove Programs dialog, click the Add/Remove Windows Components button.

3. In the Windows Component wizard, uncheck the Internet Explorer Enhanced Security Configuration box.

4. Click on Application Server and click the Details button.

5. In the Application Server details screen, click on Internet Information Services and click the Details button.

6. In the Internet Information Services details screen, click on World Wide Web Service and click the Details button.

7. In the World Wide Web Service details screen, check Active Server Pages and Server Side Includes.

■**Caution** If you already have Active Server Pages and Server Side Includes installed, you must uninstall/reinstall them or they will not be properly recognized by the service pack setup.

---

8. Click the OK buttons to close all the open details screens.

9. In the Windows Components wizard, click the Next button to install the web server extensions.

10. After the extensions are installed, click the Finish button.

11. Execute the file `MCMS_2002_SP1a.exe` to start the installation process.

12. On the Welcome screen, select Install Components.

13. When prompted to upgrade the CMS server, click the Upgrade button.

14. After the upgrade is complete, launch the DCA and proceed to the next section.

Configuring the MCMS Database

MCMS maintains all of its content in a SQL Server database. This content is then used to dynamically generate web pages upon a user request. In this section, you will configure a database for use with MCMS.

Follow these steps to configure the MCMS database:

1. On the DCA splash screen, click the Next button.

2. On the next screen, select Mixed Mode and click the Next button.

3. On the next screen, choose the same site where WSS is installed as the location for MCMS.

4. Select the Read/Write Site option and click the Next button.

5. On the SCA Web Entry Point screen, choose the SCA site on port 8080 you created earlier and click the Next button.

■**Note** If you receive a warning at this point, choose to continue.

---

6. On the MCMS System Account screen, enter the CMSSystem credentials you created earlier and click the Next button.

7. On the Select MCMS Database screen, click the Select Database button.

8. In the SQL Server Login dialog, select the server where the MCMS database is located and set credentials to gain access during the configuration process.

■**Note** The SQL Server Login dialog will try to use the CMSSystem account for access by default. You will have to uncheck the Use Trusted Connection box and supply valid credentials to access and configure the MCMS database.

---

9. Click the Options button.

10. In the Database drop-down list, select the MCMS database and click the OK button.

11. Click the Next button.

12. When prompted, choose to install the MCMS schema into the selected database.

13. On the Database Population screen, click the Next button to begin the population process.

14. On the Select Initial MCMS Administrator screen, enter credentials for the CMSAdmin account you created earlier or another account you wish to use.

15. On the MCMS Site Stager Access Configuration screen, select Yes or No based on whether or not you plan to have remote machines run Site Stager, and then click the Next button.

16. When the wizard completes, uncheck the Launch the SCA Now box and click the Finish button.

Installing Additional Components

After service pack 1 is installed, you may install the Site Manager, Site Stager, and developer tools. Service pack 1 does not offer to install these additional components. Instead, you must use the Add or Remove Programs applet to install them.

Follow these steps to install the Site Manager, Site Stager, and development tools:

1. Select Start ➤ Control Panel ➤ Add or Remove Programs.

2. In the Add or Remove programs dialog, select Microsoft Content Manager Server SP1a and click the Change/Remove button.

3. In the Installation Wizard, select the Modify option and click the Next button.

4. On the Custom Installation screen, select Developer Tools for Visual Studio .NET 2003, Site Manager, and Site Stager.

5. Click the Next button.

6. On the Summary screen, click the Install button.

Installing the Connector for SharePoint Technologies

CST allows MCMS and WSS sites to share content and functionality. The CST installation also provides some sample data that we will use in this chapter. This sample data assumes that MCMS and WSS are installed on the same virtual directory, which is why I have chosen such a configuration for this chapter.

Follow these steps to install the SharePoint Connector:

1. On the server where MCMS is installed, execute `McmsForSharePointTech.exe` to unpack the setup files.

2. Unpack the files to a directory and run the file `McmsSharePointConnector.msi` if it does not start automatically.

3. On the Welcome screen, click the Next button.

4. On the Import Sample Data screen, ensure the Import Sample Data box is checked and click the Install button.

5. After the installation is complete, click the Finish button.

Configuring Search Settings and Indexing Content

Once the connector is installed, you must configure the search and indexing services to use MCMS content. This process involves granting MCMS search permission to the Site Application Pool Identity, setting up search properties, and indexing the MCMS content. This process must be repeated if you add new MCMS sites to your installation later.

Follow these steps to configure the search settings:

1. Select Start ➤ All Programs ➤ Microsoft Content Management Server ➤ Site Manager.

2. In the Server Information dialog, enter the server name and port where you installed MCMS.

3. Click the OK button.

4. In the Logon dialog, select Log In As, enter the credentials for the CMSAdmin account, and click the Start button.

5. In the Site Manager application, select to view User Roles.

6. In the User Roles list, click the Subscribers item.

7. In the Subscribers list, right-click the MCMS Search User item and select Properties from the context menu.

8. In the Properties dialog, click the Group Members tab and click the Modify button.

9. In the Modify Members dialog, select your domain in the NT domains tree.

10. Drop down the selection list and choose Select from List of All Groups and Users.

11. When the list of users appears, double-click the account corresponding to the Site Application Pool Identity hosting your WSS installation.

12. Click the OK buttons to dismiss the dialogs and save your changes.

13. Select Start ➤ All Programs ➤ Accessories ➤ Command Prompt to open a command window.

14. In the command window, type the following to change directories:

```
cd "< drive>:\Program Files\➡
MCMS Connector for SharePoint Technologies\WSS\bin"
```

15. In the command window, execute the following to setup the SPS search properties for MCMS content:

```
SearchPropertiesSetup.exe -file "<drive>:\Program Files\➡
Microsoft Content Management Server\Server\IIS_CMS\WssIntegration\➡
SearchPropertyCollection.xml"
```

16. In the command window, execute the following to include MCMS channels in the SPS search path:

```
SearchSetup.exe -url http://<server>/channels/➡
   -user <domain>\<username>➡
   -password <password> -crawl 1
```

17. Open the SPS home page in the Internet Explorer and click the Site Settings link.

18. On the Site Settings page, select Search Settings and Indexed Content ➤ Configure Search and Indexing.

19. On the Configure Search and Indexing page, select Start Non-Portal Content Update ➤ Full to index the MCMS content.

Testing Your Installation

Once the installation is complete, you can test it to make sure all of the components installed successfully. The sample data provided with the SharePoint connector contains templates that have the same look and feel as a default WSS site as well as some external templates that utilize the SPS search. If your installation was successful, all of these features should be available.

Follow these steps to test the installation:

1. Open the Internet Explorer and navigate to http://localhost/channels. You should see the channels home page.

2. On the Channels Welcome screen, click the CmsSharePointConnector link. If your installation is successful, you should see the page shown in Figure 8-3.

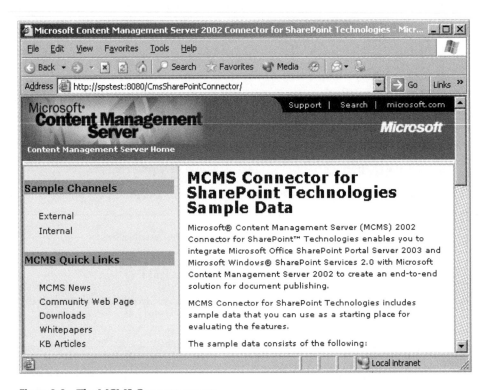

Figure 8-3. *The MCMS Connector page*

3. Click the link for the Internal sample channel.

4. Click the links to view the SharePoint News and SharePoint PR postings.

5. On the sample page, select All Sources in the source drop-down list, enter the term **News** into the simple search box, and click the green arrow. Verify that you get search results back.

6. Return to the CmsSharePointConnector page and click the link for the External sample channel.

7. On the sample page, enter the term **News** into the simple search box and click the green arrow. Verify that you get search results back.

Creating a Test WSS Site

MCMS can integrate with WSS sites in several ways. In order to experiment with the various integration techniques, you will need to create a WSS site collection. The exercises and examples in this chapter all assume this site collection is present.

1. Select Start ➤ All Programs ➤ Administrative Tools ➤ SharePoint Central Administration.

2. On the Central Administration page, select Virtual Server Configuration ➤ Create a Top-Level Web Site.

3. On the Virtual Server List page, select the virtual server where WSS is installed.

4. On the Create Top-Level Web Site page, name the site **TestMCMS** and fill in the owner information.

5. Click the OK button to create the new site.

6. On the Top-Level Site Successfully Created page, click the Template Selection Page link.

7. On the Template Selection Page, select Blank Site and click the OK button to create the site.

Authoring and Publishing Content

MCMS provides two different interfaces for authoring content: Web Authoring and the Authoring Connector. The Web Authoring interface allows end users to edit existing content or create new content based on existing templates in MCMS. The Web Authoring interface is an ASP.NET application used directly inside the Internet Explorer. The Authoring Connector is an interface that allows end users to create content using Microsoft Word and requires a special client-side installation. In this section, I will focus on using the Web Authoring interface.

Authoring and Publishing in MCMS

MCMS sites can be modified in place by switching to edit mode similar to the way in which edits are accomplished in SPS. When a page is placed in edit mode, a set of links appears based on the role of the current user. In MCMS, the link list is called the *authoring console* and it is analogous to the action list that appears on an SPS area. Figure 8-4 shows an MCMS authoring console alongside an SPS action list for a person with administrator rights to both systems.

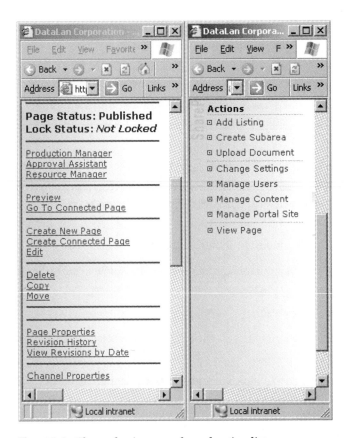

Figure 8-4. *The authoring console and action list*

The Web Authoring interface provides links that allow new pages to be created or existing pages to be edited. Additionally, there are links into the approval process that show lists of pages in production or awaiting approval. If you have set up the development environment described in this chapter, then you can already create new items based on the sample data templates.

Follow these steps to create a new page:

1. Log in to the MCMS server as a CMS administrator and navigate to
   `http://localhost/channels`.

2. On the Channels Welcome screen, click the CmsSharePointConnector link.

3. On the CST Sample Data page, click the Internal channel link.

4. On the Internal Channel page, click the Switch to Edit Site link.

5. Click the Create New Page link.

6. On the Select Template Gallery page, click the Internal folder in the Template Gallery list.

7. On the Select Template page, click the Select icon associated with the News template.

8. If prompted, select to install the Microsoft CMS HTML Editor control.

9. When the News template appears, click in the rich text box placeholder and use the font toolbar to change the font size to 10.

10. Type the following into the rich text box placeholder: **This is my first news item created using an MCMS template. The template was designed to look like a SharePoint Portal Server page.**

11. Click on the Add or Edit Image button in the page body near the image placeholder.

12. On the Select Source page, click Insert Local Image.

13. On the Insert Image page, select GIF Image from the Select File Type drop-down list.

14. Click the Browse button.

15. In the Choose File dialog, navigate to `\Program Files\Common Files\Microsoft Shared\web server extensions\60\TEMPLATE\IMAGES\newspg.gif`.

16. Click the Open button.

17. On the Insert Image page, type **News Item** into the Alternate Text field and click the Insert button.

18. Type **My first news item** into the description text box.

19. Click the Save New Page link.

20. In the Save New Page dialog, name the page **My First News Item** and click the Same As Name button.

21. Click the OK button to save the page.

After a new page is created and saved, it must go through an approval process before it becomes visible on the site. This approval process begins when the author of the new page clicks the Submit link in the authoring console. When a page is submitted for approval, it must wait for approval from an editor.

The publishing process defines three different roles: author, editor, and moderator. Authors are the users who have rights to create and edit content. Editors can approve submitted pages as well as create and edit new ones. Moderators can approve the publishing of a page to a live site as well as create and edit new ones. A submitted page must receive editor and moderator approval before it can appear on the live site. You can add individuals to any of these roles by using the Site Manager.

Follow these steps to designate roles for news items:

1. Log in to the MCMS server as a CMS administrator and select Start ➤ All Programs ➤ Microsoft Content Management Server ➤ Site Manager.

2. In the Server Information dialog, enter the server name and port where you installed MCMS.

3. Click the OK button.

4. In the Logon dialog, select the option to Log on as <User> and click the Start button.

5. In the Site Manager application, select to view User Roles.

6. In the User Roles list, click the Authors item.

7. Select File ➤ New ➤ Rights Group from the main menu.

8. After the new rights group is created, right-click the item and select Rename from the context menu.

9. Rename the group **News Authors**.

10. Right-click the item and select Properties from the context menu.

11. In the Properties dialog, click the Group Members tab and click the Modify button.

12. In the Modify Members dialog, select your domain in the NT domains tree.

13. Drop down the selection list and choose Select from List of All Groups and Users.

14. When the list of users appears, add several to the new group.

15. Click on the Group Rights tab and grant rights to the Internal channel. Figure 8-5 shows the dialog with permissions granted. You can follow these steps to add additional authors, editors, and moderators to MCMS.

Because submitted pages are not yet visible on the live site, reviewers must locate them in the production queue before they can be reviewed. Accessing the production queue is done by clicking the Production Manager link in the authoring console. Clicking this link brings up a list of pages awaiting review and approval. Using this interface, reviewers can view and approve all submitted pages for which they have rights.

Using the MCMS Pages Web Parts

The authoring console is a simple and useful interface for creating, editing, and approving pages. However, the authoring console was designed with the expectation that the user would be navigating the MCMS site content. As a result, end users may have difficulty locating and managing MCMS content when they are primarily using SharePoint technologies to manage their daily work. The MCMS Pages web parts that ship with CST are intended to provide an easy way for WSS users to manage MCMS content.

CST provides three web parts for managing MCMS content. The MCMS Page Listing web part shows a list of pages contained in an MCMS channel. The MCMS Pages Waiting for

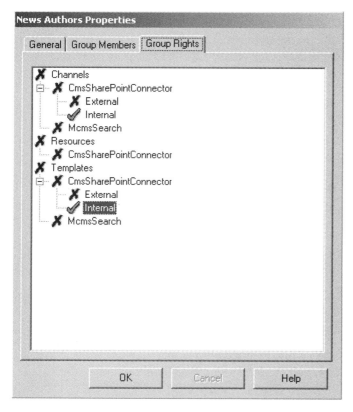

Figure 8-5. *Granting authoring permissions*

Approval web part shows a list of pages that are awaiting approval. The MCMS Pages in Production web part shows a list of pages that have not yet been published. These web parts are automatically installed in the Virtual Server Gallery during the CST installation process and can be added to any WSS site.

Follow these steps to add MCMS Pages web parts:

1. Log into your SharePoint installation as CMSAdmin.

2. Navigate to the WSS test site named TestMCMS that you created earlier.

3. On the home page of the site, select Modify Shared Page ➤ Add Web Parts ➤ Browse.

4. In the task pane, select to add parts from the Virtual Server Gallery.

5. Drag the MCMS Page Listing web part from the task pane to a zone on the WSS site.

6. Select Modify Shared Web Part from the drop-down menu associated with the web part.

7. In the property pane, expand the Custom Properties section.

8. Click the ellipsis associated with the Channel property.

9. In the Channel Information window, expand the `CmsSharePointConnector` and select the Internal folder.

10. In the Channel Information window, click the OK button to save your selection.

11. In the property pane, click the OK button. Figure 8-6 shows the MCMS Page Listing web part on the site.

Figure 8-6. *The MCMS Page Listing web part*

The MCMS Page Listing web part supports three different views of pages in the selected channel. The summary view is the default view and contains a title description and icon. The basic view is a simple list view. The detailed view is a list with more fields displayed. You can change the views for the web part in the same way as you would for any list on a WSS site. By using the MCMS Page Listing web part, end users can jump directly to pages in an MCMS channel and then access the authoring console to create, modify, or approve content.

While the MCMS Page Listing web part shows only published content, the MCMS Pages in Production and MCMS Pages Waiting for Approval web parts are used to view pages that are in the publishing process. If you drop these web parts onto the test MCMS site, you should see the news item page you created earlier. Once again, you can link directly to the page and use the authoring console to review and approve the page.

Follow these steps to review and approve a page:

1. Drop the MCMS Pages in Production and MCMS Pages Waiting for Approval web parts onto the test site.

2. In the MCMS Pages in Production web part, click on the news item page that you created earlier.

3. When the page appears, click on the Submit link in the authoring console.

4. Refresh the home page and verify the news item page now appears in the MCMS Page Listing web part.

■**Note** Because you are logged in as CMSAdmin, submitted pages are automatically approved. If you were logged in with fewer privileges, the page would first appear in the MCMS Pages Waiting for Approval web part.

Using Content from WSS Libraries

The pages we have created so far utilize fairly standard text and image placeholders. When you install CST, however, you can also utilize content from WSS Document Libraries in the web pages you create. Templates in MCMS utilize this content by including the SharePoint Library placeholder. Using this placeholder, you can include graphics, documents, and InfoPath forms in your MCMS pages. Figure 8-7 shows a simple page containing a link to a Microsoft Word document created with the SharePoint Library placeholder.

DataLan named Microsoft NY/NJ Partner of the Year

DataLan Corporation nam
ed Microsoft NY.doc   DataLan Corporation named Microsoft NY.doc

Last updated from SharePoint library: 2004-10-06 09:20:22

Figure 8-7. *Using the SharePoint Library placeholder*

While it is a simple matter to include direct links to library content, the real power of the SharePoint Library placeholder lies in using it to display the content contained within a document. Both InfoPath documents and Word documents saved in WordML format may be displayed as in-line HTML when you create and apply a style sheet to the document. This means that content creators can change web page content by simply editing an Office document.

If you want to display a Word document as in-line content, you must first save it into a WSS Document Library in XML format. Then you can create a new page using a template that contains the SharePoint Library placeholder. The internal news item that ships with CST is such a template. When you use this template, you can browse the available WSS sites and libraries looking for content to include through the placeholder. I simply navigated to a library containing a Word document that was saved as XML.

Once the document is selected, you may select from various style sheets to format the content. CST provides a default WordML style sheet named Microsoft Office WordML documents. Selecting this style sheet will display the document in much the same way as it would normally appear in Microsoft Word. Figure 8-8 shows the final page.

Because InfoPath forms are based on XML, you can also use them as sources for in-line content. Just as you do with Word documents, you must define a style sheet for use with the forms. While no default InfoPath style sheet is available with CST, you can extract one directly from an InfoPath form.

InfoPath forms can contain multiple views of the same data source. In InfoPath, views are used to present the same information in different formats based on the role of the user. This allows you to define a different interface for originators and reviewers. One of the views in InfoPath is always designated as the default and every other view is created as a transformation of the default view. This means that InfoPath must create an XSLT transformation for each new view. CST can apply XSLT transformations to InfoPath forms and generate in-line content for a page as long as the style sheet is registered in the style sheet catalog.

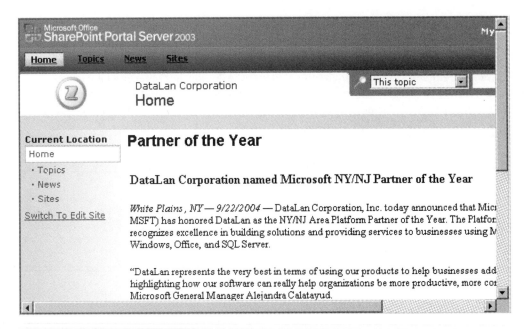

Figure 8-8. *Showing WordML documents as in-line content*

In order to register an InfoPath style sheet, you must first create a new view that will be used for the in-line content. Creating this new view will cause InfoPath to generate a new XSLT file and store it in the XSN cabinet for the form. You can easily extract the XSLT file from the XSN cabinet by either opening the XSN cabinet with WinZip or by selecting File ➤ Extract Form Files from the main InfoPath menu when you are in Design mode.

Once you have extracted the XSLT file, then it should be saved in the same folder as the sample style sheets that ship with CST. These style sheets can all be found in the directory `\Program Files\Microsoft Content Management Server\Server\IIS_CMS\WssIntegration\Dialogs\WssDocumentFinder\TemplateCatalog`. In the same directory, you will find the file `catalog.xml`, which is used by CST to map style sheets to documents. Listing 8-1 shows a modified version of the catalog file that I can use to explain the key elements.

Listing 8-1. *The Style Sheet Catalog*

```
<?xml version="1.0" standalone="yes"?>
<templateCatalog>
    <type FileExt="*">
        <template name="(None)">
            <description></description>
            <url></url>
            <sampleRenderingUrl></sampleRenderingUrl>
        </template>
    </type>
```

```
    <type FileExt=".jpg .gif .jpeg .png .bmp">
        <template name="(None)">
            <description></description>
            <url></url>
            <sampleRenderingUrl></sampleRenderingUrl>
        </template>
    </type>
    <type FileExt="contentxml">
        <template name="Case Study Microsoft Office InfoPath forms">
            <description></description>
            <url>C:\Program Files\Microsoft Content Management
Server\Server\IIS_CMS\WssIntegration\Dialogs\WssDocumentFinder
\TemplateCatalog\CaseStudyContent.xsl</url>
            <sampleRenderingUrl>
/MCMS/cms/WssIntegration/Dialogs/WssDocumentFinder/TemplateCatalog
/SampleCaseStudyContent.xml</sampleRenderingUrl>
        </template>
        <template name="Microsoft Office WordML documents">
            <description></description>
            <url>C:\Program Files\Microsoft Content Management
Server\Server\IIS_CMS\WssIntegration\Dialogs\WssDocumentFinder
\TemplateCatalog\WordNetHtml.xsl</url>
            <sampleRenderingUrl>
/MCMS/cms/WssIntegration/Dialogs/WssDocumentFinder/TemplateCatalog
/SampleWordNetHtml.xml</sampleRenderingUrl>
        </template>
    </type>
</templateCatalog>
```

The catalog file references two basic categories of documents. The first type is designated by an asterisk and simply refers to all documents. The second category is for XML documents created by InfoPath and Word. Within this second type, you can define a style sheet for any specific document. In Listing 8-1, you can see a style sheet is defined for a specific InfoPath form showing case studies and a generic style sheet for WordML documents.

After you extract and save the XSLT sheet associated with an InfoPath view, you must reference it in the catalog file. The best way to do this is to use the existing Case Study entry—which is part of the CST sample data—and modify it for your needs. At the end of the chapter you'll find an exercise that covers the complete process for creating in-line content with InfoPath forms. For now, we can use the sample data that ships with CST to investigate this technique. Getting the sample data up and running is not difficult, but it does involve several steps.

Follow these steps to use the sample InfoPath form for in-line content:

1. Start Microsoft InfoPath on the server where MCMS is installed.

2. In Microsoft InfoPath, select File ➤ Design a Form from the main menu.

3. In the Design a Form pane, click the On My Computer link.

4. In the open dialog, navigate to the file \Program Files\Microsoft Content Management Server\Sample Data\CmsSharePointConnector\SampleDocuments\CaseStudy.xsn.

5. Click the Open button.

6. When the form opens, click the Views link in the Design Tasks pane.

7. In the Views pane, click on the Case Study Content view. This is the view developed specifically for use with MCMS.

8. Select File ➤ Publish from the main menu.

9. When the Publishing Wizard starts, click the Next button.

10. On the next screen, select to publish the form to a SharePoint form library and click the Next button.

11. On the next screen, accept the default option to create a new form library and click the Next button.

12. On the next screen, enter the address of the test MCMS site you created in SharePoint.

13. On the next screen, name the new library **Case Studies** and click the Next button.

14. On the next screen, click the Add button.

15. In the Select a Field or Group dialog, select the Company field and click the OK button.

16. Click the Finish button to publish the form.

17. Close the wizard and exit InfoPath when you are done.

18. In the Internet Explorer, navigate to the test MCMS site you created in SharePoint.

19. On the Test MCMS home page, click the Documents and Lists link.

20. On the Documents and Lists page, click the link for the Case Studies form library.

21. On the Case Studies library page, click the Fill Out This Form link.

22. When the InfoPath form opens, fill it out with some test information.

23. When you have filled out the form, select File ➤ Save from the main menu.

24. In the Save As dialog, save the file as **Case Study**.

25. Close InfoPath and return to the Test MCMS site.

26. On the Test MCMS site home page, drop down the menu on the left-hand side of the MCMS Page Listing web part and select Switch to Edit Mode.

27. Drop down the same menu again and select Go To This Channel to access the Internal Channel on MCMS.

28. In the authoring console, select Create New Page.

29. On the Select Template Gallery, select the Internal folder.

30. On the Select Template page, click the Select icon associated with the News template.

31. In the rich text box placeholder and the description placeholder, type **Case Study**.

32. In the SharePoint Library placeholder, click the paperclip icon.

33. In the Placeholder Properties window, type the complete address of your Test MCMS site into the Type the URL for a Site field.

34. Click the OK button to accept the site entry.

35. When the list of files appears, click the `Case Study.xml` file.

36. Be sure the Allow Document Update Tool to Update This File box is checked and click the Next button.

37. In the layout list, select the Case Study Microsoft Office InfoPath Forms layout.

38. Click the Finish button to accept the changes.

39. In the authoring console, click the Save New Page link.

40. In the Create New Page window, enter **Case Study** in the Name field and click the Same As Name button.

41. Click the OK button to save the changes.

42. In the authoring console, click the Approve link to immediately publish the page. Figure 8-9 shows an example of the completed case study.

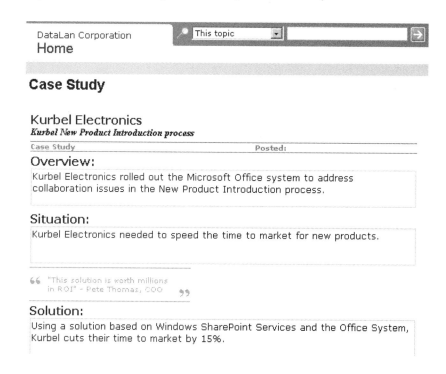

Figure 8-9. *Using an InfoPath form as in-line content*

When you use a Word or InfoPath document as a source for in-line content, you can schedule the content to update periodically in case the source document changes. In the Placeholder Properties window, you may check the Allow Document Update Tool to Update This File option. Selecting this option will ensure that the latest content is available when new pages are created. The utility `WssDocumentUpdater.exe` performs the synchronization between the designated documents and MCMS. This utility is located in the directory `\Program Files\MCMS Connector for SharePoint Technologies\CMS\bin`. As a best practice, you should schedule this utility to run periodically.

Understanding MCMS Templates

MCMS sites rely on templates to provide the framework for web pages. Authors may use a single template as the basis for many pages. It is this system of templates that allows business users to create and edit content without the involvement of the IT department. Templates, however, must be created by technical personnel before they can be used to create pages. Furthermore, creating a quality template involves more than just technical skills because the design must support the look and feel required by the business. Therefore, you'll find that templates may keep business people from having to understand technology, but it won't keep technical people from having to understand the business.

Understanding the CmsSharePointConnector Solution

If you have installed the development support for MCMS, then you can create templates using Visual Studio. In the New Project dialog, you will find a new folder for Content Management Server projects with three project types: MCMS Web Application, MCMS Web Service, and MCMS Empty Web Project. All of these projects are just MCMS versions of the standard projects normally found in Visual Studio.

Although you can certainly create templates from scratch by starting a new project, CST ships with a Visual Studio solution named `CmsSharePointConnector` that gives you all of the support necessary to create templates specifically for use with SharePoint technologies. The main file for this solution is located at `\Program Files\Microsoft Content Management Server\Sample Data\CmsSharePointConnector\CmsSharePointConnector.sln`.

If you open the `CmsSharePointConnector` solution in Visual Studio .NET, you will see that it consists of two different projects. The `McmsSpsWebControlLibrary` project consists of controls that support SharePoint-style navigation elements in the templates and the `CmsSharePointConnector` project—which has the same name as the overall solution—contains the main set of custom templates. The most important thing to understand about this solution is that it creates templates that look and feel like SharePoint pages, but they are not actually SharePoint pages. All pages created from these templates will be under MCMS control, not SharePoint control.

The main templates that you will work with are contained in the `Templates` folder under the `CmsSharePointConnector` project. If you open this folder, you'll see the templates that we used earlier to author new pages. If you open any of these templates in Visual Studio .NET, you'll notice that they are an ugly collection of table elements and large rectangles that function as placeholder controls. Properly arranging these controls on a page is what allows an

MCMS page to look like a SharePoint page. Figure 8-10 shows the template we used earlier to author internal news items. If you look closely, you can see how the arrangement of elements in the template mimics a typical SPS page.

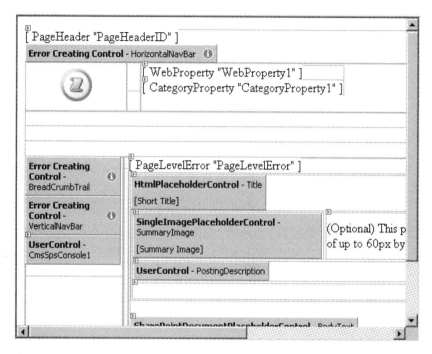

Figure 8-10. *The internal news item template*

Understanding Templates

While the templates provided in the CmsSharePointConnector project are a good starting point, you may want to create your own templates. You can choose to create new templates in a new MCMS project, or you can simply add your templates to the existing CmsSharePointConnector project. If you intend to create templates specifically for use with SharePoint, then I strongly recommend that you simply include them in the CmsSharePointConnector project because it already contains all of the supporting elements you need.

Creating a new template begins by examining the existing template structure available in MCMS. You can see all of the existing templates in Visual Studio .NET using the Template Explorer window. The Template Explorer is available by selecting View ➤ Other Windows ➤ MCMS Template Explorer from the main Visual Studio .NET menu. The Template Explorer lists the available templates in a hierarchy of folders. The folders that contain the templates are known as Template Galleries. Figure 8-11 shows the Template Explorer.

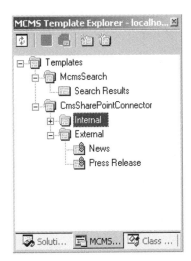

Figure 8-11. *The Template Explorer*

In the Template Explorer, you can create new template galleries and templates by right-clicking an existing item and selecting the appropriate item from the context menu. When you first create a new template, you will notice that the icon in the Template Explorer appears as a ripped page with a check mark. Additionally, the name of the template is bold. Figure 8-12 shows an example.

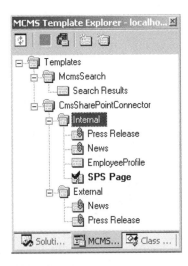

Figure 8-12. *A new template icon*

The ripped page icon means that the template has not yet been associated with an MCMS Template File. An MCMS Template File is added to the project using the New Item dialog and is essentially a specialized ASP.NET page. The MCMS Template File implements the layout of the template and is bound to the template through the `TemplateFile` property of the template. Once the `TemplateFile` property is set, the icon changes from ripped to whole.

The check mark icon appears because the template is currently checked out for editing. Templates may be checked out by a single developer to prevent anyone else from making changes. You can check a template in and out by right-clicking the template and selecting the appropriate menu item.

The bold name appears next to the template because it has not been saved. Templates will not be available for creating content until they have been saved. I find it a good idea to save frequently while creating templates.

Understanding Placeholders

Once you have associated an MCMS Template File with a template, you must arrange placeholders on the design surface. Adding placeholders is actually a multistep process that begins by setting values in the `PlaceholderDefinitions` property of the template. The `PlaceholderDefinitions` property is used to create a collection that represents all the different kinds of content you want to add to the template.

Because the `PlaceholderDefinitions` property is a collection, you must click the ellipsis associated with the property. Then you are presented with a dialog that allows you to create multiple definitions for the template. With CST installed, MCMS supports seven different types of placeholders: HTML, XML, Attachment, Image, Office Attachment, Office HTML, and SharePoint Document.

Placeholder definitions are associated with the template, not the MCMS Template File. Their role is to define the set of possible content types in the template. Actually implementing the placeholder definition is accomplished by dragging and dropping controls from the toolbox onto the MCMS Template File design surface. When an MCMS Template File is opened in design mode, the toolbox will contain a Content Management Server palette. Figure 8-13 shows the Content Management Server palette in Visual Studio .NET.

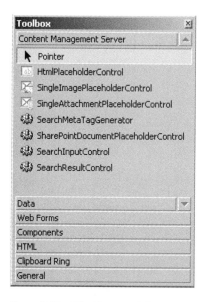

Figure 8-13. *The Content Management Server palette*

When a placeholder control is dropped onto the design surface of the MCMS Template File, it must be bound to one of the placeholder definitions in the template. This is accomplished using the `PlaceholderToBind` property of the control. After binding the control, designing the template is a simple matter of arranging the controls on the design surface. Once the design is completed, you can save the templates and build the project.

The HTML Placeholder Control

The HTML Placeholder Control is truly the workhorse of MCMS templates. This control can contain any kind of content that can be represented in HTML. This means that authors can use this placeholder to insert text or graphics. Template designers use this control when they are unsure of exactly what kind of content an author may want to include.

The Single Attachment Placeholder Control

The Single Attachment Placeholder Control allows an author to upload a file into a web page and display a link. Authors use this placeholder to show links to files from a web page. During the authoring process, MCMS will upload and store the file in the MCMS database.

The Single Image Placeholder Control

The Single Image Placeholder Control allows an author to upload an image file to a web page. This control is used to show just one image on a page. If authors want to display multiple images, they generally use the HTML placeholder. As with documents, the image is uploaded to the MCMS database during the authoring process.

The SharePoint Document Placeholder Control

The SharePoint Document Placeholder Control is used to link a document from a WSS library to a web page. This is the placeholder to use if you want to provide links to a document or generate in-line content. During the authoring process, the target document is uploaded to the MCMS database, but running the document update utility regularly helps keep changes to the document synchronized.

The Search Input and Search Results Controls

The Search Input Control is used to add search capabilities to a web page. The Search Results Control is used to display the results of a search. The external sample pages that ship with CST utilize these controls.

The Search Meta Tag Generator Control

The Search Meta Tag Generator Control is used to generate data that can be used to index MCMS pages for searching. During the setup of the development environment, we created a link between the MCMS channel structure and the SPS search engine. When SPS indexes the MCMS channel structure, it collects keyword information from pages with this control.

Understanding User Controls

Along with placeholder controls, MCMS templates also make use of user controls to add additional functionality like navigation or visual elements. The most common example of a user control is a console, which is a standard part of every MCMS project. The Default Console is a user control that implements the MCMS authoring console on a template. The templates defined by CST created their own authoring consoles. These consoles are better suited to the mixed SharePoint/MCMS environment.

Exercise 8-1. MCMS and SharePoint

The CMS Connector for SharePoint Technologies provides a significant level of integration between MCMS and SharePoint sites. CST allows you to use content from WSS libraries when authoring, searching, and indexing MCMS pages. Additionally, you can participate in the authoring and publishing process through web parts hosted in WSS sites. In this exercise, you will create a template that uses an InfoPath form to generate in-line content. The template and form will create an employee profile page that will contain basic information about an employee.

Creating the Employee Profile Template

The first step in creating the employee profile page is to build a template. In this section, you will use the existing sample project that ships with CST to create a template. The template will host a SharePoint Document Placeholder that will convert InfoPath form information to in-line content.

Follow these steps to create a new MCMS template:

1. Start Visual Studio .NET.

2. In the main menu, select File ➤ Open ➤ Project.

3. In the Open Project dialog, navigate to `\Program Files\Microsoft Content Management Server\ Sample Data\CmsSharePointConnector\CmsSharePointConnector.sln` and click the Open button.

4. In Visual Studio .NET, select View ➤ Other Windows ➤ MCMS Template Explorer.

5. In the Template Explorer, expand the CmsSharePointConnector folder.

6. Right-click the Internal folder and select New Template from the context menu.

7. Rename the new template **EmployeeProfile**.

8. Right-click the EmployeeProfile template and select Save from the context menu.

9. Right-click the EmployeeProfile template and select Properties from the context menu.

10. In the Properties window, click the ellipsis associated with the `PlaceholderDefinitions` property.

11. In the Placeholder Definition Collection Editor, click the down arrow next to the Add button.

12. Select to add a SharePoint Document Placeholder definition to the template.

13. Change the name of the placeholder to **EmployeeProfile**.

14. Click the OK button to save your changes.

15. Select Project ➤ Add New Item from the main menu.

16. In the Add New Item dialog, open the Content Management Server folder.

17. Select the MCMS Template File item from the Templates list.

18. Name the file **EmployeeProfile.aspx** and click the Open button.

19. Select File ➤ Save All from the main menu.

20. In the Template Explorer, right-click the EmployeeProfile template and select Properties from the context menu.

21. In the Properties window, click the ellipsis associated with the `TemplateFile` property.

22. In the Select File dialog, select the `EmployeeProfile.aspx` file and click the Select button.

23. Right-click the EmployeeProfile template and select Save from the context menu.

24. Select View ➤ Solution Explorer from the main menu.

25. Drag the `CmsSpsConsole.ascx` control from the Console folder in the Solution Explorer and drop it on the design surface of the `EmployeeProfile.aspx` page.

26. Select View ➤ Toolbox from the main menu.

27. In the toolbox, click on the Content Management Server palette.

28. Drag the SharePoint Document Placeholder control from the toolbox and drop it directly to the right of the Default Console control.

29. Right-click the SharePoint Document Placeholder control and select Properties from the context menu.

30. In the Properties window, drop down the list associated with the `PlaceholderToBind` property and select `EmployeeProfile`.

31. Select Build ➤ Build Solution from the main menu.

32. In the Template Explorer, right-click the EmployeeProfile template and select Check In from the context menu.

33. Exit Visual Studio .NET.

Creating the Employee Profile Form

The next step in the project is to create the InfoPath form that will contain the employee profile. In this section, you will build a form with two views. The default view will be used to fill in the form; the second view will be used to generate the style sheet necessary to create the in-line content.

Follow these steps to create the employee profile form:

1. Start Microsoft InfoPath and select File ➤ Design a Form from the main menu.

2. In the Design a Form pane, select New Blank Form.

3. In the Design Tasks pane, click the Layout link.

4. In the Layout pane, click the Table with Title layout.

5. When the table is inserted, click in the area marked Click to Add a Title.

6. Enter the text **Employee Profile**.

7. Click in the area marked Click to Add Form Content.

8. In the Layout pane, click the Two-Column Table layout.

9. Repeat this process until you have six two-column tables in the form.

10. In the left-hand column cells, enter labels for the form as **Name**, **Title**, **Phone**, **E-Mail**, **Skills**, and **Other**.

11. In the Layout pane, click the Controls link.

12. In the Controls pane, drag a Text Box control into each of the cells in the right-hand column.

13. Select Format ➤ Color Schemes from the main menu.

14. In the Color Schemes pane, select the Blue color scheme.

15. Select View ➤ Manage Views from the main menu.

16. In the Views pane, click the Add a New View link.

17. In the Add View dialog, name the new view **Content** and click the OK button.

18. In the Views pane, click the View 1 view.

19. Select Edit ➤ Select All from the main menu.

20. Select Edit ➤ Copy from the main menu.

21. In the Views pane, click the Content view.

22. Select Edit ➤ Paste from the main menu.

23. Right-click any of the text fields in the Content view and select Text Box Properties from the context menu.

24. In the Text Box Properties dialog, click the Display tab.

25. On the Display tab, check the Read-Only box.

26. Click the OK button to save the changes.

27. Repeat the steps to set the Read-Only property for each text field. Figure 8-14 shows the final form.

28. Select File ➤ Extract Form Files from the main menu.

29. In the Browse for Folder dialog, select the My Documents folder.

30. Click the OK button to extract the form files.

31. Select File ➤ Publish from the main menu.

32. When the Publishing Wizard starts, click the Next button.

33. On the next screen, select to publish the form to a SharePoint form library and click the Next button.

34. On the next screen, accept the default option to create a new form library and click the Next button.

35. On the next screen, enter the address of the Test MCMS site you created in SharePoint.

36. On the next screen, name the new library **Profiles** and click the Next button.

37. Click the Finish button to publish the form.

38. Close the wizard and exit InfoPath when you are done.

Employee Profile
Name	
Title	
Phone	
E-mail	
Skills	
Other	

Figure 8-14. *The Employee Profile form*

Adding the Style Sheet to the Catalog

Once you have extracted the style sheet from the InfoPath form, it must be added to the style sheet catalog. This process involves saving the extracted style sheet and making edits to the catalog.xml file. This process will make the style sheet available to authors who are using your template.

Follow these steps to add the style sheet to the catalog:

1. Open the Window File Explorer and navigate to the My Documents folder.

2. Locate the file Content.xsl. This is the style sheet that creates the Content view of the InfoPath form.

3. Copy the file Content.xsl into the folder \Program Files\Microsoft Content Management Server\ Server\IIS_CMS\WssIntegration\Dialogs\WssDocumentFinder\TemplateCatalog.

4. In this same directory, right-click the file catalog.xml and select Edit with Visual Studio .NET 2003 from the context menu.

5. In Visual Studio .NET, select Edit ➤ Find and Replace ➤ Find.

6. In the Find dialog, type **FileExt="contentxml"** and click the Find Next button.

7. Add the following code to create a new template definition for the Employee Profile form:

■**Caution** Be sure to put the contents of the <url> tag on a single line. It is broken in the following listing due to space constraints. Also replace the [drive] token with your drive letter.

```
<template name="Employee Profiles">
    <description>Displays the employee profile in line.</description>
    <url>[drive]:\Program Files\Microsoft Content Management
    Server\Server\IIS_CMS\WssIntegration\Dialogs\WssDocumentFinder
    \TemplateCatalog\Content.xsl</url>
    <sampleRenderingUrl></sampleRenderingUrl>
</template>
```

8. Select File ➤ Save All from the menu and exit Visual Studio .NET.

Creating an Employee Profile

Once the style sheet is available from the catalog, you can create a new page. The content for the new page will be entered in the InfoPath form and saved in the form library. After the content is saved, you will create a new MCMS page based on the content.

Follow these steps to create a new employee profile:

1. In the Internet Explorer, navigate to the test MCMS site you created in SharePoint.

2. On the Test MCMS home page, click the Documents and Lists link.

3. On the Documents and Lists page, click the link for the Profiles form library.

4. On the Profiles library page, click the Fill Out This Form link.

5. When the InfoPath form opens, fill it out with information about yourself.

6. When you have filled out the form, select File ➤ Save from the main menu.

7. In the Save as dialog, save the file as **My Profile**.

8. Close InfoPath and return to the Test MCMS site.

9. On the Test MCMS site home page, drop down the menu on the left-hand side of the MCMS Page Listing web part and select Switch to Edit Mode.

10. Drop down the same menu again and select Go To This Channel to access the Internal Channel on MCMS.

11. In the authoring console, select Create New Page.

12. On the Select Template Gallery, select the Internal folder.

13. On the Select template page, click the Select icon associated with the EmployeeProfile template.

14. In the SharePoint Library placeholder, click the paperclip icon.

15. In the Placeholder Properties window, type the complete address of your Test MCMS site into the Type the URL for a Site field.

16. Click the OK button to accept the site entry.

17. Select the Profiles library from the list of available libraries.

18. When the list of files appears, click the `My Profile.xml` file.

19. Be sure the Allow Document Update Tool to Update This File box is checked and click the Next button.

20. In the layout list, select Employee Profiles.

21. Click the Finish button to accept the changes.

22. In the authoring console, click the Save New Page link.

23. In the Create New Page window, enter **My Profile** in the Name field and click the Same As Name button.

24. Click the OK button to save the changes.

25. In the authoring console, click the Approve link to immediately publish the page.

Index

forums.apress.com

FOR PROFESSIONALS BY PROFESSIONALS™

JOIN THE APRESS FORUMS AND BE PART OF OUR COMMUNITY. You'll find discussions that cover topics of interest to IT professionals, programmers, and enthusiasts just like you. If you post a query to one of our forums, you can expect that some of the best minds in the business—especially Apress authors, who all write with *The Expert's Voice™*—will chime in to help you. Why not aim to become one of our most valuable participants (MVPs) and win cool stuff? Here's a sampling of what you'll find:

DATABASES
Data drives everything.

Share information, exchange ideas, and discuss any database programming or administration issues.

INTERNET TECHNOLOGIES AND NETWORKING
Try living without plumbing (and eventually IPv6).

Talk about networking topics including protocols, design, administration, wireless, wired, storage, backup, certifications, trends, and new technologies.

JAVA
We've come a long way from the old Oak tree.

Hang out and discuss Java in whatever flavor you choose: J2SE, J2EE, J2ME, Jakarta, and so on.

MAC OS X
All about the Zen of OS X.

OS X is both the present and the future for Mac apps. Make suggestions, offer up ideas, or boast about your new hardware.

OPEN SOURCE
Source code is good; understanding (open) source is better.

Discuss open source technologies and related topics such as PHP, MySQL, Linux, Perl, Apache, Python, and more.

PROGRAMMING/BUSINESS
Unfortunately, it is.

Talk about the Apress line of books that cover software methodology, best practices, and how programmers interact with the "suits."

WEB DEVELOPMENT/DESIGN
Ugly doesn't cut it anymore, and CGI is absurd.

Help is in sight for your site. Find design solutions for your projects and get ideas for building an interactive Web site.

SECURITY
Lots of bad guys out there—the good guys need help.

Discuss computer and network security issues here. Just don't let anyone else know the answers!

TECHNOLOGY IN ACTION
Cool things. Fun things.

It's after hours. It's time to play. Whether you're into LEGO® MINDSTORMS™ or turning an old PC into a DVR, this is where technology turns into fun.

WINDOWS
No defenestration here.

Ask questions about all aspects of Windows programming, get help on Microsoft technologies covered in Apress books, or provide feedback on any Apress Windows book.

HOW TO PARTICIPATE:

Go to the Apress Forums site at **http://forums.apress.com/**.

Click the New User link.